SOCIAL MOBILITY IN KERALA

Anthropology, Culture and Society

Series Editors:
Dr Richard Wilson, University of Sussex and
Professor Thomas Hylland Eriksen, University of Oslo

SOCIAL MOBILITY IN KERALA
Modernity and Identity in Conflict

FILIPPO OSELLA AND CAROLINE OSELLA

Pluto Press

LONDON • STERLING, VIRGINIA

First published 2000 by Pluto Press
345 Archway Road, London N6 5AA
and 22883 Quicksilver Drive, Sterling, VA 20166-2012, USA

www.plutobooks.com

British Library Cataloguing in Publication Data
A catalogue record for this book is available from
the British Library

Library of Congress Cataloging-in-Publication Data
Social mobility in Kerala : modernity and identity in conflict / [edited
by] Filippo Osella and Caroline Osella.
    p. cm. — (Anthropology, culture, and society)
Includes bibliographical references (p.)
 ISBN 0-7453-1694-8 (hardback) — ISBN 0-7453-1693-X (paperback)
 1. Ezhavas. 2. Social mobility—India—Kerala. I. Osella, Filippo.
II. Osella, Caroline. III. Series.
 DS432.E95 S63 2000
 305.5'13'095483—dc21
                        00-009109

ISBN   0 7453 1694 8 hardback
ISBN   0 7453 1693 X paperback

Designed and produced for Pluto Press by Chase Publishing Services
Typeset from disk by Gilbert Composing Services, Leighton Buzzard
Printed in the European Union by TJ International, Padstow, England

CONTENTS

LIST OF TABLES

LIST OF MAPS

DEDICATION

We would like to dedicate this book, first, to our families – who have patiently borne the long separations and bouts of bad temper during writing which mark the anthropologist's craft – and most especially to our long-awaited and much-loved daughter Anna, who now begins to share the adventures and trials of fieldwork and writing up with us. We would also like to record fond memories of two 'aunties' who helped us to make this work happen, and who we very much regret not having the chance to show the final manuscript to: Zia Rina, whose correspondence with us was interrupted when she died suddenly in 1990 in Torino; and Mrs Chandrika, late of Palayam, Thiruvananthapuram, who took us under her wing when we first arrived in Kerala in 1989.

ACKNOWLEDGEMENTS

A manuscript in preparation as long as this one – rewritten several times and covering seven years of fieldwork – collects many debts of gratitude, only a few of which we can single out here. So let us first offer a general and sincere thank you to the many people in various places who have participated in the work and made it possible. We have received generous financial support for various periods of fieldwork and writing up from the period June 1989 to September 1996 from: the Economic and Social Research Council of Great Britain; the London School of Economics; the Leverhulme Trust; the Nuffield Foundation; and the Wenner-Gren Foundation. We have been affiliated to the Centre for Development Studies, Thiruvananthapuram, Kerala; the Madras Institute for Development Studies, Chennai; and the Centre d'Études de l'Inde et de l'Asie du sud, Paris.

We must mention for particular thanks those who guided our studies as undergraduate and graduate students, offering inspiration, advice and encouragement along the way and helping us navigate the vast ocean that is South Asian scholarship: to Chris Fuller and Jonathan Parry of the LSE, heartfelt thanks for everything. Another special 'thank you' which must be given goes to Michael Carrithers at Durham, UK. As head of department during our first academic jobs he was always supportive of us, in ways and to an extent which we will never be able to repay: for taking us on as job-sharers, thereby allowing us time to write; for granting special leave to permit further fieldwork; for reading parts of the manuscript; for suggesting new angles to help the work connect to ongoing debates; for general encouragement and advice – sincere gratitude.

We also owe particular thanks to those who undertook to read the manuscript in its entirety and comment upon it: Chris Fuller of the LSE, London; P.R. Radhakrishnan of MIDS, Chennai; Thomas Isaac of CDS, Thiruvananthapuram; Yasushi Uchiyamada, of FASID, Tokyo: all of these we thank unreservedly for their most kind help and constructive suggestions. We are also grateful to several colleagues who have read and commented upon parts of the manuscript: Celia Busby; James Carrier; Michael Carrithers; Simon Coleman; Gilles Tarabout. Various parts of it have also been presented to seminars at MIDS, Chennai, at CEIAS, Paris, at LSE, London, at the

University of Edinburgh, and at the University of Durham. We wish to thank all those who offered suggestions for improvements, while acknowledging that errors and shortcomings remain entirely our own. Recently we have enjoyed material support in preparation of the final manuscript from our home institutions, the Social Anthropology Subject Group at the University of Sussex and the Department of Anthropology and Sociology at SOAS. Cindy Noel and Suzanna Cassidy helped us with vital editorial and proofing tasks and Sue Rowland prepared the maps.

Finally, while space does not permit us to mention the very many people in Kerala who have taken us into their homes, spoken with us, met us in their offices, invited us to share their social and familial lives, we would like to mention one particular friend. Anil – Chandrasekhar T. – first met with us in 1989 for Malayalam conversation lessons. He has since helped us on and off with various parts of our research; we have shared some important moments in our lives and now our children – Anna (kutty) and Sanjay (kunja) – are beginning the second generation of a much valued transnational friendship.

PREFACE

This book comes out of a total of three years' residence in a rural *panchayat* in Kerala, south India. From the beginning of our first fieldwork, we made it explicit to people that the purpose of our residences was study, and that we would be writing about our experiences in 'Valiyagramam'. We told those who spoke with us that they should have nothing to fear, as anything told us would be in confidence from other villagers; we promised that before publication we would first change the names of, 'this place and all the people here, so that nobody could understand where it is or who you are'. People have been extremely free with us in giving information and in letting us into the sometimes intimate details of their family lives. This book will certainly be read by some villagers, who may often think that they recognise each other's stories; we warn Valiyagramam readers that we have changed not only names but also, on occasion, certain other identifying details. To non-villagers, we must also explain that we have changed several place-names: that of the *panchayat* and the two villages which comprise it and the names of all junctions, neighbourhoods and temples around the *panchayat*. Mindful of the ever-growing tourist traffic which charter flights now bring into Kerala, and the increasing tendency to promote and seek out ever more 'authentic' experience (see for example the UK *Independent on Sunday* newspaper's 8.12.96 travel section's proposition of the Sabarimala Aiyappan pilgrimage as a spectacle of difference), we have also changed the names of several nearby temples. We have also (reluctantly) changed the names of the four major towns between which the *panchayat* stands. These changes, we hope, do not detract from understanding of the milieu in which the *panchayat* finds itself; those familiar with the area will easily recognise the approximate location.

1 INTRODUCTION

THREE FAMILY STORIES

Ceru Mannattu family

In 1990 Advocate Remini suggested, 'Come and talk to my husband's brother: he knows all the family history and has time to talk.' Remini's work at the district court, her duties as *panchayat* member and Congress Party worker, and her practice of moving frequently between her natal home and her husband's home 5 km away meant that she was difficult to track down. Rather than find her at one of her homes we would more often pass her along the road, driving in her Ambassador car into town, to the city high court, or to the nearby prestigious Puthenkulangara Devi temple where her family worship and make regular cash donations. Remini's is one of the influential and wealthy families in the south Indian village where we were staying: her father, after military service, had been manager of his maternal uncle's Nilgiris tea plantation before retiring back to the village in the late 1960s, where he opened a profitable ration-shop. Villagers recalled that not only had the family been the first, in the 1970s, to buy a car, but they had – scandalously – permitted their girls to have driving lessons, a spectacle which other villagers had come out of their houses to see. The eldest of the five sisters had married wearing 25 sovereigns' (200 grammes) worth of gold jewellery, including a gold waist-chain: commonplace in the 1990s, when dowries often top 101 sovereigns (808 grammes) but rare in the 1970s. Remini herself had married into a similarly well-placed family whose stories we also wanted to hear.

Finally, late one rainy afternoon in 1995, preparing to tell us the story of his famous great-uncle, Remini's brother-in-law sat back on the verandah of the family's old-style teak *nalukettu*. *Nalukettus*, generally inhabited by families from the traditional elite, are increasingly rare these days as once-wealthy families despair of rising maintenance costs and abandon them. Looking not at us but at the large cow-shed opposite, he began to speak in English:

Nowadays you see many families around here with big mansions, but they are all very recently built. Before they built these houses, some of them were living in thatched

1

huts: their prosperity is all new. Now they play at being big families, but they were nothing ten years ago. Their families have no history, whereas our family is famous around here. You can tell the name of our great-uncle K.V. Krishnan to anybody around here and they will have heard of him.

K.V. Krishnan lived from 1883 to 1953 and is a prominent person around these parts, remembered as a person and as an institution. From a very modest background, he left here to work in a plantation as *kangany*, where he was taught by one of his labourers to read and write in Malayalam: he had been illiterate until then. Although he spoke no English he could always guess what the Europeans wanted and so he gained their esteem and trust. With time he started earning and began buying land here in his home village, but his European boss advised him instead to invest in plantations and helped him buy 500 acres of land next to the Travancore Tea and Rubber Company. In those days, Brahmans held all the land as *Brahmaswam*; it was all forest and they never went there, knew nothing about it. You couldn't buy, but if you took them gold coins, according to how many you gave they would say 'You can have 200 or 300 acres in a certain place.' K.V. got land, labourers felled trees and planted paddy for the first two years and after that the plantation was started. Many people from here went to work for him.

In his plantation grounds he built a handloom weaving factory to make cloth for his workers; at the township which came up at the junction he built a shopping complex and rented out all the shops except one, run by his brother and selling the cloth made on his looms. In the 1920s he also started the first bus service from Kottayam to Kumily (Kerala's high ranges), with two or three buses. He was supplying European plantations with everything they needed.

K.V. Krishnan was the biggest landlord in his home village and also had property in many other places: a textile shop in Kottayam; an ex-royal palace in the state capital; a 750-acre cashew plantation where he constructed a cashew factory, the first in that area. K.V. Krishnan built bungalows for himself and his family inside his own plantation but didn't live there until one and a half years before his death: before that, he was obliged to live in company quarters at Mundakkayam, where he continued to work.

In the plantations only European owners had cars; they used to sell them and buy a new one every four or five years. K.V. Krishnan was allowed to buy one of these cars second hand, but, unlike the Europeans, he was not permitted to employ a driver, so he had to learn to drive. He was the first person here to own a car; people would hear it and come out to stand and watch him pass. If a European car approached on the plantation roads, he had to get off the road, stand by the car and let them go by.

In 1923 there was a great flood and famine here. The richest man in the area was the Brahman from the big house next to the temple. So when famine came people assembled outside his house to beg for help, but he felt threatened by the crowd and didn't give anything. K.V. Krishnan, driving home from the plantation, passed by and saw the crowd and immediately sent his assistant into town to buy rice and provisions. He distributed them in person in front of the Brahman's house while standing on his car: the Rajavu came to know this fact.

The founders of the first SNDP (Sri Narayana Dharma Paripalam Yogam, i.e. society for the preservation of the moral law of Sri Narayana Guru) college approached K.V. Krishnan, who gave 10 acres of land plus Rs100,000, the biggest-ever donation; with that money they built and equipped the chemistry laboratories. The only condition put on the donation was that in future any family member should get admission to the college. He never became involved with the SNDP reform movement; he had so many businesses that he had no time for politics.

Before dying, he partitioned all his property providing for all his dependants, including driver, watchman, servants. Some received 5 or 10 acres of plantation land and now they are rich; the wealth of people who received from him has increased ever since, while others have gone down. He died in the district hospital on the 23 April 1953 at the age of 70 and was buried in his own estate, on the first plot of land he ever bought. There is a memorial there where someone lights a lamp every day. His last car – a Chevrolet – is also preserved there, and somebody looks after it.

Warriattu family

Geographically close, but socially far distant from the *nalukettu* in its spacious grounds where we heard K.V. Krishnan's story, is Keshavan's sparsely furnished two-roomed brick house, standing in a densely inhabited lane near the paddy fields. During 1989, walking through the village to our rented house near a dispensary, we had often seen Keshavan waiting outside: over 60, thin and wiry, with a hollow chest and a racking cough, the physical privations of life as a manual labourer have left him an invalid. When we first called to visit him, he was alone. Embarrassed and apologetic for having no refreshments to offer, he turned to talk in coarse village Malayalam of the past:

My mother died when I was 10 years old and my father remarried and went away, leaving me alone in this house, so I went to work; I had no schooling. My next-door neighbour went to work in Ceylon and got loads of money: once he was picking grass for a cow and found some gold which he put in the grass basket before falling immediately unconscious. When his nephews came looking for him they found the basket, covered the gold with grass, and took it straight home to hide. Only after that did they return to bring their sick uncle home! That whole family got very rich – including the nephews – when the uncle died.

Other villagers told us that Keshavan's neighbour had gone to Ceylon as a *kangany* and revealed that Keshavan himself had also passed a spell in Ceylon as a plantation labourer, returning home none the better for his brief period of migration, penniless.

My father was in agriculture but I chose to become a ferry-man. I worked transporting pepper, coir, chilli, from Kochi (a port city) to Thiruvananthapuram (the state capital). My job was very tough: I used to carry a quintal of wood, which was a terrible strain, but the ferry work paid good money: enough to buy furniture and things for the house. I used to go as far as Kozhicode where it's really tough because there's a tidal lake. When they built a bridge, the ferry work all stopped and lorries came. Sivagiri (a pilgrimage centre) is a good place because there are caves and water coming out of the rocks. The water there is always flowing, you just went along with it. I don't have much interest in religion, I don't really believe in these things. There used to be some family shrines around here, but we destroyed them all.

When Keshavan's 22-year-old son Premadasan came to us to ask for a loan towards going to seek work in Mumbai, we readily offered him his train fare. Having already failed pre-degree exams three times, he had given up on study, but, like many young men, had found no regular local employment. Having passed his SSLC (Secondary School Leaving Certificate), he was unwilling to go for manual work. Premadasan was confident and cheerful, telling us that he had friends already in Mumbai, that he was going with three others, and that within one week they would all find good work and make some money. 'Here there are people with MSc degrees just sitting doing nothing at the junction. What job will I ever get here?' He told us that his grandmother was afraid, having read about gangs which abducted the healthy and removed their kidneys to sell to wealthy Arabs for transplant. Laughing off this possibility, he said, 'I might even become an underworld king myself!'

After one week a letter came from Mumbai: 'We've taken a room in a Malayali building. I've got a job as a trainee air-conditioner mechanic: Rs600 per month with an increase after four months' training. We're all four working and earning. Don't worry, we won't lose our kidneys. Love from Premadasan.' We and the family heard nothing else for two months until Premadasan came home thin and ill. Shamefaced, embarrassed for the money he had borrowed and was unable to repay and for the failure of his Mumbai dreams and big-talk, he sat on our verandah and spoke sadly in *Manglish* about his experiences:

We got to Mumbai and phoned our friends who took us to their house; they were all in one room and they gave us the other. The bathroom was next to us but we only got water from 5 till 7 in the morning and we only had one bucket. After one week we were all thin: we had *kanji* twice a day, then bread and coffee. We learnt to make a sort of vegetable curry by throwing everything together into the pot – it didn't taste good. We couldn't afford to buy fish or meat. Every Sunday they hold VIP weddings in this hall, with fish, chicken, *biryanis*. There was a disco with western music. On Sundays we used to go and watch; we could eat there too. They all spoke English, so we used to pretend to be distant relatives and smuggle ourselves in. Up there it's all diseases: chickenpox, jaundice, everything. In the morning you can see even women sitting and shitting openly. There was water coming into the room where we stayed; it was so damp and there were all sorts of insects. I didn't like Mumbai at all – too hot and humid.

In Mumbai we didn't know the language and had to speak dog-English to everyone. They call us Madrassi; they don't know anything about Kerala. Everyone from India goes to Mumbai. There are lots of Goans – running shops; Punjabis – taxi-drivers; Gujaratis – they're all rich; then there are lots of Tamils and Malayalis, ducking and diving. There are loads of villains, but we kept out of their way: Shiv Sena is huge there, they're big thugs. Fashion is big there: girls are all *modern* girls with tight jeans; boys have coffee-brown dyed hair. Everything you can get in the USA you can get in Mumbai – things with 'Made in USA' on them, *duplicates*.

I got a job as a trainee air-conditioner mechanic, a helper. The man doing the job got Rs1000 a day for it but I got just Rs25 daily off him, for crawling through the pipes: it was so hot and dark. Liju got a job in a factory grinding metal for Rs25 a day; he had headaches and was quite ill. Joey and Thampy were getting Rs20 per day in a soda-bottle factory: nobody was giving us any money. We decided to get back our deposit, spend what money we had, and then come home.

Thampy's elder brother came through Mumbai on his way to the Gulf and found us;

he was swearing like mad at us and told us to come home. We'd paid Rs4000 deposit for the room, Rs150 per month for rent plus Rs50 per month for water. We wanted our deposit back, but the landlord – a Bangalore man with a Maruti car – wouldn't give it. At the train station there was 3 km of platform full of people coming away from Mumbai and waiting to get a train; we had to stand two nights and one day to get tickets. Liju and I came home first because we were ill. Thampy and Joey will wait to get the deposit back and then come.

There is work – we got jobs – but the wages are no good and the work's too hard. There are a few good companies to work for, but most are thieves. You need a lot of money to live there: Rs49 just for four fruit juices! You travel 140 km a day just to go to work; leave the house at 7 a.m. and get back at 7 p.m. – how can you live like that? I won't go further than the river-bank now: here there's clean water and air.

In 1998 Premadasan had attempted leaving the village again. He has still not found steady employment but is reluctant to abandon hopes of a better life than his father's or to go for casual manual labour. This leaves him as one of many chronically under-employed young men who 'sit doing nothing at the junction'. As nightmares of the Mumbai experience fade, dreams of getting out and finding regular work surface again. He has started to help out in a ladies' shop owned by a neighbouring family who manage a string of small shops in the Persian Gulf state of Oman. Like many others, Premadasan sees his only hope as a *chance* taking him beyond Mumbai – where wages are low and in rupees – to a place where wages are reputedly fabulously high and come in a solid foreign currency.

Kuttiyil

The Kuttiyil family who own the shop where Premadasan helps out were close neighbours of ours in 1990 when Suresh, at 23 the youngest of five brothers, was called to Muscat. We were invited to the main house for his send-off. This house, the first in the neighbourhood to be reconstructed during the early 1980s building boom, is one of four impressive brick and concrete structures standing in a walled-off roadside plot, all built according to plans brought from the Gulf and modified to fit *taccasastram* requirements. From 1989 to the present, there has always been building work going on, as the brothers construct, extend and improve their respective residences. While the wives and children sleep in their own houses and cook separately, the house where mother lives with the eldest daughter-in-law is the hub of the family. The television, video, stereo and fridge-freezer are all kept in this main house, which is also richly furnished with a three-piece suite in red velvet, a large polished dining table and many ornaments in a glass display case. Despite the constant flow of people streaming through night and day, the house is kept spotless and tidy. In time, as years pass and cash is accumulated, each house will be fitted out and furnished like mother's, and a new house will be constructed for Suresh, who has yet to marry.

Suresh's departure was to be at 8.45 a.m., the auspicious moment advised by the astrologer, although his flight was not until late evening. That morning, mother and daughters-in-law passed around tea and snacks to a crowd of relatives and neighbours milling excitedly around the house: admiring Suresh's smart black moulded plastic suitcase with combination lock; adjusting his going-away outfit; constantly checking the time, anxious not to let the *muhurtam* pass: poring over the magical air ticket in its shiny folder for the umpteenth time; teasing Suresh about his film-star style in his passport photograph. As Suresh's mother pressed her son to eat two more *idli*, she spoke:

Some families have enough money; they don't need to go to the Gulf but can stay and look after their fields. If we stay in our own place we wouldn't have a chance to rise in our situation. If you have Gulf money, you can live well. Everyone here is interested to go, but some families are too poor: you need at least Rs25,000 to go. There is jealousy from families who can't afford to go and also within families – if one member goes, he must call others.

The Kuttiyil family worked at the turn of the century as servants for wealthy caste-fellows and as petty traders. Menfolk visited temple festivals and fairs selling posters, small toys and cheap ornaments. Some family branches are still involved in this itinerant petty trade. Family women undertook dressmaking or did casual labour. Suresh's father saved enough capital to open a permanent ladies' shop in Krisnakara town and send Rajesh, eldest son, to work as a shop-assistant in Mumbai. When the 1970s Gulf boom arrived, the chance came for Rajesh to go; other brothers have followed. One brother stays in Valiyagramam to man the shop in town and do the family's marketing and other 'public' jobs which respectable women cannot do.

Suresh chewed miserably on his *idli*, not looking at all like a man interested in going to the Gulf. He had already said his goodbyes to friends the night before, furtively sharing a bottle of brandy, sitting behind a pile of logs outside the wood-mill. These boys had grown up knit closely together, attending neighbourhood schools, playing in the lanes and running between each other's wooden or unplastered brick two-roomed houses from one unfenced compound to another. Now their paths were diverging: most were struggling half-heartedly with further study; some were already in dead-end jobs or back-breaking manual labour. Almost all wished that they could have a chance to go to the Gulf, flying on an aeroplane, dressed in new ready-made shirt and pants, and returning in glory having made some real money.

Seven months later a polished Ambassador taxi left the village at 4 a.m. for Thiruvananthapuram airport. All day neighbours asked one another, 'Has Rajesh come yet?', and continually watched the junction. In the late afternoon the taxi arrived, its roof-rack gratifyingly laden with cardboard boxes, cases and bags whose contents were the subject of the neighbours' feverish speculation. Eldest brother Rajesh got out, and the small crowd gathered in the lane took careful note of the gold watch on his right wrist, the one-sovereign chain around his neck and his large signet ring. Older villagers noted how Rajesh had aged since his last visit home – five years beofre – remarking that he had become thinner and darker. Young men carefully scrutinised his hair-style, the cut of his trousers, his Lacoste polo shirt and his gleaming black mock-croc moccasins: avid followers of fashion all, they knew that what came from the Gulf this month would be *de rigueur* fashion wear in all Kerala by next month.

During his visit, Rajesh went many times to town: treating friends to drinks in the town's air-conditioned bar; taking family children by taxi to the ice-cream parlour. Rajesh bought a brand new 'Bullet' brand motorbike, which – a neighbour recounted – he had paid for with cash notes (over Rs30,000). After a few days, when the hectic visiting and gift-giving had died down, we went to talk to Rajesh. A younger sister, whose fate was probably to marry a Gulf migrant, stood in the kitchen doorway frowning and listening intently as Rajesh spoke, mainly in English, with words and phrases in Malayalam, Hindi and Arabic thrown in:

Six years ago I went to Muscat through a Mumbai *agent* : salaries are lower there, but conditions are better. Kuwait used to be the best place for money, now it's Saudi. For a 'free visa', where you can go to any Gulf country and do any job, you need to pay Rs25,000 then buy your ticket on top. Otherwise you go with an Arab sponsor who promises you a job and accommodation; you have to surrender your passport so that you can't walk out for a better job.

Malayalis there are mostly in construction work; it's better to have your own business, your freedom. Employees get problems like being asked to work longer hours, getting paid less, being told that they've also got to go to the Arab's home and work there doing cooking or housework or something. I started out as a salesman but now I've got my own business; the *Araby* is the owner on paper, because foreign nationals can't own property. I run the business and give him commission: it's rare for them to cheat, they're honest. I've got a supermarket selling clothes, electronics, everything – that's where Suresh's working now. Everything you get here, you can get there from a Malayali wholesaler, but the tapioca will cost Rs60 per kg, where here it's Rs4.

Where we live, there's no Europeans – they're in the cities in officer jobs – just Filipinos, Pakistanis, Bengalis. The Arabs don't mix with us at all; we mix with Pakistanis and with other Malayalis. Houses are all different too: office workers get air-conditioned concrete houses; ordinary workers have brick, wood or metal sheeting, and have to buy air-conditioning units and fit them themselves. The heat is the main problem there. Then the law is different, we don't have equality with Arabs. If you marry an Omani girl you can get citizenship but you must become a Muslim, wear a cap, get circumcised. In Muscat there are temples and churches; in Saudi other religions are forbidden – Muslims get more consideration in the Gulf. The worst treatment is given to our people, Hindus: they call us *Kaffirs* or *Baniyas*. Nobody in this family is interested to settle there: our wives and children are all here.

The ticket fare to come home is Riyals 250, Rs15,000: before the Gulf War it was only Rs8000. You only come home every four or five years, otherwise you can't save. It's been a sudden development: before the Gulf, Christians used to be poor. They take their wives to work as nurses: Christians like a working wife, but a Hindu loses prestige

if he has his wife working abroad; a Hindu woman should stay in the house. If a
Christian has a rupee he'll invest it and make it into two; Hindus have to waste a lot of
money on families.

'*PROGRESSINU VENDI*' (FOR THE SAKE OF PROGRESS): THE IZHAVA SEARCH FOR SOCIAL MOBILITY AND MODERNITY

This is a book about the modern search for upward social mobility: processes
which it involves, ideologies which support or thwart it, and about what
happens to the people involved in it. All the people above – Advocate Remini,
K.V. Krishnan, Keshavan, Premadasan, Rajesh, Suresh – come from one
rural area and belong to one caste in India's south-western state, Kerala.
That caste – Izhavas – consisted in the mid-nineteenth century of a small
landowning and titled elite and a large mass of landless and small tenants
who were largely illiterate, considered untouchable, and who eked out a
living by manual labour and petty trade. During the twentieth century,
Izhavas have pursued mobility in many social arenas, both as a newly united
caste and as individual families, and have expanded their horizons beyond
the confines of state and nation.

One of the earliest doctoral theses submitted to the London School of
Economics' Department of Social Anthropology was entitled 'Culture
Change in South-Western India'. This 1937 thesis, documenting and
reflecting upon the century's recent rapid social changes and their effects
upon the Izhava community, was written by A. Aiyappan, himself an Izhava
and later to become a prominent social anthropologist. His work captures
prevailing moods: in his first monograph, noting progress in education,
health care, employment and so on, and acknowledging a cultural
interchange during late colonialism which he saw as partly fruitful, he
confidently foresaw the possibility of the abolition of caste, 'it is only a matter
of time for the superstructures to crumble' (1944: 194). Twenty years later
(1965), *Social revolution in a Kerala village* charted the Izhava caste's
continuing progress since Indian independence in 1947 and the 1957
election of a Communist state government in Kerala, whose reforms
included programmes of land redistribution, free education and health care,
and an end to all caste discrimination. Aiyappan again methodically
recorded and commented upon the continuing progress of his community,
noting with satisfaction that while things were by no means perfect, it could
be assumed that beneficial change would continue with continuing
modernisation.

At the end of the century, then, this book can be seen as an attempt
at taking stock of Aiyappan's predictions and expectations for the future
of his community. We will consider how successful the Izhava mobility
project has been and look at the effects within a society of a widespread ethos
of mobility, now lexicalised in Malayalam as *progress*. We will look at
practices which Izhavas self-consciously undertake or avoid 'for the sake

of progress' ('*progressinu vendi*'). Throughout, in order better to understand present experience, we will refer to the recent history partly charted by Aiyappan.

Modernity, together with a generalised commitment to progress, appears as integral to Izhavas' self-defined identities, embedded in community identity – forged and articulated from the mid-nineteenth century onwards through a long process of internal reforms and mobilisation, in a dialogue between local ideas of justice and equality and European-derived notions of modernity and reform (cf. Prakash 1996, 1999; Chatterjee 1993; Oddie 1995; Pandian 1995; Hardgrave 1969; O'Hanlon 1985; Hardiman 1987). Miller writes that 'what does indeed make Trinidadians modern is the fragility of their self-creation' (1994a: 293): if modernity is taken by many to be characterised by reflexivity, alienation and self-doubt, then the post-colonies are laboratories of modernity as much for the identity formations they foster as for their wilder excesses in capitalist production (cf. Breman 1991; Kelly 1991; Gilroy 1993; cf. Friedman 1990). Miller argues 'it would be hard to find comparable examples of unremitting rupture, alienation or the denigration of custom in Europe' (1994: 293). Izhavas are then hyper-examples of the processes discussed by Miller, in as much as they consciously chose as a group total repudiation of their nineteenth-century selves, leaving them with an 'identity gap'. This gap they chose to fill with a sense of themselves as 'modern', standing near to Kerala's 'progressive' Christian communities and against high-caste Hindus (Brahmans, Nayars) whose own particular form of modern self-consciousness took the form of cultivating essentialised identities rooted in 'tradition' and 'authenticity' (cf. Friedman 1990).[1] At the same time, after the reform movement's first flush, Izhavas find themselves increasingly searching for forms of symbolic capital whose referents are Nayar practice. While we admit as real the possibility of accepting history as only artificially periodicised, and modernity as a chimera (evidenced by the impossibility of agreement among theorists on its defining characteristics or time-scale), we will be exploring the argument that Izhava lives are as exemplary as any other twentieth-century lives and that, in their avowedly modern orientation towards progress and in their hyper-reflexivity, Izhavas go further and throw light upon the qualities of modernity itself, whether we take that to be an unachievable goal, a working project or a theoretical and folk-pragmatic concept. The ethnography offers a complex and not entirely predictable picture of modernity. We find rupture and rapid change, but also continuities and a sense of appropriateness: Izhavas see themselves has having always had a substantial 'affinity' with modernity and progress. Modernity and progress are experienced not as linear, positive trajectories, but as ambivalent: material advancement sometimes brings social advancement, but often involves suffering and separation, leading simultaneously to exclusion and stigmatisation of community members who fail to live up to group endeavour. Modernity and progress also transcend modernist reason, tinged with luck and magic.

The story of this community is specific and unique – different, for example, from that of the Nadars, a similarly placed caste in neighbouring Tamil Nadu (see Hardgrave 1969; Templeman 1996) but also, we argue, an archetypal one. It represents one of the possible workings out of modernity in a place at the so-called peripheries of modern capitalism; actually, we believe, a central part of this century's global story in which all of us are implicated (cf. for example Miller 1994a; Gardner 1995: 269ff). As a social group openly committed to the active pursuit of mobility in both cultural and economic life, the experience of the Izhavas provides much food for thought for those interested in exploring at a general level issues of stratification and mobility or evaluating the successes and failures of modernisation and recent economic liberalisation processes, as well as for those interested in Kerala's 'social experiment' programmes of redistribution and promotion of equality. The Izhavas' story is well worth close scrutiny outside the narrow confines of Indian anthropology.

Another thread running through our argument and ethnography is the question of identity. Our analysis will involve a degree of artificial breaking down of categories, the better to examine and unravel the threads of caste, class, religious status, gender and family name which mesh to make up the social status of heterogeneous families in different areas of social life. Identity has at least four levels of meaning and association: for the person, ontologically; for others, looking at and placing the person within various social arenas; for the community, presenting a group face to itself and to other groups; finally, analytically, for us as outsiders looking in. Within these four levels, identity is always multiple, and always composed of interwoven threads of caste, class, religion, party affiliation, family, house name, occupation, gender, age and locality. One of these threads – caste – is something not found in postcolonial and late modern societies outside South Asia and its diaspora. Caste identity and status are explicitly ascribed through and accorded to a group or to persons as members of a group: in matters of caste, a person's identity is as dependent upon the behaviour of their neighbours as upon themselves. Attempts to shift identity or status must be worked out in relation to the group. A subjective caste identity, as a group identity, is also a strong example of the 'group within' (Daniel 1984; Roland 1988; Kurtz 1992). Unlike some commentators, we do not take this to make South Asian identity qualitatively different from other identities: we take Izhava 'selves' to be, like all 'selves', not a unified subject or agent but a constantly shifting combination of roles and statuses, of consciousness in constant reaction to the environment, loosely and only superficially unified around the apparent singularity of the person, located within a single body (see for example Daniel 1984; Dirks 1992; Muralidharan 1996; Moore 1994; Kondo 1990; Bradley 1996). And we see several parallels between caste and ethnicity, caste in no way making the South Asian experience unique and incompatible with other forms of differentiation.

We will see throughout that sometimes class issues are presented as though they were caste issues and vice versa, and will turn to the work of Pierre Bourdieu for a way out of the sterile impasse of debates about whether the 'real' issue is caste or class. Political debates around reservation or positive discrimination for India's 'Backward Classes' which argued over whether 'Backwardness' was primarily economic or social, have concluded that it is clearly a matter of both, while academic writers have found that a disaggregated approach may still be convenient for analysis but fail to capture realities. An example is the vexed question in sociological literature of the relationship of class to statuses such as 'race' and 'sex'. While early work held categories as separate and tended to see different statuses operating in different arenas (see for example the work of Myrdal cited in Warner et al. 1994), and later work acknowledged an intersection or interaction between categories, most recent (post-1980s) work suggests that categories actively participate in and shape each other, such that for example, 'race is ... the modality in which class is "lived" ' (Hall 1980, cited in Bradley 1996: 126). As Fernandes writes, 'The question ... is how to ... move beyond an "interaction" or "interplay" between discrete identities, terms that continue to suggest static distinctions between categories of social analysis' (1997: 6).

We can then usefully underwrite and explore connections between 'categories', understanding their separateness to be an analytical fiction, while understanding the issues they raise at a broader level by means of a more general analytic notion of capital accumulation, where capital includes not only economic, but also symbolic, social and cultural components (see for example Bourdieu 1990: 112ff; Bourdieu & Wacquant 1992: 118ff; cf. Beteille 1991: 20, 'We require a more extended concept of capital ... that calls for a considerable change in our analytic strategy.'). While Bourdieu analyses capital as something which is present to a greater or lesser degree, or absent, we will extend the metaphor further to differentiate between positive capital, that which is considered desirable within the mainstream, and negative capital, a sort of negative balance to be erased or negative equity which needs to be compensated.

Moving on, we will take the position that environment, social identities and consciousness are strongly interconnected so that there are many points of correspondence between the world 'out there' and the self 'in here'. While we do not wish to see Izhavas as liberal individuals, whether that be the free agents of Enlightenment myth or the romantic radicals sometimes apparent in the work of 'Subaltern Studies' historians, nor do we wish to see them as locked in by structures, their lives and consciousness totally determined by social position and ideology (O'Hanlon 1988; Sivaramakrishnan 1995). Another plank in our theoretical orientation is the idea of agents using creative 'strategies' (see for example Bourdieu & Wacquant 1992: 128ff; Bouveresse 1995: 583ff; Mahar et al. 1990: 17ff). We try throughout, perhaps not always successfully, to steer a careful course between the twin perils of subjectivism and objectivism (for example Bourdieu 1990: 30–51), by presenting Izhavas as agents making choices which both makes good sense in view of their historical and social locations and represents a set of options from a set of possibilities which itself is not limitless; they are more likely to make certain choices from the set of possibilities than others. Another way of looking at this is through the notion of 'habitus', where social position over-determines practice via embodied common-sense knowledge (Bourdieu 1990: 52ff; Bouveresse 1995: 581).[2] Habitus is not determinist and must be understood as contributing to a general direction, not a precise trajectory (Bouveresse 1995: 586).[3] Bourdieu's point about 'double historicity', by which he refers to the identification of social being with history, means that the social histories of the groups to which someone belongs, together with people's own personal life-trajectory, suggest particular responses to circumstances and predispose them towards certain responses or strategies: finally, then, it is in the bodies of persons that the multiple strands of history come together (Codd 1990: 139): the habitus excludes liberal philosophy's subject, but not the historicised and historical agent (Bourdieu & Wacquant 1992: 140). We will move between several time-frames: for example individual life-cycle; familial group mobility cycle; twentieth-century history.

This leads us on to argue that while it is not possible to read off linear correspondences between social positions and consciousness, it may sometimes be possible to trace some connections, through ethnography and history, and to make global connections between social groups occupying similar structural locations. Erikson and Goldthorpe (1994) in a retrospective of general sociological literature on social mobility, outline several phases. First, they present variants of dominant post-1960s liberal theory proposing that industrialisation brings absolute and ever-increasing upward mobility and of this hypothesis' opposite, Marxist proletarianisation theory. Empirical studies following up these positions have led to more refined and tentative claims being made. First, that mobility may increase or decrease in different historical and geographical circumstances, so that post-eighteenth-century apparent mobility increases (in Europe and the USA) associated with industrialisation do not represent a general or a continuing tendency. Second, that periods of rapid upheaval may produce temporary effects of mobility, but that longer-term trends may tend towards stasis, as social strata close over time. An important thread in these debates has been that of whether mobility rates for industrialised societies are constant and comparable; crucial data in this regard has been provided both by studies of intergenerational mobility and of occupational ranking, showing remarkable cross-national similarities. Problems with evaluating empirical data are many; for example, the very existence of increased mobility itself remains hotly disputed, as sociologists argue about what constitutes mobility; movement ('infiltration') of individuals into higher social strata; the abolition of certain strata and evolution of new ones; re-evaluation of strata (see for example Sorotkin 1994). Some argued that rates of mobility remained constant throughout time and place, as it is normal in industrial societies for children to find occupations in sectors different from those of the parents (see for example Lipset et al. 1994).

In any case, a broad consensus can be summarised thus: that all societies at all times have some forms of inequalities; that formal stratification 'systems' rely upon several variables, by no means all economic;[4] that mobility is most pronounced in the middle of status and class hierarchies, notably among blue-collar workers, and is least likely at extremes, as among agricultural labourers and professionals; that mobility correlates (highly) with education and (less surely so) with a 'mobility ethos' (Gilbert & Kahl 1982; Grusky 1994a and 1994b). The Kerala experience recounted in these pages will confirm that India fits into these general frameworks.

While we follow the work of Bourdieu in many respects, in one particular methodological point we differ. As Barnard (1990: 77ff) points out, 'Bourdieu's analyses have never been directed at groups per se but at a completely different constructed object, the field'. Barnard takes our fellow-ethnographer Rabinow to task for not having learnt Bourdieu's radical lesson of looking not for groups, but for fields within which relations are played out. We are choosing to examine an intersection of the two by looking at one group – Izhavas – in interaction with other groups, all of whom occupy positions within various spheres of social life constituting fields in which struggles for capital are played out. While a field is, for Bourdieu, the primary focus of analysis, being, 'spaces of objective relations that are specific and irreducible ... follow[ing] specific logics', a field is also defined as 'a network, or a configuration, of objective relations between positions' (Bourdieu & Wacquant 1992: 97). The importance of the field is that it defines the 'game', 'a capital does not exist and function except in relation to a field', while allowing in history, highlighting the idea of competition and movements between groups, 'the field is also a field of struggles' (Bourdieu & Wacquant 1992: 101). While we start from the point of view of a group's practice and experience, we will always think of the group in relation to those who surround them, and see them acting within fields which are, of course, also occupied by others.

We have chosen to work outwards to fields from a particular group because of the reality and salience of caste, especially for ex-untouchable and *sudra* groups, a point made strongly by, for example, Pandian, who takes postcolonial historians (especially those of the Cambridge school) to task for 'expel[ling] caste identities from their accounts' (1995: 387). While we in no way wish to reproduce the style of colonial accounts or take the power of the king or the censor to name and classify (Duncan 1990: 182ff), and while we fully accept that caste as we see it today is at least partly a colonial construction, we follow Pandian and those among whom we worked in giving it close consideration (Inden 1990; Dirks 1987, 1992; Muralidharan 1996).[5] We strongly believe that caste remains a legitimate subject of analysis and that a study taking off from the point of view of a group which constitutes itself and is constituted by others as a caste is valid; caste's existence and continuing importance in daily life will also be apparent in the ethnography to come. In a focus on caste, we are in no way claiming any sort of high ground for our own, caste-less society; as Dirks argues, 'India's postcolonial condition is not its precolonial fault' (1992: 76), while other status distinctions play similar roles to caste in non-caste societies, which remain riddled with the discriminations and prejudices built around 'race', class and gender (for example Bradley 1996; Grusky 1994a: 194).

We also reject both the idea that caste itself defines the total or major experience of being a Hindu Indian, and that India represents something unique or unfathomable. While our method is to present detailed ethno-graphy contextualised within some local history, in the hope of presenting 'little things about many people, systematically bound together' (Bourdieu 1976: 420, quoted in Barnard 1990: 78), we hold fast to the possibility that our work can be used by others who wish to construct wider, generalising frames. While a wider vision is beyond the scope of a single ethnography, we will occasionally use ourselves, socially positioned subjects, with particular social backgrounds and life-experiences, to hint at some of the possibilities which we see. The search for upward social mobility is a theme which we hold to be a common twentieth-century experience of many communities, status groups and classes dispersed around the globe; the struggle for upward mobility via capital accumulation is a universal game with many players, and many of the game's processes and underpinnings are shared across different parts of the globe.[6] With these general issues always in the back of our minds, we turn now to the story of a part of one community in one part of the modern world as we have been helped to understand it.

Until the beginning of the twentieth century, while Izhavas worked as wood-cutters, boatmen, tenant-cultivators, small traders, teachers and Ayurvedic physicians, a large part of the caste either worked as agricultural labourers or concentrated on the extremely low-status 'traditional' caste occupation of tending coconut palms and exploitation of their products: coir, jaggery, toddy and arrack. Politically and economically weak, stigmatised as 'toddy-tappers' and considered unapproachable, Izhavas were associated with other manual-labouring untouchable castes such as Pulayas, agrestic slaves who worked in the paddy fields. The late nineteenth century rise in demand and prices for coconut products, the growth and diversification of the colonial economy, and migration (especially to Malaysia) saw the rise within the Izhava community of a small middle class who joined the caste's existing elite. Under their influence, several social reform and pressure group movements grew up throughout the 1920s and 1930s, the most successful being the Sri Narayana Dharma Paripalana (SNDP) Yogam, or the society for the preservation of the moral law of Sri Narayana Guru. This organisation, under the Guru's spiritual leadership, started a state-wide process of transformation and radical reform of the caste's social,

religious and economic endeavours. This was accompanied by a mass
campaign for the abolition of untouchability and to obtain political
recognition, part of the general wave of social protest movements sweeping
India at the time.

Advocate Remini's family, like her husband's family, made their fortunes
at the beginning of the twentieth century, when the expansion of capitalist
production under colonialism drew many into plantations and the new
opportunities offered by an expanding international commodity trade. While
they are now part of the rural elite – educated and cultured professionals –
three generations ago their family fortunes were not yet made and their
households consisted of illiterate untouchable labourers. Some years later, in
the 1930s and 1940s, Premadasan's father and neighbour attempted – with
little success – to ride the bandwagon of migration within the British
colonies. Keshavan failed to reach a high-earning position, perhaps because
of his unwillingness to act as a *kangany* for the colonial planters, unlike the
greedy nephews in his story who put gold before moral social relations.
Keshavan contented himself with withdrawal from nineteenth-century
village patterns of agrarian employment, taking the opportunity for
increased security, autonomy and dignity offered by the moderately secure
and decently paid work available on the ferries through expanding local
trade. Keshavan's son, having tried an option – internal migration within
India – through which many families prospered during the post-
independence economic restructuring of the 1950s and 1960s, has realised
that rupee wage rates, increasingly bad living conditions in the metropolises,
and rising costs of living in Kerala make this option no longer a viable route
to increased wealth and prestige. Since the 1970s, this road has been
superseded by migration to the Persian Gulf, the means by which Suresh's
family has managed to construct houses for its brides, buy private education
for its grand-children and fill the house with the consumer goods so desired
throughout Kerala.

While they are of the same caste, an enormous social gap exists between
Advocate Remini's family – who openly mock the newly Gulf-rich as
uncultured, flashy and over-lavish spenders, ridiculing their concrete
mansions and gold watches as *nouveau-riche* ostentations – and Suresh's
family – former servants and agricultural labourers who count no
professionals or graduates among their number. Yet in its day, Vallatu
family's huge *nalukettu* with its four-cow cow-shed and rambling grounds
must have seemed as gaudily ostentatious to the then local elite, the high-
caste Hindus who were entitled by tradition to live in such houses, as any
marbled Gulf mansion may seem now. The lavish dowries and jewels
provided by Remini's father to his daughters were certainly derided as the
unnecessary expenditures of the *nouveaux riches*, keen to buy status. Many
villagers probably mocked the ration-shop owner's desire to make his
daughters into advocates and schoolteachers, as many now sneer when they
see Suresh's nephews and nieces in their sky-blue uniforms, waiting for the

school bus to take them to the convent school in town where wealthy
Christians send their children and where teaching is done in the prestige
language, English. Such criticisms and derision are ignored by the upwardly
mobile as sour-grapes: *progress*, for the many who eagerly seek it, is a long-
term strategic family project, while refusal to 'know one's place' within
village caste hierarchies belonging to the nineteenth century is no sin. Since
Narayana Guru exhorted his caste-mates to seek self-improvement, and
since the caste took up the project of mobility in earnest as a group goal, it
has actually become a virtue.

At the beginning of the twentieth century, as Izhavas' existing
stigmatised caste identity was repudiated, and as class mobility was sought, a
new group identity centred around generalised ideals of 'progress' and
'mobility' was formed and new imperatives were set: education, respectable
employment, thrift and accumulation of wealth, abolition of untouchability,
entry into the mainstream Hindu fold. The project has been partially
successful: Izhavas have managed to gain access to education, public office
and temples, all barred to them in the nineteenth century; with the
introduction of universal franchise, they have also been able to project and
promote their caste interests at a wider political level. While the hated
'*avarna*' tag remains, Izhavas have gone some way towards re-defining
themselves as non-untouchables. At the same time, new economic
opportunities have significantly increased economic differentiation within
the caste.

THE SETTING

Kerala

Those whose lives are represented in this book live in a rural part of
Kerala, formed in 1956 by the unification of formerly British administered
Malabar with Malayalam-speaking districts of south Kanara and the
erstwhile princely states of Travancore and Cochin, ten years after the
latter had become part of the Indian Union (see Maps 1 and 2). Kerala is a
narrow strip, with a 580 km coastline, and an east–west spread of 120 km,
covering 38,864 square km. It is bounded on the west by the Arabian Sea
and separated from Tamil Nadu on the east by the high ranges of the Ghats
(see Map 3). These are forested and plantationed (tea, rubber, coffee) hills
which run at an average height of 950 m, but which reach over 2000 m at
several points. Land is divided by geographers and Malayalis alike into three
natural longitudinal divisions: *tira pradesam,* a low-lying coastal and
backwater strip; *sammatala pradesam,* a central zone from 30–200 m,
characterised by red laterite soil and scrubland; and *mala pradesam* or hill/
mountain country, formerly thickly forested, now less so. Kerala has 44
rivers and many lakes, the largest of which – the Vembanad – covers 200
square km. This wealth of natural resources, yielding lush vegetation and
permitting dense population settlement, has contributed to Kerala's

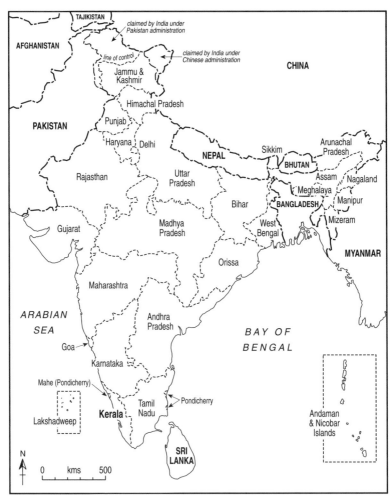

Map 1. India showing Kerala

reputation as 'God's own country', a sort of earthly paradise nowadays aggressively marketed for international tourism (cf. Miller 1954; Mencher 1966a; Menon & Rajan 1989).

Development theorists have been particularly interested in Kerala as a state which, despite low GDP and per capita income, scores high on social development indices such as birth rates, literacy and provision of social services (see Government of Kerala 1993; Franke 1994; Franke & Chasin 1994). Kerala has appeared to some as a paradigm of cheap social development which could be applied elsewhere; to others it is a unique experiment (Jeffrey 1993). Critical appraisals demonstrate that some cornerstones of Kerala development, for example land reforms, bypassed the poorest section

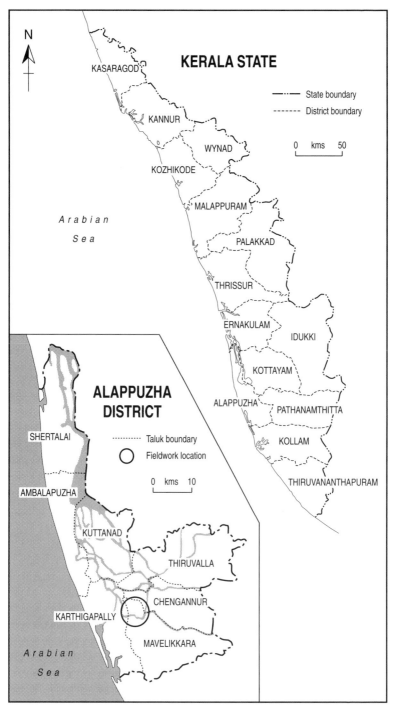

Map 2. Kerala showing Alappuzha District and fieldwork location

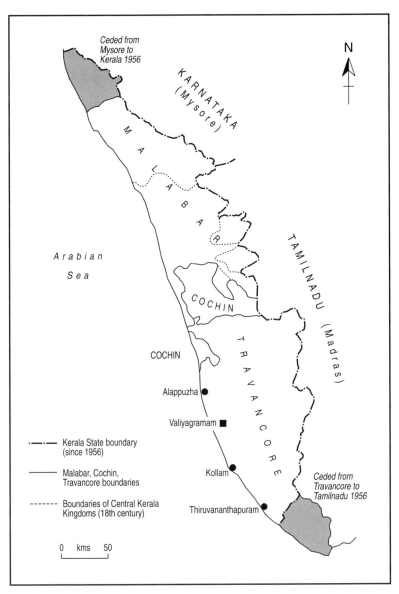

Map 3. Pre-unification Kerala

of the population (Krishnaji 1979; Radhakrishnan 1980, 1983, 1989; Herring 1980, 1983, M.A. Oommen 1994) and that caste continues to influence education and employment opportunities (Sivanandan 1979). Others point out that the 'Kerala model' depended upon a particular reading of specific indices and a generalised picture which overlooks the conditions of poverty still experienced by many Malayalis (Mencher 1980, 1994; Nieuwenhuys 1991; Mohandas 1994; Kurien 1995). Many papers at the 1994 International Congress on Kerala Studies (AKG Centre 1994) critically examine this 'Kerala model', the assumptions behind it and the political motivations behind its promotion. Our experience from fieldwork is that the benefits of social development are highly unevenly distributed and are grounded as much in factors of chance such as private investment or precarious foreign remittances as in government-led and grassroots-controlled reforms (cf. for example Raghavan 1994; Kurien 1995; Isaac & Tharakan 1995).

Nor in our experience do Kerala villagers content themselves with literacy classes or local health dispensaries, but want to participate directly in and receive full benefits from *progress* as they define it, which would mean striving to bring their standards of living up to those enjoyed not only by the affluent Indian middle classes but by those who set the international pace, particularly in consumption – notably Arabs, Europeans and North Americans. Theories of development which implicitly set acceptable standards of living for Malayali villagers different to those enjoyed in 'developed' regions deny co-evalness and the reality of one complex world (see for example Appadurai 1990b; Ahmad 1992; Gardner 1995). While Malayalis are generally proud of their state's achievements and reputation, the villagers we know – who criticise the GATT agreements, discuss political developments in eastern Europe, and make plans to migrate to west Asia – do not want to be part of a 'Kerala model', but of one complex interconnected world: like them, we insist upon Kerala's central location within wider global processes.

Valiyagramam – Punjakara Panchayat, 'The Village'

The data on which this book is based are drawn from three periods of joint fieldwork (June 1989 to June 1991; December 1994 to June 1995; December 1995 to June 1996) within one rural *panchayat* in central Travancore whose population at the 1991 census was 27,569. Valiyagramam *panchayat* is formally split into two named villages administered by two village offices keeping separate records of land-holdings, land taxes, government subsidies, pensions and so on. Ignoring stereotypical ideas about what constitutes a 'village' or village life, we follow local usage in referring to the *panchayat* – large, densely populated, unbounded, well-connected and developed as it may be – as 'the village' (*ii gramam* or *ii naadu*, this village, this land, cf. Daniel 1984: 61).

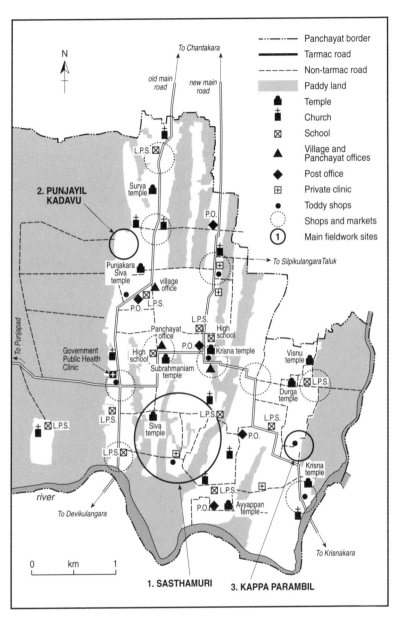

Map 4. Valiyagramam showing fieldwork areas, roads and landmarks

During our residencies, we worked and socialised with families from all communities and undertook intensive fieldwork involving closer interaction and basic house-to-house surveys in three areas (see Map 4). Sasthamuri, where we lived from 1989 to 1991, is a highly differentiated area of 176 households near to the main road, a major temple and the main market: it is populated by Izhavas, Christians and Nayars, some of whom live in large two-storeyed mansions and some in thatched huts. The second area, Punjayil Kadavau, is a *Harijan colony* (areas where members of ex-untouchable Scheduled Castes are housed under near-segregation) formed in the 1970s, a clearly demarcated area in the north-west, bordering onto the *punja*. Almost all the 85 homes in this poor neighbourhood, inhabited mostly by Pulayas living alongside a handful of poorer Christian and Izhava families, are labourers' thatched huts. The third area, Kappa Parambil, is a distinct Izhava-only area at the south-east near to *virippu* and a popular Durga temple and named after the large Izhava family, comprising 46 households, which spreads over several acres of land there and whose members live in thatched huts, small brick houses or single-storey bungalows.

Quantitative data on the village population were collected ward by ward over several lengthy interviews with *panchayat* members and older 'knowledgeable' people from various castes. Going through electoral rolls, these informants were able to provide complete breakdowns of households within their ward identified by caste/community. For each ward we then cross-checked directly a random sample of the households for which members' names did not offer any obvious clues as to community affiliation. In no case did this data contradict the original information given by informants, and we therefore consider it reliable. An additional general survey of households belonging to communities not well represented in the three intensive fieldwork areas (including Christian households) was conducted among a selected sample of households. Among the four main castes/communities (Christians, Nayars, Izhavas and Pulayas) there is only minimal variation in family size (0.75 more children per household among Pulayas), while the developmental cycle of the household follows a similar pattern among all four. Plus-and-minus variations between percentage of households and population in the ward among these four communities can be ascribed to temporary variations in household composition, usually accounted for by reason of relatively high or low incidence of migration. Among Christians, Nayars and Izhavas – all communities with a high incidence of migration – it is common to find households composed either of older parents alone (sons and daughters residing outside of the village) or of a woman alone plus her children (cf. Gulati 1983, 1993). This situation is not found among Pulayas who, because of economic and social constraints, have a much lower degree of migration.

The *panchayat* covers 5577 acres of *tira pradesam*, bounded on two sides by a large river: to the south lies the prosperous town of Krisnakara, where the

Block Development Office, railway station and many modern glass-fronted shops (some with air-conditioning) are situated. Krisnakara was an important town in the petty princely state of Pandalam (mythical childhood home of the popular South Indian deity Aiyappan) until 1812, when it was absorbed into Travancore State, the latter incorporated into Kerala as part of the Indian union in 1957. To Valiyagramam's eastern border is the Christian-dominated Silpikulangara *taluk*; on the west side, an artificial irrigation canal separates Valiyagramam's paddy fields from those of Punjapad village. The northern border is not demarcated by any boundary, and there Valiyagramam runs into Chantakara *panchayat*, an area famous for its many Muslim metal traders. On Valiyagramam's west side spread 2985 acres of single-crop irrigated paddy land, *punja*; to the east are 758 acres of double-crop land, *virippu*; between the two lies a long narrow strip of 1834 acres of *parambu*, prime garden land used for habitation and for cultivation of trees such as coconut, banana, jackfruit, areca, mango and cashew; root vegetables such as tapioca and various types of yam; and secondary cash crops such as pepper (Map 5). While many families, mostly from Christian and lower-caste Hindu communities, live around the *punja* and the *virippu*, the *parambu* is the village proper where temples, churches and old houses are to be found and where higher-status Christian and Hindu families live.

A Village Tour

There are two roads running north to south through the village, from Chantakara to Krisnakara: an original old main road, now a secondary

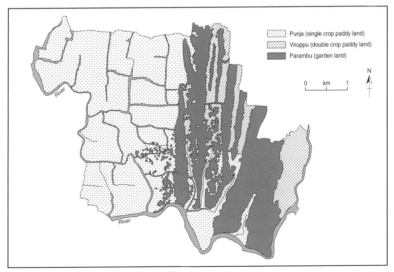

Map 5. Valiagramam showing land types

tarmac road with light traffic, running on the western side through
Valiyagramam's old heart, separating the paddy fields from the inhabited
garden land; and a new major road carrying much traffic, a primary
highway on the eastern side (see Map 4). In between are many tarmac
secondary roads along which autos run, themselves crossed by scores of
narrow dirt tracks hidden among the ubiquitous coconut and banana trees
and snaking around and behind houses, so that it is possible to walk directly
off-road between almost any two parts of the village. These are the informal
paths taken by children who run safely in and out of each other's compounds
far from traffic, and by women, who are thereby able to range far visiting
neighbours and families, calling at the back doors without ever appearing in
public spaces.

Valiyagramam's northern end is a mostly Christian area with good brick
and concrete housing and Marthoma (Syrian Protestant), Jacoba (Syrian
Catholic) and Roman Catholic churches. Any of the small lanes and dirt-
tracks to the right (west) leads first into areas where ex-untouchables live –
mostly Pulayas, most of whom work as agricultural labourers – and then into
the *punja*: Punjayil Kadavu is here. Valiyagramam's *punja* (2 m below sea level)
floods during monsoon and forms the south-east corner of Kuttanad, Kerala's
rice-growing region.[7] Near the paddy fields, *Krishi Bhavan* (a government
office) dispenses advice, gives small grants (for example coconut plants),
administers subsidies on fertiliser and checks agricultural land plot boundaries. In the paddy fields stand small Hindu shrines, dedicated to ancestors and
fierce deities, and modest Christian chapels. These are the places of worship of
the ex-untouchables, mostly Pulayas and Parayans, who experience
continued discrimination and segregation, be they Hindu or Christian.[8]

Near the village office, the southernmost western lane makes an important junction with the old main road. Known as '*Pulaya pokkunnu mukku*', 'the
junction where the Pulayas go', it marks the boundary beyond which – in the
days when unapproachability was strictly enforced – Pulayas could not pass.
In 1983 a Nayar woman tried to prevent an Izhava girl from bathing in
Punjakara temple tank here; in the ensuing clashes between the Rashtriya
Swayasevak Sangh (RSS) and Communist Party of India (Marxist), a murder
took place in the temple grounds. Around Punjakara temple – a mainly
Nayar, Brahman and Christian area – stand several *nalukettus*: one has a
small disused temple and *kalari* attached; another, with a huge paddy store,
belongs to the Koickal family, the area's former *janmi*, primary landlord and
Nayar chieftain; yet another, two-storeyed, has recently been bought from its
Nayar advocate owner by a member of the Vira-Saiva caste, a former lowly
papadam-maker whose son is in the USA. The oldest and biggest traditional
house in the village, the two-storeyed Velathumpadi palace of Edapalli
Rajah, the absentee Brahman landlord who held many acres here (as in
many other villages) now stands empty apart from a colony of bats; a
collection box appealing for money to maintain the house stands fruitlessly
outside. Nearby stands one of the largest new two-storey mansions in the

village, owned by an Izhava, an ex-Gulf migrant with two sons still in the Gulf. A small road leading east from here is populated by 44 Izhava households belonging to one large family, allegedly involved in illegal liquor distilling. The village's newest *gurumandiram* shrine is half way up this road.

The new main road is busier: state and private buses going to Thiruvalla, Krisnakara, Chantakara or Changannasseri pass every ten minutes; two or three buses a day go to more distant destinations such as the state capital Thiruvananthapuram or the busy port city of Kochi. Houses along this road are mostly large, belonging to Nayars and Christians; many are Gulf mansions. Along this road stand Valiyagramam's major ration shop and the main Post Office, where people throng in the mornings waiting for news about family or a job, or for that all-important money order from the Gulf. Turning off here is Sasthamuri: a small road of Izhava and Marthomite Christian houses leads down to an area densely populated by Izhavas. Our first rented house (1989–91) was on this street.

Back at Puthenmookku junction on the main road stands a long two-storey concrete building, owned by a local Christian whose old-style lock-up shops include two popular provision stores (one Christian and one Izhava owned) and a video rental business run by three young men. Next door stands the main toddy shop, set discreetly back off the road; in the early morning outside here the meat market is held. Village men are served by seven toddy shops, licensed by the state government to sell *kallu* and – until the 1996 state government ban – *charayam*.[9] These are supplemented by a number of even more discreet unlicensed house-based stills whose owners are periodically rounded up and fined when the excise department comes to make a raid. Most of those involved in the liquor trade – as toddy-tappers, contractors, or shop-owners – are Izhavas.

Back at the roadside come four or five small sheds where poor Christians sell jaggery and eggs – hen and duck, local and imported – an occupation especially associated with their community. A shrine to the Jacobite saint Parumala Thirumeni leads to another row of lock-ups including a provision shop; a barber, member of the Izhavati caste, who will cut hair in his shop for men of any caste and who cuts hair in the home for Izhavas and Christians; the largest and most popular fruit and vegetable shop in the village, owned and run by a prosperous Izhava family. Next door stands Valiyagramam's biggest meals hotel and tea-shop, the Christian-owned 'Hotel Paradise', and two workshops owned by members of the Kollan (blacksmith) caste: a motor mechanic's and a smithy.

On the opposite side of the road is a brand-new shopping complex (row of shops), built in 1994 by the *panchayat*, with an open space behind where a fish and petty trade market takes place each afternoon. Among this complex's modern-style shops with glass doors and signboards outside are a pharmacy; a video and music studio; a ladies' store and ready-made clothes shop; the village's most popular bakery, owned by the Izhava family who run the greengrocer's opposite; an electrical shop; and a driving school. A laminating and screen-printing business and a travel agency and ISD/STD telephone booth are both owned by a wealthy Christian entrepreneur. Next to this prestigious shopping complex remain a few of the older petty shops which were there before, selling loose cigarettes and renting out chairs and *mandapams* for weddings.

Just past these shops stand two enormous Christian-owned mansions with double garages, air-conditioning, large compounds and high boundary walls. These houses are almost always empty. Their owners are settled in the USA, and come home occasionally to open up the houses for a wedding or baptism, better celebrated in the natal village than a strange land. Valiyagramam is full of empty houses temporarily abandoned by owners who are working away: in 1994, one week's enquiries brought us a choice of six houses to rent. Near here is a double-storeyed building housing a marble business and a *cool bar* (shop with fridge, selling cold drinks) owned by an Izhava ex-Mumbai-migrant. Perched on top of this building is a huge satellite dish: satellite and cable TV are recently available to the village's wealthier residents, who already have colour TVs and VCRs.

Towards the south end of the main road, a small lane leads into a Christian and Izhava area at the village's eastern borders, including the Izhava colony known as 'Kappa Parambil'. A Christian-owned match factory here provides employment to many of the village's poorer men and women, either in the workshop or as outworkers. The factory's owner lives in one of the village's largest mansions; his children are settled in the USA. At the junction here is the second village office, a motor mechanic's workshop, a beauty parlour, the Cooperative Bank, and a new diesel workshop opened by a Gulf-returned Izhava; and an important landmark, Dharmananda *asram*.

Shrines to the Virgin Mary and St Don Bosco mark the village's southern-most boundary, where Krisnakara town begins at Pallikara bridge. Hindu fisherfolk and Roman Catholic converts live here in small huts and houses along the river banks; a fish market is held daily. Elephants are often found here being scrubbed clean by their *pappan*; they may work in local wood mills or as temple elephants.

Valiyagramam has two main markets and several *mukkus* where people gather. At each junction there will be at least a small Hindu or Christian shrine (often both) and a wooden hut with a makeshift bench outside where tea, *naranga vellam*, bananas and single *beedis* or cigarettes can be bought and consumed; popular Malayalam serial-story weeklies such as *Mangalam* and a few sachets of toothpaste and shampoo hang from pegs on wires strung across the front of these huts. At busier junctions men stand in the evenings cooking chilli omelettes or *dosa* from handcarts for the many men passing by on their way home from market or toddy-shop.

Larger junctions have medical practices, public offices, daily petty markets and a queue of autos and taxis always waiting hopefully. They have rows of small concrete purpose-built shops, open-fronted during daytime with metal shutters drawn down at night. Price-controlled government *ration* shops and privately run provision shops both sell rice, lentils, chilli, onions, sugar, tea, coconuts, cooking spices and kerosene. *Tuni* shops have ready-made clothes as well as bales of cloth, *lungis* and *mundus*. White-coated staff at *medical stores* – Ayurvedic and allopathic – offer a range of medicines, tonics, shampoos, toothpastes and food supplements. Stationery shops sell not just paper, pens and exercise books for school students, but also plastic and glass bangles, cheap metal earrings, hair slides, nail varnish, soap, shampoo, toothpaste, plastic buckets and jugs, washing powder, disinfectant, incense and cooking spices. Bakeries sell bread, cakes, sweets, ready-made fried snacks such as banana chips, tea, dried milk, cooking spices, incense, soap, and shampoo and toothpaste in sachets. Some bakeries announce by painted signs outside that they are also *cool bars*, which means that they own a blender and a fridge, and that cold soft drinks (fruit juices or sodas) can be bought there.

Small *hotels* offer meals, snacks and non-alcoholic drinks; there are many video and music cassette rental libraries; several beauty parlours; an electrical shop; laundry and dry-cleaning agencies; and six or seven ISD/STD booths, from which metred telephone calls can be made to any part of the globe. A recently opened supermarket, a self-service shop whose clientele is mostly Christians and Gulf returnees, has shelves crammed with a variety of items unavailable elsewhere, such as frozen ready-made *chapati* with *chilli chicken*. The old country cinema burnt down in 1993 and has not been replaced, the owner – a Christian ex-Gulf entrepreneur – concentrating upon his second business: a print shop offering desk-top publishing with the latest computer technology. People prefer to visit one of Krisnakara's two 'proper' cinemas, while increasing numbers have access to television.

Businesses found only in town include *cold-stores* (shops with deep freezes selling frozen meat, etc.), bookstores, foreign liquor stores and commercial jewellers (several Thattans ply their trade locally from small houses-cum-workshops). Newspapers are read at the tea-shop or delivered to the house;[10] milk and yoghurt are bought from neighbours or the Milk Cooperative. All daily and many occasional purchases can be made locally – many people hardly ever visit Chantakara or Krisnakara towns, although both are within walking distance, just 3 km from the village 'centre'.

LOCAL COMMUNITIES

Izhavas (the biggest single community in Kerala) live in a state whose population covers a variety of Muslim, Christian and Hindu *communities* (*samudayangal*). While there are only a handful of Muslim families, Valiyagramam is a mixed village in which Izhavas are the third-largest group. Families of traditionally high status – Brahmans and aristocratic Nayars – live largely in the village interior, near to temples; other communities live scattered, the wealthier tending to move to large roadside plots. Residential areas are divided between a few *colonies* and the mixed areas, by far the majority.

Table 1.1 Village Population by Community

Community	Total number of households	Aiyappan's tripartite division
Brahman		
Nambutiri	29	A
Potti	3	A
Tamil	5	A
Embran	1	A
Ambalavasi (temple servants)		
Mussattu	3	A
Warrier	1	A
Unni	7	A
Other twice-born		
Varma	23	A
Reddiar	2	A
Sudra		
Nayar	1311	A
Maran	16	A
Nayar washer	19	A
Nayar barber	19	A
Viswakarmam (artisans)		
Tacchasari	129	B
Kalasari	6	B
Tattan	8	B
Kollan	16	B
Avarna jati		
Izhava	1256	B
Nadar	3	B
Kanian	12	B
Pandaram	27	B
Tandan	109	B
Tatchan	20	B
Velan	8	B
Hindu Pulaya	488	C
Parayan	15	C
Pannar	2	C
Kuruvar	15	C
Christian		
Forward Christian	1446	A
Pulaya Christian	92	C
Latin Catholic	252	A/C
Muslim	22	B
Total	5365	

Most Izhavas live alongside the high-caste Hindus, Nayars and Brahmans who until recently openly kept them as untouchables, ordering them off the road and excluding them from temples. Izhavas keep some distance from – but may still work alongside – the very lowest-caste Hindus (Pulayas and Parayas) who have, despite official anti-discrimination legislation, remained – men and women alike – tied to agricultural and other manual labour and to a degraded status. Izhavas also live alongside Christian families, some of whom were Izhava converts (many to the Protestant Marthoma Church) during the pre-1936 days of untouchability, and many of whom provide the most spectacular examples of upward mobility this century within the village. Table 1.1 shows local communities grouped into eight locally salient groups. Aiyappan (1944: 31) groups Hindu communities into three, a tripartite division which still holds good today: 'A' group consists of higher castes, the *savarnas* recognised under the modern state as 'forward' castes; 'B' group includes Izhavas and consists mostly of *avarna* groups classified as 'Other Backward Communities'; 'C' group comprises those of lowest status, recognised as 'Scheduled Castes'.

Villagers are differentiated by both community and class. Since building or extending and improving a family house is a universal imperative, housing is a good indicator of a family's condition.

Housing

Housing can be classified into four types: *nalukettus*, 'traditional' high-status teak houses; 'modern' high-status housing, one- or two-storeyed and built in European style of expensive materials; middle-status low-cost brick and tile houses, from two to six rooms, sometimes plastered; low-status housing, temporary shelters of cheap wood or, more commonly, coconut thatch. Wealthy villagers (the top 5 percent, most of whom are Christians) live in three- or four-bedroomed concrete two-storey homes set in large enclosed plots (half to one acre) of prime garden land, often guarded by dogs chained in kennels outside. Compounds are gardens of coconut and banana, mango and jackfruit, and have cow-sheds for one or more cows. These houses have solid front doors and cast-iron gates which are locked at night, large verandahs and balconies, and glass at the windows; water from outside wells is brought to European-style bathrooms by electric pumps; interiors are well furnished with sofas, beds, easy-chairs and (often imported) consumer goods such as fridges, TVs and videos. Most of these houses have been constructed since the 1970s. They have large kitchens with tiled or marbled floors, containing sinks with taps, fridges, ovens or hobs running on bottled gas, mixers, *idli*-makers, a range of plastic storage boxes, steel tiffin-tins and stainless-steel saucepans, including pressure cookers. Many have two kitchens: one large and European-style with shining marble or granite work-tops and stainless-steel sinks; one smaller and Indian-style with grinding stones and open fireplace attached. House servants do the heavy work (laundry, cleaning) and help out in the kitchen. Wealthy families eat from pyrex or melamine plates and drink from good glasses. When we visit them, they offer tea or coffee (the latter – increasingly expensive – fast becoming a luxury item) in melamine or china cups and saucers. If it is hot, they may offer lime juice made with cool water, bottled and kept in the fridge. Bakery-bought cakes and snacks or labour-intensive home-made treats such as halva are served on melamine or china plates.

A house which does not offer a Gulf mansion's comforts but which is highly prestigious to own is the nineteenth- and early twentieth-century high-status home: the *nalukettu*, a single-storey house of costly teak wood around a central courtyard, with large verandahs running along external walls where lower-caste servants, dependants and visitors were (and are) kept. Of the few *nalukettus* remaining, most are inhabited by Brahmans and Ksatriyas, a few by Nayars and one by a Scheduled Caste family with sons in the US, who bought the house when its Nayar advocate owner moved to Kochi city. Variations are half- and quarter-*nalukettus*, common among Nayar and Christian families, and two-storeyed *kottarams*, of which there are just three. While *nalukettus* offer rudimentary facilities (outside bathrooms, basic kitchens, small dark rooms) these houses carry enormous symbolic capital, suggesting old wealth, high status and *dharmic* living. Built according to *taccasastram*, these houses were denied to non-*savarna* Hindus under sumptuary restrictions prevalent until the early twentieth century. The high-caste communities who were permitted to reside in such comfort and style guarded their privileges jealously, punishing infringements with violence (Jeffrey 1994: 62; Mathew 1989: 76; Kooiman 1989: 148–154).

The bottom 30 percent includes a significant proportion of Izhavas and almost everybody in the *Harijan colonies* where Pulayas and other Scheduled Caste families live side by side with a few Izhava and Christian families, sharing one well between twelve houses and relatively distant from facilities like bus-stops and clinics. The housing of the poor is scattered throughout the village; small thatched huts are found in each of the three neighbour-hoods where we worked, sometimes right next door to a two-storeyed Gulf mansion, sometimes in the compound of wealthier neighbours as squatters (cf. Uchiyamada 1995). Poor villagers live on tiny unbounded land plots of less than ten cents (0.1 acre) in one- or two-roomed coconut-thatch mud-floor huts with open doorways, usually no larger than 3 m × 3 m and rebuilt each year after monsoon. Very few now live in wooden shacks, common during the 1950s and 1960s; since the 1970s, those who can afford to improve their housing move immediately into brick, constructing an earthen-floored two-roomed house. Coconut and banana trees are less thickly planted in poor neighbourhoods; most people's only garden will be a small row of tapioca. These homes have no kitchens, latrines or bathrooms, and little or no furniture: chairs are borrowed for special occasions, while residents sleep on woven mats on the mud floor. Labourers' huts provide basic shelter rather than housing: these families cook, eat, wash and often sleep outdoors, next to the canals and paddy land which provide their meagre livelihood. Those in thatched huts have no kitchen: water is fetched from shared wells; food preparation and cooking are done outside, using not coconut husk but *chuttu*. These families own one or two aluminium pans and eat from steel tiffin-tins or sometimes straight from the cooking pot; they drink water from metal tumblers. On some days these villagers do not cook or eat rice at all. Visitors are often a source of embarrassment for those who – having nothing to give – feel themselves unable to meet basic local hospitality expectations. A glass may be hurriedly borrowed from a neighbour, and black tea offered apologetically: few of the poorest buy milk. Since cooking fuel is expensive and not to be wasted making tea, children get sent to the nearest tea-shop to bring back glasses of weak, sweet tea and tea-shop snacks like fried banana in batter, put on account to be settled later when cash is available.

The majority of villagers fall somewhere between these two extremes. Middle-status accommodation divides between basic brick and tile housing – walls unplastered, windows unglazed, floors of beaten earth – and better quality accommodation with concrete floors, glazed windows, plastered walls and more than two rooms. These two types of houses generally sit in unbounded plots of 10 to 20 cents. Smaller houses have one coconut-thatch screened area within the compound as bathroom and another over an ash-pit as latrine. The majority now have a double outhouse housing both toilet and bathroom (room with tap and bucket); a few larger houses have inside facilities. There will be three or four coconut and banana trees, a couple of lines of tapioca, a few chickens and perhaps a goat. Outside *Harijan colonies* every house has its own well and most are electrified; few have electric water pumps, water buckets being pulled by hand. Better-off villagers own wooden beds, dining tables and a few cane chairs; those less well-off own one bed and perhaps one table with a couple of cheap metal chairs. Villagers in brick houses have small concrete-floor kitchens with open hearths, where cooking is done over coconut husks, supplemented by one or two kerosene stoves. These families fetch water in plastic buckets from the compound well. They own five or six saucepans (one or two stainless steel, the rest being aluminium), several steel tiffin-tins, and an *idli*-steamer. They eat from thin metal plates, drink from metal beakers or cheap glasses. Visitors are likely to be served sweet weak tea (if the milk has not run out) and a few of the small local bananas costing a few rupees per kilo always kept in stock at home. Simple home-made snacks like jackfruit chips may be offered.

Wealthier villagers keep cows, middle to poorer ones keep goats; almost everybody keeps chickens and occasionally rabbits. Diet varies enormously: labouring families rely as much on roots (tapioca, yams) as on rice, make do with tea from the tea-shop (buying milk is expensive) for breakfast, and rarely eat side-curries. Everybody aspires to eat rice at least once a day; not everybody manages to do this all year round. Breakfast – for those who eat it

– is *dosa, idli* or *puttu,* accompanied by sweet milky tea. Main meals consist of *choru,* fried fish, *sambar* and one or two side curries; common secondary meals are *kanjichammundi* or *kappachammundi.* Meat – buffalo, beef, goat, chicken – comes secondary to fish; only Brahmans are vegetarian, and even high-status Nayars eat buffalo meat or beef; small fish and frogs caught in the paddy fields are delicacies which can be eaten or sold to cold stores. Almost all fresh vegetables in this area are imported from neighbouring Tamil Nadu.

IZHAVAS, OTHERS AND US

We first went to Kerala – newly-married – in 1989, for doctoral fieldwork. We planned to stay in a rural area and not to over-specialise, hoping to mix with everybody and try to understand as much as possible in general about the place we were staying, learning Malayalam and pursuing the 'classic ideal' of anthropological fieldwork. After six months in the state capital following a taught Malayalam course,[11] we moved into Valiyagramam, a zone chosen after preliminary library research and advice from academic contacts[12] as an area which was multi-community and involved in paddy agriculture.

We moved to Valiyagramam with Anil (Puliyadi Veedu Chandrasekhar T.), at that time a 19-year-old history undergraduate who had been giving us Malayalam conversation practice and declared himself bored enough with city life and intrigued enough at the possibility of seeing 'fieldwork' and 'village life' to come and stay with us. While we had some mighty fights with each other during our time together (something surely not unique but missing from most anthropological accounts of fieldwork), we all three mostly enjoyed the privileged situation of learning and novelty which we found ourselves in, and developed a relationship with Valiyagramam which made us keen to return.[13] Returning in 1995, Anil was away studying and we saw him only briefly during his vacation. This worked out well in that we wanted to work concentratedly and unmediated among Izhavas: many Izhavas related better to us alone than accompanied by Anil, a high-status Nayar (cf. Berreman 1972: xix–lvii). We also wanted to work on our language skills, by then getting better but needing the boost of total immersion. Working without assistance and as much as possible in Malayalam, we improved our language skills, strengthened existing social ties and also ventured into new parts of the *panchayat* (where we had not worked with Anil) to develop new relationships, notably within Izhava colonies. Returning for six months in 1996 to focus on Bhadrakali temple festivals we again worked with Anil, by now qualified with BA and MA (Sociology) and a first-class diploma but still waiting for a full-time post. This time round there were no fights and through Anil we were able to meet with high-status Nayar families who the previous year had held us somewhat suspiciously at arm's length. Anil now holds a temporary position as Public Health Inspector, where he uses his experience of fieldwork; he continues to send us written translations of Malayalam documents, magazine articles and so on (our reading skills are rudimentary).

In 1989 we wanted to mix with all communities and avoid identification with any group: we optimistically hoped to become friends of everybody and enemies of no one, while maintaining good faith. Sheer novelty value guaranteed us at least one invitation into the homes of most villagers; we accepted all invitations and began to forge our own dense social networks. While struggling to achieve balance we found that our relationships with members of different groups were rooted in different bases. Brahmans and many Nayars related to us as fellow-scholars and bearers of 'culture', people with whom they could discuss aspects of Kerala culture, especially Hinduism. Christians welcomed us into their networks as co-religionists and as bearers of a European identity associated with progress, education, modernity, power and wealth. Members of Communist parties embraced us as fellow-socialists, although they were often disappointed at our refusal to be drawn into disputes and our determination to be even-handed, giving house-room to members of Congress, RSS and other political adversaries. After initial suspicions, we met with very low-status ex-untouchable groups as arbiters: if we – apparently wealthy and educated – considered them to 'have culture', to be people worth socialising with and people whose stories should be heard, some benefit might come to them; in time Filippo met as friend and confidant with some Pulaya young men. While our acceptance of food and drink within Pulaya colonies was initially tolerated as the eccentricity of the ignorant, many people became uncomfortable with our rejection – increasingly difficult to hide – of caste hierarchies and discrimination.

During first fieldwork, erring on the side of caution, Filippo did not drink alcohol, missing a large part of male sociality. Later, Filippo took drinks with men of all communities except Brahmans and had regular close 'drinking friends' among Izhavas, Christians and Pulayas. Caroline had open female friends from Christian and Izhava communities, all educated and somewhat rebellious young women who were not afraid of being tainted as immoral by contact with a *madamma*.[14] Several other young women were happy to meet Caroline in their homes but feigned diffidence when meeting along the road. Finally, we are still not sure of the significance of the fact that while members of Nayar, Izhava and Christian families often asked us for cash loans (sometimes given, sometimes not; sometimes returned, sometimes not), no Brahman and only one Pulaya family ever did.

We have experienced fieldwork in a multi-community area as forcing us to use skills of negotiation, time-management and extreme flexibility in self-presentation no less complex than those which we need to call upon when in Europe, where we also move in several distinct and unintegrated social arenas and more often than not find ourselves behind a mask. We would often slink out from the Pulaya colony where we listened to indignant talk of landlords and caste prejudice to steal directly into the house of a Nayar RSS activist, where we would hear about the insincerity and laziness of ex-untouchable labourers; Filippo would listen appreciatively to an orthodox Brahman diatribe against alcohol in the afternoon before sneaking furtively away after dusk to a bar in town with some Christian men; a bad day early on was the one in which we surreptitiously attended a Nayar funeral and a Brahman wedding within the space of a few hours: 'Most inauspicious', grumbled Anil. Managing all this made us aware at once both of how far gossip networks stretched and of how little many of the social worlds of Valiyagramam overlapped. People had commonly never been inside the house – sometimes not even into that part of the village – where others who were well known to them at work or in politics lived. Conveniently for all, things done after dusk (when most people stay at home) remained generally hidden, as acknowledged by the Malayalam saying, 'How interesting it is to go around at night and see the movements of all the fine people who are so upstanding by day.' Certain pieces of information travelled far; others remained locked into the communities where they originated. Sometimes we felt forced to drop our equivocation: our public attendance alongside a handful of male Communist Party men at an inter-caste love marriage brought widespread disapprobation, especially upon Caroline; no other woman had attended this scandalous event. For the most part, however, we have managed to remain on good terms and in ongoing contact with many people from all communities.

Amidst all this, we retained interests in stratification and class and undertook house-to-house surveys and intensive interviews in neighbour-hoods of labourers and ex-untouchables. While our original plan was that Caroline would work with Pulayas and Filippo with Izhavas we found that in a segregated society we would understand and integrate better, fight stereotyping of 'westerners' and ultimately have easier lives if we worked together and tried to follow local expectations of gendered behaviour. We also found ourselves drawn easily towards and accepted among Izhavas, while being with Pulayas was initially hard work, eventually (by 1996) limited to Filippo's friendships with some men. Pulayas, overwhelmingly employed as casual labourers, subject to the grossest discrimination and living in conditions of extreme hardship at the village margins, are often suspicious of outsiders, and put us (and Anil) to many tests before offering qualified acceptance of our presence in their *colonies*. Filippo over time partially bridged the gap but Caroline's status as educated and childless professional woman and the taboos placed upon the 'respectable' eventually proved insurmountable obstacles (cf. Fernandes 1997: 147f). While some groups of Pulaya men forged good relationships with Filippo, Pulaya women were never sure what to do with Caroline; women of other communities constantly chided her not to accompany Filippo on visits to 'those regions' of the village. A crucial factor was Caroline's falling female status since 1989, from auspicious newly married bride to childless (hence presumed barren) woman. Ribald teasing and jokes about her failure to produce a child gave way to frank questioning about 'the problem'. By 1996 she was openly excluded by some families from auspicious occasions, seen as dangerous to pregnant women and small children – a state of inauspiciousness suffered more strongly among certain groups, Pulaya labourers being one. In short, we have never doubted that who we are influences who we can work with and among, and the subsequent experience of fieldwork (see Rosaldo 1993: 19ff; Kondo 1990: 3ff).

As ethnic Europeans, we had, should we wish to activate it, a 'ready-made' affinity with local Christians; when Anil lived with us we had an entry, should we have wanted it, into the Nayar community; from the very beginning, however, it was among Izhavas that we felt our strongest affinities and feelings of *simpatia* which seemed to be mirrored. In retrospect the attraction seems hardly surprising when we look at the social backgrounds of most Izhavas and of ourselves: many points of contact enabled us to forge our deepest and most affectionate relationships from within this upwardly mobile group, who stand at and are pushing against the boundaries of distinctions: between the 'respectable' and the 'non-respectable', between 'unskilled labourers' and 'skilled workers', between the 'cultured' and the 'uncultured'.

While 'culture of poverty' theories have long been discredited, anthropologists still take interest in and find broad validity in generalising theories of culture (see for example Parkin 1979; Bourdieu 1990, 1994). We have suggested that broader sociological literature on social mobility is relevant in India and that we must consider Kerala within a global network. Our fieldwork experiences also reinforce suggestions that, cultural differences notwithstanding, global links can be made between those from similar structural positions: that our affinity with the broad mass of Izhavas is often a question of coming from similarly placed class fractions, sharing similar mobility aspirations and being in similar structural locations with regard to strands of culture. Izhavas stand above the mass of Pulayas who remain tied to agricultural labour but below the ranks of those assured middle to high community and class status, the Christian and Nayar clerks, shopkeepers and schoolteachers: they are a lower-middle community in caste terms, who generally fit into sociologists' 'upper-lower class categories', the 'respectable and self-improving poor'. When Paramu sat us down and quizzed us, 'Are you the first people in your families to go for education?'; when we met Suresh on leave from the Gulf and thought of the visits of our own glamorous out-migrating relations; when Vanitha joyfully showed us around her gleaming newly-built house, spotlessly clean; at these moments and countless others we experienced feelings of mutual recognition and understanding which did not occur when, for example, a Brahman talked about his family pedigree, a Nayar showed us over his ancestral properties, or a graduate Pulaya complained of being trapped in casual labour through continuing discrimination. We believe that our own experiences as mobile members of mobile social groups has given us a particular insight into the processes and problems of social mobility (cf. Rosaldo 1993: 19ff).[15] We each bring to our understanding of this ethnography, then, specific individual insights gained from our own life-experiences and an implicit comparative frame of reference. What we offer here is our particular view of the particular Izhavas we met in Kerala, in the hope that those whose lives are laid out here will forgive us our failures and will feel that overall we have done a good and fair job.

CONCLUSIONS

Izhava history and the family stories we tell here contradict stereotypical but all-too-familiar images of an unchanging India of insular and self-contained villages and a passive rural peasantry: images representing Indian lives as substantially different from the putatively dynamic and mobile lives led by those in developed countries. Valiyagramam residents are active subjects, planning and working to improve their own and their children's lives while participating in global movements of labour and capital. They are ready to leave Valiyagramam: to go to unfamiliar parts of Kerala, metropolitan India and even abroad, in pursuit of *progress – progressinu vendi*. A familiar local saying is that, 'Life is a competition'; in this competition some attain success, becoming business people, professionals or high-status public servants; others are left behind. Through the lives of Izhava families within one village, we will focus on areas of particular relevance for long-term projects of social mobility and suggest some processes which have been at work.

Family, personal and community mobility trajectories are inscribed upon a person's life-cycle and identity; mobility can be traced by following such movements. The order in which we will look at the various fields we have chosen bear a rough correspondence both to an imaginary life-cycle and to parallel processes of capital accumulation and conversion or conservation. Chapter 2 discusses employment, the first challenge to face young men like Premadasan: the business of making a living, preferably in some occupation better than that of one's father and ideally in some employment permitting accumulation of significant savings. Time and again migration has provided an answer to this imperative. Female employment has also been an important prestige barometer, most women claiming 'housewife' status and female participation in manual labour or unskilled work being a marker of poverty and indicative of a weak prestige position. Chapter 3 focuses on the next stage in a young man's life, delayed until he is settled in secure employment and has made some contribution to his parents' household, that is, marriage, another arena important for family status, as strategic alliances are made and prestigious dowries displayed. Chapter 4 considers one central process in which employment income is used and cash begins to be converted into symbolic and sometimes cultural capital: consumption, covering both longer-term investments and more ephemeral purchases. This chapter highlights the central and necessary goal of all long-term projects of social mobility: conversion over time of wealth – economic capital – into status and prestige through judicious accumulation of symbolic and cultural capital. Chapter 5 analyses an area of social life providing privileged arenas for those seeking to assert reputation: religion. While a group's religious practices are weakly indicative of relative prestige, the religious domain acts as a specific and highly prestigious opportunity for strategic consumption, specifically opportunities to 'sponsor' festivals and sacrifices. In contrast to arenas of production and consumption, in which class mobility takes priority, religion is a sphere in which Izhava caste status is foregrounded. It therefore becomes an arena for competition and confrontation with high-caste Hindus who widely resist and resent Izhava attempts to participate in religious life on an equal footing, as 'Hindus'. This leads us on to a field of great importance this century for the would-be mobile, and in which the struggle for power – arguably, following Bourdieu (for example 1990: 122f, 1994: 56), the most valuable of goods – is openly manifested. Chapter 6 examines Izhava political participation, considering both macro-levels, when Izhavas band together to protect or defend group interests, and micro-levels, where families and individuals seek involvement in agencies of locally exercised power. Like religion, politics is an arena in which mature men convert wealth into prestige; consolidate their position within the locality (often after a lifetime of working away); and manipulate relations of patronage and clientism in attempts to enhance status. Finally, we turn towards micro-politics or personal interaction, crucial to Izhava longer-term ambitions of mobility away from an untouchable past, and a field in which individual subjects act in small but significant ways to undermine or assert caste hierarchies. Chapter 7 examines friendship and 'passing' as Nayar or Christian: some ways in which Izhavas seek to subvert the strong barrier of caste threatening to undermine successes in class mobility. We also consider ways in which caste prejudice and hierarchy continues, turning both to the question of what is 'community identity' in the 1990s, and – following recently intensifying debates on the nature of 1990s caste – to the more abstract question of the putative prevalence of social and cognitive principles of hierarchy which work against social fluidity and mobility.

2 WORKING FOR PROGRESS

PURSUING CAPITAL THROUGH THRIFT, INDUSTRY AND PRESTIGE

All caste-hereditary occupations continue to be accorded a degree of innateness and naturalness, and to act as a sign of essentialised identity. Over the century Izhavas have struggled to disassociate themselves from what has been assumed to be their 'natural' occupation: toddy-tapping. The damage done to the Izhava cause of abolition of untouchability by associations with liquor was recognised early on in Narayana Guru's famous 1921 injunction that, liquor being poison, Izhavas should not make it, give it or sell it. This advice was promulgated by 'respectable' Izhavas keen for caste mobility and through SNDP campaigns for alternative employment. While Izhavas strongly resist being labelled as people whose caste-specific nature predisposes them towards alcohol or coconut-related work and whose chief characteristic is drunkenness, negative stereotypes continue to link them to the figure of the toddy-tapper and the distiller. At the same time, making and selling of alcohol can be a profitable economic activity.

As a result of reform processes in which Izhava identity as degraded toddy-tapper was erased – consigned to an unreformed past – all that remained was a modernist orientation towards the future, specifically towards broad goals of progress and mobility, to be achieved through reformed and rationalised social practices and capital accumulation. In this way, 'mobility' itself came to be both an imperative and a dominant public identity for Izhavas, previous and possible alternative identities suppressed or relegated to private spheres. In this project of social mobility, paid employment has been central on two counts: as income generation, offering a moment of accumulation of capital; and for the prestige attached to an occupation; during the twentieth century Izhavas have assiduously sought wealth and prestige through thrift and industry.

Far from being a narrowly focused Sanskritising body, the SNDP – formed as a universalist reform movement at the turn of the last century but soon adopted as the official voice of the Izhavas – had a strong economic programme, urging members to seek new forms of employment and wealth-generating schemes. When the SNDP set up in Valiyagramam during the 1930s, village Izhavas were clear that they wanted an end to back-breaking, stigmatised and badly remunerated manual labour and to insecurity of tenure. The SNDP took charge of centralising commerce of coconuts and derived products while acting as a lending bank to relieve indebtedness with local landlords. Following land reform programmes initiated in 1957 by the Communist-led government, the SNDP also organized Izhava tenants' claims over the land on which they lived or worked.

Some occupations – liquor trade, unskilled migration – have low long-term prestige but offer chances of substantial economic capital accumulation, then to be converted into symbolic and cultural capital at a later stage in household development or by following generations. Other occupations – such as school-teaching – require heavy investment in education and offer low financial returns but command high prestige. According to a family's current situation, strategies seeking to maximise economic or symbolic capital are followed. Most Izhava families start out with little or no wealth and have accumulation of cash and property as first priority.

Determination to move away from identification with the caste-specific occupation and from manual labour in general, and especially to escape from labour relations entwined within village caste hierarchies, such as are especially found in agriculture, has often led Izhavas outside local arenas in search of work. It has also encouraged them towards innovation and take-up of new employment opportunities de-linked from rural caste relations – ferry work, military service – and to favour occupations which enable autonomy – petty trade. Izhava intermediate caste status enables participation in many arenas effectively barred to Scheduled Castes.

IZHAVAS AND OTHERS

While class and employment always have a cultural dimension, the pre-eminent reference group in this field is that with substantial wealth; in Valiyagramam (as in Kerala generally) this group nowadays overlaps heavily with the Christian community, admired for their ability to 'turn one rupee into two'. Christians have a history of acting as innovators: clearing and settling jungle land; taking up new opportunities such as migration and plantations; launching banking and investment companies; opening private schools, colleges and hospitals. This, with strong orientations towards values of 'westernisation' and 'modernisation' reinforces Christians' position as standard-bearers of class mobility, status achieved rather than ascribed. Izhavas, like Christians, often pride themselves upon their thrift and industriousness, characteristics (they hold) not shared by orthodox Hindus, stereotypically held to loathe labour and waste money in lavish status-seeking. When Izhavas seek avenues for capital accumulation and class mobility, they look towards Christians. The SNDP has followed Churches in investing heavily in schools and colleges where community members are given admission preference under 'management quotas'.

Dignity (*manam*) is strongly bound up with caste status and rooted in forms of ossified symbolic and cultural capital such as family name and religious practice, independent of current economic capital – poor Brahmans can receive respect merely by virtue of caste and lifestyle. For Izhavas, an *avarna* caste historically less attached to Brahmans in service relationships, the major reference group for prestige accumulation and caste mobility is what they refer to as 'Hindus' or '*savarnas*', meaning Nayars. Occupations commanding prestige and strongly associated with the Nayar community, albeit generating limited income and scope for economic mobility, are attractive to those with modest economic capital who wish to convert it into prestige. Only families already in a moderately good condition can consider such jobs; remaining within the local economy does little to satisfy the mobility ambitions of the many.

The poor – those having negative economic capital – are the indebted asset-less manual labourers who live precariously from hand to mouth, dwelling in thatched huts, working for uncertain daily wages and suffering long periods of annual unemployment. In Kerala (as in India as a whole) this group coincides very closely with Scheduled Caste communities: day-labourers tend to be drawn mostly from the Scheduled Castes, and members of Scheduled Castes are overwhelmingly employed as casual labourers. This group, acting as a negative reference point, is where caste and class coalesce. The continuing association of untouchability and low ritual status with manual and degraded labour and with poverty – a negative balance of any form of capital – is a sign of the particular nature of Scheduled Caste status, reminding us of the tenacity of the disadvantage and discrimination attached to it, making it qualitatively different from any other status and fixing the sociologists' general 'agricultural labour = immobility' equation in a more forceful manner than is found elsewhere (Featherman & Hauser 1994: 272). Unlike members of the Scheduled Classes, those many Izhavas who are forced to undertake badly paid and negatively valued manual (especially agricultural) labour are widely assumed to be doing it out of the exigencies of poverty and against their true 'nature'.

While the balance sought between wealth and prestige differs according to current situations and strategies, all aspire eventually towards occupations permitting build-up of significant amounts of both wealth and prestige which can be transmitted to the next generation. As in other societies, professionals are considered maximal achievers (Sorensen 1994: 231): people who are also in a position to use their influence and connections to further enhance their life-chances, for example by becoming powerful patrons (Hobbs 1996: 149). Those reaching the highest positions enhance their fortunes further by moving to the metropolises or overseas, from where they are a source of prestige and – sometimes – financial aid, for relatives. As Bourdieu points out, capital has a multiplier effect, being convertible and re-convertible (for example 1990: 118ff). Given the high costs of higher education, opportunities among Izhavas to reach such a position are limited, restricted to a handful of already wealthy families.

WOMEN, MEN AND WORK

Work is important in the life-cycle: through different relationships to work, gender and maturity are expressed. Group drives towards mobility are inscribed upon trajectories travelled by gendered individuals: young women's adoption of nurturing and housewifely roles, whether accompanied or not by withdrawal from public arenas of work, confirms personal status while contributing towards family prestige; female participation in or withdrawal from certain types of paid employment are indices of family status. A broad gendered division of labour exists in the work of pursuing familial and personal mobility, in which young men's primary duty is accumulation of wealth and young women's the pursuit of reputation, female withdrawal from labour being a relatively cheap and easily achievable form of prestige.

Women and Work

We cannot present accurate figures for female labour participation, largely because of the dominance among Izhavas of the 'housewife' (*vittukari*) ethic. Heuzé (1992: 19) remarks that census figures claiming 15 percent of Indian workers as women represent under-estimation. We found several women who responded in house-to-house surveys as 'housewife' also engaged in casual or occasional work – assembling matchboxes at home, acting as a life-insurance agent, doing seasonal agricultural work for wealthier relatives. It is however true that a large proportion of Izhava women – we estimate 50 percent to 70 percent – do not work outside the home, while most of those who do are engaged in decidedly non-prestigious and non-remunerative manual labour.

Professional employment is ungendered, allowing women to participate without necessarily losing status; low-status work is highly gendered and is thought to say something about both the type of woman who does it and the type of family she comes from. Male or female, lawyers, doctors, lecturers and school-teachers have their personal name and status augmented by gender-neutral titles (Advocate, Doctor, *Saar*). The prestige of professional occupations is so high – as is the existing social status of the women involved – that negative effects are limited; significant material benefits render professional women largely indifferent to criticism. Low-status and poorly paid manual labour is, by contrast, highly gendered: within agricultural labour, transplanting seedlings and weeding is 'women's work'; dress-making, matchbox assembling and prostitution are exclusively female, highly feminised and very low-income occupations. Women working in such feminised spheres suffer stigmatised social status in relation to the middle classes, as do their menfolk: failed householders who cannot support families without a female contribution or maintain the home properly, which requires a *vittukari* (cf. Fernandes 1997: 137ff).

Suja, 19, working for Rs400 a month at a *sari* showroom in town and Shobha, 22, working for 'almost nothing' (Rs100–50) from home as a dressmaker, are both dowry-less daughters of widows. Sheena, 24, teaching in a local nursery for Rs300 per month, plans to give up employment on marriage. Ponamma, a childless divorcee, 32, fell back upon her BA degree to take work in a private tutorial college in town, earning Rs500 per month. Devaki, 40 years old, was abandoned by her husband when pregnant; with a teenaged daughter to support, she works as house-servant for a wealthy Christian family, supplementing this Rs200 monthly income with seasonal agricultural work and spells at a match-factory. All of these women struggle to assert respectability – specifically that sense of feminine honour which articulates with family prestige – within the wider community; the majority of women who work do so, like these, from financial hardship, not choice (cf. Vera-Sanso 1995; Kapadia 1995). Valiyagramam has one or two female professionals like Advocate Remini, a handful of women (largely from the 'educated Left') working as school-teachers or clerks, and an increasing number of younger women – generally from very poor families – working in new occupations such as shop assistant, laboratory technician, beautician, telephone booth operator. These latter occupations are replacing manual labour – specifically agricultural labour and house service – among poorer sections of the community. We have observed between 1989 and 1995 both a mushrooming of service jobs, as more and more shops and bureaux open, and a dramatic drop in the number of Izhava women coming for paddy harvest, contributing to a labour shortage and facilitating the gradual introduction of mechanisation. Meanwhile, almost all of Valiyagramam's house servants are live-in unmarried women from relatively depressed eastern hilly areas.

Ideas about prestigious styles of womanhood are based upon the bourgeois 'housewife' ethic which has developed over the twentieth century (Arunima 1995; Mathew 1995; Isaac 1995), itself over-determined by the ghostly figure of the *andarjanam*, the nineteenth-century 'lady of the inside': the Nambutiri Brahman woman who never left her house, and who still serves as a point of distinction for Hindu women between themselves and Christians. Migrants whose mothers and wives formerly went for paddy field work now proudly assert 'our women don't know anything about agriculture and never went to the fields. They stay in the house.' Discussing a forthcoming marriage in a neighbouring family less than 200 metres away, a woman in her fifties asked us what their house looked like; she had never seen it. Her husband, seeing our surprise, boasted, 'She's always just around this compound; since she came here 40 years ago, she never goes anywhere.' Most women are in no way 'public' figures and many hardly ever move outside the neighbourhood, hired transport taking them door to door to weddings or family visits. These limitations are not necessarily perceived or experienced as hardships: jostling on public buses or travelling un-accompanied can be unpleasant experiences for women, while a claim to 'houseboundness' is a claim to symbolic capital.

The personal parts of an adult woman's identity (as opposed to those parts derived from natal family, husband and so on) do not depend, as do a man's, upon wealth, occupation, connections, landowning; but upon physical appearance, sense of modesty and – importantly – maternity. All stages in the female life-cycle are encompassed by a division – marked linguistically by suffixes to personal names and embodied in distinctive physical and dress styles – between non-reproductive virginal pre-motherhood (*kutti* or *mol*, daughter) and reproductive, non-virginal post-motherhood (*amma* or *mama*, mother). All girls are considered future mothers, while all females undertake mothering behaviour for the household (domestic service, feeding, child care, religious protection); first delivery simply concretises a status which is latent in all females and has been anticipated for many years. In the dominant ethic, women's work is not income-provision, but mothering work, in its widest sense of nurturing.[1]

Those families who allow their daughters to study or even work away, and their daughters-in-law to follow migrant husbands, are often harshly criticised: Hindu girls generally study at local colleges; Hindu wives stay in the village with parents or in-laws. Some married couples meet only once every four years because of this, but most agree that this is better, 'The Gulf (Mumbai, Chennai or Gujarat, wherever) is no place for a woman' the common explanation. In most families, men and boys undertake daily marketing: although the *andarajanam* ideal has weakened, woman's place, in the absence of economic necessity, is widely considered to be in the kitchen, while women – including those in employment – identify themselves closely with home and family.

Conventions on female movement are complex: families have spaces defined as 'inside' – minimally house and compound, often a wider area of two to five related adjacent family houses; only adult men travel un-accompanied outside the limits of this space. While the limits of 'own space' for working women are necessarily extended beyond the house to include the workplace and the paths leading there, most villagers define permissible space more narrowly, criticising those who travel, accompanied or not. The reality of Izhava women's lives, of which a proportion include outside work, means that double standards must operate. When a teenage girl became pregnant, women, several themselves studying or employed, blamed the girl's mother (an insurance agent) for being 'never at home', but 'always out at work'.

The 'housewife' tag and appeals to prestige made by those not in paid employment covers a wide spectrum of activities and social statuses. Much domestic labour takes place outside the house: all clothes washing – a robust task involving bending, stretching and hitching up the dress – is done outside, ideally in secluded or screened areas to avoid the gaze of passing men; fish is cleaned at outside taps; the twice-daily sweep extends beyond the house interior and into courtyard and compound. Given that 'inside/outside' divisions are bounded not by the house but by familial plot(s) of land, many jobs can be presented as 'inside' work, but those with house servants pass tasks on, preferring to stay shielded within the house walls.

Wealthier women describing themselves as 'not working' spend most of their day indoors, the larger part of their labour consisting of cooking meals and helping children with homework; servants undertake cleaning, laundry and food preparation. Such women have large amounts of leisure time, spent watching videos or reading, socialising with children and female relations or making luxury treats such as ice-cream. Women from non-wealthy families describing themselves as 'not working' actually labour inside and outside the house from morning to night. Having no servant, indoor meal preparation is only one of many tasks which may include: sweeping and laundry; watering plants and weeding the compound; mending coconut-thatch fencing marking house boundaries; milking and washing the cow; collecting fallen cashew fruits and nuts; stitching and mending clothing. Given that most homes stand on plots of productive garden land used to grow fruit, tubers and vegetables, and given that all families keep some livestock, the labour involved in 'housework' can be substantial. The self-assigned category 'housewife' and the prestigious 'no work' self-description refer, then, to confinement within the family compound and/or non-performance of paid labour or employment.

Restrictions are seen as no hardship by most housewives, who are not generally keen to swap their home-centred lives for the drudgery involved in the 'double shift'. When Caroline asked one childless graduate wife if she had ever felt bored at home with her husband away in the Gulf and no children of her own yet, and whether she had ever thought that she might have liked to use her commerce degree to take some respectable office job, Jayasri had laughed. She had asked, 'Whatever for?' adding, 'The family is doing well, thanks to God; there is no need for me to work.' Smiling, she continued:

I know you Christians send your women out to work, but we Hindus don't; you Christian women go here and there but we must stay in the house to keep our dignity, otherwise people gossip. It is our custom. It's a question of what you're used to, habit. When our husbands go away, we aren't lonely, we have his family here. And the Gulf is not suitable for family life; we women and children are better here, it's our place, isn't it?

She looked embarrassed to mention the ever-scandalous behaviour of Christians, whose migrant workers not only routinely took their wives with them, but even sent them out to work, as Hindus remark, 'as nurses to the Arabs'. For Izhavas, struggling against *avarna* status towards respectable

'Hindu' identity, scruples common among Nayar families about what is suitable for womenfolk must be followed.

Many Kerala Christian women work outside the state as nurses; recently women from Hindu communities – mostly Scheduled Castes – have taken up employment as nurses or auxiliary workers. Hindus explained their anti-pathy towards sending their daughters for nursing not in terms of purity but of respectability: nurses work night shifts, need to talk to strange men, stay away from their families in hostels and so on. A common view is that unlike Hindus, who understand that a respectable and respected wife's place is at home with her husband's family, Christians care so much about *cash* that they put it before running their families decently, putting female reputation and safety at risk for the sake of money. While men may defer accumulation of prestige until sufficient cash wealth has been built up, women's first priority, as bearers of a heavy load of family symbolic capital, must always be their prestige. If they are to work it should be in some occupation considered unequivocally respectable, such as school-teaching; benefits should be high enough to outweigh possible prestige losses. High female literacy rates and participation in higher education, like the two-child family norm, are indicators of *culture*, not enabling conditions for employment. While villagers often make favourable comparisons between themselves and other Indian states, pointing to female illiteracy and high birth rates as examples of 'backwardness', qualifications are more relevant on marriage than employment markets. Women college students joke that they will be ready for marriage when they have, 'BA and MA, that is Master of *Adukkalla*'. Questions about employment status meet with the joke response, 'IAS' (Indian *Adukkalla* Service, a parody on the high-prestige and high-earning Indian Administrative Service). The majority of housewives are matricu-lates; many are graduates or even postgraduates who never had any intention of going out to work.

A Working Housewife

Sarasamma, who has worked all her married life as a clerk in a Cooperative Society, hopes that her daughter will become a school-teacher, both because it is a good profession for a woman (respectable; decent hours; you can work near home; holidays when your children have them; good pension) and because it will bring the dowry down. Sarasamma herself married only at 30, being very dark-skinned and unable to offer a suitably compensatory dowry.

Living in a nuclear family with no domestic help, Sarasamma works extremely hard. Up at 4 a.m. every day to sweep, pull water, do laundry, morning *puja*, make cooked breakfast and the lunchtime meal, she has already done four hours' labour before going to work. She jokes that she likes getting to the office for a rest, adding that life is like that for all working women and that they would not have it any other way, because to be at home would be boring. This was confirmed whenever Caroline interviewed local female school-teachers and clerks, all of whom described their day more or less as above: while women pay public lip-service to the housewife/seclusion ethos, those with a chance for respectable salaried employment are happy to take it. In the evening Sarasamma sweeps again, pulls more water, does house *puja*, cooks the evening meal and makes ground rice batter for next day's breakfast. We have often seen her fall asleep in the middle of reading or watching television while she waits for dinner to cook. After dinner she sometimes reads aloud from the *Bhagavatham*, while on Fridays she visits the Durga temple, both 'labours of love' undertaken for the family benefit.

Sarasamma's double shift is more burdensome than that of her counterpart in developed countries because water must be drawn in buckets from a well, spices ground by hand, laundry beaten clean in cold water; she told Caroline, 'In your place, you have machines to help you do the housework: we are our own machines!' While an increasing number of families own electric water pumps and mixer-grinders, in 1995 only one household had a twin-tub washing machine. Fewer and fewer have servants, and they tend to be part-time or occasional helpers, for example with laundry (live-in servants can cost Rs600 to Rs700 per month). Like many women over 40, Sarasamma suffers from painful joints leaving her almost in tears when scraping coconut or doing the laundry. Yet she never uses the electric *mixi*, preferring to grind spices and coconut onerously by hand between two heavy stones because, 'When you cook with a *mixi*, the taste isn't there.' Sarasamma's monthly cash contribution to domestic finances does not lessen the nurturing contribution expected of her as her 'real' job, nor does she herself try to minimise her housework; on the contrary, like many working women, she is at pains to show that her family in no way suffers from the decision to work outside the home.

Men and Work

For prestige reasons and because of Kerala's extremely high rate of unemployment, parents of all communities place great hopes on education: almost all Izhava boys sit (and often re-sit many times) degree entrance exams. Even less well-off manual labouring families find the necessary cash to enrol their sons at pre-degree college and patiently budget year after year for books, smart clothes and bus travel. Pulaya youths combine study and leisure with occasional paid casual labour as soon as they can work (age 10 to 14); Asari (craftsmen) youths start learning the family trade and helping out in workshops virtually from toddlerhood; initiated Brahman youths help their fathers in ritual work; most teenaged boys from the Izhava community, having neither family occupation nor crushing poverty, are put under no pressure to contribute to household expenses or take up any occupation.

Such things are deferred either until their education is successfully completed or until their family tire of paying for chances to re-sit examinations and change courses, which usually happens only after every possible option to get a paper qualification has been tried, at which point the family resigns itself to the fact that the boy will either become a manual worker or have to look for a *chance* elsewhere.

Srijith's story is not at all untypical. After passing his SSLC at the third attempt with minimal marks (215/600), he took BA entrance exams twice before securing admission on a management quota for Economics at a local private college. His family paid Rs10,000 *donation* to the management committee (considerably less than the going rate of Rs25,000 for 'outsiders', because Srijith's father is an SNDP official). Srijith deferred second-year examinations, knowing that otherwise he would fail, and sat the year again. When he failed to get entry to the third year, his father and mother's brother paid Rs15,000 donation to secure a place at a TTC (Technical Training College) for a two-year electrical engineering course. In 1991, aged 22 Srijith was not confident of passing first-year exams, and was hoping to defer and re-sit the year. He admitted that he never applied himself to his studies, regularly cutting classes and spending book monies on shirt-pieces and entertainments in town, but felt that he was unable to remedy his academic failures, as he did not have the head/will for study (*manasilla*). In 1993, after another examination failure, Srijith's mother's brother took him to Saudi Arabia where he now works as a waiter in an international hotel.

Many boys take their studies lightly, arguing that even a degree will not help them to get a job and that their only hope of finding employment is to wait for and seize any *chance* which might come up to get out of Kerala. Young Izhava men are under an imperative towards individual action related to quests for employment. They can expect advice and practical help (connections and money) from elders, but must take seriously upon themselves the responsibility – in high-unemployment Kerala, a burden – of finding paid work. To this end, chains of relatives and friends in mutual self-help are formed, and the slightest hint of a *chance* is followed up. When Sahadevan, working in a resort hotel, heard that there would shortly be vacancies for waiters, he immediately notified two friends, who gathered hotel and catering training certificates together and went to ask to be considered before any formal calls for applications were announced. When Binu heard that there would soon be a great shortage of qualified health inspectors in state government, he left for Gujarat to enrol for the two-year diploma course; two cousins followed. By 1996, when all three had obtained temporary posts, Binu then took a friend of his to the college to arrange enrolment, help find accommodation and make introductions.

For young Izhava men, keen to show themselves living up to the community's mobility ideal and impatient to become part of the consuming classes, the source of wealth, while not irrelevant, is of lesser importance than the amount. Money which is 'New', Gulf-earned, gained through running a *blade* (informal loan company), achieved by hard labour and saving or via semi-legal means, is all good money. Illegal money – from smuggling or cheating on a property deal – is at least better than no money at all. One young Izhava, working as a sales representative, told us: 'These Hindus (Nayars) want to go to the office in a white *mundu*, drink tea, talk to the secretary, and be called *Saar*; nobody calls me *Saar* but I earn Rs 3000 a month.' In 1990, this was a good salary: a school-teacher could have hoped to earn half this amount. Izhava men who are willing to make money under whatever constraints transgress 'official' insistence on the primacy for all Hindus of *manam*: many lie about the work they are doing. Male identity is built partly upon occupation and wealth, while the identity of a household depends heavily upon the occupation of the man of the house. An Izhava family in which the wife is a practising medical doctor, while her husband – an 'artist' – is substantially unemployed, has little prestige; the enormous status usually accorded to members of the medical profession cannot compensate for the gender imbalance perceived in this couple or for the failure of the putative head of the family to maintain his household. The imperatives of finding employment and earning money then also hold significance for young Izhava men extending beyond their public persona and familial status and into their personal sense of masculine identity.

Pulayas, Artisans and Brahmans are drawn early into a world of sexually segregated work, based upon strict gendered divisions of labour (in the manual, craft and ritual spheres respectively). The resulting gendered and casted occcupations, (labourer, artisan, priest) are strong sources of personal identity, and provide clearly defined activity-based male roles: Izhava *payyanmar* have no such role available. Moving through their teens and twenties, preparing for adult life, a spell of military service or a period of migration has been one common means of bridging the gap – temporal and categorical – between *payyan*-hood and becoming an adult man. Taking up an occupation and earning money for the family offers a means of con-solidating both an adult sense of self and a masculine identity, given that earning is 'man's work'. Young men and their families think long and hard and consider many options in their search for decent employment. Before considering the options which have been open to young Izhava men throughout the twentieth century, we will briefly mention important nineteenth-century developments which set the stage for changes in and expansion of the economy.

SOME IMPACTS OF COLONIALISM ON THE TRAVANCORE ECONOMY

As the family stories told in Chapter 1 show, Izhavas are involved in national and international flows of labour and capital; Kerala villages have played an important part in the world economy for hundreds of years, through the pepper trade, for example, considered by many as a crucial factor in world history (see for example Chaudhuri 1990: 6). In the 100 years after the end of the fifteenth century, following the arrival of Vasco da Gama's fleet in Kozhikode (north Kerala) the Portuguese, followed by the Dutch, Danish, French and British, all established trading stations and factories along the Kerala coast. A qualitative change in trading relationships is later marked by direct penetration of colonialism in Travancore, the British East India Company beginning to trade directly in south Kerala in the late seventeenth century.[2] During the eighteenth century, Travancore and the East India Company were drawn progressively closer through a combination of commercial and military treaties. In 1795, following the end of the Second Mysorean Wars and the defeat of Tippu Sultan, the Travancore Rajah signed a treaty of perpetual alliance with the Company, agreeing to pay for the stationing of Company troops and expenses incurred in campaigns against Tippu, and to accept the presence of a British Political Resident. The final act towards the establishment of British Paramountcy in Travancore came ten years later when British troops intervened twice: first to quell a rebellion of local troops (1805) and then brutally to crush the famous 1808–9 revolt against foreign interference, led by the *Dewan* Velu Thampi. By agreeing to permanent disbandment of the local army, stationing of Company troops in Thiruvananthapuram, payment of costs of the military campaign against the rebel *Dewan*, settlement of outstanding debts to the Company and deferral of all important state decisions for approval by a British Political Resident, the Rajah to all effects relinquished his authority. As the nature and balance of this relationship changed, a colonial framework was set for important restructuring of the economy; this in turn provided the context for major social changes at the turn of the twentieth century (Sobhanan 1977; Vijayamohan 1979; Yesudas 1977; Aiya 1989).

The reforms introduced in Travancore from the first British Residency onward (Col. Macaulay 1800–10) were aimed in two directions. They entailed provisions directed towards 'modernisation' of the state administrative structure, creating a more efficient and comprehensive revenue system while enlarging the revenue base: an efficiently organised tax-collecting state would overcome problems in paying tributes to colonial power. Meanwhile, measures such as the introduction of private landed properties (1865) and abolition of state monopolies promoted an economic climate ultimately favouring direct involvement of colonial capital (Isaac & Tharakan 1986a). The East India Company had been investing in spice plantations in north Malabar since 1798. In 1824 the British Crown introduced laws facilitating grants of land to Europeans in India, while in the 1840s coffee (later also tea and rubber) production regions were created in Wyanad, Nilgiris, Coorg and Travancore. The first Travancore plantation was started when William Huxham opened a coffee estate on hill ranges east of Kollam in 1830. Travancore, by virtue of its low taxation, the 1818 Wasteland Act and the 1865 private property acts, became renowned for the generous concessions it offered European planters.[3] By the 1920s, 60 percent of the whole area under tea cultivation in Kerala and 85 percent in Travancore was controlled by European firms (Isaac & Tharakan 1986a: 10; Ravi Raman 1991: 244, 249; George & Tharakan 1985). With the establishment of the Public Works Department (created during the 1860 famine to provide food-for-work schemes), the Travancore government also spent large amounts of money on building infrastructures such as roads and bridges to facilitate development of plantations in new areas. Plantation companies operating in Travancore grew from 3 in 1905 to 61 in 1935 (Kooimann 1989: 123–4; Lemercinier 1994: 176).

Several social reforms were promoted from the mid-nineteenth century onwards by colonial powers and missionaries, such as promotion of education, abolition of slavery, promulgation of laws excluding low-caste converts from untouchability rules and progressive curtailment of the powers of the traditional landed upper-caste aristocracy. These must all be seen in the context of the progressive commercialisation of Travancore's economy, in particular against the development of European-owned plantations and the need for cheap, docile, mobile labour. Plantation workers were soil-slaves freed by the abolition of slavery of 1855, tribal peoples and poor under-tenants, including many Izhavas impoverished by changes in the land revenue system and succesive famines in 1860 and 1876–8 (Ravi Raman 1991: 246ff; cf. Kooiman 1989: 135ff). Mateer reported, 'Sudra [Nayar] masters complained of the planters taking away their labourers' (1883: 236), while an economic survey conducted in neighbouring Cochin State recorded a high shortage of agricultural labourers due to migration to plantations (Subbarama Aiyar 1918: 145). That among plantation owners were found many prominent colonial administrators (for example General Cullen) and missionaries (for example John Cox, London Mission Society; H. Baker, Church Mission Society; Caldwell, Society for the Propagation of Gospel) suggests the strong articulation or convergence of interests between these three groups (Mateer 1883: 226ff; Kooiman 1989: 117ff). Christian converts, counting many Izhavas in their numbers, 'educated by the Mission proved themselves of great service to the new industry', wrote Rev. Mateer, 'became overseers, confidential clerks and managers to European planters' (1883: 236; see also Kooiman 1989: 135ff).

While progressive integration of Travancore into the wider colonial economy was marked in hilly areas by development of export-oriented crops (rubber, tea, coffee, spices) the fastest-growing crop in the plains was coconut. This tree is especially associated with the Izhava community, whose caste-specific right (*avakasam*) was to tend the tree, and who are mythically reputed to have brought coconut plants with them when they migrated from Sri Lanka to Kerala (Aiyappan 1944: 16–18). Production of coconut-derived products such as copra, oil and coir grew alongside expansion of coconut cultivation. In 1859 in Alapuzha the American James Darragh started the first coir weaving unit. Although the coir industry was dominated by local entrepreneurs – mostly Izhavas – European traders monopolised the export market by controlling baling presses. After a period of rapid growth, the coir trade suffered badly during the 1930s Great Depression leaving many families in penury (Isaac & Tharakan 1986a: 8, 16; Isaac 1985, 1990; Isaac et al. 1992; Raman Mahadevan 1991: 178ff; Nieuwenhuys 1994: 121ff, 174ff).

This development of commercial agriculture encouraged rapid expansion of trade, exports and imports increasing ten-fold from 1870–1939, also facilitated by the abolition of government monopolies over trade and of inter-port duties. The main beneficiaries of this development were European trading firms, virtually monopolising export of plantation products. Local merchants – mostly Christians – already relegated to a secondary position by pre-colonial monopoly laws, acted mostly as sub-agents to large European traders (Isaac & Tharakan 1986a: 3–8). Despite heavy Izhava involvement in coconut cultivation and trade, they were unable to reap full benefits. Far from consisting of self-contained villages full of subsistence farmers, the Kerala countryside was enmeshed in unequal transnational economic relation-ships.

THE GROWTH OF IZHAVA MIDDLE CLASSES

Developments in nineteenth-century Travancore society affected Izhavas in several ways. Although changes in the land revenue system meant expulsion of sub/under- tenants,[4] the community gained from the missionary-inspired abolition of several special taxes (for example poll-tax, cottage-tax) and customary dues to upper caste landowners and village heads. From 1834, Izhavas involved in the liquor business – a sector of the economy they dominated – profited from the introduction of new *abkari* regulations, the trade previously having been run according to the *Amani* system – collection of revenue by goverment officers directly from cultivators/producers. The government launched a system based upon contracts leased to the highest bidders, similar to that introduced in parts of India under direct rule. Contractors ran fixed numbers of shops, collecting monthly rent instalments from sub-contractors, and were bound to buy from producers *kallu* and *akkani* and to sell arrack and toddy at fixed rates. In 1878 the *Abkari* Department was taken over directly by the *Dewan*'s office, which acquired the power to assign by licence exclusive right of manufacture and sale of fermented liquors to suitable renters. Development of the liquor business is shown by increases in *akbari* revenues, from Rs42,584 in 1834 to Rs190,041 in 1880 (Mateer 1883: 280–1; Aiya 1906: 502–4; cf. Hardiman 1987: 110–11; Oddie 1978: 205ff).

Other economic opportunities emerged with Travancore's assimilation into the colonial economy. Following increased demand on world markets, many coastal Izhavas became small-scale producers and traders of coconut products (Isaac & Tharakan 1986a: 6–7). Under the labour-hungry plantation economy, many Izhavas found work as coolies or *kanganys*.

Those with (English) education, while still barred from government service, could aspire to more prestigious and better paid white-collar jobs; establishment of the Public Works Department provided new opportunities beyond village labour relations. Following the 1865 Land Act some Izhavas, investing wealth accumulated over this period, began to emerge as large landowners.

Along Kerala's western coastal belt, where Izhavas are the dominant community, lives an upper stratum of high-status, titled, wealthy families. The nineteenth-century growing Izhava middle-class was not entirely drawn from an established elite. Many villagers remember or know as mytho-histories stories of Izhavas like Advocate Remini's family, who 'came up' during this period. The most famous aristocratic and wealthy coastal families are Alummoottil and Komalezhattu: more than one villager told us of the latter's solid gold models of *kappa, chena* and *chembu* plants. This image – ornamental display of manufactured golden versions of humble root plants which still provide staple foodstuffs for those too poor to eat rice, suggests the family's links with new industries while hinting at suspicions about the artificiality of quick fortunes made through involvement in modern capitalism (cf. Taussig 1980).[5]

Alummoottil is exemplary of the rising bourgeoisie which built substantial fortunes post-1870 from new opportunities.[6] Kuttakkakaran Sekharan Channar, *valiyammavan* of the activist T.K. Madhavan, was a major *abkari* contractor in Travancore, still now remembered for being 'wealthier than the Rajavu' and 'minting money'. A prominent tax-payer who was close to the *Dewan*, he enjoyed the Rajah's protection and was reputedly visited by him. The family lived in a *nalukettu* before building the area's first European-style two-storeyed building. Visiting this house, we found no golden tapioca but many family portraits, including European faces. Kuttakkakaran Sekharan Channar acquired extensive paddy and coconut gardens in several villages, including Valiyagramam. His successor as *karnavan*, Koccu Kunja Channar, abandoned the *abkari* business to concentrate upon the higher-status occupation of agriculture.[7] Kuttakkakaran Sekharan Channar is said to have had twelve elephants with Nayar *mahouts*. Although extremely rich, pollution rules prevalent until the late 1930s required Channar, on approaching temples, to dismount and walk the back alleys while his Nayar *mahout* rode past on elephant-back. Commenting on this well-known episode, an Izhava villager remarked upon the anomaly that, 'His servant could do what he couldn't.'

Unsurprisingly, we see a clear attachment to values of modernity among this rising bourgeoisie who profited directly from the expansion of colonial capitalism: a relationship strikingly illustrated by K.V. Krishnan's tomb (see Chapter 1), where his Chevrolet is lovingly preserved and tended alongside his spirit. The relationship sometimes involves direct involvement with modernisation processes: English education; plantation employment; *abkari* business; opening factories; learning to drive; providing not only for nephews ('traditional' matrilineal system) but also for wife and sons. It also takes the form of close connection with those taken to represent hyper-modern values, Europeans themselves: Alummootil built a European-style house, and has several inter-marriages with Europeans. In K.V. Krishnan's story (Chapter 1) the latter appear as dominators controlling plantation workers' lives but also proffering advice and gifts, while providing models of styles of doing business, living life and asserting status alternative to those practised by local landed high castes. Relationships may also, significantly, be with local Christians who, closest to Europeans, are the first to become modern entrepreneurs, seizing new employment and business opportunities. Europeans and local Christians offered examples of autonomy, entrepreneurship and self-help: inspirations taken, along with wider modern values, into official Izhava rhetoric during the 1920s and 1930s social reform movements (Jeffrey 1974, 1993: 96–117). Izhavas turned their backs on the nineteenth-century agrarian order to become agents of modernity in new forms of employment.

THE LOCAL ECONOMY

Valiyagramam lies in Kerala's central zone between hilly plantation land and coastal coir belt. With more than 65 percent of village land suited to paddy cultivation and the remaining garden land to cultivation of coconut gardens, root vegetables and fruit trees, it was agriculture which dominated the village economy to the end of the 1940s. While we are conscious of difficulties in identifying clear-cut class divisions in an agrarian context in terms of ownership/non-ownership of the means of production,[8] the situation was one in which, broadly speaking, class and caste coincided and reinforced each other (cf. Beteille 1965: 191 ff; Gough 1981; Oommen 1985, 1990: 245–53). As Table 2.1 shows,[9] until 1910 most of Valiyagramam *punja* was held by upper castes, particularly Nayars. Partition of previously indivisible ancestral estates, fear of land reforms and labour militancy, permanent emigration, opening of new employment avenues (for example schools, government service), decline in paddy cultivation's profitability and indebtedness are all factors contributing over many years to progressive land sales by upper-caste landowners. Until the late 1950s the main buyers were Christians (generally medium to large traders-cum-money lenders) recently replaced by migrants of all communities (cf. Varghese 1970: 190–1; Fuller 1976a: 30; Sivanandan 1979: 475; Jeffrey 1994: 204; Radhakrishnan 1983: 145; Franke 1992: 94).

Pulayas and (to a lesser extent) Izhavas were, at the turn of the century, engaged in paddy agriculture. Izhavas, unlike Pulayas and other untouchable groups, were also already involved in a variety of other occupations. They worked not only as labourers but also as self-cultivating tenants or sub-tenants of paddy land, as boatmen, as cultivators of coconut gardens and as

Table 2.1 Holdings of Single-Crop Paddy Land (*punja*)

Community	1910 (acres)	% (of total)	1959 (acres)	% (of total)	1990 (acres)	% (of total)	Community as % of population in 1990
Nayars	1714	65.4	999	45.5	855	39	25
Christians	385	14.7	993	45.3	1005	45.8	27
Brahmans	299	11.4	90	4.1	26	1.2	0.7
Kshatriya	102	3.9	43	2	8	0.4	0.5
Izhavas	**100**	**3.8**	**55**	**2.5**	**252**	**11.5**	**23**
Pulayas	0.5	0.02	4	0.2	25	1.1	11
Others	22	0.85	8	0.4	21	1	12.8
Total	2622.5	100	2192	100	2192	100	100

Table 2.2 Holdings of Garden Land (*parambu*) in 1910

Community	Acres	% (of total)
Brahmans	1.69	1
Kshatriyas	2.89	1.8
Nayars	68.66	43.1
Christians	46.61	29.3
Izhavas	**37.91**	**23.2**
Thandans	0.96	0.6
Pulayas	0.96	0.6
Total	158.68	100

producers and traders of coconut derived products and of country liquor (cf. Aiyappan 1944: 105–6, 1965: Rajendran 1974: 25; Isaac & Tharakan 1986a: 7; Radhakrishnan 1989: 34–5; Menon 1994: 74ff). An upper section, by reason of wealth and/or influence, came into the position to acquire titles (*Channar, Panikkar* and *Tandar*) from local rulers. Fortunes were made from provision of military services and militia to local rulers, ownership of coconut gardens or control of *abkari* business. These families owned private temples, lived in *nalukettus*, paid taxes and acquired honours from rulers; Advocate Remini's family belong to this group (cf. Rajendran 1974: 25–6; Rao 1987: 23; cf. Bayly 1984). An indication of economic differentiation is given in Table 2.2, showing holdings of *parambu* in Sasthamuri. While both Izhavas and Pulayas held only a negligible amount of *punja* (Table 2.1), Izhavas – unlike Pulayas – were far from landless, the third-largest holders of garden land.

PRESENT EMPLOYMENT IN VALIYAGRAMAM

Table 2.3 brings us up to date, presenting primary occupations for Nayar, Izhava and Christian men from Sasthamuri and Pulaya men from Punjayil Kadavau, surveyed between 1989 and 1995. The two main sources of occupational income are agriculture and migration. While declining in economic importance, agriculture and landownership continue to interest the majority. Many have agriculture as a secondary occupation; income from this may be nil, land being used to keep the household self-sufficient in rice: any surplus sold is likely to be small (cf. Heuzé 1992). Migration is the major source of the recent past's economic and social change. Not only does it involve large numbers of villagers (30 percent of men in Sasthamuri),[10] but it, especially Gulf migration, has also brought large amounts of remittances and 'foreign goods' into the local economy, as throughout Kerala. While farming, through association with the figure of the traditional high-caste Hindu landlord, is allied to Nayars and to the village economy, and hence especially with status mobility, migration – an innovative and individualistic

Table 2.3 Male Primary Occupation

Occupation	Nayar	Christian	Izhava	Pulaya	Total (%)
Agricultural/manual labour	8 (7%)	6 (7.1%)	29 (23.3%)	65 (50.5%)	108 (23.8%)
Skilled labour (for example ploughman)	1 (0.9%)	11 (13%)	6 (4.8%)	15 (11.7%)	33 (7.3%)
Technical employment (for example electrician)	0	2 (2.3%)	11 (8.8%)	4 (3.1%)	17 (3.7%)
Petty trade	21 (18.3%)	8 (9.5%)	21 (16.9%)	9 (7%)	59 (13%)
Farming	18 (15.7%)	1 (1.1%)	0	0	19 (4.2%)
Low government employment	15 (13%)	2 (2.3%)	8 (6.4%)	3 (2.3%)	28 (6.1%)
Teaching	9 (7.8%)	2 (2.3%)	4 (3.2%)	0	15 (3.3%)
Military and police	9 (7.8%)	4 (4.7%)	13 (10.4%)	5 (3.8%)	31 (6.8%)
Skilled factory work	2 (1.8%)	0	3 (2.4%)	0	5 (1.1%)
High government employment	5 (4.3%)	6 (7.1%)	1 (0.8%)	0	12 (2.6%)
Big trade	5 (4.3%)	0	0	0	5 (1.1%)
Migrated in India (unskilled)	1 (0.9%)	7 (8.3%)	17 (13.7%)	19 (14.7%)	44 (9.7%)
Migrated in India (skilled/professional)	5 (4.3%)	3 (3.5%)	0	0	8 (1.7%)
Migrated in the Gulf (unskilled)	5 (4.3%)	13 (15.4%)	10 (8%)	6 (4.6%)	34 (7.5%)
Migrated in the Gulf (skilled/professional)	5 (4.3%)	14 (16.6%)	1 (0.8%)	0	20 (4.4%)
Others	6 (5.3%)	5 (5.9%)	0	3 (2.3%)	14 (3%)
Total men	115	84	124	129	452

solution looking beyond the local economy – is especially associated with the group which first took it up, the Christian community, and with class mobility.

The largest proportion of wealthy villagers (looking at income from employment, property and savings) is found among Christians, who emerge overall as the wealthiest local community. Among upper castes there is more economic differentiation than in the past: although only a few from the old landed elite are now impoverished, these groups have generally lost political and economic dominance. Processes of economic differentiation among lower castes have been fairly contained but noticeable. Among Izhavas especially there are several households, notably those of migrants, which, while they cannot be described as affluent, are now relatively well off. Meanwhile, the bounties of economic liberalisation and Gulf migration have so far failed to trickle down to poorer villagers. While inflation has bitten badly into already low purchasing power, no new jobs have been created and safety nets against poverty provided by state government subsidies have been reduced. This progressive and speeded-up economic differentiation is all too evident to those labourers who, during the 1995 paddy harvest, were supervised by a landowner sitting not in the traditional thatched shelter but in his air-conditioned, Omani-registered Mercedes car.

Pulayas, the group from which Izhavas strive to distance themselves, are for the great majority (62 percent), still employed either as permanent or seasonal/semi-permanent agricultural labourers. In either case, as agricultural labour (*krisipani*) provides only 90 to 100 work-days a year, work in fields and gardens is coupled with casual day-labouring (*kulipani*) in the building trade, in brick factories and with head-load work (cf. Narayana & Nair 1989: 28; Gopikuttan 1990). While Izhava men and women have been increasingly withdrawing from agricultural labour, in 1968 in Kerala as a whole, 40 percent of Izhavas returned their occupation as 'agricultural/ related labour', as did 23.3 percent of Izhava men surveyed in Valiyagramam in 1990 (1968 Government Survey Report cited in Sivanandan 1979: 478). The Izhava project of withdrawal from manual labour is, then, far from complete, while the broad correlation of caste/class at the level of an identification between agricultural labour and untouchability still stands. Sociological work on occupational mobility points out that agricultural labouring families experience the least mobility, while a generalised decline in agriculture is associated with a temporary upsurge in general mobility (for example Lipset et al. 1994: 250; Erikson & Goldthorpe 1994: 307; Featherman & Hauser 1994: 272).

Nayars and Christians are taken by Izhavas to be imitated in economic endeavour and style. Although many Nayars (23.6 percent) are employed in agriculture, only 8 percent are day-labourers, while 15.7 percent are full-time 'farmers' (owner-cultivators who do not themselves perform manual work in the fields). Compared to other groups, Nayars have also the largest proportion of government servants (25 percent), 12 percent of whom are middle- to high-ranking officers. Christians also participate in government service, having a proportionally higher number of men occupying high-ranking posts. Of those Nayars involved in trade (22.6 percent), a fifth are large-scale commodity traders (of rice, paddy and coconut oil in particular). While our sample does not include any Christian large traders, who tend to move to the village peripheries near main highways, or into town, several local families have made good this way. Of Nayar migrants (21.6 percent), a significant proportion (20 percent) has skilled or professional employment. The greatest single source of employment and wealth among Christians is migration (48.5 percent excluding military), almost half in well-paid skilled and professional jobs.

Table 2.3 indicates that Izhava occupations are spread between four major categories. The three largest areas of employment are agricultural and manual labour (23.3 percent), petty trade (16.9 percent), migration (23 percent) and military/police (10 percent). Agricultural or manual labour represents, then, a large and unsuccessful section of the community, those whose occupation offers neither wealth nor prestige and who have failed to find mobility, remaining dangerously close to Pulayas. The other main categories are all occupations associated with Nayars and Christians and – importantly – permitting autonomy, representing escape from work patterns requiring relations with higher-caste people.

CASE STUDIES

We can now consider some particular cases illustrating how a variety of factors – from education and social contacts to global movements of international capitalism – have influenced Izhava families' fortunes across generations. These cases make plain that, far from demonstrating peasant fatalism in the face of uncontrollable forces, villagers have employment strategies, calculating and planning towards mobility; but, their efforts notwithstanding, one factor which villagers themselves recognise as crucial is *chance*. Chapter 1's family stories make this clear: all tried to make good; all shared a readiness to take chances and risks outside the village. Differences between successful migrants K.V. Krishnan and Kuttiyil and the unsuccessful Keshavan and Premadasan lie partly in timing and luck, in making the right contacts and riding waves of opportunity during boom periods: sometimes good strategy is not enough.

Consolidating Status after Accumulating Wealth

Biju, an only child of 16, lives in a comfortable two-storeyed three-bed-roomed modern house. He had just matriculated in June 1995; with good enough results, his parents planned to send him to college in Thiruvalla, a Christian-dominated town 15 km away whose many colleges are of higher standard than those available locally. Biju's father hopes that his son will get the grades for medicine or engineering. Having consolidated wealth in previous generations, this family is now pursuing maximal achiever status. Biju's mother, an economics graduate, is a housewife with one live-in servant; father, Sadashivan, BSc Engineering and MBA, works as an engineer for Kerala State Electricity Board. Sadashivan 'moves among Nayars'; his roadside house at the edge of a Nayar-dominated part of the village stands near the popular Kottakara Durga temple where he is committee president. Sadashivan's brother, a Bachelor of Ayurvedic Medicine (BAMS), lives next door in a similarly grand and well-furnished house, working from home in a private practice inherited from his father; his wife, also a graduate housewife, has recently been elected as *panchayat* member on a seat reserved for women. One of the men's sisters, a graduate, works as a clerk in a prestigious SNDP college; her husband, an engineering diploma holder, works in the Telephone Department. Elder sister, who studied to pre-degree level, is a housewife married to an electrician working in Dubai.

Sadashivan's father and father's brother were both *vaidyan*s who built up thriving practices after marrying into Valiyagramam in the 1930s and settling there, as was common custom before the matrilineal system collapsed. Sadashivan's mother's father and mother's elder brother were both described to us by him as farmers and copra traders; other Izhavas told us that they had actually owned toddy businesses and sold liquor. This was how they had made the money enabling them to educate their children well and make good strategic marriages: Sadashivan's mother's sister married a wealthy farmer; mother's brother became a traffic inspector.

The marriage between Sadashivan's mother – from a liquor trading family – and father – from a family of *vaidyan*s – is a common calculated move: first, alliances are often made in which wealth is traded off against status, large dowries 'buying' girls into families of higher prestige (cf. Warner et al. 1994: 191). Second, affinities exist between alcohol and Ayurveda: *kashayam* and *arishtam* medicines are alcohol-based. We have met several people who described themselves to us as *vaidyan*s, later to find that they were involved in *vattu*. The tools of the trade of the *vaidyan* and of the illegal distiller are similar: he who knows the technique of distilling medicines is also able to distil liquor. The story of this family, moving from the liquor trade at the turn of the century via Ayurveda and on to become professionals by the end of it is an exceptional example of fulfilment of the ideal of mobility: not all have been so fortunate.

Success and Failure Waxing and Waning through Generations

Warriattu family employment history begins at the turn of the twentieth century with a pair of polyandrous brothers from Sasthamuri, one in the military and one remaining home to look after the family copra business and land. When the business failed during the 1930s depression, the brothers were financially ruined. They first took up a bullock cart for transporting copra and then became ferrymen, along with several of their relatives in the area.

Between them, this pair had seven sons and one daughter: the younger children suffered from interruption of their education when family fortunes fell. Two elder of the seven sons are permanently settled in Calcutta: one, with matriculation and diploma, is a typist; the other, a B.Comm. graduate, works as a telephonist. Another matriculate brother spent over 20 years in military service while a fourth, after failing matriculation, spent a short and unsuccessful spell in Calcutta before returning to Valiyagramam to open a welding workshop where he trains young men. Another brother, primary educated, retired from work as a permanent (attached) agricultural labourer, while a sixth worked as a *compounder* in the local government hospital.

The seventh son (Madhavan) together with his sister (Pankajakshi) had an exchange marriage in the 1940s with another pair of siblings (Mohannan and Kalyani) children of a nearby small *vaidyan* and tenant farmer related to the family. Madhavan, primary educated, is a retired ferryman with five sons and two daughters. Kalyani never went to the fields, but helped out with the family harvest. This couple have seen their children's futures improve over time. Their eldest son, primary educated, works as a contract driver for lorry owners; his wife, officially 'housewife', goes to the paddy fields during harvest. Eldest daughter, primary educated, married a tailor and undertakes agricultural labour. These two eldest siblings and their families live jointly at some distance from the original two-roomed family house which has recently been extended as fortunes have flourished over the last ten years, thanks to second son, Rejish. He failed to matriculate, learnt welding at his FB's workshop before going to Mumbai, from where he was recruited to Qatar. He learnt motor mechanics before going on to a better-paid job in Saudi, where he eventually plans to open his own workshop with five of his in-laws. His wife, a non-matriculate 'genuine' housewife, and baby daughter (whom he has hardly seen) live with his parents in the family house. While Madhavan complains that his son is not sending enough money to the parental home, Rejish sends money secretly to his wife who makes substantial monthly deposits to an assurance policy, unbeknown to her in-laws.

The third son, another non-matriculate, spent eight years in Pune working in a tyre factory before returning to Valiyagramam to be trained as an electrician, where he now makes a fair living; he is likely to go to the Gulf. The fourth son, non-matriculate, has been in the army for five years in a post found by his paternal uncle. He has taken difficult and unpopular postings, refusing the favoured option of Chennai, with an eye both to saving money and to making a career. Finally, youngest brother Sanjay, a matriculate who failed degree entrance examinations three times at private colleges, spent just six months in the army before coming home, explaining privately that he had left because he could stand neither the discipline and hard work nor being ordered around by a 'North Indian Harijan who kept calling me an ignorant Madrassi'. He was then sent by his enterprising elder brothers to their FB in Calcutta to look for work and learn English. He has gone for several interviews for hotel work, but, having neither experience nor a recognised qualification, has been unsuccessful and is is now pinning his hopes upon being called to the Gulf by his elder brother.

The second couple in the 1940s exchange marriage, *vaidyan*'s son Mohannan and Pankajakshi, sister to seven brothers, are settled nearby and have not seen their household do so well. Mohannan worked alongside brother-in-law Madhavan as a ferryman until 1983, when he retired at 55 on a small pension, in severe ill health after two heart attacks. Pankajakshi, officially a housewife, used to do agricultural labour but now is out of the house much of the day selling insurance and collecting premiums for Peerless Assurance. We are reminded that household mobility often involves loosening kinship obligations by the fact that her niece (Rejish's wife), makes her secret deposits of Gulf remittances with an – unrelated – agent of a rival company, LIC. This couple's only son has been a disappointment and has so far failed to contribute much to struggling household finances. Having failed SSLC he began, to the family's chagrin, working as a head-load worker; his parents persuaded him to go to Mumbai with his elder sister's husband. He was back three months later, the *company job* promised by brother-in-law having turned out to consist of packing toys in a small shed for twelve hours daily. He was next dispatched to maternal uncles in Calcutta. Failing to find work there he returned to Valiyagramam to work as a daily wage manual labourer. He often stands at the junction in the evenings with his work-mates, somewhat the worse for drink: unlike his cousin Sanjay, he has little prospect of improving his situation.

His two sisters also spend much of their time in their natal home, although both are married to Mumbai migrants, a pair of brothers. Elder sister took typing and stitching classes after failing SSLC before marrying a low-grade factory worker who cannot support his non-working wife and 7-year-old daughter in the city. Second sister married at 17 after failing SSLC; her husband, currently unemployed, sent her and her small son back to her parents' house complaining that he had never received the full amount of dowry. Long spells of separation and lack of contact since 1990 between this woman – full-time in the village – and her husband – in Mumbai – leads us to think that divorce is in the offing. All this is much to the shame and anguish of the parents who hoped and planned, worked and saved, for better things; they cannot but compare their fortunes and their children with those of their siblings Madhavan and Kalyani, alongside whom they were married. Luck, temperament and good connections have made a difference, as has having five mobility-hungry sons rather than two daughters to marry and one unambitious son. The difficulties suffered by Warriattu family are exacerbated by the fact that, living in Sasthamuri, a mixed area, they are always forced to keep an eye on their prestige and are subject to constant appraisal by others. Izhava families living in relative isolation from others are able to look first to material advantage, consolidating financial well-being and projecting their identity mainly to supportive family and caste-fellows.

The Advantages of Being out of the Eye of Other Communities

Kappa Parambil is a highly particular family, consisting of a demarcated area containing 46 related households – all offshoots from one original family – whose five branches are densely related to each other through continued cross-cousin marriages. Only a handful of households not part of this family live in the area, while most members of the family live together here. This has several implications. Kappa Parambil is a self-contained and self-consciously strong unit whose members have a strong family identity from which they derive great material and moral support: many are in business together or have helped each other find work, leading to long migration and military chains. While enormous internal economic differentiation exists, family members work hard to mitigate this for the sake of unity. Family strength and solidarity, coupled with isolation from other castes – and other Izhavas – has allowed the family to innovate and adopt its own ethos, which often deviates from dominant ideals: individuals and households are answerable mainly to the family. Those members involved in low-prestige occupations such as liquor-brewing and building-site work suffer less stigmatisation than do non-family counterparts in other parts of Valiyagramam, where households keep face and pace, competing with other Izhavas and with the dominant Nayar and Christian communities. Interestingly, Kappa Parambil, isolated from Nayars, retains the perceptibly modernist outlook promulgated by early self-respect movements, striving for class mobility as a priority over status: Kappa Parambil has, for example, a high proportion of working women and migrants and several women working as or studying to become nurses, still an extremely rare phenomenon among village Hindus. A few examples of employment strategies from some households within this huge and complexly interrelated family, will give a sense of the importance of mutual help and disregard for outside opinion.

The 'core' family, where the oldest man of the main branch lives, reside in a 1970s four-roomed brick and plaster house. This household head spent many years in military service before returning to Valiyagramam to take over the local toddy-shop. He had previously shared a wife with his younger brother but on retirement built a separate house and took his own wife, a matriculate and diploma shorthand-typist from the eastern hilly area. Together the couple run a photocopy shop and typing institute in town. Here we see one household ignore taboos on polyandry, liquor-selling and women working, all for the sake of its financial progress.

One of the other original houses, a spacious 1960s-built six-roomed building, is headed by two sisters in their seventies. The elder never married, worked as a touring actress, a profession still now tinged with scandal in mainstream society. Her sister, a widow, was married to a military man. Their eldest son, after a spell in the military, has been in Muscat (Oman) working as a driver for 14 years, his wife living in Kappa Parambil and working as a pharmacist at the government hospital. Their daughter, recently matriculated, plans to take a physics degree. Second son is currently home for two years from Muscat while he builds a new house; his wife works as a bank clerk in town. Two daughters – matriculate housewives – have marrried out, respectively to a policeman and a Saudi migrant.

A nearby household, a 1970s-built four-roomed brick and plaster house, is headed by a working widow, a veterinary attendant whose husband was a small farmer. Her eldest son (a matriculate) is in Dubai with his housewife wife; eldest daughter, a matriculate housewife, married a bank clerk. The middle son, a matriculate and diploma holder, worked as a typist in Delhi, Dubai and – recently – Muscat, where he was called by his cousin; his wife, a nurse, also works in Muscat. The next sister, married to a cloth wholesaler, studied for a BSc and BEd and works as a school-teacher in a government primary school. Youngest sister, graduate housewife and new mother, was engaged to a local military man when another villager, working in Saudi as an electrician, proposed marriage. The first engagement was pragmatically called off, scandal notwithstanding, to enable the better match. In these households we again see a disregard for bourgeois morality relating to womenfolk and a willingness to embrace new and unusual forms of employment; family cooperation has also been crucial.

Next door lives another widow, an outworker who assembles boxes and puts splinters of wood into frames to be dipped as matches. Her husband was a military man who died before the minimum 15 years' service, leaving her without a pension. The family clubbed together to repay the Rs 5000 loan outstanding on the two-roomed brick house. Two daughters, both matriculates but pre-degree failures, work as shop assistants, one earning Rs 500 per month writing bills in a *sari* showroom in town and the other working in a local ready-made garment shop for Rs 300 per month.

Around the corner stands a thatched hut whose owner is an illiterate retired ferryman living with his wife, a retired agricultural labourer. This couple do odd jobs for wealthier family members and help those with land at harvest-time. Two daughters of the house, non-matriculates, work as agricultural and building site labourers, and have children but no husbands. One daughter's son, after failing matriculation, is doing casual labour; the other daughter's son is studying to become an electrician, while his sister is a nursing student.

In a nearby 1950s-built four-roomed brick and plaster house with verandah lives a woman who was polyandrously married to two brothers.

One brother stayed at home to farm; the other was in military service, working as a compounder in Singapore. On retirement, he worked for a while in a private hospital before opening his own medical store. He has recently sold the shop to retire, at 75. One son, a matriculate, works for an airline at Ernakulam airport; the next two, who failed matriculation, work in a local edible oil refinery and as an auto-rickshaw driver respectively.

Along the lane is a 1970s-built brick and concrete house with verandah whose household head, now farming half an acre of paddy land, spent 21 years in the Indian Air Force as a fitter before going to Muscat where his wife – also his cross-cousin – was working. After taking a nursing diploma in Mumbai, she has been a staff nurse in a Muscat government hospital for 15 years. Her husband worked there as a shopkeeper and as a telephone operator for a transport company before coming back to Valiyagramam to look after his mother-in-law and school-going daughter, who spends two months a year with her mother, during the school holidays.

Kappa Parambil family live in an exceptional situation within the village, and are considered an exceptional family; many Izhavas speak disparagingly of them as failing to 'play the game' of seeking group social mobility, for example, by allowing their women to work as nurses or by continuing to run a toddy-shop. The family has, we found, much in common with Izhavas living in Izhava-dominated villages towards the coastal coir belt, where we found a similar relaxed atmosphere and sense of self-worth. Kappa Parambil supports claims that in single-caste areas, class mobility is privileged over caste status or prestige (Kapadia 1995). Most Valiyagramam Izhavas live in mixed areas and choose to keep their eyes on the dominant communities, who in turn keep their eyes upon Izhavas. The consequent impulse to accumulate not only cash but also respect and prestige within the wider Hindu community has led many to compete in arenas of employment with Nayars, chasing employment which does not offer spectacular financial rewards but is considered respectable or status-enhancing.

Privileging Education and Culture

In 1953 Sasthamuri Prabhakaran's father, a small tenant farmer and petty pepper trader, died leaving the family in penury. Although high-status, titled Izhavas – *Channars* – they were asset-less, father's business having made losses and left debts. Younger brother, then 14, left school and, 'did hard labour to get an income; that was the only family income ... we had nothing ... for five or six months we ate nothing but tapioca.' Elder brother Prabhakaran worked part time doing *chitty fund* accounts while taking SSLC and TTC to become a primary school-teacher. Finding no local employment, he worked for short spells as a tally-clerk in Kochi docks and as clerk in various plantations in Tamil Nadu and Karnataka. In 1957, when the first Communist government was elected, Prabhakaran obtained state government employment as a primary school-teacher. He paid for his sister to make a good marriage to a welder, helped his brother build a two-roomed brick house and then finally himself married (at 36) Pankajakshi, also an orphan from a titled but impoverished family. The pair determined to make good their families' *manam*.

Prabhakaran's two children are Shijini, BA and MA at 23, currently studying BEd; and Shaji, 22, an enthusiastic Democratic Youth Federation of India (DYFI) and Kerala Sastra Sahitya Parishad (KSSP) member who has completed ITC and is currently an apprentice draughtsman in Alapuzha. This family, in line with their status, has eschewed chances of greater income in favour of a balance between cash and prestige, making many sacrifices for the children's education. They seem to be thriving in their modest four-roomed brick and plaster house, and are making plans for pragmatic, prestigious and advantageous marriages of their children into respectable families connected with education or engineering.

FOUR TYPES OF EMPLOYMENT

Rather than offer pedestrian analyses of these case studies, which offer clear examples of different employment strategies aimed in different ways towards satisfying various Izhava families' mobility goals, we turn to look more closely at four important categories of employment. Toddy-tapping is significant as the so-called caste-specific occupation of Izhavas, and is – for most – to be avoided at all costs, for what it represents in terms of the repudiated past. Agricultural and manual labour is no less to be avoided, both as part of the degraded past and as a form of employment particularly associated with untouchability. Public service provides occupations giving not only income but also prestige, favoured among Nayars; migration – favoured especially among Christians – is increasingly popular, offering considerable and unique advantages in terms both of capital accumulation and identity formation.

Toddy-tapping and Coconuts: Izhava Nature?

In Table 2.3, only two men are officially involved in the liquor business, the caste-specific and supposedly 'traditional' occupation of Izhavas: one as toddy-tapper and another running a toddy-shop. Several (unrecorded) others make their living illicitly and discreetly distilling and selling liquor. Those families involved in toddy-tapping or the illicit liquor trade tend to live in *colonies*, segregated from other Izhavas; certain neighbourhoods have a far higher concentration of Izhavas involved in the liquor trade than our samples.

Census reports, gazetteers, manuals and histories of Travancore and Kerala published towards the end of the nineteenth century describe

Travancore Izhavas as a community closely associated with tending coconut gardens, the production and commerce of coconut-derived and palmyra-derived products, and production and sale of country liquor (Mateer 1883: 85; Aiya 1906: 401; Menon 1993 [orig. 1937]).[11] The 1881 Travancore census showed around 25 percent of all surveyed men engaged in extraction, production and sale of toddy, suggesting the economic importance of these activities. Mateer (1883: 85) describes Izhavas' main occupation as culture of the coconut palm and manufacture of toddy and arrack. Izhavas are introduced by Thurston & Rangachari (1909: 392ff) as 'toddy-drawing castes', and described by Aiya (1906, II: 401) as 'engaged in ... cultivation of the coconut palm and ... industries connected with its produces ... toddy-drawing is another important occupation'. A section of Padmanabha Menon's 1937 (1993: 423ff) history, headed by the derogatory term '*Chegos*' (surviving today as an insulting epithet), designates Izhavas' 'traditional occupation' as toddy-tapping, and is illustrated by two photographs: one of 'Izhuvas with toddy-drawing pots' and one of Narayana Guru, 'under whose guidance ... the community is making rapid strides' (Menon 1993: 443). This dramatic counterposition of photographic images evokes the community's adoption and public projection, under the SNDP, of a modernist myth of linear progress from toddy-tapper to reformed Narayana Guru supporter. Whether they actually gave up tapping or not, the percentage of Izhava men recorded in censuses as following their 'traditional occupation' of toddy-drawing decreased from from 20 percent in 1911 to 8 percent in 1921 and just 4 percent in 1931 (Kumar 1994: 90; Lemercinier 1994: 201). The anthropologist A. Aiyappan, himself an Izhava, strenuously denied that toddy-tappping had ever been the caste's 'traditional occupation' (Aiyappan 1944: 106–7).

One famous story, reproduced in many sources and told to us many times, and always by SNDP officials in their attempt to explain to us the enormity of caste stereotyping and discrimination, concerns SNDP founder Dr Palpu. He and his brother were English-educated by missionaries at home in the 1870s, government schools being banned to even wealthy Izhavas, as untouchables. In 1884 Palpu came second in the all-Travancore medical entrance test; as an Izhava, his application to medical college was rejected and his – substantial – fee not refunded. He passed his finals from Chennai Medical College in 1889, and joined Mysore government service in 1891. Visiting Travancore as a qualified medical doctor, he went to the palace and pleaded to be permitted to return to his home state and to serve the Rajah. The Rajah's response was (in some versions) to offer Palpu a patch of land with coconut trees on it, and the promise that he could tend them tax-free (i.e. tap toddy from them), since customary law permitted Palpu only that as an occupation. In other versions, the haughty Rajah first tells Dr Palpu, 'Yes, you can serve me. Here there's plenty of work for you to do', before having him taken outside, shown the coconut trees in the royal compound, and told, 'There's plenty of trees here for you to climb.'[12]

Colonial material such as gazetteers and missionaries' accounts labelled Izhavas, on the understanding that castes were primarily defined in relation to occupation and religious practices, contributing to the persistence of stereotypes about Izhavas common among other communities. While current Malayali discourses on personhood and caste identities differ from European essentialist conceptions of the self in according great importance to environment and permitting a high degree of malleability to the person, discourses about qualities (*gunams*), some of which are assumed to be hereditary and stable, are available to talk about that part of persons' natures which is essentialised, *swabhavangal*. Caste nature, including a relationship or affinity (*bandham*) with certain substances and a propensity towards certain occupations, is still now widely assumed to be part of the more stable parts of the person. Outside the community, alcohol and toddy-tapping continue to be central to attributed Izhava identity. Of the many derogatory names for and negative stereotypes heard in private from others, most continue to associate Izhavas overwhelmingly with making and excessive drinking of alcohol: as Pulayas are assumed to have an essential relationship – a *bandham* – with the paddy fields, Izhavas are commonly assumed to have one with alcohol.

When the state government proposed (in 1996) a blanket ban on arrack, it was common to hear comments like the following from members of other communities: 'It's a good idea, but it will never work. Our place is full of Chovans and they'll all be brewing like mad. They'll be the ones who are laughing, making money on the sly' (20-year-old Nayar woman). A joke (told to us by a Christian) again illustrates the force of the alcohol connection: an Izhava man interviews a prospective bridegroom for his daughter; the groom's response to enquiries about his job is that he is 'in the air-force'. Impressed, the man gives his daughter a substantial dowry, only to discover after the wedding that his new son-in-law is part of the village 'air-force', in the air up a tree, tapping toddy.[13] This common epithet 'air-force' insults Izhavas in several ways by suggesting, first, that they are high in the air up a tree, thereby associating them with 'tree-climbers' like the low-status Scheduled Caste Thandans whose caste occupation is coconut-picking; second, that they are up a tree because they are tapping toddy; third, that they are 'high in the sky', i.e. drunk. It also mockingly evokes two popular sources of Izhava employment: the armed services and migration, the latter involving being part of the Gulf 'air-force', forever taking a plane, leaving or returning to the village. The derogatory nickname *air-force* then manages to conflate old and new stereotypes, playing on several aspects of Izhava identity and making the status-quoist claims both that Izhavas are inappropriately ambitious for mobility and that they are wilfully deceitful in self-presentation, claiming higher status than they are entitled to. Izhavas are clearly identifiable as the group described by Bourdieu as '*déclassé*', '*parvenu*', picked up by others for their 'jarring notes' (Bourdieu 1984: 109ff; Mahar et al. 1990: 20; cf. Sorotkin on 'status discrepancies', 1994: 255–7).

Since Narayana Guru urged caste members to give up this 'degrading occupation', toddy-tappers or 'Chettu Izhavas' (from the verb *chettuka*), liquor contractors and those involved in illegal distilling have become targets of strong criticism by high-status and educated Left Izhavas alike, who argue that the group as a whole continues to be dragged down by the participation of some members in the liquor trade, and consequently distance themselves from any interaction with *Chettus* or *Vattus*, refusing marriage or commensality. However, among most Izhavas – as among other communities – liquor is seen as a fairly harmless substance whose consumption helps men make a difficult life more bearable, while being a central part of male sociality. A trip to the *sharppu*, centre of relaxation, gossip, politics and *chitty funds*, a strictly gendered space where men can drink with friends after a hard day's work, is considered a working man's legitimate right and pleasure,[14] while a bottle of 'foreign' liquor (commonly brandy or whisky) is a treat to be shared. Military men are issued daily rations of spirits; ex-servicemen can buy good quality liquor at subsidised prices and most military men continue to take a daily peg, often arguing it to be medicinal. Reformed Izhavas attempt to marginalise Chettu Izhavas as a degraded sub-group separated from the wider community, while other Izhavas continue to mix with them, consume their products, and may even marry with them if other factors are advantageous. Most make finer distinctions: between those who tap, those who distil, those who sell from their own homes, those who own licensed toddy-shops and so on: Izhavas who still accept the 1930s SNDP-inspired blanket condemnation of all involvement with alcohol are few. A division between 'country' and 'foreign' alcohol, and association of the latter with values of westernisation, modernity, sophistication and wealth has partially redeemed the status of those involved (as sellers or consumers) with this end of the trade, while a trip in a taxi with friends to an air-conditioned bar in one of the nearby towns, a practice common among wealthy and sophisticated Christian men, is becoming a marker of distinction. Those who make a good living in the liquor trade by moving into the lucrative hotel or bar business are admired for their entrepreneurial skills and would be considered by many as a 'good catch' in the marriage stakes. While only one or two local SNDP officials are involved in the toddy trade, at least one high-ranking SNDP official is a liquor baron; we have already suggested that parts of the aristocratic elite and the nineteenth-century new bourgeoisie alike owed their fortunes to control of the *abkari* trade.

We visited relatives of Prabhakaran, a teetotaller Communist Party activist, in a coir-belt Izhava-dominated village. The annual festival was due to take place that afternoon at the village's main temple, dedicated to Mudiamma (a form of Durga) and to Gurudevan; we were to take food first with Prabhakaran's relatives. Greeting us warmly at the door and ushering us in, Sukumaran asked Filippo, 'Will you take a small drink (*oru cheriya hot*) before the meal?' and guided him, with Prabhakaran, into a side room. Prabhakaran looked nervously around the room where father, sons, and son-in-law sat in front of a bottle of good imported brandy; refusing a drink, Prabhakaran good-humouredly wagged his finger, declaiming, 'Sri Narayana Guru said, "Don't make it, sell it or use it." ' Sukumaran's riposte, as he filled Filippo's glass to the brim, was, 'Don't worry, Sri Narayana Guru didn't come to this house today.' At the festival, Prabhakaran was one of few men not the worse for drink. Since alcohol plays a part in both celebration and in masculine sociality, Nayar-dominated festivals and Christian weddings and baptisms all have a similar boozy atmosphere: only Izhavas have been forced, through their ascribed association with alcohol, on to the defensive about this common part of everyday life.

Sivan, working as a toddy-tapper, and Velayuthan, running a licensed toddy-shop, explained to us the processes of toddy extraction and the system of production and distribution which has been in force since the 1950s. Krisnakara *taluk* has 72 shops under control of one main contractor, divided between two 'ranges' of 36 shops each, each range providing employment for 186 tappers; numbers of shops and tappers are fixed by law. Valiyagramam has five licensed shops which, since the state government's 1996 blanket ban on *charayam*, have licences to sell only toddy. Each of the village's 33 licensed tappers has responsibility for ten coconut trees, which he taps three times daily for five months on, five months off. Contractors bid at public auctions for the right to hold alcohol licences and subcontract the right to sell toddy at licensed shops. In 1996, the going rate for a licence for a Valiyagramam shop was Rs40,000, while the annual increases in state income from toddy-shop auctions ranged from 32 percent to 95 percent (*Indian Express* 12.3.96). Shop-owners arrange with and pay directly to coconut tree owners Rs50 per month for tapping, appointing tappers as direct employees to do the work. Shop-owners pay taxes of Rs32 per tree and wages to employees based upon union rates for basic daily allowances plus bonus according to the quantity of toddy brought in. Sivan told us that a tree may yield from 1 to 4 litres a day, more in the rainy season and less in the hot season: the maximum he has ever tapped from one tree was 8 litres.

Kerala's toddy-tappers have been highly organised and unionised since the 1940s, fighting for and obtaining holiday and sickness leave, retirement and dependants' payments, house-building loans and – importantly – minimum wages. If Sivan taps 15 litres, he receives Rs85 for a day's work; during the hot season, when he taps barely 3 litres, he receives just Rs30 daily. A survey in the Malabar area claims that there toddy-tappers and their families are as educated, wealthy and 'respectable' in their behaviour as other parts of the community, sometimes earning more than blue-collar factory workers (Kannan 1988). In Valiyagramam, the picture appears less optimistic: tappers are at a socioeconomic level comparable not to blue-collar workers but to manual labourers. Sivan lives in a sparsely furnished, small two-roomed unplastered brick house. When he goes to work he is scantily dressed in a vest and towel, with the tools of his trade – a bone, knife, pot and wooden box – suspended from his waist; his appearance at once contrasts unfavourably with that of the village school-teachers (in white *mundus* and shirts) and that of the factory workers (in smart trousers and shirts) and is instantly recognisable as that of the toddy-tapper. The continuing stigmatising by the Izhava middle class of those involved in toddy-tapping therefore also owes something to its status as manual labour and as a caste-bound occupation, categories of employment associated with those unable to escape the village economy, a group increasingly identified with Scheduled Caste status. As such, and as the occupation ascribed by Brahmans, Nayars and Christians as uniquely and solely fit for Izhavas, tapping represents a profound failure of mobility ambitions.

Even worse, according to the reformed and successful, are those running illegal stills from home: regular and public excise department raids notwithstanding, it took us many months to learn anything about this trade and we still, after ten years, know little about it. We know of a few distillers' colonies and of a couple of widows who distil and sell from home, but we have never been permitted to see the process. Problems with this occupation derive not so much from illegality as from desecration of the home, ideally a repository of morality and family prestige, and a place of the 'inside', where the family's women are protected from the 'outside'. People continue to make associations between trading in alcohol from the house and a degraded past. Karthikeyan, an Izhava in his sixties, said disgustedly:

In the bad old days, our people sold the toddy they tapped directly from their houses. Nayars would come to the house, call for toddy, and our women would serve it. Some of them would then call for our women to go in the back room with them, and we let them do it: what else could we do? This is no secret: our houses were toddy shops and our women were prostituted.

While involvement in the *vattu* business today in no way necessarily means involvement in prostitution, images of the trade – as with toddy-tapping – continue to be over-determined by a past experienced and remembered as degraded and humiliating, to be rejected and erased.

Agricultural and Manual Labour: Poverty and Stigma

At the bottom end of the occupational scale – both in terms of prestige and wealth – stands agricultural and manual labour, a badly paid and severely degraded occupation (cf. Heuzé 1992: 15, 18). Izhavas, who cannot always avoid doing manual labour, draw a series of extremely fine distinctions based upon differences in the tasks performed and the social relations around them. Being the leader of a head-load gang is better than being an ordinary worker; ploughing is more prestigious than spraying pesticide; the trusted agricultural labourer who holds the position of *nokkakaran* is not a mere labourer. Pulayas especially often mock these attempts by labouring Izhavas to introduce distinction and difference into what is generally lumped together as one category, 'casual manual labour' (*pani*, opposed to *joli*, salaried permanent employment). A joke we heard many times runs: an Izhava man interviews prospective bridegrooms for his daughter; one man's response to enquiries about his job is that he is in the road-works, doing casual manual labour. Seeing prospective father-in-law's face drop, the would-be groom's accompanying party hurries to offer reassurance, clarifying, 'He's not the one who carries the basket of earth on his head, or the one who digs the hole.' Father-in-law brightens, asking, 'Well, then?' 'He's the one who holds the shovel and basket for the other two.' Father-in-law satisfied, the marriage is arranged. Like the 'air-force' joke above, this joke mocks Izhava mobility ambitions while also suggesting that they can be adequately fulfilled by very little. Izhavas here are again denied the possibility of genuine and substantial mobility, tied to manual labour in the same way that 'air-force' jokes tie them to alcohol production and use (cf. Huber, cited in Roediger 1994: 137, on 'hillbilly', 'redneck' and 'redbones').

Attached labour, based upon semi-permanent relations with particular families and valued among Pulayas for the economic security it brings and for the chance of linking family status to that of the patron, is considered the lowest-prestige option among Izhavas, struggling for independence. Attached agricultural labour means being at an employer's beck and call throughout the year, continues to require 'extra duties' (for example giving assistance at weddings) and is associated with annual reciprocal gift exchanges, openly pervaded by the ideology of patronage (cf. Harriss 1982: 238; Osella & Osella 1996). Agricultural work permitting autonomy such as ploughing or head-loading is preferred, often supplemented by small businesses such as selling wood, coconuts, copra or coconut husks. While those working contractually might find employment for fewer days per annum than do permanent labourers, this can be compensated by relatively higher wages. A casual labourer in 1995 would receive Rs50–60 a day for fencing a plot of garden land; permanent labourers would receive Rs35–40 for the same task.[15] The process of paddy cultivation is such that on particular occasions (for example harvest, transplanting) there is always a demand for labour. In between times, labourers can travel to other labouring jobs wherever they are available, for example with road building contractors, or brick factory owners, throughout the district. Independence involves a continual scramble for work, but is possible.

Another significant opposition is drawn between agricultural and non-agricultural manual labour. If nowadays it is shameful for an Izhava to work as a manual labourer, it is even more shameful and degrading to work in the paddy fields, especially the *punja*, alongside Pulayas. Because ideas about qualities stress the importance of environment (*samsa gunam*), it is widely claimed that in being with people of lower caste one becomes like them in habits and appearance (described as dirty, violent, dark-skinned and so on; Osella & Osella forthcoming). A retired head-teacher and SNDP branch president accused his caste fellows who work as agricultural labourers of being 'uncultured, bad, gangsters', using the same vocabulary and tone of contempt used minutes earlier to talk about Pulayas. Educated and high-status Izhavas consider fellow caste members who work as agricultural labourers as a hindrance to the advancement of the caste as a whole, 'letting the side down'. The obvious tension for those working in the paddy fields – between economic necessity and remaining faithful to their rejection of 'demeaning' work and an undesirable identity – is often mediated by seeking employment with an Izhava landowner (possibly a relative or fellow party member) or by working in gangs excluding Pulayas (cf. Warner et al. 1994: 194; Roediger 1994: 61ff, 136ff). As soon as other economic opportunities arise, Izhavas withdraw altogether from agricultural manual work. Table 2.3, showing Izhava involvement in agricultural labour of around 30 percent, fails to capture this increasing trend: while many of the over-50s (men and women) are involved in such work, none of the under-25s are, or appear likely to be. These late twentieth-century changes become dramatically apparent at harvest time.

In 1990 and 1991 we saw bus-loads of labourers coming in from surrounding villages to work the paddy harvest, while many Valiyagramam labourers themselves travelled around Kuttanad to work in villages where they have kin links. Under union agreements, a landowner cannot turn away workers who come for harvest: work must be given to whoever turns up on the day. In 1990/1 up to 20–25 workers – two or three gangs – would come to harvest plots of one acre of paddy land. It took half a day for cutting and one day to thresh, chaff and bundle the straw, after which head-load workers would be readily available to transport paddy and straw to the house; within two to three days, the whole process would be finished.

In 1994/5, landowners were going around before harvest to solicit labour, trying to pre-arrange with local workers a gang of at least five or six people. Workers, in high demand, would cut paddy and move on to other fields, waiting to do threshing and sifting until all cutting work had been done; it was also difficult to find head-load workers for transport. A plot of one acre initially observed in 1990/1 now took ten days to harvest, everything done by just one gang of eight women. Some landowners were using threshing machines and negotiations were under way for the introduction of further mechanisation, in the form of combine harvesters.[16] Labourers working as *nokkakarans* for non-labouring landowners have been increasingly buying land themselves and by 1995 were prioritising their own plots of land for harvest before coming to work anybody else's; it seems likely that they will eventually withdraw altogether from working for others, rejecting altogether the status of 'labourer' and becoming a 'working farmer'. The 1995 labour shortage during the paddy harvest was widely attributed to the withdrawal of Izhavas, particularly women, many of whom now have sons and husbands in the Gulf.

Playing it Safe by Balancing Income and Prestige

Reductions in landholding size and increased cultivation costs brought about by higher labourers' wages and introduction of fertilisers and pesticides have only partly been compensated by introduction of HYV (high yielding variety) paddy and have therefore diminished profits from paddy cultivation, (cf. Harriss 1982: Ch. 5). Although only a minority of landowners depend on agriculture for their livelihood (in Sasthamuri only 19 out of 452 men are full time 'farmers', all but one Nayars) and everyone considers paddy cultivation a costly burden, 'farming' retains a high aura of prestige, heavily associated with ideas of patronage and the figure of the white-clad upper-caste landowner of the past, the *janmi*. Heuzé argues that India as a whole remains a peasant culture, identifying common composite figures also found in Valiyagramam, such as the 'factory-worker/peasant' and the 'government-official/peasant' (1992: 17–18); while many Izhavas of the 1950s and 1960s invested savings in paddy land, lately farming is losing its glamour. Increasingly, young men – sons of part-time 'farmers' – loathe going to the fields, even to supervise the work of labourers, considering the entire business of agriculture as uncultured and *backward*. While India as a whole may remain characterised by agriculture, in Valiyagramam as increasingly in Kerala as a whole, the referent for young men is the world of paid employment.

Being a public servant means holding a prestigious, permanent, salaried, white-collar position, and is unambiguously a *joli*, the *joli* par excellence, standing in opposition to *pani*, casual labour. As Heuzé points out (1992: 23) such employees, from the lowest-grade *peon* to the highest-level administrator, tend to gain cachet from their salaried status rather than the specific task performed. Security and fringe benefits aside, government employment holds great symbolic importance, lending prestige through assumed association with centres of power. The services of government servants, even a government hospital *peon*, are always sought by villagers whenever they need to approach state bureaucracy. This is a good opportunity for public employees to make extra income and build up clientele ready for competition in local prestige and political arenas. Such positions hold extra significance for Izhavas, who fought hard at the turn of the century for access to public employment, the jealously guarded prerogative of forward Hindu castes. Reservation of positions within state government service for OBCs has helped Izhavas gain a foothold, mostly at lower levels (cf. Radhakrishnan 1993). While reserved posts in central government have been proposed since the formation of independent India, delays in implementation due to disputes over the nature and extent of these reservations mean that Izhavas, like other non-forward castes, tend to be poorly represented. As part of the backward classes, Izhavas stand outside that 85 percent of the uppermost echelon of the central bureaucracy composed of dominant classes (see for example Chatterji 1996: 302). Table 2.3 shows that just 7.2 percent of

Izhavas have 'government jobs', compared to 17.3 percent of Nayars. While young Izhavas yearn to participate in the high-prestige government employment sector, they see their best opportunities coming from the private sector and outside the village. They are also aware of extremely high levels of competition for places: in 1994, several local graduates appeared, as part of what one estimated as '10,000–15,000 other people', at a public examination for a government clerk's post, requiring just SSLC qualification; there were 100 places.

Teaching in primary or secondary schools is another occupation endowed with relative prestige but generating little income: in 1991 the salary of a government primary school-teacher with 30 years of service was Rs2500 monthly. Uniquely among *avarna* communities, Izhavas have a tradition of village vernacular teachers, *asans*, and it is not uncommon to hear Izhava teachers claiming descent from high-status *asan* families, ultimately trying to establish a continuity between themselves and Brahmanical traditions of teaching and learning (even today, a high proportion of local high-school teachers are Brahmans). The importance ascribed by Narayana Guru to education as a fundamental instrument for both the enlightenment and the progress of the caste constitutes Izhava teachers as standard bearers of SNDP orthodoxy, frequently given official positions in the local *karayogam*. The low number of Izhava teachers locally is partly attributable to difficulties in finding teaching jobs. Places in government schools are limited by low turnover and high demand; political connections are necessary to obtain such jobs. Private *management schools* are ever expanding, but jobs are reserved for members of the community – sometimes the family – running the school; locally, these schools all belong to the Christian and Nayar communities. While Izhava teachers can obtain employment by giving a *donation*, many Gulf migrants are willing to pay to procure a teaching job and hence professional status for their wives. The profession is therefore becoming increasingly feminised while *donations* are running locally as high as Rs100,000, far exceeding Gulf migration costs. Qualified young Izhava men prefer to invest family savings in migration.

Bucking national trends, the military continues to attract Izhava men, most of whom join as *jawans*, retiring as soon as they are eligible for pension after 15 years' service. While Christians and Nayars began to join the army during the Second World War, Izhavas joined only later, after independence. The benefits of a military career are still many: it is respectable, permanent and secure employment which, regardless of relatively low pay, allows savings of a good part of the salary. Joining the army need not require payment of large *donations*, relatives of servicemen taking priority in recruitment. Military personnel, during and after service, benefit from perks such as low-interest loans and buying goods at lower prices in special military outlets. Finally, a good retirement payment and secure pension are available after relatively short service. Military personnel return to Valiyagramam with the sophistication of those who, having spent several years in different parts of north India, have learnt to speak Hindi and sometimes English, and have a *modern* outlook on life. Besides the obvious economic security and prestige derived from holding permanent and non-labouring government employment, army careers hold further attractions: Nayars are historically the caste most closely associated with martial endeavour, said to have constituted the backbone of various Rajahs' armies. As part of their effort to sustain claims for higher status, Izhavas have tried to establish a martial past for themselves. Much SNDP-inspired history gives prominence to Izhava military skills and the feats of Izhava chivalric heroes such as Aromal Chegavar, Unniarcha and Aromal Unni, protagonists of well-known folk songs,[17] their exploits captured in popular films. Izhavas discussing the caste's past status often pointed out that the commanders of Kayamkulam Rajah's militia included many wealthy, high-status Izhavas. By establishing an 'affinity' (*bandham*) between themselves and military skills, Izhavas try to establish military 'qualities' and continuity between them-selves and Nayars. All this notwithstanding, the youngest generation of otherwise unskilled Izhava men with only basic education prefers to look for better-paid work, taking army employment only when other migration opportunities are not available.

Trade is another popular and respectable activity, albeit for the majority not a particularly renumerative one. Those in petty trade usually run small shops (groceries, tea shops, pan shops, fancy shops) opened either after retirement or at the end of a period of migration. Sometimes, money sent by migrants allows relatives to abandon manual labour and to set themselves up in more prestigious independent self-employment. In the majority of cases, however, trade is only a secondary activity supplementing other income. This area of the economy, which is booming as the village's new *shopping complex* testifies, is perhaps the most open to innovations and fashions, especially since the beginning of Gulf migration. Throughout the 1980s the trend was to open *cool bars*, small shops with a blender and a fridge selling cool drinks and a few 'bakery items'. By the end of the 1980s, music cassette shops and photography studios were mushrooming; by 1995, many of these had expanded into hiring and making videos. The latest 1990s fashions were ISD/STD telephone booths and beauty parlours (for women and men).[18]

Migration: A Special Category

Migration, internal and external, has been a significant feature of life in Valiyagramam (as in Kerala as a whole) for more than a century: a popular joke runs that the first astronauts to reach the moon found a Malayali there, running a tea-shop. The slumps and famines of the twentieth century's first half and the chronic unemployment of the second, have provoked the same response: migration provides an escape from poverty and unemployment. At the same time, migration often proves a privileged site of capital accumulation – a *chance* – in which a lucky few accelerate the process of mobility through rapid amassing of wealth.

From the turn of the century, many Christians and some Izhavas were migrating to plantations on the high ranges of Kerala and abroad to Malaysia and Sri Lanka. By the 1930s, Christians made a 'gold rush' to the virgin mountains of north Malabar.[19] From the Second World War, Christians and Nayars, followed later by Izhavas, left to join the army. By the 1950s, after the Travancore-Cochin State joined the Indian Union, new national employment opportunities opened up for villagers. More than a hundred years of progressive education policies followed by Travancore and Cochin States had created a pool of skilled, educated people able to take up employment in the administrative service and nationalised industries of newly independent India; many clerks and typists went to the cities; some joined the railways. Migration to metropolitan centres, first Chennai and later Calcutta, Mumbai and Delhi, also represented – for those with no certificate of formal education or technical skills, no land of their own and the prospect of being forced to work as casual manual labourers – a way not only to escape unemployment and to seek better fortunes elsewhere, but also to save face and preserve prestige.

Migration helps prestige damage limitation in several ways. First, it facilitates concealment of one's occupation, indicated by the number of migrant respondents who gave vague or incorrect answers to our survey questions. Many told us and neighbours only that they were 'working in a company'; others claimed to be in white-collar jobs, showing posed photographs of themselves at a desk, pen in hand, only their working clothes and muddy boots suggesting their true occupation. As one wood merchant commented, 'When someone tells you he works for an un-named *company*, it means he is only doing *kulipani*'.[20] Second, by splitting the moment and site of wealth accumulation from its moment of consumption, it enables and encourages a focus upon the results of employment. Families send sons, after examination failures, to stay with relatives in north India; the shame of working as a labourer is lessened if done away from the village. Working away also offers autonomy and dignity by disentangling Izhavas from lopsided social relations of production with other villagers: the returned migrant manual worker, when he goes around the village, can comport himself as the putative equal of his Nayar or Christian neighbour, whereas the Izhava employed within the village must face his employers, and offer a degree of deference. If, as Heuzé suggests, caste follows the logic of uniting under one system of control both production and reproduction (1992: 22), migration, more than any other form of employment, shatters this unity.

Migration within India

A considerable number of Izhava migrants are working in various industrial centres and cities in north India, mostly as unskilled and low-paid labourers in places such as Gujarat prawn factories or tyre re-treading workshops in

Mumbai and Pune. These jobs are mainly seasonal, with bad working conditions and low pay, around Rs800–2500 per month; living conditions are generally worse than those enjoyed in the village. Such migrants often leave children and wives behind to move between in-laws and the natal family.

While manual work is generally spurned, despised and regarded as an indicator of low status, permanent factory work ranks for villagers of every community second only to government or bank and clerical jobs. Skilled factory work, unlike traditional manual work, entails a degree of formal knowledge and education: it is a *joli* and not a *pani*. Prestige surrounding blue-collar work also derives from the salaries it can generate, the average being almost double that of a school teacher, around Rs3000 – Rs5000. In Kerala, with its extremely limited industrial base, these skilled blue-collar jobs are almost impossible to find. The few available, mostly in public sector industries, are generally kept for satisfaction of politicians' clientele. Even so, *donations* are required, which could run up to Rs150,000 (for example Rs100,000 for an electrician's job in a power station). A skilled worker, lacking political connections and capital, has no choice but to seek employment elsewhere. Since the early 1960s, workers holding technical/ vocational training – electricians, welders, fitters, plumbers – or those with secretarial skills have been finding employment in the various industrial areas of north India, notably Maharashtra, Madhya Pradesh, Orissa and Gujarat.

Migrants holding permanent skilled/technical employment can earn monthly salaries of over Rs4000 plus annual bonuses equal to two months' salary and in some cases other benefits such as rent-free accommodation. These better-paid migrants and their families tend to be settled away, maintaining little or no contact with the village. Many express, during their rare visits, the desire and intention to return to Valiyagramam on retirement. While some of those who migrated before the 1960s have done so, high costs of land and living in Kerala now make it extremely difficult for others to return. A good number of young Izhavas are now working locally in skilled/ technical positions, having learned their skills by studying at Industrial Training Institutes in town or through a period of apprenticeship with local artisans, (generally from Viswakarma communities). These are mostly doing badly paid jobs in small workshops, taken on in the hope of gaining experience while waiting for migration, no longer within India, but to the Gulf.

Gulf migrants

During the last 20 years, as a result of the Gulf countries economic boom, international migration has received a considerable boost, reaching its peak numerically and remittance-wise, between 1979 and 1984 (Nayyar 1989: 107, 1994: 25; Birks et al. 1986; Amjad 1989: 4). It is estimated that in 1983 50 percent of Indians working in Gulf states were from Kerala (Nair

1989: 343).[21] During 1980–1, at the height of Gulf migration, Gulf revenues were estimated to constitute up to 28 percent of Kerala's GDP, rising to 50 percent in areas of high migration (P.A. Kurien 1994: 765).

Gulf migration from Valiyagramam fits the Kerala profile: it is almost exclusively a male phenomenon, migrants being typically under 35, unmarried or recently married and with education at or below SSLC (Prakash 1978; Matthew & Nair 1978; Nair 1986: 72; Gulati 1983: 2218). Due to laws preventing naturalisation of migrants and linking visas to work contracts, migration periods are usually limited. When work contracts end, visas are terminated; if a migrant wants to take up another contract he must re-commence the whole process, returning to India to apply for a new contract and visa. Those in unskilled or semi-skilled jobs – the majority of Valiyagramam's migrants – unlike their professional/skilled counterparts, have great difficulties in obtaining long-term contracts and visas; migration consists of a series of stretches in the Gulf (average four to six years) alternating with periods in the village between contracts. Given the short-term nature of most Gulf jobs and, since 1995, the promulgation in some countries of laws linking residence visas for dependants to the migrant's job and income, migrants' families are usually left behind. A substantial part of earnings are remitted regularly or brought back as savings at the end of the migration period.

Migration expenses, while considerable by Valiyagramam standards and often exposing families of prospective migrants to considerable financial strain, can be recouped, given the size of the salaries, in a relatively short time. We were quoted total costs in 1991 (air fare, *agent*'s fee and visa) ranging between Rs10,000 (pre-Gulf war) to Rs20,000. Most migrants quoted costs of around Rs15,000, representing Rs8000 air fare, the balance handed over to an *agent* to cover administration. One migrant told us:

The Arab who sponsors you gets Rs30,000–40,000 for sponsorship; the brokers used to take all the commission they got from us, plus a fee from the Arabs for finding workers! The Arab sponsors didn't realise that the visa had a value, they gave it free. Now they demand money for sponsoring.

By late 1990s, a minimum of Rs25,000 was needed for procuring a visa and job through a relative or friend; otherwise the intervention of an *agent* and an 'Arab sponsor' are required, in which case the amount of money needed (for visas, agencies, travel fares and so on) doubles up. These amounts of cash are seldom readily available; after selling or mortgaging gold and land, near relatives are asked to meet part of the expenses. The promise of a job in the Gulf or a loan to cover part of migration expenses commonly form part of marriage negotiations: prospective husbands ask for higher dowries than usual on the understanding that in return they will help, through contacts or cash, migration of a brother or close relative of the bride.

The first Valiyagramam Gulf migrants were educated and professionally qualified villagers, mostly Nayars and Christians, especially those resident at the time in urban centres where Gulf-based companies and employment agencies were recruiting. Still now, the Christian community has a higher proportion of Gulf migrants; this is not altogether surprising, given that this is the wealthiest community and that Gulf migration requires a considerable amount of capital to cover initial expenses. By reason of differential access to education, professionals, middle-rank managers, white-collar and skilled workers are not uncommon among Christian and Nayar Gulf migrants. With the exception of a small number of Izhavas, mostly skilled industrial workers who were already working outside Kerala and whose qualifications were in demand, Izhava men are relative newcomers to Gulf migration, where they are mostly employed as semi-skilled and manual labourers, particularly in the construction business. From the mid 1980s, a decline in the demand for labour resulting from a slow-down of Gulf economies has made employment more difficult to come by and less economically attractive. Not only have salaries relatively decreased but migration expenses have increased considerably. While these factors have contributed to a relative slow-down, even the lowest Gulf wages continue to be more than double an average local salary. According to figures collected from migrants on leave, labourers in 1991 earned between Rs2000–4000 per month; skilled workers Rs4000–6000; qualified computer operators about Rs8000–10,000; professionals above Rs10,000.[22]

Gulf migration has particular and significant effects both for the families involved and for those left behind. By the chance it offers of rapid and vast accumulation (by village standards) it accelerates processes of social change and differentiation. Gulf migrants do not settle away but must sooner or later return, where new-found wealth may dramatically alter their status and relationships with others, offering chances to forge new identities. We will see in the following chapters how, and in what arenas, wealth is legitimised and converted into symbolic and cultural capital.

CONCLUSIONS

Izhavas as a group have, over the course of the twentieth century, strategically attempted to move away from two forms of labour associated with stigmatised identities: manual – especially agricultural – labour and toddy-tapping; Izhava women have meanwhile followed their Nayar counterparts in adopting the bourgeois 'housewife' ethic and Hindu 'seclusion' identity. While many households succeed in entering new arenas and taking up new opportunities offered by an expanding and diversifying economy and growing state and service sectors, a proportion of families remain within these spheres: impoverished, dominated, stigmatised and associated with negative stereotypes, their very existence is hidden within the caste's public face. These families face increasing exclusion as a result of increased expectations and a generalised ethos of mobility: while a young man in the 1940s could be proud of his escape from degraded labour by his decision to become a ferryman, that man's son in the 1990s will not be content with the present-day equivalent of his father's job, viz., driving a tempo van. His educational level will probably be higher and his expectations will certainly be so. The middle-range of 'respectable' salaried jobs suitable for the matriculates and graduates of this generation are under pressure as the ranks of the educated unemployed swell. Such jobs, with their modest incomes, also fail to address adequately an increasingly important arena, that of consumption, equally the subject of continually increasing expectations. While Izhavas in single community areas are under less strain, those in mixed areas, where they compete with Christians for cash and Nayars for prestige, find themselves hard-pressed. Migration is seen as a solution to many problems: the need for ever-increasing amounts of cash; local unemployment; impossibility of achieving a satisfactory production-defined status.

Earning money and owning cash are also important signs of an individual Izhava man's success and masculinity. The process of transformation of a cash-rich successful young man into a socio-moral person, a man who mediates successfully between self and public interest, runs concomitant with and shares the predicaments of the growth-cycle into manhood. First comes a moment of accumulation, corresponding to youth (*payyan*-hood) and possibly to migration, in which a young man has few responsibilities and no dependents outside the immediate household: his goal at this point as a member of a mobile group is to find employment and earn cash, in better-paid and more prestigious work than his father. Later comes a period of fuller integration, in which youth must move towards an adult social status, marrying and taking a place within the community. Attention then can and should turn outwards towards the wider community, where symbolic capital can be built up and claims to status validated. The first stage of a young man's movement towards all this is consolidation of a house and family unit, a process beginning in marriage and fatherhood. An intimate connection also exists between employment status and marriage, tied together by dowry (Heuzé 1992: 24). Inflationary dowry rates in Kerala have led to a situation described locally as groom-price or 'buying a boy', *payyan vangikkuka*, in which grooms' earning capacities are carefully weighed and in which a 'dowry scale' based upon employment statuses runs from USA migrant down to local manual labourer. Thus, employment also has important ramifications for ambitions to pursue mobility through strategic marriage, to which we will now turn.

3   MARRIAGE AND MOBILITY

For all Malayalis, marriage and parenthood are requirements of mature adult status, while a primary duty of the household group is to 'send away' its daughters in marriage. The major goal of those with least wealth and prestige is simply to see their sons and daughters married, the marriage itself being an end rather than a means to further benefits; but among the majority of families, arranging a marriage is also a chance for mobility and prestige through strategic alliance and expenditure. Most families find themselves sooner or later faced with the prospect of arranging a marriage for a younger member. As various prospective partners are considered and their merits in terms of benefit to the wider group weighed up, family members discuss priorities – Gulf-employed groom; graduate bride; titled family; non-working mother; public servant father; wealthy household – and try to make their arguments heard until consensus is reached (cf. Bourdieu 1977, 1990:147ff). Which factors are prioritised depends upon the family's current strategy and priorities, which may vary over time. As in the field of employment, families may decide to maximise prestige or wealth, or seek a balance between the two; it may have so little initial capital itself that its goal hardly extends beyond the arrangement of a wedding.

As a group seeking caste mobility, Izhavas have adopted practices favoured as accumulators of group status and prominent among Nayars, such as asymmetrical alliance stranger-marriage with payment of substantial dowry. Practices held within dominant *savarna* society and in Izhava public discourses alike as negative are avoided, practised in secret or with a sense of shame. An alliance never sought but often approved of post facto if other conditions are right is a love-match. For individual Izhava families, a self-arranged 'love marriage' may provide a better catch on the marriage market than would be available under normal rules. It is not surprising to find that those who need to watch their cash take up marriage practices widely considered non-prestigious: cross-cousin marriages; low-dowried local marriages; polyandry; divorce and non-advantageous love marriages. In strategic arranged marriages, two ideals are held in tension: the oft-quoted principle that families should be exactly matched in every way, and asymmetrical alliance, in practice the preferred prestige option (cf. Parry 1979: 247ff; Pocock 1993; cf. Donnan 1993: 326–7). A family's first consideration – strategic use of marriage to enhance or consolidate family mobility – is sometimes in tension with a second – mobility of the group as a whole. Families follow the path of most benefit for themselves and call upon post facto rationalisations appealing back to discourses upholding isogamy or hypergamy respectively to argue that they did 'the right thing'; appeals to the twin modernist ideals of *progress* and class mobility can add respectability even to love marriages.

We have argued that group mobility, partly dependent upon community solidarity, is both enhanced and undermined by the successes of its elite and upper middle class, who stand apart from and may detach themselves from the group, like the Alummoottil family or Engineer Sadashivan, foregrounding class or occupational status; similarly, titled families making marriages may also seek to detach themselves and claim higher prestige. As a modern community which officially abolished sub-castes to permit and encourage marriage between any group members, Izhavas officially cannot accept the principle of hierarchy within: in theory and SNDP rhetoric all Izhavas are equal. Marriage arrangements highlight how community ideals of unified and singular identity remain at odds with realities of internal differentiation, as high-status families marry between themselves while those unable to compete with ever-escalating dowry rates are, like the toddy-tappers and manual labourers of the last chapter, marginalised within the wider community. Again, we will sketch out some late nineteenth-century and early twentieth-century history necessary to set the scene for the current situation.

REFORM OF THE IZHAVA MARRIAGE SYSTEM: ENDOGAMY AND MONOGAMY

We have seen in Chapter 2 that female identity is heavily based upon qualities of nurturance and protection, and that adult women are differentiated by name as 'daughters' and 'mothers', not as wives. In contrast to other parts of India, Malayalis do not elaborate a status of 'auspicious married woman': *sumangali* and its equivalent *mangalastri* pop up in romantic cinema songs, never in everyday speech or interviews (cf. for example Madan 1993: 291; Reynolds 1991; Nishimura 1994). Given the historical absence or underplaying among the matrilineal communities of what is widely understood as 'marriage', this is not surprising: for much of Kerala's history, what elsewhere stood as a formal tie has been ambiguous and weak (see for example Gough 1959a; Fuller 1976a). While women and female children are certainly characterised by the ambivalence commonly associated to them in ethnographic literature and may be vessels of good or bad luck for the household, 'auspicious female' appears more as a residual category covering all females neither young widows nor childless[1] (cf. for example Gatwood 1991; Marglin 1985; Fuller 1980; Kondos 1986: 191; Tapper 1979; Shulman 1980: 139; Beck 1981).

Under the matrilineal system prevalent among Nayars and sections of Izhavas until twentieth-century reforms (*marumukkattayam*), whereby property was passed from a man to his sister's son,[2] a pre-pubertal 'mock' primary marriage (*talikettukalyanam*), gave way to secondary – often polyandrous – relationships (*sambhandam*) (see for example Aiyappan 1941; Gough 1955, 1961; Fuller 1976a; Dumont 1983: 109–12; Moore 1988; cf. Good 1991). High-prestige *karanavans* utilised the sexuality of their sisters and sisters' daughters, younger brothers and sisters' sons, for status mobility and political purposes. Hypergamous *sambandham* unions permitted 'refinement' of the *tharavadu*, children born to such unions embodying qualities relatively superior to those of their mother and mother's brother. This betterment had obvious status repercussions. Nayar *tharavadus* whose women had repeated *sambandham* unions with Brahman men claimed higher Illakkar status: (Aiya 1989: 349). Even now, the highest status Nayars are those who have proven Brahman ancestry (cf. Tambiah 1973; Dirks 1987: 222–8; F Osella 1993: 42ff). Matrilineal Izhavas similarly underwent both *talikettu* and *sambandham* rites, allowing for unions outside of the caste. This historical fact of exogamy remains ambivalent and open to many interpretations: Izhavas now commonly remember the past as one in which their women were sometimes 'prostituted' to Nayar men, yet Izhavas often boast that their women in Tallassery are famous for their beauty, which – given that female beauty is largely assimilated to pallor of skin-tone – appears to refer to the results of past liaisons with Europeans.[3]

Changes in Izhava marriage practices must be seen in the context of wider political and ideological pressures for reforms exercised from the middle of the nineteenth century onwards throughout all matrilineal Hindu communities and arising from economic changes outlined in Chapter 2 (Panikkar 1995: 176ff). While Nayar caste associations (first Keraliya Nayar Samajam, later Nayar Service Society [NSS]), as part of campaigns for marriage and inheritance regulations reform and against Brahmanical 'tyranny', encouraged members to break *sambandham* unions with Brahmans and to marry only within caste (for example Jeffrey 1994: 243ff; Fuller 1976a: 75), Izhavas also began to unify, adopting ideologies of self-respect and caste pride. As monogamous caste-endogamous marriage became a norm, Izhavas joined in general condemnation of Nayar women as 'prostitutes to Brahman men'. Once again, Izhavas followed Nayars in the pursuit of 'dignity' and status.

In line with general drives towards state modernisation, the colonial administration also wanted reforms, bringing Travancore marriage and inheritance into line with British-administered south India. These reforms were granted wider social relevance. Colonel Munro, Political Resident and *Dewan* (1810–19) was convinced that Travancore society could not be rid of social 'evils' merely by administrative reform, arguing that political system 'immorality' could 'in some degrees be ascribed to the perverted system of their domestic relations ... the parental ties and affections that in other countries connect and unite ... have in Travancore no existence' (Munro in Yesudas 1977: 368). This assessment was shared by missionaries like Rev. Mateer (in Travancore 1859–91) who concluded, 'the natural relationship and reciprocal love of parents and children are interfered with and perverted by this pernicious law ... the love and care and discipline of the father are systematically absent' (Mateer 1991b: 180; cf. Jeffrey 1993: 40). Matriliny's impact was held to be a generalised lack of morality 'sensuality and lust are fostered and encouraged by these usages ... the whole country becomes saturated with immorality and vices' (Mateer 1991b: 182; cf. Stivens 1996). The residential system of *tharavadu*, in which property was held jointly and undivided by all family members under trusteeship of the oldest male member (*karanavan*), was not spared criticism: '[it] naturally tends to discourage individual activity, personal exertion, and independence of spirit' (Mateer 1991b: 182).

During this same period, the newly formed NSS, partly reacting to European ideological pressures and partly giving voice to sentiments harboured by a growing mass comprising junior members of impoverished Nayar *tharavadus* and members of new bourgeoisies, began to agitate for partition of ancestral properties and introduction of new inheritance laws (Jeffrey 1994: 164ff; Fuller 1976a: 137; Panikkar 1995: 176ff). Narayana Guru's teacher Chattampi Swamikal (1855–1924), a Nayar *sannyasi* active in Thiruvananthapuram area, campaigned for eradication of 'irrational' and 'wasteful' customs such as *talikettukalyanam*. In an explosion of magazines and newspapers, prose writers took up social themes and rationalist perspectives examining and criticising features of Travancore life such as caste and the matrilineal joint family, and ridiculing ritual practices held to be based in superstition. In 1889 Chandu Menon wrote what is widely credited as the first Malayalam novel, *Indulekha*, satirising and criticising *sambandham* marriages, a central plank of the matrilineal system (Leela Devi 1978; Kumar 1994: 86). This novel also played a key role in promulgating the new taste and ethos, offering an English-educated hero and heroine who fused the best of indigenous and European thought to make rational critique of existing society (Panikkar 1995: 123ff). Educated middle-class Izhavas joined their Nayar counterparts in pressing for reforms to the matrilineal system, by now openly resented and ridiculed as 'backward', 'irrational' and 'immoral'. This campaign became a prominent part of the wider Izhava reform project, reinforced by calls from Narayana Guru and the SNDP for Izhavas to abandon expensive and suddenly 'unorthodox' ritual practices (Rajendran 1974: 38). This period of great social upheaval and change corresponds to what Bourdieu – who denies that 'rational choice' is the usual human decision-making condition – identifies as an exceptional time of 'crisis, in which the routine adjustment of subjective and objective structures is brutally disrupted ... when "rational choice" may take over' (Bourdieu & Wacquant 1992: 131).

In 1899 the Travancore Wills Act gave male members of matrilineal communities the right to will half of acquired property to wives and children: disputes – leading even to assassinations – between men's sons and sister's sons, are common themes in matrilineal family histories and Malayali mythology. Alummoottil Koccu Kunja Channar was allegedly assassinated by his sister's sons because he was planning to leave the greater part of his wealth to his wife and children. The 1912 and 1925 Nayar Acts, recognising de jure *sambandham* unions and providing for full inheritance of self-acquired property by wives and children and partitioning of joint matrilineal properties, paved the way for similar legislation in 1925 regarding matrilineal Izhavas. The 1956 Indian Hindu Succession Act and the 1976 Kerala Joint Hindu Family System (Abolition) Act were the final nails in the coffin of matrilineal joint families (Jeffrey 1993: 41ff). This period saw a shift to dowried virilocal monogamous marriages (as among Christians) and introduction (promoted by caste associations) of new forms of marriage ceremonies.

We feel that caste endogamy as an unspoken consideration in all current marriage arrangements stems not from the fact that this is a 'rule' so basic as to be taken for granted as from the fact that no upper castes in the area are willing to marry Izhavas.[4] Moral and caste-solidary statements such as, 'we marry within the *jati* because we love it' are weakened when read against recent history, against intra-community jockeying for position between families and against the all-important mobility imperative. To some extent, Izhavas these days marry within the *jati* because they are generally constrained to do so. They remain ambivalent about caste endogamy: while generally voicing strong caste pride and resentment towards higher-caste Hindus, condemning past liaisons as rape or prostitution, the potentially prestigious referent for inter-caste unions (the old *sambandham* prototypically between Nayar women and Brahman men) is widely romanticised in popular film and talk.

LOVE-MATCHES: WILD CARDS

Exogamy, which means love matches, is an unpredictable affair bringing about the best or the worst of alliances or simply, as among labouring Scheduled Castes, providing husbands and wives for those whose families are in no position to pay dowries and arrange a wedding. Marriages with Europeans, among both elite and ordinary Izhavas, have offered particularly spectacular mobility opportunities. Izhavas had and continue to have many intermarriages with ethnic Europeans despite the comparative rarity of contact opportunities in the postcolonial situation; between 1989 and 1995, we recorded three Izhava-European marriages in Valiyagramam. This is in line with Izhavas' particular orientation (shared with Christians) towards those (particularly English-speakers, i.e. including north Americans and

Australians) who have been seen not only as rapacious colonisers and – post-GATT – as neo-imperialists but also, as we have suggested, as facilitators of new economic opportunities and – through actions of missionaries and reforming residents – as upholders of modern universalist values in opposition to oppressive caste Hindu orthodoxy. At the end of the twentieth century, European-descent English-speakers' imputed[5] position as apparently globally wealthy and hegemonic puts them, for many Izhavas, at the top of all possible class hierarchies. Images of European and North American affluence available through media representations and occasional sightings of tourists are reinforced by migrants' participation in the deeply unequal social relations of capitalism. Many village migrants work as subordinates to Europeans in factories and hotels in Gulf states; some workers have been sent to UK or Germany for training. The glamour of white skin and its role as signifier of global wealth and power provide further attraction.[6]

Returning to K.V. Krishnan's plantation story (Chapter 1), we remember that he was permitted to buy a second-hand car without a driver which he was forced to quit when a European passed by. His story exactly parallels that recounted (Chapter 2) about Alummoottil Kuttakkakaran Sekharan Channar, forced to dismount his elephant in the presence of putatively superior Nayars. The thoroughly modern occupational and 'racial' hierarchies of the twentieth century are presented by storytellers not as new indignities, but as a continuation of existing feudal patterns. In narrative, the segregated and highly stratified world of the plantation is made to mirror traditional caste hierarchy with the Izhava clerk forced to move out of the road to allow the European planter to pass by just as he was obliged, outside the plantation, by unapproachability restrictions to get out of the road as Brahmans or Nayars approached. As the brothers of Chapter 1 know, in the Gulf where Europeans and Malayali Christians hold well-paid professional posts, are semi-permanently settled in air-conditioned accommodation provided by employers, and are treated favourably as 'people of the book' by the Muslim elite, most Izhavas find themselves still on the bottom rung: labouring on short-term contracts, living packed together in non-air-conditioned small camps at the peripheries of elegant and unapproachable towns, separated from their families for years, their religious identity alien and inferior to that of Muslims and Christians alike. Intermarriage transgresses such boundaries. Marriage with a grandchild of those powerful enough 100 years ago to command not only an Izhava's labour but also his person, ordering him out of the road as 'unapproachable', like marriage to those who currently command Izhava labour and persons, can be both a road to mobility and a potent symbolic capture of power.

Anticipating later Ambedkarist moves, the early SNDP called for resistance to caste and untouchability through inter-caste marriage. The first out-marriage celebrated at Narayana Guru's Sivagiri *asram* headquarters (1927) was between an Izhava man and a German woman (Pereira 1989: 161). The Malayali press often presents photographs and stories of similar marriages, a number of which are celebrated at Sivagiri where Gurudevan sits in *sammadhi*; such marriages are in perfect remembrance of the saint's famous universalist and anti-caste maxim, first delivered at the 1921 All Kerala Fraternity Conference and later to become the SNDP slogan, found written on SNDP offices, Gurumandirams and so on all across Kerala:

> One Caste, One Religion, One God for Humankind
> Of the same blood and form, there is no difference;
> Animals of the same caste alone procreate;
> Viewed thus all humanity belongs to one caste.

While Christian families also often view marriage with Europeans favourably, legitimised on grounds of religious compatibility, possibilities of appealing to SNDP rhetoric and the memory of Gurudevan enables Izhavas to accept and legitimise such marriages, in contrast to Nayar and Brahman communities; if there have been any *savarna* Hindu–European unions in Valiyagramam they are well concealed. Izhava families, like Christian families, boast of European relatives; the elite family Alummoottil proudly displays wedding photographs of such liaisons.

We have argued that in the postcolony local Christians have partly taken up some roles left vacant by departing Europeans, extending Izhava relationships as co-adherents of modernity and referents for class status to Christians. It is therefore not surprising that while Christians may be reluctant to accept marriage with Izhavas, for Izhavas marriage with Christians presents little problem. Intermarriage with Nayars is also valued for the transgressive and exhilarating breaking of caste taboos which it affords and for the prestige thereby 'captured'. We have recorded several Izhava–Nayar intermarriages, openly referred to by neighbours and family with some pride. In reality, the only love marriages which cannot be regularised and which draw upon themselves the full weight of community disapprobation – supposedly applicable to all love marriages – are those viewed as disadvantageous and potential sources of family embarrassment rather than pride, be they with lower castes or with partners from poor families holding little prospects. Those who marry members of the Scheduled Castes (male or female) are invariably constrained to leave the area and live among in-laws; an indication of the continuing force of 'untouchable' status is that even a Pulaya professional from an extremely wealthy family would be considered wholly unsuitable and such a marriage could never be rehabilitated, as can those with Nayars, Christians or Europeans. Modernity's universalism stretches only so far.

ARRANGED MARRIAGE STRATEGIES: CHOICE OF SPOUSE

Marriage as a monogamous stable relationship, comparatively recent, is today as in the rest of India arranged by groups and accompanied by payments and gifts; within this, a variety of forms are found. This is partly due to the existence of three major referents for 'marriage' and several ways of classifying payments from bride's to groom's family. The first referent is south Indian alliance, a relationship of affinity continuing through time between groups. In its classical form it takes the shape of bilateral cross-cousin marriage, as is usually said to be already implied within Dravidian kinship terminologies, and is both grounded in and productive of equality between two groups which make no division between wife-givers and wife-takers, and which implies (although in practice not preferred) sibling-exchange. The alliance model may be expanded to include situations in which geographical areas 'exchange women' bilaterally between themselves. The second model, the sanskritic *kanyadan* ideal of a gift of a virgin to a superior group, is, as has been widely noted, increasingly hegemonic and is itself not incompatible with certain forms of south Indian cross-cousin marriage alliance. Notably, when a preference exists, as in Kerala, for the matrilateral variety, this leads to a situation in which at least three groups 'circulate women' unilaterally among themselves, with clear distinctions between wife-givers and wife-takers (see Parry 1979; Trautmann 1981; Dumont 1983; Fruzzetti 1982; Gough 1961; Trawick 1990; Good 1991 for details and discussions). The third referent is the old matrilineal system, which consisted of a 'set' of rituals concerned with female sexuality, fertility and auspiciousness and with the legitimisation of children. The rituals included a pre-pubertal *talikettukalyanam*, a *tali*-tying ceremony for girls; a *thiranthakulikalyanam*, first-menstruation rite; and a *sambandham*, cloth-giving rite marking acceptance of a sexual liaison (Panikkar 1918; Aiyyappan 1941; Gough 1955; Fuller 1976: 105–6; Moore 1988; cf. Dumont 1983: 109–12; Good 1991: 7). This system differentiated between two types of affines: *enangar* being those people connected through *talikettukalyanam* and performance of other reciprocal ritual functions and *bandhukkar* being those connected through *sambhandam* unions (cf. Dumont: 1983: 117 ff). Nowadays, the *enangar* category has disappeared, while the *tali*-tyer and the sexual partner are the same man, who takes on both functions simultaneously in a single ceremony in which both *tali* and cloth are presented.

Meanwhile, gifts or payments made by the girl's family may be presented officially as affinal presentations (in line with *kanyadan* ideology) or as *stridanam*, commonly understood as girl's 'share' or pre mortem inheritance; unofficially, payments may be referred to as 'groom-price'. In the matrilineal system, those who tied a girl's *tali* received substantial compensation of cloth, foodstuffs and cash; this may also have some bearing on present-day payments (Mencher & Goldberg 1967). Gifts commonly include land given by father; land given by mother as part of unilineally transmitted female property; gold jewellery bought by parents or gifted by other relatives; cash raised by parents, brothers or a wider group; clothes bought by mother; ritual items gifted by mother and mother's brother's wife; and consumer goods bought by father.

Looking more closely at local categories of marriage will make clearer their implications and possible referents, as will a fuller description of the process of arranging a marriage, from negotiations to ceremony. Finally, some case studies will highlight issues of capital-maximising strategy and ways in which different strategies can be justified post hoc.

Cross-cousin Marriage and Polyandry

Despite the apparent existence in Malayalam of Dravidian terminology favouring cross-cousin alliances, this may always have been a second-best option for those unable to conduct hypergamous unions.[7] With the introduction of laws allowing partition of family properties in 1925, the arrangement of marriage alliances between cross-cousins appeared to be a strategy favouring conservation of undivided properties (Fuller 1976a: 83ff); we found some (scant) evidence to show that cross-cousin marriage was relatively more common in the previous two generations than now. For most 1990s Izhavas, marrying someone classified as cross-cousin is unequivocally 'poor people's marriage', a second-rate arrangement maintaining the status quo between two families. Out of more than 300 Izhava marriages recorded, less than 5 percent are between (direct or classificatory) *murapennu* and *muracherukkan*[8] and most of these are in older generations.

Sadhasivan, retired school-teacher, summarised popular opinion: 'marrying a relative has some advantages because the two families know each other and there is no cheating, but it is not good because there is no change, you stay in the same position as before'. For those with limited financial resources and (or) the burden of having to providing dowries for several daughters, this type of marriage has the advantage of requiring minimal costs; wedding expenses are considerably less than other marriages and dowry is relatively low – a few gold ornaments (3–5 *pavans*: 24–40 grammes) plus the girl's 'share' of her mother's land, if any, totalling less than Rs20,000. Polyandry is another arrangement once relatively popular among Izhavas, that has now almost disappeared (Aiyappan 1935, 1944: 98ff). There have been no polyandrous marriages in Valiyagramam for at least 20 years, but there are still women resident in the village who live or have lived as wives of two brothers; the youngest is in her forties. While Aiyappan (1944: 103) reports imbalances between female sexual needs and male capabilities as justification, Valiyagramam Izhavas account for polyandry by reason of economic factors. It is usually a temporary arrangement involving two brothers unable to bear the costs of two marriages and two households; as Berreman (1993) points out, polyandry may represent a phase in a domestic group's developmental cycle. The form in Valiyagramam is that an elder brother marries one women, 'shared' after marriage by younger brother, who defers or may never complete his own marriage. In all the cases we came across, one brother would spend long spells away – for example working as a travelling petty-merchant or in the military. In one household, a woman is married to two brothers who work in the Gulf for alternating periods. Usually, when younger brother has saved enough money he takes his own wife and starts an independent household: children born during the polyandrous relation continue to live with mother and her permanent partner, the elder brother. People born of such marriages are referred to in 'village language' as *thalayude mackal*, 'children of a mother', i.e. their paternity is uncertain. Sometimes such offspring presented themselves to us as children of the elder brother, maintaining that younger brother had remained unmarried; sometimes they would present themselves to us as 'having two fathers'.

Families like Kappa Parambil, where we found three times the usual rate of cross-cousin marriages and a considerable number of polyandrous relations, confirm the benefit of such low expense marriages in early stages of long-term mobility strategies. Possible economic advantages are generally outweighed by the new bourgeois orthodoxy defining marriage as necessarily monogamous: polyandry is almost universally, unequivocally condemned as uncultured, shameful and backward. Akin to toddy-tapping and agricultural manual labour, it is an indicator and reminder of the past from which Izhavas try to distance themselves. Its effective removal from the arena of possible marriage strategies places yet another burden upon the poor, denied the possibility of setting up households run upon financial contributions from two adult men rather than one. Cross-cousin marriage is more ambiguous; many middle-aged Izhavas maintain that 'people preferred to marry cross-cousins' for the prestige associated with practices perceived as formerly common among Nayars. For younger Izhavas, oriented more towards the *modern* lifestyle of Christians, this marriage has strong connotations of shame, to a greater degree than among young Nayars. Although relationships between cross-cousins continue to be an arena for institutionalised flirting (celebrated in fiction and films), all cousins are increasingly considered in Christian or north Indian idiom as (*cousin*) sisters and (*cousin*) brothers.

As alliances between relatives or close neighbours drop, marriages increasingly fall into two extremes: a minority of love matches made by elopement or with familial approval, in arranged marriage style; and stranger-alliance where families play for high stakes, seeking to maximise prestige and/or wealth in the interests of mobility.

Marrying a Stranger: Within the Village

Marriages within a neighbourhood, usually meaning among loosely related families, are unequivocally considered 'poor people's marriages' and take place between couples who would not be 'good catches' in the prestige marriage market. In line with reform and mobility imperatives, the vast majority of marriages are conducted among unrelated families with a marked preference for spouses from outside Valiyagramam. In the areas surveyed, less than 20 percent of Izhavas marry within the village and those who do almost all belong to labouring classes. The same groups who find themselves in the latter part of this century with suddenly stigmatised identities in production arenas experience similar processes in the field of reproduction. While intra-village marriage does not yet carry the negative symbolic load of polyandry or cross-cousin marriage, it is clearly disliked and coming under increasing pressure as a marriage among those considered 'our own people'.

This dislike was rationalised by Thankamma, a 55-year-old widow: 'It is bad for men to marry nearby because you always have in-laws peeping around. For women, you cannot go away if you have an argument. Also if you come from far away nobody will know your past.'(cf. Kapadia 1993b). While revealing widespread distrust of in-laws, Thankamma's statement exposes the limits of local unions. If both spouses come from the same village, their respective families know each other's history: this consideration greatly curtails the possibility of deceiving prospective in-laws during marriage negotiations. This is common and accepted: by boosting 'capitals', bride and groom's families try respectively to reduce and increase dowry size and force through an advantageous match.[9] While this appears to be the exact opposite of material on South Asian Muslim marriages presented by Donnan (1993: 310, 314, 320–1), in which obtaining accurate information about prospective in-laws is highly valued and associated with preferred marriage to kin or known families, it echoes Bourdieu's analysis of marriage strategies suggesting the importance of bluff in obtaining prestigious affines (for example 1977, 1990: 121). Moreover, cooperative collusion between in-laws to enable re-shaping of identities and aggrandisement of status is not possible when both parties are known to other villagers. Two families who are party to an alliance mirror and reflect each other's idealised eminence for mutual benefit. Affines pay frequent reciprocal visits to each other, arriving in taxis dressed in their best (womenfolk loaded with jewellery) and trying to appear equal to inflated claims about them which will have been passed around the village by their in-laws. It is possible to claim of an unknown family from 20 km distance that their house is enormous, their menfolk well-employed and their women virtuous beyond compare: no such boast can be made of affines from the other side of the village, whose position and reputation will be known all too well by neighbours. When Sundaran's daughter was to marry, the group going to the groom's house to fix dates was strictly limited, leaving several relatives and neighbours who had expected to be called disappointed. Sundaran remarked, 'The less of us who go, the better; the ones who come might start talking to the groom's people and find some scandal which they'll spread around here.'

While Donnan's informants, who routinely practise not only village endogamy but also marry close relatives, appear to express the exactly opposite point of view (1993: 314), it later becomes clear (1993: 327) that while this is expressed as a general practice, those with aspirations to prestige are expected to marry outsiders and to range far afield. Differences between less wealthy hill-dwelling Muslims and plains-dwelling upwardly mobile Izhavas are partly, then, questions of relative capacity for risky and costly hypergamy. Alliances favoured among the majority of Donnan's informants, 'non-change' marriages in which risks of deception are reduced to a minimum, are attractive only to those Izhavas who have limited resources and cannot afford to 'gamble' in new alliances beyond village boundaries. As Divagaran's daughter said, talking about Kappa Parambil's refusal to abandon cross-cousin marriage:

The women from down there move only from one house to another ... it's very bad (*mosham*), low-class behaviour ... it shows their low nature (*citta swabhavam*) ... things used to be like that when there was matriliny, but it's not good ... nowadays we should go out and make links with other families, for progress.

Going beyond family and village to make links with other Izhavas follows SNDP and reformists' logic of unifying the caste and making it the wider unit of exchange. Village exogamy effectively draws Izhavas together in wide affinal networks, reinforcing modern caste identity and solidarity, while a narrow village-bound perspective, associated with the pre-reform situation, reinforces and focuses upon 'backward' localised kin and lineage-based identities.

Marrying a Stranger: Outside the Village

Marriages outside the village, offering the best opportunities for new alliances and strategies maximising mobility, are by far the preferred option, accounting for about three-quarters of all Izhava unions we recorded. Family connections are crucial to the unfolding of successful strategies: the wider they are, the larger the number of prospective grooms or brides from whom to choose. Families with limited networks of contacts and/or lacking connections commensurable to their marriage ambitions resort to the help of brokers (*maman* or *mami*),[10] also sought by those wanting to hide negative characteristics which might hinder good alliances, such as financial difficulties, family scandals or physical flaws (illnesses, birth defects, bad 'character' and so on).

Risks in stranger-marriages are great, often involving breach of pre-marriage agreements. Common cases are those of husbands finding their wife's family unable (or unwilling) to pay the promised dowry in full, or wives discovering their husband's job to be unprestigious and badly paid. In one notorious case, a village bride discovered after some months that her new husband was not in the Gulf, but Mumbai; he had been posting letters to a friend in the Gulf, who had then posted them on to Kerala. Amicable solutions to conflicts between affines previously unknown to each other, who live at some distance, and who cannot count on mediatory interventions of common relations, are often impossible to reach; divorce follows almost inevitably. Family contacts are usually reliable sources of information on prospective in-laws, reducing risks of deception by strangers. Since affines are principal sources of contacts with other villages, marriages are often arranged through them. 'If your mother comes from a village or your sister is married there', Vasudevan explained, 'when you want to marry, your relatives there look around to find you a match. This is why there are many people married into the same places. We sent women to a place, then the *ammavanmar* knew the place and took women from there, there was *bandham*' (cf. Donnan 1993: 321).

Data we collected confirms that about three-quarters of all recorded 'outsider' marriages were conducted in just two areas, both Izhava-dominated: the hilly regions east and south-east of Krisnakara and the western coastal belt. The percentages of men and women from Valiyagramam taking a spouse from these two areas is almost identical, but this does not imply symmetrical alliance. The east of the country is generally devalued in relation to the west. Moving east from the coastal belt and plains – the major urban, industrial business and paddy areas – into hilly and mountainous areas, living conditions become harsher, land more inhospitable and Izhavas living there are considered less 'cultured' and lower in status. Hill-dwellers are often said to be *pothu-malakkar*, ignorant and uncouth (cf. Aiyappan 1944: 22), notions reinforced by the fact that the coastal belt has many villages where Izhavas are the 'dominant caste' and has always been the residence of the wealthy, high-status Izhava elite of Travancore. The coastal zone, unlike the eastern hills, is a centre of Izhava influence and power. Families whose resources are limited but sufficient to construct 'outsider' alliances marry sons and daughters to the less prestigious hilly area and repeat marriages there. Many poorer Izhavas in Valiyagramam used to work as agricultural labourers; when Izhavas from the hills came for harvest, marriage relations between the two areas developed giving families the chance to get to know and trust each other. Following non-risk strategies of 'marry people you know', alliances continue regardless of the fact that hardly any Izhavas now come into Valiyagramam for harvest. Such matches can be publicly presented as prestigious stranger-marriages while actually offering both sides the security of repeat alliance. There are also important economic advantages to liaisons with less-favoured areas. Men from the hills are willing to take 'cultured' brides from the favoured flat-lands for relatively low dowries, while brides from the east are keen to move into villages such as Valiyagramam where living conditions are easier and prestige higher. Families in hilly regions are keen to throw off 'hillbilly' reputations and make affinal links with the plains (cf. Donnan 1993: 317–18). One old man said frankly, 'You get good dowries from there: they don't have water and the climate is bad, but they have money, and they like to come here.' Marriages to the hills, then, represent a 'poor person's' stranger-marriage, just one step up from village endogamy, with financial advantages for those watching cash.

Meanwhile, wealthier and better-status Izhavas conduct marriages in the coastal area. As a family's capital grows, the upwardly mobile tend first to begin taking wives from the east, using the dowries to send their own sisters and daughters westwards. Later, they try to break alliances with the hilly regions and to conduct all marriages along the coastal zone.

Types of Alliance Sought

In marriage, as in employment, those families at the bottom of the community have been harmed rather than helped by group mobility strategies. Whoever has even a little wealth and wishes to be even a minimal player in the prestige game is forced to adopt the prestigious stranger-alliance model, costing them dear. As with employment, Kappa Parambil family again uses its solidarity and strength to buck dominant trends in favour of maximising and consolidating material wealth. Kappa Parambil counts a high proportion of cross-cousin, repeat and polyandrous marriages, strategies which have brought upon the family the opprobrium of local Izhavas, but enabled it to conserve properties and cash and build family strength.

Izhavas have a strong publicly expressed preference for isogamy, claiming that, 'All Izhavas are equal and can marry', and 'You should look for a family like your own to marry with': these statements are in line with SNDP orthodoxy (including abolition of sub-caste differentiation) and reflect south Indian alliance ideology. This public preference stands in tension with actual very strong leanings towards hypergamy with substantial marriage payments, and with attitudes in practice towards marriage alliance which seek to maximise not stability and equality but mobility and differentiation. While informants argue that equality in wealth is the only thing to be checked, ensuring desirable marriages of equals, in practice asymmetrical alliance is widely preferred. Families with boys to marry commonly accept hypergamous marriages for sons in order to raise the dowry necessary to send daughters 'up'. Apart from questions of geography, families seeking advantageous stranger-marriages need to decide what sort of partners they want and what balance they wish to strike between material and symbolic advantage. While hypergamy classically refers to relative status, hence to caste and sub-caste, hierarchies of occupation and material wealth shade into those of status, while 'blood' and 'wealth' are not always in conflict (Pocock 1993: 336–7).

Regarding questions of relative status, Izhava subdivisions resemble those of Nayars (Fuller 1976a: 38–43, 1975: 283–312). During the pre-reform period, apart from stable and continuing endogamous actual sub-*jatis* based upon occupations of barber/priest and washerman respectively, the remainder split and re-formed around 'ad-hoc' and unstable subdivisions amounting to no more than individuals or groups of families who accumulated wealth and land, claimed higher status for themselves and henceforth tried to refuse marriage with outsiders (cf. Yalman 1967: 189–

224; Ahmad 1973). The process also occurred by default at the caste's lower end: Izhava families who by reason of poor economic circumstances had to take servants' positions and were in some cases burdened with demeaning ritual roles, came to be regarded as separate groups and kept apart by ordinary Izhavas. High degrees of confusion and ambiguity concerning the existence and role of subdivisions reflect two opposite phenomena. On one side, destruction of the old kingly order conferring titles and honours combined with a strong ideology of equality has blurred intra-caste hierarchy, proof of which is most villagers' genuine ignorance regarding subdivisions, especially among the young. Although some regional differences exist (for example between south Kerala Izhavas and north Kerala Tiyyas), internal subdivision of endogamous regional groups into exo-gamous 'Illams' (houses, localised lineages; see Aiya 1989: 399 and Aiyappan 1944: 63–6) has completely disappeared. The SNDP has been by and large successful in unifying formerly endogamous regional groups (Tiyyas, Chovans and Izhavas) into a state-wide caste. While marriages between Travancore Izhavas and Malabar Tiyyas are rare, they do occasionally take place, as love marriages needing little rehabilitation or as sought-for alliances between wealthy elite families.

Izhava public discourse conforms to SNDP orthodoxy so that informants assert that sub-castes have been abolished, making all Izhavas equal status; in reality, elite and titled Izhavas often behave as and may be considered – by themselves and others – as an endogamous status group. Similarly, many try to draw a status line between the mainstream and Chetti Izhavas involved in toddy-tapping or alcohol trade. Families from these groups are often forced into intermarriage with each other in the absence of alliance partners from the wider community. Those involved at higher levels of the trade, who may accumulate substantial wealth, may be able to make outside marriages, especially if, having made their money, they withdraw from associations with liquor. That these are recent (post-reform) and unstable distinctions is clear by the double identity of several elite Izhava families, known to have made their fortunes through involvement in the liquor trade, yet also titled and unequivocally of the highest status. Titled families – Channar, Pannikker, Thandar – of which there are a handful in Valiyagramam, few in the hills and very many in the coastal belt, often prefer to marry from similarly high-status families regardless of wealth, preserving family 'name and fame'. Titled Izhavas do not form a sub-*jati*; titles indicate rank and prestige of individual families with means (wealth and influence) to have positions of superiority within their community recognised by the Travancore Rajavu. While Aiyappan argued that titles cease to be effective marks of distinction once they cannot be sustained by lifestyles appropriate to rank (Aiyappan op.cit.: 52), we find that titles still represent a significant element of symbolic capital (cf. Pocock 1993: 339).

At the same time, class status is extremely important to Izhavas, both because of their commitment to modernity and official repudiation – as *avarnas* – of caste as a valid marker of hierarchy, and also because their very identity and group project has, since the turn of the twentieth century, centred upon generalised modernist ideals of mobility and *progress*. Impoverished elite Izhava families cannot content themselves with past glories or the prestige of a big name, as very many Nayar and Brahman families do. Group identity and relationship to the imagined past is not rooted in images of glorious landowning and titled days gone by but continues to be linked to toddy-tapping, poverty, untouchability and manual labour, associated with stigma and ambivalence. Families considering themselves as having high prestige within the community through title, education or family name but whose holdings and income are meagre often hope to rectify what they experience in the class-conscious and increasingly consumption-oriented village as an anomaly between prestige and wealth. Conversely, the wealthy but low status may look to maximise prestige in alliance-making, seeking to capture the symbolic capital of a title or famous family name. 'Trade-off' marriages between old name and new money are fairly common. On the other hand, the latter group may choose to consolidate wealth and increase opportunities for further accumulation, in which case business connections and class status will be prioritised over family name. Newly wealthy families wishing to expand business prospects may choose to defer conversion until the next generation, in the meantime making sound financially motivated decisions. Alliances between contractors and suppliers, families in the liquor trade and Gulf migrant families are common examples.

Achieving balance between prestige and wealth is what most families claim to do. In practice, marriages of equals, a 'conservation strategy' in Bourdieu's terms (Wilkes 1990: 121, 128; Bourdieu & Wacquant 1992: 99), tend to be undertaken by two distinct groups: the Izhava elite, families already having significant wealth and prestige, and those who already enjoy moderate levels of wealth and prestige and wish to continue to maintain balance. Elite families marry repeatedly among themselves, carefully matching and conserving prestigious family names and wealth. As highly educated city-resident professionals they also generally marry from the cities; families like the Alummoottil fall into this group. The village Izhava elite is small, so families often cast the net wide for suitable matches; the alliance between Advocate Remini's natal and affinal households, both wealthy and long respectable ex-plantation people, and between her and her husband, both high-earning advocates, is a typical local elite marriage. Other families seeking 'balanced' marriage come from sections of the community who make similar choices in employment. School-teachers, clerks and so on often prefer not to risk or 'trade off' either of their modest levels of wealth and prestige for greater gains but to consolidate their position, comfortable and respectable on all fronts, in isogamous alliance.

Expenses for families wishing to give their daughters in stranger-marriages are high, the largest part being taken up by cash payments to grooms' families and brides' gold jewellery. The latter, it is well understood, represents not an inalienable gift to the bride but a means of showing to maximum advantage the payment made, conferring prestige upon both donor and recipient. After a few months of initial display, in which young couples visit both sets of relatives dressed in their best clothes, brides bedecked with wedding jewellery, newly married young women revert to wearing one or two necklaces rather than five or six, four or six bangles instead of ten or twelve; a large part of a bride's gold is commonly sold or at least mortgaged within a year of the wedding.

While gold along with other gifts and cash payments are referred to by villagers as an undifferentiated category, *stridhanam*, and while we follow local usage in talking about 'dowry', it is clear that such use of cash and gold is neither female property nor an unreciprocal and unusable affinal gift, but what Caplan (1993: 359ff) calls 'bridegroom price', a revolving societal fund or 'circulating pool of resources' continuously alienated and exchanged among households. The association of this practice with caste made by Caplan holds partly good, since 'dowry' has, according to informants, escalated in scale and become prominent since unification of the caste and subsequent opening up of a caste-wide marriage market. However, extreme variation in dowries within the caste means that there are in effect several funds of varying size, circulating within restricted groups and operating at different social levels. That 'groom-price', a payment dependent as much upon the qualities of the groom as any other factor, is more apt, is recognised by villagers and marriage brokers alike; the latter talk frankly to parents of would-be grooms of their son's 'value' or 'worth', strongly related to his employment status, while the former often complain that nowadays marriage consists of '*payyan vangikkuka*'. While the dowry a family is able to pay gives a groom's worth, it also, as Sharma (1984) notes, measures a bride's worth, and forecasts what type of groom she can expect to marry. Like Caplan, Sharma draws a correlation between caste and dowry, noting dowry inflation and arguing that erosion of sub-caste barriers and increasing use of socioeconomic factors to measure status has led to hypergamous competition, with families 'bidding' for desirable alliances. The fantastically high and escalating dowries which we see in Kerala are then functions of the state's modernity – abandonment of village endogamy and sub-castes and embracing of new forms of employment and wider identities.

The ethnographic case studies which follow show the extent to which Travancore Izhavas, having spurned forms of isogamous or localised alliance in the name of modernity and social reform, have created within the caste a fierce hypergamous marriage market in which opportunities to display and augment prestige are maximised. Families and individuals negotiate and manoeuvre within this treacherous market, seeking to mitigate its disadvantages and ensure best possible outcomes for their families.

ARRANGING A WEDDING

When families wish to arrange a marriage, word is spread through available networks, if necessary supplemented by a broker; matrimonial agencies and advertisements are avoided in favour of some level of personal relationship and presumed knowledge. Weddings with already known families or existing affines are relatively simple from here on: a 'small' dowry is agreed and families arrange a date-fixing ceremony or 'engagement' (*nischayam*). When families are trying to arrange marriage with strangers from outside the process is more complicated: a series of meetings and negotiations begins in which families try to boost their own wealth and status, presenting themselves in the best possible light, while trying to uncover the truth about potential alliance partners, aware that they are also exaggerating their desirability.

Boys' parties make first approaches to girls' families and a first informal meeting takes place away from either home between one or two of the menfolk, when photographs are usually exchanged. These meetings, potentially fraught, are ripe with comic possibilities, since, to avoid possible loss of face in case of refusal, meetings are ideally held in neutral public places and secretly, actually a near-impossibility. We have often seen the fathers of marriageable boys or girls in town standing outside a bank or *sari* shop and talking intently with one or two strangers; at the end of the conversation, both sides slink furtively away. Like other villagers, we will later innocently ask, 'Who was that we saw you talking to today in the street?', generally provoking laughter and warnings to keep the 'secret'. After such meetings, menfolk return home to discuss the proposal with family members; if everything seems encouraging first meetings take place at the girl's house. This is the sign for hectic activity: the house's occupants are warned to be ready for surprise inspection, since groom's parties commonly ignore arrangements and arrive unannounced, hoping to catch the family out in its 'natural' state. This period is a tremendous strain on the girl's family: all members, but especially mothers and daughters, must limit outings, lest the *party* arrive to find them away – a great shame leading to suspicion that these are not good home-loving people after all but frivolous gadabouts; the house must always be clean and tidy; a prestigious new tea-set may be bought for guests; menfolk avoid lounging around in vest and *lungi* or inviting too many friends home, and should definitely avoid daytime drinking. Meanwhile, the would-be bride may be bought a new *nighty*, be lent or bought new jewellery and beautified, usually at home, but, in wealthier and more sophisticated families, despatched to a beauty parlour for facial skin-bleaching and superfluous hair removal.

As few as two or as many as ten of the boy's menfolk – occasionally also senior womenfolk – come on a *penpakam*: a chance to see the girl's house, assess her family's economic condition and *culture* and exchange a few words with her when she appears briefly to serve tea and snacks. Senior men may tentatively suggest dowry figures at this point and horoscopes or at least *nakshatram*s are exchanged for matching by the families' respective astrologers. In some cases, dowry figures may not be openly discussed at all, as 'vulgar': this leads to considerable strain upon the girl's side, since it is fully understood that something will be expected, but it is difficult to gauge how much. The prospective groom may or may not attend this meeting: in many cases he is working away and trusts his family to proceed with arrangements in his absence. Grooms working in the Gulf or in military service come home on short leave with several sets of arrangements made, going to see and meet two or three prospective brides just days before selecting one and finalising the wedding. Such swiftly made arrangments are no matter for comment; once a family decides to enter the marriage market, both sides hope to avoid protracted negotiations and conclude matters quickly. If two families feel comfortable with each other after the *penpakam*, the girl's menfolk and possibly some senior women go to the boy's house. If all is going well, photographs and full horoscopes will by now have been exchanged and families ask prospective marriage partners for formal assent or refusal, visiting astrologers for horoscope-matching and advice.

During final negotiations in which dowry figures may or still may not be discussed, details of the *nischayam* are decided. While Nayars hold both a simple fixing and wedding at the bride's home, Christians hold one ceremony in each place: usually the fixing (a larger ceremony than among Nayars) at the bride's home and the wedding at the boy's; Izhavas generally hold fixings at the boy's home and weddings at the girl's. At smaller Izhava weddings this ceremony is, as with Nayars, a simple affair consisting of a handful of the bride's family (minimally F, MB and FB) visiting the groom's house for snacks and tea. An astrologer of the Kanian or Izhava caste, having matched bride and groom's horoscopes, reads out the marriage agreement and suggests several auspicious times before the families agree a date. These used to be men-only affairs, but the bride's senior women (M, MBW, FZ) increasingly also attend. Another fast-growing practice, following Christians, is setting up tables and a marquee outside the house to serve a larger range of snacks (*idli-sambar* and sweets or even a full rice meal) to 30–40 people. At such fixings the auspicious moment for the wedding is likely to be calculated by somebody of higher status than the local Kanian (an OBC). In Valiyagramam, this would likely be Hanuman Tantri, a noted local Izhava astrologer who has studied Brahmanic rituals and who fixes new deities in Izhava temples. Some families consult a high-status professional *savarna* astrologer, such as a member of the Warrier or even Brahman caste, to match horoscopes, in which case he will not attend the fixing personally but will suggest suitable dates.

At this point, the bride's family now commonly renovate and whitewash the house, making minor repairs and improvements ready for critical inspection by in-laws. Monies are gathered together to pay for expenses covering dowry, jewellery, new clothing for close family members, the bride's trousseau and the wedding feast. The groom's side must minimally buy the bride her all-important gold *tali* and a complete outfit, including shoes and underwear: before leaving for his house, she should be clothed entirely by him.[11] They also commonly buy the bride a wedding ring and a gold chain for her *tali* plus gifts for the bride's household: in wealthy weddings gold rings, chains and watches for brides' younger brothers and mother, more commonly shirts and *saris*. In striking contrast to turn of the twentieth century Izhavas, critical of lavish expenditure and seeking 'rational' conservation of capital, searching to distinguish their ceremonies from the 'wasteful' ones performed among the Nayar community, Izhavas now continue to raise their marriage expenses in competitive hierarchies. The habitus is not rational, but reasonable, making socially appropriate choices; only in times of exceptional crisis does 'rationality' partly take over (Bourdieu & Wacquant 1992: 129–31). Increasingly, wealthy families with sons seek to augment the prestigious display element on the groom's side: at a high-status coir belt marriage the bride wore 101 sovereigns of gold (808 grammes), while the groom's side presented 15 sovereigns (120 grammes) to their new affines in the form of gold rings and watches for her male relatives.

Both sides send hundreds of invitations, commissioning several different types from local printers: gold-bordered engraved cards in English reserved for VIP guests; flimsy single-leaf papers in Malayalam for college friends of bride and groom; most invitees receiving something in the middle. Fashions change fast, arriving from the cities: high-status families spend high and show prestige by commissioning the latest and most elaborate designs, such as transparent PVC cards screen-printed with scenes from the Mahabharata, or double-cards embossed in gold, green and red outside and delicately lined with rich tissue paper inside. Bride and groom may be referred to by grandiose titles such as '*Sow.*' and '*Chir*', ('*Sowbhagyavati*' and '*Chiranjeevi*', auspicious woman and hero) baffling recipients. To avoid bad luck the bulk of wedding purchases, including the bride's *sari* and gold, are made at the last moment. Highest-status men and women do this in style by taxi, going to the most prestigious city shops; those with relatives take lengthy trips, staying over. Medium- and low-prestige families shop less far afield, in Krisnakara, Chantakara or Kayamkulam. Everyone buys gold locally from somebody known and trusted, which often means a community member.

Dowries nowadays often greatly exceed what could be a woman's share of ancestral properties and are commensurate to how much a family is prepared and able to invest in the fulfilment of status aspirations. The range of acceptable items has increased to include houses, cars, motorbikes, stereos, television sets, videos, cameras, fridges, electrical cooking gadgets, thermal casserole dishes and so on. Within a few days of marriage, a bride's family visit her in her new home in a ceremony known as *adukkulla kanan*, seeing the kitchen. This visit was previously accompanied by small gifts of cooking pots and sweets; it has now become common to take far more expensive household items. One family took with them a metal *almirah* costing Rs8000, only to be told by their new in-laws that it was not acceptable and that a refrigerator – minimum cost Rs12,000 – would be more appropriate (cf. Kapadia 1993b; Caplan 1993; Billig 1992). The inclusion of new items and inflation of dowry rates since the 1970s appear to be directly related to the expansion of migration.

Calculation of dowry is highly complex. The bride's beauty, education, employment and the status, prestige, wealth and connections of her family and relatives are weighed against similar parameters on the groom's side, complicated bargains following lengthy negotiations. These variations make it almost impossible to present a precise scale of dowry 'rates'. As an approximate guide, in 1995 a minimal dowry, given between two labouring or low-class and low-status families or for 'small' marriages such as those within the village would hold a total value of Rs15,000 to Rs40,000. An average 'respectable' amount, given by those of mid status and wealth or for stranger-alliances would total around Rs80,000–200,000, probably divided between land, gold, and cash; one lakh (Rs100,000) is a very common figure for middle-class marriages.[12] A high-prestige and high-wealth dowry, given between migrants, professionals or business people, would amount to anything upwards of Rs200,000 and is constantly escalating. The magic 101 *pavans* of gold amounted in 1995 to a cash equivalent of approximately Rs350,000; by 1996, its value was Rs404,000. Families like to give as large a proportion as possible in the form of gold jewellery, for maximum effect. As one woman told us, 'When you go to a wedding you look at the gold: it's all you can see; we can never be sure how much cash or other things are given, so it's important to have a lot of gold.' On a scale determined by gold, women agreed that fewer than 15 bangles marks the wedding as that of a 'small' or 'ordinary' party'; 15 to 25 bangles is 'medium' or 'good'; while anything over 30 is decidedly 'good' or 'very good'.

Girls' mothers may have property in their natal village as their 'share', which they pass to their daughters. Most mothers try to save to buy a few pieces of gold for daughters' weddings; they may also have gold put by from their own wedding to pass on. But, unlike some parts of Tamil Nadu, many women no longer have property of their own to pass on to their daughters, and mother–daughter inheritance is becoming rarer (cf. Nishimura 1994). The bulk of a dowry consists of land given by the father, together with gold and cash raised through contributions from close family. Since many prospective grooms do not want land in a village they and their wives may rarely visit, land is often sold and cash equivalent given; often, cash is given up-front and land mortgaged to be sold later. Gold and land making up the bride's share and her maternal property should remain in her name and control throughout her life; the rest – cash and goods making the dowry gift – going to the husband and his family. In practice most women lose control of the whole dowry; gold and land might be sold or mortgaged to provide money for husband's sister's dowry, to pay for husband's brother's migration and so on. While a newly wed bride living with her husband and his relatives is in no position to refuse to relinquish control over her dowry, her contribution may give her some leverage in the family (cf. Visvanathan 1989). So far, Kerala's fantastic escalation of dowry does not seem to have been accompanied by widespread severe ill-treatment of brides: divorce is fairly common and the usual remedy for post-marital dowry dispute.

Scale and Style of Wedding

Marriages take place only during auspicious times and tend to cluster around two periods: the pre-monsoon hot season, and the post-monsoon Onam festival, Kerala's major 'new year'. Weddings, talked about and remembered by participants and outsiders, are rare and special occasions, usually a once-in-a-lifetime chance. This is especially true for the bride's family, facing a unique opportunity to build and show symbolic capital. The actual ceremony is then a dramatic public perfomance of a family's wealth, status and style objectified, and an important piece of identity-work for that family. Villagers say that you hear a Christian wedding, noted for the Mass and for hymns sung by a choir and acompanied by music; smell a Muslim wedding, marked by the use of rose-water, perfumes and fragrant *biryani*; and see a Hindu wedding, for the gold and silk saris. An element of spectacle is important: Advocate Remini's wedding (Chapter 1) is commonly referred to as the first in Valiyagramam in which 101 *pavans* of gold were *seen*, giving her family a unique point of distinction over status rivals. Apart from the level of expenditure – specifically the amount of gold worn by the bride – there exist several other clear signs of distinction, looked for and understood or decoded by guests who, seated on folding chairs in front of a stage, represent the audience being played to. Certain practices or styles are associated with certain communities and hence hold negative or positive prestige connotations, while also suggesting a family's particular orientation and strategy and would-be identity.

All Brahmans and many Nayars marry at home; the bride's house is the most popular choice for Izhava marriages: cheaper than using hired premises and more prestigious than using the *gurumandiram*, inescapably associated with 'Izhava-ness'. Poorer Izhavas, whose homes are unsuitable to receive guests, use this least popular venue with its small attached dining hall, costing very little to hire. Notwithstanding the fact that guests at modest weddings are generally few – 100–200 – still three or more sittings are required at small houses or *gurumandirams* to serve food to all: *tali*-tyings at such functions are followed by undignified scrums to get served. Higher-status weddings are at home with a large marquee outside, at public temples with dining halls or in other large hired premises such as the village high school or the huge Dharmananda *asram*. At these weddings food is served to anything upwards of 300 guests in just one or two sittings. While dining halls large enough to accommodate everybody in one sitting (as found in city 'marriage halls') are most prestigious, since no respected guests are kept waiting to eat, no such venue is available locally; in any case, two sittings is acceptable among Hindus because serving the groom's party first means demonstrating respect, hence is *cultured* behaviour.

Catering at the smallest-scale weddings is done exclusively by family members; women (sometimes also young men) come together the night before to grind spices, scrape coconut and chop vegetables. On the day itself, family men stir huge steaming brass pans – borrowed or hired – full of *sambar, parippu* and *payasam*. Many families can call upon some workers to help in preparations; when helpers are poor caste-mates' payment can be token – a new cloth. Sometimes impoverished Nayars who make their living as caterers are paid to cook; marriages at temples or *asrams* are catered by staff assisted by family members; a very few elite families make use of professional town-based catering companies, for the most part Christian-owned. There is little scope for shaving or boosting expenses by economising or elaborating on wedding food, nor much room for innovation. For Izhavas as for Nayars, standardised full vegetarian rice meals served upon banana leaves (costing Rs 3 each) and accompanied by boiled warm water must be served to at least 100 guests. The only real variations between poor and wealthy Hindu wedding feasts are the number of *papads*, side-curries and puddings served: at the bottom end one *papad*, around five side-curries and one or two puddings are served. Marks of luxury weddings include generous replenishing of *papads* with all four main courses (lentils, *sambar*, pudding and sour-curry) plus up to ten side curries and four puddings.

Fewer and fewer families draw attention to caste status by calling upon the man holding traditional caste rights (*avagasham*), dating back before reform processes, to perform life-cycle rites: the barber/priest (Izhavatti *jati*, a subdivision considered 'at the bottom' of Izhavas). As many Izhavattis, 'barbers by birth', now practise their trade, if at all, in modern saloons, refusing to come to houses or to take up ritual roles, some neighbourhoods are no longer even served. In those that are, the compromise taken by most families is to call the Izhvatti to decorate the *kalyanamandapam* with paddy and coconut-flower, red and white flowers, incense, and so on (*ashtamangalyam*), items which it is then the Izhavatti's right to take home as payment along with some small *daksina* cash. Somebody more prestigious officiates for the actual ceremony; we have seen few marriages actually celebrated by an Izhavatti. If a wedding is at a *gurumandiram*, the likely celebrant is a local SNDP official, a 'patron'. In house and temple functions, senior family men take on the job, essentially consisting of instructing the couple and handing the *tali* to the groom. At high-status weddings, district-level SNDP officials or holy men of good repute may officiate. At public Durga temples – a highly prestigious choice since Nayars commonly marry here – bride and groom are handed *prasadam* by Brahman priests before the wedding. Another mark of a family's *culture* or prestige level is the number of people involved in instructing the couple when to sit, stand, garland and so on, and the degree of disagreement. Weddings of the poor are often accompanied by large numbers of – often drunken – senior men arguing and making suggestions about procedure and timing while local SNDP officials try to take control of the situation; elite weddings have clear hierarchical structures with one recognised and important man such as a regional SNDP official 'in charge' of rituals, deferred to by others.

The least wealthy – the manual labouring classes – brides' families hold *tea parties* a few days before the wedding, setting up a few hired trestle tables and metal folding chairs outside the house within an area screened off by *saris*. *Tea parties* have two purposes: those who do not wish to compromise their own standing by attending a low-prestige wedding, or who consider themselves of too high status publicly to take a rice meal from the family, can still show some care and attachment (*sneham*) towards the household by discreetly taking tea and snacks. More importantly for the bride's family, visitors to a *tea party* leave small cash *donations* as they leave, anything from Rs11 to Rs101. Over several days, family patrons and *well-wishers* – high-status or wealthy neighbours and caste-fellows – arrive in small groups at any daylight hour to be seated at separate tables, unlike the wedding proper where people sit in undifferentiated lines. A small plantain leaf is placed before guests by the bride's father, who then serves tea, one or two of Kerala's ubiquitous small bananas, and *bakery items* – shop-bought snacks including biscuits, *halva*, *mikksu*. High-prestige guests begrudgingly eat a little of whatever is on offer, often spurning all but the banana;[13] others, who plan to attend the wedding but have come specifically to make a financial contribution, politely eat everything. Before leaving, *tea party* guests press into the bride's father's hands an envelope containing cash, whisked straight into the house for examination of its contents. For poor families, this is a tense time: they rely upon *tea parties* to make up cash deficits for wedding purchases.

While even the poorest of Nayars and Christians do not hold *tea parties*, the practice is common among Thandans and Pulayas and widely considered by mainstream village society a shameful thing for a family to be forced to do, a form of 'low-class' behaviour associated with members of untouchable castes. In reality, all families of all communities rely upon and receive cash contributions and gifts at weddings; what is shameful is the soliciting, via *tea party* invitations, of such contributions from a wider public. Given before the wedding, cash appears unequivocally as a contribution towards expenses; given on the day, it can be presented as an unsolicited gift. In the Izhava-dominated coastal belt, *pattu-kalyanam* (song celebration) *tea parties* at which popular film songs are broadcast are spoken of as part of Izhava traditions of mutual help, in no way shameful. This again suggests the degree to which Valiyagramam Izhava behaviour is conditioned by the presence of other communities.

Just as *tea parties*, actually an Izhava practice in coastal areas, are attributed locally to non-prestigious style belonging to Pulayas, therefore to be avoided, styles used locally in Christian and Nayar weddings are picked up as pieces of symbolic capital which, through their origin, dialectically negate 'Izhava-ness', an identity which the aspiring middle classes find increasingly constraining. Markers of distinction referring to particular orientations but freely borrowed between communities are clearly recognised by villagers. Christians very often serve light refreshments (for example *halva*, wedding cake, branded soft drinks such as Rasna), favouring shop-bought rather than home-made items. They also, in common with city-dwellers, hold wedding receptions in marriage halls. Holding a reception not at home or temple but in a hired hall, welcoming guests with a glass of Rasna or a bottle of soda, and sending them away with a Cadbury's chocolate eclair sweet, usually stapled to a card 'with compliments of the bride and groom', are recognisably *modern* practices associated with Christian weddings, indicative when practised among village Izhavas both of class status and high sophistication.

Izhavas sometimes say that the only difference between their marriage ceremony and that of Nayars is the *sari*. A new ceremony was devised during the 1920s by the NSS which combined Nayar nineteenth-century pre-puberty auspiciousness *tali*-tying ceremony with the cloth giving (*puduvakoda*) marking the beginning of a sexual relationship (*sambandham*). Nayar grooms now tie a gold *tali* to the bride and present her with cloth: both a silk *sari*, which she changes into after the ceremony to wear at the reception, and a *cassavu-mundu*, the 'traditional' late nineteenth-century gold-bordered dress which she changes into after the reception for photographs. After the abolition of matriliny, the SNDP similarly devised an Izhava ceremony designed to require only simple prayers and *tali*-tying and minimise 'irrational' expense. One complete outfit, including the silk *sari*, is brought to an Izhava bride's house on the wedding morning by the groom's sister, who then helps dress the bride (cf. Good 1991). At some recent Izhava weddings, instead of coming out of the house for *tali*-tying already dressed in the groom's *sari* as laid down by SNDP reformed ceremony, the bride wears her own new silk sari and is presented with the groom's *sari* by him during the ceremony, in which case she changes into it before the reception. Not only does this practice speak of wealth, involving two costly *saris* being worn within the space of 30 minutes, but it borrows the 'Nayar style' of ceremony. Many village Izhavas also use 'Nayar-style' *talis*, small simple gold ornaments shaped like a single leaf. Proper 'Izhava *talis*', much larger ornaments, are circular, leaf or heart shaped, filigree or solid, and decorated (before the 'gold-boom', Izhavas used gold-plated silver for their *talis*, hence larger and more decorated pieces of metal). Nowadays, if large 'Izhava *talis*' are used (commonly seen on wives of Gulf-migrants), they are enamelled, engraved, studded with jewels and made of solid gold.

'Izhava-style' weddings are regarded by most Valiyagramam Izhavas as low-status affairs. As in other areas of social life, the mobility imperative which prefers adoption of prestigious Nayar and Christian practices is at odds with the emphasising of Izhava caste identity – at best ambivalent, at worst still associated to 'drunken toddy-tapper'. One issue here is the degree of involvement and visibility of the SNDP, necessarily – as the caste association – involved in all weddings. Weddings of the poor and low status commonly take place on SNDP premises, organised by village SNDP officials and sanctified by *Gurudevan*. Elite weddings are almost indistinguishable from those of Nayars, the SNDP's only public part being the discreet handing over of the marriage certificate after signing of the register. In between, much depends upon whether those attending representing the SNDP are local-level activists or office-bearers from district or even state-level; it is also important to see whether they are present as organisers and 'helpers' – patrons – or as distinguished guests and putative equals. Apart from the single *sari* and large Izhava *tali*, recognisably 'Izhava style' practices avoided by the seriously mobile include an altar to *Gurudevan* next to the *mandapam*, group prayers to *Gurudevan* during the ceremony, and speeches on the joys and duties of married life by SNDP officials.

In pragmatic fashion, however, Izhavas do not undertake wholesale rejection of 'Izhava-style' or adoption of prestigious Nayar and Christian or high-class styles. Two practices regarded with horror and sneering by Nayars but continued regardless by Izhavas, who regard Nayar scruples as motivated by an un-modern and irrational desire to put manners before all, are the public registering of cash gifts at the wedding and dowry registration. Izhavas view Nayar arguments – that registration of the amount of dowry is shameful – as a ludicrous piece of risk-taking with things which should be treated carefully: daughters and cash. A Nayar bride has proof, via NSS marriage registers, only of her 'share', the land passed to her, making her less able to divorce. Izhava women regard themselves as more valued and protected by their families and as more likely to be well-treated by in-laws because divorcing Izhava women are able to claim back more of the dowry. SNDP marriage registers effectively register dowry by the expedient of converting amounts of cash given into gold equivalent 'gifts' (thereby also converting groom-price into *stridhanam*). All Izhavas register both the marriage and the full dowry, signing their local SNDP branch's book after the ceremony and being presented with certificates and lifetime SNDP membership. Unhappy women can, aided by SNDP mediation, return to their parents with most of the dowry and eventually re-marry.

Nayar and Christian concealment or discretion about cash gifts is similarly regarded as uneccessary hypocrisy. At all but the wealthiest Izhava weddings, trestle tables are set up outside marquees or dining halls, manned by male relatives of the bride and spread with betel nut and cigarettes. Male wedding guests bring cash gifts which are openly recorded in a book, to be reciprocated when a wedding comes in the donor's family. The wealthiest Izhavas, like their Nayar and Christian counterparts, expect no cash but only token wedding gifts, presented by females to the bride and consisting of gift-wrapped luxury items like china or melamine tea-sets, ice-cream dishes, ornaments for the glass display cabinet, wall plaques and so on. It is not uncommon for brides to have ten or more tea-sets stored – unpacked – at home, testimony to wealth and prestige (cf. Nishimura 1994). Few Izhava families then find themselves in the position of putting prestige before finance – only those aspects of Nayar and Christian style which can be adopted reasonably cheaply and easily are widely taken up. The following marriage case studies will again demonstrate a variety of strategies and remind us of the community's heterogeneity.

STUDIES IN MODERN MARRIAGE

A Love Marriage

When we met Aruna in 1990 she was – unusually – single and working at 24. She was employed by a well-known women's magazine, but had ambitions to do *serious* journalism. Speaking confidently in fluent English, she told us that she was in no hurry to ruin her life by marrying and expressed relief that her mother, a widow who could offer little dowry and exercise no authority over the working daughter who maintained her, was in no position to argue. (This might of course have been a face-saving exercise.) In her free time, Aruna often visited the East–West centre. This is a universalist institution which grew out of the Narayana Gurukula Move-ment and the University for the Science of the Absolute, founded by Narayana Guru in 1924 after his Alwaye *asram* hosted a 'conference of all religions'. The foundation, with many international centres across the globe offering courses to Indians and non-Indians in meditation, Advaitic philosophy and so on, is itself a development of the Brahmavidya Mandiram founded at Sivagiri, Varkala in 1963 by Nataraja Guru, disciple of Narayana Guru and son of Dr Palpu, founding SNDP member. The current guru, Nitya Chaitanya Yathi, normally resident in Ootacamund, was a *sishya* of Nataraja Guru, hence heir by direct guru lineage to Narayana Guru's universalist tradition. He and Nataraja Guru have undertaken several foreign tours and count many Europeans, North Americans and Australians among their disciples (Nataraja Guru 1968, 1989, 1990; Yati 1991).

In 1995, we heard that Aruna had recently married a German national, manager in an engineering company and – like her – frequenter of the East–West centre and devotee of Guru Nitya Chaitanya Yati. They had met at the centre. Aruna's family and neighbours presented the marriage as something of a coup, stressing the groom's high occupational status and telling us that Aruna would now be living in style in Germany. Even neighbours who sniggered, suggesting that we would all have expected no more of this '*modern girl*' than that she would make a love-marriage with a foreigner, were also pleased to see that she had at last married and married very comfortably. Importantly, the couple did not have a poorly attended register-office wedding, common practice for 'shameful' love marriages, but a sanctified marriage in the presence of families and friends from both sides at Sivagiri, *Gurudevan*'s most important spiritual home. By 1996, this marriage was already being re-cast not as *love-marriage* but as arranged alliance. Aruna's cousin told us the re-worked wedding narrative:

That *sahippu* was always coming to Kerala to see Yathi; he's a great devotee, like Aruna. The *sahippu* was a bit sad, a quiet one; he wasn't married. Yathi called Aruna and the man together, telling them that it was his will to see them married. Aruna admitted that she liked the *sahippu* but had been afraid to tell anybody; the *sahippu* said that he had wanted to marry Aruna for a long time. Yathi had known all this, although nobody else did. Yathi called Aruna's mother and brothers and arranged everything.

Aruna's aunt told us that her family had been happy, but worried.

Aruna had nothing, not even a pair of earrings. That *sahippu* immediately showed the family his sincerity by depositing Rs200,000 in a bank account in Aruna's name and giving her 15 *pavans* (120 grammes) of gold for the wedding. They came round to visit all the relatives after the wedding; he's a nice man. All this good thing was Yathi's doing.

Two Izhava-style Weddings

Making the best of things

A very poor Izhava family where both mother and father work as casual labourers married their daughter at 16, right after failing matriculation (SSLC). Apart from Brahmans, who commonly marry their daughters in their teens, most village marriages involve brides of at least 19, usually older, and grooms nearer 30 than 20. This groom was just 22, an SSLC failed shop assistant, son of labouring parents living in the bride's mother's natal village: while presented as an 'outsider' stranger-marriage, the two families were actually already well known to each other. Dowry was the minimal 3 *pavans* (24 grammes) of gold needed to make the wedding-ornaments – earrings, one neck chain, a hairpiece and two thin bangles, plus a ring for the groom – supplemented by Rs10,000 in cash, making Rs20,000 in total. Wedding monies were raised by pawning the bride's mother's gold chain (1 sovereign, 8 grammes, raises around Rs1500 loan) at a *blade*, augmented by a loan taken out with the SNDP against the price of future coconut harvests from the family's six trees and topped up at the last minute by loans and contributions raised at a *tea party*. In 1995, four years after the marriage, the bride's parents were still in debt.

The wedding was held at the bride's home, a two-roomed unplastered brick house. The meal (with only one *payasam*) was served, unusually, before the marriage; some guests arrived after the food just to watch the ceremony. All catering was done by family members. Taped music played throughout, something we have only otherwise seen at Pulaya weddings . Many Izhava neighbours snubbed the marriage as a function which they would lose prestige by attending, going only to the *tea party* to make discreet contributions to expenses; the total number of wedding guests was under 200. Instead of the usual silk *sari* costing anything upwards of Rs2000, the bride wore a Rs120 nylon one. There were only two cars from the groom's side, most guests coming by rickshaw. At the *mandapam*, a crowd of older relatives pushed forwards and argued about correct procedures, shouting conflicting advice to the couple. After *tali*-tying, the wedding went straight on to mutual garlanding followed by gift-giving by a few friends and family. As the couple made to leave, everyone realised that they had forgotten to do *panigraham*, the giving of the bride's hand by her father to the groom, symbolic of *kanyadanam*. It was hastily performed.

The style and scale of this wedding were less prestigious even than some Pulaya labourers' weddings we have attended, but the atmosphere throughout was similar: celebratory but a little subdued, as close family members in debt worried about costs and about how they would repay loans, while everybody experienced the embarrassment of a low-cost version of a ceremony designed to be done on a lavish scale. Women guests, who would usually discuss at length the richness and beauty of the wedding *sari* and gold, asking from where it had been bought and how much it had cost, found themselves with little to say. Many had no gold jewellery or silk *saris* of their own to wear; those who did found themselves over-dressed, in contrast to most weddings, where female guests openly compete in the lavishness of their *saris* and the amount of gold they wear (a practice nonetheless commonly criticised by women as '*fashion-show*'). Male guests, who normally help themselves liberally to areca-nut and cigarettes at the bride's father's expense, and who use weddings for intense networking, searching out job opportunities for sons or bridegrooms for daughters and angling for introductions to VIP guests, also found themselves at a loss: local men from the street mingled with the bride's labouring family and in-laws. Common wedding conversations, along the lines of, 'Do you see that man? He's the bride's uncle who works in Pune', or 'Did you hear that the groom's cousin will be taking him to the Gulf soon?' became redundant. After the ceremony there was no spectacle of a roll-call of family and guests for photographs, nor any other function: guests soon drifted away.

Marrying locally

In 1995, Kappa Parambil family married a girl, 21, who had failed her SSLC, to a distant affinal relation, an army private aged 28, from the other side of the village. Thirty men and around ten women, including the bride's MBW and MBD (who had been largely instrumental in arranging the marriage) attended the date-fixing ceremony where a full vegetarian *sappadu* was served after the Kanian suggested suitable wedding dates. At Kappa Parambil three weeks later, 300 guests were served in two sittings with a two-*payasam* feast, prepared the night before by family women and cooked on the day by family men. There was only one wedding taxi, reserved for bride and groom; a jeep ferried guests across the village in relays. The ceremony, conducted at the bride's MB home, was officiated by a local SNDP official and included sung prayers to *Gurudevan*. There was neither photographer nor video crew but a relative with a camera who took one roll of film. The dowry included no cash or land, the full amount being given as 20 *pavans* (160 grammes) of gold jewellery, worth around Rs70,000 at the time.

Three Mobility-oriented Alliances

Chasing dowry

Mani Kuttan is a 27-year-old army private, one of five brothers from a *naluvittu* family having a fairly 'big name' among Izhavas but no particular wealth. From the start, Mani Kuttan's parents were determined to go for maximum dowry, while Mani Kuttan declared his only criterion to be the girl's looks. Mani Kuttan saw several times, and liked, a matriculate girl found by a broker; she was very beautiful, and her family were willing for the match. Mani Kuttan's family scorned the 20 *pavans* and Rs50,000 cash on offer saying that with their family name and one son in the Gulf, Mani Kuttan was worth more. Another broker found a girl to the family's liking: 19, matriculate with a technical qualification, she was working as a laboratory technician earning Rs500 a month. Her family were offering 25 *pavans* (200 grammes) on marriage and a further 1 lakh cash (Rs100,000) to be paid within one year of the wedding. While his parents were very keen, Mani Kuttan was not: the girl was both hugely fat and dark, not considered at all attractive. To Mani Kuttan's relief, as negotiations proceeded the girl's family lowered their dowry offer, claiming that 20 *pavans* (160 grammes) and Rs75,000 would be sufficient because their daughter would be working and earning for the family. Mani Kuttan looked on in satisfaction as his father explained to us, 'Expenses on our side will come to at least Rs30,000; the bride's *sari* costs Rs3000; then we have to pay for a 3 *pavan* (24 grammes) chain for her *tali*, presents for her family and taxis from this house.' Mani Kuttan's leave ended and his family discontinued negotiations until next year's season. In 1996, Mani Kuttan came home on leave determined to conclude a marriage and equally determined not to be swayed by his parents. After many arguments, his parents stopped passing details on to brokers and told Mani Kuttan to find his own wife. Eventually, a match was arranged via a distant maternal relation to a 21-year-old girl from the hilly south-east, a B Comm. student at a private college. The bride brought Rs75,000 cash and 11 pavans of gold (88 grammes, worth around Rs44,000); both parents and son declared themselves satisfied.

Pursuing status

Among the guests at the first wedding described above ('making the best of things'), while nobody from any of the big 'four families' (*naluvittumar*) were present, women from Kuttiyil (the successful Gulf migrant family from Chapter 1) were. During our early months in Valiyagramam we had often noticed social distance between Kuttiyil and their closest neighbours, the 'four families', which we had put down to the strained relations resulting when one family suddenly enriches itself while others, formerly close, are left behind. After this wedding we found out that Kuttiyil belong – or used to belong – to an Izhava subdivision considered very low status by 'ordinary' Izhavas. Despite SNDP reforms and Izhavas' assertion that, apart from the Izhavatti barber sub-group, the caste is no longer subdivided, families like Kuttiyil – eventually described to us by neighbours as 'servants' and 'messengers' – continue to be held at a distance. Kuttiyil have – by local Izhava standards – enormous wealth, but almost no prestige. Most family members also have extremely dark skin, something almost universally devalued among Izhavas (as among other non Scheduled Castes) as 'ugly', and associated to low-caste status, 'making you look like a *Harijan*' and so on (Osella & Osella 1996).

Kuttiyil has carefully managed its marriage strategies, making local alliances spread carefully between neighbours with lower and higher degrees of status, husbanding dowry money to be used for maximum effect. The family knows that it will not achieve a status leap in one generation, so there is little sense in dispersing its wealth in trying to play prestige stranger-alliance at this point. One daughter from Kuttiyil managed to marry into a nearby *naluvittumar* family, allegedly for a larger than expected amount of dowry; she wore 20 *pavans* of gold (160 grammes), but rumours claim that another 1 lakh (Rs100,000) in cash discreetly changed hands. Another daughter married into a family across the village described as 'ordinary Izhavas', i.e. a mainstream family. Hypergamous alliance with 'respectable' local Izhavas will, over time, help Kuttiyil to integrate within the neighbourhood: both Kuttiyil's 'ordinary' Izhava affines and the higher-status 'four families' are now obliged to give and receive reciprocal house invitations for certain functions (baby namings, weddings and so on). Presumably one incentive (apart from dowry) for the 'four families' to accept this marriage was the hope of employment opportunities and connections to the all-important Gulf. Since Kuttiyil run their own business in Oman, potential migrants among affines do not need to worry about working hard under a *Sahippu* or an *Araby*, but would be in the relatively luxurious position of working among other Malayali Izhavas. That they would be working not only for affines who – as wife-givers – are putatively inferior but also for those who used to be their low-status 'servants' are ironies probably not lost on Kuttiyil.

Kuttiyil's younger son Anil love-married a Protestant Christian girl from the other side of the village. Their illicit relationship became public in 1991; Mini's family took her out from college, beat her, and threatened violence to Anil. Communist Party officials called in as mediators between the two families (both Communist supporters) visited Anil's home and warned him that the *romance* must stop and could never lead to anything. After another two years of secret *romance* Mini's brother, who supported her, came by night to Kuttiyil warning that the family were planning a quick wedding; the engagement was to be within the week. The couple eloped, returning after some weeks to Anil's home. Rather than complain about losing dowry Kuttiyil graciously welcomed Mini in, and have helped her transform herself into a model Hindu daughter-in-law wearing *pottu* and *sindooram*, allowing her to light the family holy oil lamp each evening. She has been encouraged to continue her studies and is working for a technical qualification with a view to employment as a laboratory technician.

The elder sons took wives from their own subdivision: girls from extremely poor families living in thatched huts alongside very low-status fishermen in Kollam district and described by villagers as 'practically dowry-less'. One daughter-in-law wore six bangles, a hair-piece, earrings and two necklaces, totalling 5 *pavans* (40 grammes, around Rs20,000) at her wedding. In the game of status strategy, Kuttiyil have succeeded in renouncing their degrading former occupations ('servants' and itinerant vendors), making money and obtaining the house filled with consumer goods which is many Malayalis' dream. Through wealth and Gulf connections they have also become potential patrons to those who claim status superiority. What the family has not yet been able to change, as malicious outsiders gleefully note, is their 'blackness' (*karutta*). When people finally spoke to us about Kuttiyil's low status, many thought we had already inferred it from the physical features many family members share: dark skin, broad noses, very curly hair. Status has, under the influence of European 'racial sciences' and colonial racial hierarchies, become essentialised and racialised, making the bodies and the interior of the person – 'essential qualities' and 'nature' – the final frontier on which mobility struggles are inscribed.

These daughters-in-law may have been poor but, like the Christian girl Mini who was welcomed in, they are exceptionally 'white', with the features (small or thin nose, high forehead, straight hair) widely admired by villagers (Osella & Osella 1996). These girls' dowry was their 'good looks' and the promise they give Kuttiyil in the very long-term of ridding itself of its hated 'darkness' which is holding back its claims to prestige, its self- and public images, and the chances of its girls – undesirably dark – in marriage. Current family members are often said by neighbours to be indistinguishable from Pulayas: after a couple of generations of careful marriage, grandchildren will be fair, possibly even able to 'pass' as Nayars. At that time, with wealth, education and beauty on their side, grand-daughters may easily be able to make advantageous marriages with 'ordinary' Izhavas, clearing the way for grandsons to take Izhava wives and eventually lifting the status of the whole family away from degraded subdivision and into 'Izhava proper'.

Modernity and mobility

Komalan, retired headmaster of a government primary school, and his wife Indira, government primary school teacher, have two daughters and one son. Komalan's father and mother were both *naluvittumar*, his tenant-cultivator father owning an acre of garden land planted with coconuts. Illiterate but in a better position than many of his caste-fellows, he paid for his son's studies at an NSS-run Teachers' Training College in town. While Komalan lives in a neighbourhood of predominantly poor Izhavas, his six-room brick and plaster house is larger and better maintained than those surrounding it. There is a water pump, gas cooker and fridge; dining room with tables and chairs; living room furnished with two upholstered vinyl sofas and several armchairs; a telephone stands on one small table and a colour television on another. As in many fashionable middle-class houses, a bad-tempered white Pomeranian dog, doted on and petted, runs around the rooms. Relations between Komalan and his neighbours, mostly poorer relatives, are strained. He does not let them use his telephone; more importantly, when they come every Sunday to watch the Malayalam film on his colour television he keeps them sitting on the doorstep. Komalan says that his neighbours are 'ignorant' and 'invasive'; he keeps to himself, preferring to mix socially with (middle-class) Nayar and Christian neighbours.

Komalan's son Anil Kumar, 29, graduated in chemistry but, unable to find a job, works as a salesman with a Christian Honda dealer in Krisnakara. The elder daughter Meena, 28, with BSc in mathematics and BEd married a USA-resident green-card holder in 1991. Komalan had begun looking for a husband for Meena while she was in her final year BEd. He immediately excluded Valiyagramam and surrounds from inquiries. He knew he could hope for a better match outside the area: Meena, a beautiful, pale-skinned double-graduate daughter of two school-teachers, had studied not – like most villagers – at the private college in Chantakara, but in the prestigious city of Bangalore, where she had obtained not only a more valuable paper qualification but also a degree of polish and *culture* that most village girls do not have. Meena held considerable value in the marriage market. Eventually, Meena's mother's brother found a very attractive match: a retired plantation supervisor living in Ootacamud was looking for a wife for his younger son Sahadevan. Sahadevan lives in New York, working as a clerk in a super-market; he had been taken to the USA by his elder brother, married to a hospital-employed nurse. The two families were put in touch with each other and horoscopes and photographs exchanged.

Two months later Sahadevan came on leave to Kerala, arriving one afternoon at Komalan's house accompanied by his brother and mother's brother. He came out of the taxi wearing Ray-Ban sunglasses and a baseball hat, corduroy jeans, T-shirt and Nike trainers while his brother, holding a video-camera, filmed the meeting; Sahadevan was eventually introduced to a shy-looking Meena, the third prospective bride he had seen that day. Impressed by her good-looks and qualifications as well as by the substantial dowry on offer, Sahadevan agreed there and then to the marriage. As in the case of most migrants, the wedding was arranged in haste: Sahadevan's leave could not be extended beyond another month.

For the wedding Komalan rented Dharmananda Asram marriage hall, a prestigious location on account both of high costs and size. Although many of Komalan's Izhava neighbours snubbed the wedding, it became – with over 800 guests – one of the largest of the year. Among the guests were many Christians and Nayars, friends and colleagues of Komalan and his wife. The groom arrived in an air-conditioned Ambassador car, dressed in a cream silk shirt and matching silk *mundu*. Meena, hair full of jasmine, carefully made-up by a professional beautician and wearing a heavy red silk and gold *sari*, walked shyly in looking like the ideal Hindu bride shown in jewellery shop advertisements, accompanied by the lights of two video-crews and two sets of professional photographers hired for the event.[14] The groom's relatives counted several sophisticated short-haired women among their number, some scandalously dressed in sunglasses and sleeveless *sari* blouses, never seen on local women. Several of the groom's men had expensive foreign cameras and were shooting rolls and rolls of film. Although the total amount of dowry remained anybody's guess, rumours putting it as high as four lakhs (Rs400,000), everybody agreed that Meena was wearing 101 *pavans* (808 grammes) of gold ornaments, a magical amount standard in elite and city marriages but in 1991 still a rarity in Valiyagramam.

After the wedding, Meena and Sahadevan left for Ootacamud; from there they visited Kanyakumari and Coimbatore on honeymoon, another unusual and scandalous notion for most villagers. After three weeks, Sahadevan returned to the USA; within six months he arranged a visa and Meena joined him; she has not been back to the village since. When we visited the family in 1995, Anil told us proudly that he had become an *ammavan*, while his mother passed around an album of pictures recently arrived from the USA, showing the progress of her grandson. Meena, her son and husband were expected soon, hopefully for Onam. Anil had been once to the USA to visit and is now counting time while confidently waiting to be 'called' to the USA by his brother-in-law. Komalan is very pleased with developments: he paid the highest dowry he could afford but now, when Anil himself goes to the USA to become a green-card holder, the money will come back. With both son and daughter in the USA, marrying the younger daughter Beena will be easy and relatively inexpensive. Komalan and his wife will soon loosen local ties further as they begin the peripatetic life common to migrants' parents, moving between the village and the USA.

CONCLUSIONS

Marriage reforms, unification of the caste and the abolition of matriliny have encouraged expansion of affinal ties and formation of a wide-ranging marriage market this century. An ever-decreasing number of marriages are arranged within the kin group and village as Izhavas look outside for more advantageous 'stranger' alliances. This has been accompanied by moves towards more prestigious styles of marriage, as isogamous alliance is spurned in favour of hypergamy and marriage is spoken of in *kanyadanam* idiom. This last development both legitimises and actually sanctifies payment of large amounts to wife-takers, enabling 'groom price' and the subtle extortion which often accompanies it to be euphemised and converted into a prestigious unsolicited affinal gift between families thereby deemed to be 'respectable' and 'cultured'.

It is comparatively rare among Izhavas with mobility aspirations to find 'marriages of equals', since marriage is one of the major mobility strategies; despite the high risks involved, most feel under a compulsion to make strategic use of it and few are in a position to renounce the opportunities it offers. Factors are traded off in the overall long-term interests of the group, and are 'juggled' according to the particular strategy being played out at each particular marriage. While the underlying strategic motives for making a particular match may remain implicit and hidden, several public discourses – rooted in different ideological sources – can be called upon post hoc publicly to justify marriage choice (cf. Bourdieu 1990: 159). All informants claimed that ideally the two families in a potential alliance should be matched as equal, while the boy should be slightly higher than the girl in education, age, height, salary (if both working). Since 'marriages of equals' carry lower dowries than asymmetrical alliances, appeal can then be made to one version of orthodoxy – as represented by official reform discourses such as the SNDP view of marriage – which states that to receive dowry (as opposed to the 'girl's share', which is acceptable) is a shameful practice which only the corrupt and impoverished would resort to. The convenient fact that dowry between equals will be lower can also be turned into a prestige issue and a moral virtue also for the girl's family: 'We don't need to buy good husbands for our daughters; because we are a respected family, our women are also respected, and so the grooms will come anyway.'

Marrying up is by now the usual pattern and requires no justification from the girl's side; her family take pride in saying 'We sent our daughter to a good family', following the view of marriage as an alliance with a superior family effected by means of the daughter. Although hypergamous marriage into another caste may be a matter if not of shame at least of regret, even this can be something to be proud of for the girl's family, since it replicates the behaviour of the higher castes in former times and conforms to the dominant discourse, which sees women as a means by which to increase family prestige and to effect useful alliances with higher-status families. Like old-time Nayars who consider themselves favoured by having had contact with Brahmans, a girl's family are generally convinced that their daughter and her children will benefit from exposure to more refined ways. There is no requirement on a bride's family to justify marriage to patently superior outsiders, since everybody fully understands that to give your daughter up means full success in the marriage stakes. It shows that the girl and her family are acceptable partners for valued superiors, that the family did the 'best thing' for their daughter and for the advancement of the family. Full scorn is reserved for hypogamous marriages, which 'lower the woman', if they don't actually prove that she was never any good in the first place and which violate every rule of correct hierarchy within *jati* and gender and the mobility imperative. In the last analysis, intermarriage with Europeans shows that Izhava family mobility ambitions override orthodoxy and adherence to the caste hierarchies which have most often been experienced from the wrong side by Izhavas.

Again we find that the poor suffer from the community's mobility ethic, being shamed into abandoning strategies (cross-cousin and polyandrous marriages) harking back to the Izhava unreformed past and finding themselves increasingly forced to run up debts and take risks with their children by at least pretending to participate in the dowried stranger-marriage alliance game. At the same time, their attempts can only ever be pale imitations of the real thing, increasing their discomfort and the stigmatisation. Those who can and do participate fully in the practice of using marriage as a means to mobility take a broad view and a very long-term orientation, prioritising not the transient immediate household but the enduring family unit (*kutumbam*): the plans of Kuttiyil and of Komalan will take another two generations to mature fully, the eventual benefits of current alliances – higher status, residence abroad – being enjoyed by the grandchildren of those who spend the money and take such pains to make marriage arrangements.

Izhava class and status mobility ambitions are rooted in ever-expanding horizons. In the nineteenth century Kuttakkakaran Sekharan Channar (Chapter 2) played on a strictly local stage, competing with high-caste Hindu neighbours and asserting wealth and prestige within southern Travancore by buying an elephant, usually the prerogative of Nayars. In the early twentieth century, K.V. Krishnan (Chapter 1) moved into a wider arena, leaving behind his natal village for the high-range plantations and looking beyond the styles of local Nayars towards the colonial British; buying and driving foreign cars, he became a pace-setter on grand scale, part of the India-wide consumption elite. In the late twentieth century, the stage has expanded still further and Izhavas look beyond India towards international innovators and a global stage, competing with Non-Resident Indians (NRIs), Arabs and Europeans. In the arena of consumption behaviour to which we will now turn, this century's rapid expansion of horizons and aspirations becomes most clear.

4 CONSUMPTION: PROMISES OF ESCAPE

Izhavas' abstracted ideals and identity of mobility, as applied to units of 'family' and 'community', only make sense when objectified and measured over time, when strategies' success can be evaluated. Marriage is the important first stage towards setting up a new household: a unit of objectification through which social mobility can be gauged, differences between original and new units explicitly revealing the degree of mobility achieved over generations. A new household plainly concretises wealth and prestige in the size and quality of the house and the extent and location of landholdings, as do the people in the house who, with their particular possessions, culture and behaviour, are embodiments of 'family' and 'community' mobility.

Izhava strategic consumption practices are highly focused upon improving and refining these objectifications: extending and decorating houses; buying land; providing household members with goods and services calculated to demonstrate, achieve or facilitate social mobility, understood as a very long-term project extending well beyond the lifetime of those who accumulate the initial cash (cf. Carrier & Heyman 1997; Wilk 1989, 1994: 102; Rowland 1994: 155ff). Indeed, the lion's share of household spending for the benefit of persons is often channelled towards children, representing the family's progress to date, its still-growing and evolving changes in wealth and prestige, and its future mobility ambitions.

Upwardly mobile Izhavas, non-mobile, would-be mobile and already high-prestige professionals all participate, to greater or lesser degrees, and in different styles and arenas, in strategic consumption. A clear local distinction exists between transient forms such as fashion, oriented towards the person and the body, and especially associated with the young and the low-status, and more widely valued long-term and fixed forms such as land and housing, oriented towards values of permanency and the household group. Consumer durables, as relatively affordable portable property associated with domestic life, stand between the two extremes. Longer-term consumption practices articulate with the pan-Indian figure of the householder, the mature man-in-the-world associated with values of social reproduction (Madan 1987;

Dumont 1970a). Mobility trajectories also clearly articulate with life-cycles, as people's spending patterns change over time, young men spending cash freely on ephemeral and personal pleasures of fashion and cinema, young would-be householders buying domestic and luxury goods, and mature householders channelling substantial wealth into future-oriented investment in housing and children.

Consumption is an important arena for capital conversion and prestige embodiment: as the range and cost of goods available to villagers continues to increase, this role can only grow. While many Izhavas, especially among the locally employed less wealthy sections of the educated Left (school-teachers, petty government employees) remain highly critical of escalating consumption levels, many more welcome the opportunity to participate, competing with Nayar and Christian neighbours. We have seen that Izhavas as a group have historically resisted being defined by their putative role in production, refusing the 'toddy-tapper' label; for many 1990s workers, employed in low-prestige sectors as manual labourers, auto-drivers, shop assistants, tailors and so on, there is still no benefit in a social identity defined in terms of relations of production. Production continues to retain characteristics linking it to status: Izhava caste status is still linked to definitions of the community as 'toddy-tappers'; the most popular form of employment among Brahmans is school-teaching; most agricultural labourers are Pulayas. All this makes employment a less promising and significant arena for escape from caste hierarchy and for construction of a new identity than consumption. The increasing importance of consumption is also linked both to migration and to economic liberalisation, which have brought new and more expensive goods into the village. For migrant workers in particular, who form the vanguard of consumption activity, sites of production are hidden, far removed from the village; this works to their advantage as public attention turns upon spending behaviour where they take a prominent role in consumption, rather than upon their labour, likely to be low or unskilled work.

A focus on consumption works to the advantage of all those with cash to spend. The prestige associated with both Nayar and Christian communities is partly rooted in community orientations to consumption, Nayars being associated with the lavish spending nineteenth-century landowner-patron (*janmi thamburan*), and Christians with twentieth-century innovations in general and the cash-rich *planter* in particular. For the aspirantly mobile, Miller's characterisation of consumption as an empowering and ultimately egalitarian act which allows consumers, 'to employ their resources for the self-construction of their individual and social identity' rings true to hopes (1995a: 42). However, constraints posed by caste status remain such that ex-untouchables such as Izhavas cannot hope to adopt a wholly new identity simply by changing consumption patterns (see Campbell 1995: 113). Yet again we find that a mobility strategy – consumption – largely excludes those living at or below subsistence levels, the poor and weak, traditionally excluded and of low status and now unable to participate in all but one or two specialised (and often marginal) consumption arenas. 'Consumption, as a means for self-realisation and incorporation of symbolic value' simultaneously creates, according to Gell, 'a negative self whose contours are defined by the economically imposed limits of increasing personal consumption indefinitely' (1988: 46–7; cf. Grusky 1994a). Participating in certain consumption arenas (for example private education) and specific style(s) also allows consumers eventually to gain further economic benefits, simultaneously penalising and excluding non-consumers. The politics of consumption are, then, not exclusively politics of identity but also of inequality (Carrier & Heyman 1997) and yet again we find that the multiplier effects of capital give a headstart in the mobility game to those who already have something (Bourdieu 1990: 118ff).

FASHION AND THE POOR

The poorest villagers, meaning almost all Pulayas and a good proportion of Izhavas, are strongly rooted within the local economy, working as manual and agricultural labourers or providing services like dressmaking and housework; they rely upon employers or neighbourhood patrons for loans, their purchases largely limited to what can be bought locally and consisting mostly of subsistence items. It makes little difference to a widow like Mohanna, doing outwork for a match factory and whose daughter works at the market making children's clothes, whether her family is stigmatised for its lowly position in production or in consumption, in which it hardly participates: the results are the same. Those who have little cash nevertheless participate in consumption, albeit on a smaller scale and often in different arenas from the mainstream. It is the most excluded section of village population – ex-untouchable manual labourers – who act as the vanguard of certain styles of clothing, hairstyles and music.

While both sexes participate in fashion, women, who dress in *Kairali-style* (*sari* or *churidar*) remain largely limited to changing patterns in fabrics and colours; while men, who may dress in *Kairali* (*mundu* or *lungi*, sandals) or *European-style* (pants, shoes) clothing, have more avenues open. Those excluded from buying originals copy prestigious patterns, but increasing diversification of male clothing styles is making this difficult: while fake designer labels can be bought in the cities to be sewn into tailored clothes and while a manual labourer can have a copy of a film hero's shirt made by a local 'stitching centre', he can less easily duplicate a Raymonds or Van Heusen shirt, whose material is exclusive and whose finishing is recognisably different from that of the local tailor. A Gulf-imported Lacoste polo shirt, be it authentic or a cheaper duplicate, is completely out of reach. Alternative styles which do not depend upon expensive ready-mades or unattainable imports are taken up.

Denied the opportunity to participate in many arenas, fashion – something cheap and transient, and which is oriented towards the individual, modernity and the external world, away from caste, agriculture and the village – is one domain in which the low-status reign. Young Pulayas in particular appropriate styles from films – Hindi, Tamil and Malayalam – and competitively exaggerate them. At festivals where all young people try to be 'sharp' and 'shine',[1] Pulayas stand out: dressed and coiffed with utmost care, young women wear up-to-the-minute *sari* blouses and the latest cheap fashion accessories such as hair-slides and imitation jewellery, while young men sport extreme haircuts and clothing. While women remain constrained to local dress styles, fashion being expressed in changing designs and especially fabrics of *churidars* and *saris*, young men experiment with hyper-fashion: the baggiest baggies, African cuts (Apache Indian style) in their hair, and extravagant shirt designs. All this is reminiscent of the vanguard roles of the working class, particularly the black working class, in British fashion, popular music and 'street style', while bringing us close to the worlds of Miller's Trinidadian *saga* boys and of the Congolese *sapeur* (Gilroy 1993: 72ff; Miller 1994a, 1994b: 75; Friedman 1994: 176ff; cf. Maher 1987; Rowland 1994). A red satin shirt or puff-sleeved lurex sari blouse take the wearer far away from the person in old and shabby clothing who labours in the paddy fields (cf. Gell 1986). Bright synthetic shirts, baggy trousers and cheap trainers are also worn in defiant opposition to the sober white cotton shirt, *mundu* and *cerippu* of the high-caste Hindu.

This fashion vanguard has recently been addressed in south India by a series of movies celebrating the youth culture partly born of the cinema. The Malayali film *Street*, released in 1994, features ragga-inspired male clothing styles,[2] rap music ('the new wave music for a new generation', announces the cassette) and lyrics in Manglish such as 'Streetil Tharikidathom', celebrating the life of the street with a *sambhashanam* including the line, 'I did so many rubbish things in my life'. The big Tamil hit of 1995, 'Kaadhalan', centres around Prabhu Deva, a hero with bleached hair, Ray-Ban shades and a red bandana who would not look out of place in any metropolitan inner city. One of the film's hit songs, 'Urvasi, Take It Easy', celebrates oppositional youth street culture and transience, satirising grandmothers, pilgrims, elder brothers and examination failures, and advising the young to face modern life's pressures and celebrate physicality with a 'Take it easy policy' (cf. Miller 1994a).

When one Pulaya couple announced their intention to marry, young boys in the *Harijan colony* where they live burst into the latest Tamil film-songs whenever one of the pair passed by, teasing them further by accompanying their singing with lascivious disco or break-dancing and improvisation, changing the song lyrics to include the names of the betrothed. This degree of celebration of freedom, romance and physicality is not generally found in mainstream society, which demands restraint and adherence to bourgeois notions of respectability.

Young Izhavas dress carefully and participate less enthusiastically in cinema culture, maintaining with care a line between themselves and

Pulayas. Premadasan's son went to Mumbai in 1989 joking that he might become an underworld king, modelling his style upon that of the Mumbai film villain or *goonda*; these days he has no such *filmi* ambitions, and favours appropriately more subdued self-presentation. Meena warned us to be careful of a young man with the latest haircut and a shirt so fashionably baggy it almost reached his knees; she could tell, she assured us, that he was no good, because he was always extremely fashionable (*bhaiyankara chettu*). Being extremely fashionable is widely associated in the mainstream with low-life and with *Harijan style*, and it is here that the situation diverges from that in the Congo: an Yves St Laurent suit is an item of cost and quality whether worn by African *sapeur* or Parisian businessman; a Malayali labourer's shiny shirt has little value outside its own highly limited sphere (cf. Kopytoff 1986; Parry & Bloch 1989). Villagers also refer to something known rudely as *Pandy style*, Tamil style, another non-prestigious mode of self-presentation which they identify as something taken up by Pulayas of all ages, consisting of a preference for bright colours and strong designs in clothing, said to be favoured by those with dark skin. Among most people outside of *Harijan colonies* where Pulayas and a few Izhavas live segregated from the rest of the village, fashion vanguardism is enjoyed on film, its use in daily life limited. Past the age of 25, most Izhava young people, like their Nayar and Christian counterparts, abandon hyper-fashion altogether.

In 1995, Tamil director Mani Ratnam had two big all-India hits, both shown (in Tamil versions) at local cinemas. The hero of *Bombay*, actor Aravind Swami, is pale-skinned, with straight hair and an aquiline nose. His character, a high-caste Hindu working as a journalist in Mumbai, an educated man of substance and status, works as investigator and peacemaker during a period of communal violence. For the hit love song ('Kannalanae') he wears a horizontally striped jersey shirt which would appeal to mainstream European or North American tastes in casual wear or sportswear. When romance turns to passion, bourgeois hero and heroine are replaced for the sexy song ('Andha Arabi Kadaloram'), by a dancing couple in lavish red, white and gold, who uninhibitedly express sexual desire and a more general sense of bodily freedom, in contrast to the hero and heroine's restraint and timidity (cf. Miller 1991). The male dancer, wearing an outfit reminiscent of Michael Jackson's 'Bad' period, is a clone of Deva, hero of the film *Kaadhalan* with its 'take it easy policy' message. With his extremely curly hair, darker skin tone, street-style baggy clothes and lubricious dancing, he is identifiably of different origins and style from the hero: we read his style as modern, young and working class (cf. Pandian 1992 on M.G. Ramachandran's 'proletarian appeal').

Among the middle-class young men around Valiyagramam who bought *Bombay*'s romantic-hero style horizontally striped polo shirts (available at Rs400 from air-conditioned Raymond's Suiting showrooms in Thiruvananthapuram or Ernakulam cities), were a Nayar travel agent, a Christian rice-mill owner and an Izhava electrician. Baggies, loose shirt with gold thread and Michael-Jackson style kiss-curl dangling on the forehead, as worn by *Bombay*'s sexy dance hero, were not much seen outside of the day-labourers' colonies. The hyper-fashionable and outrageous heroes of *Kaadhalan* and of *Bombay*'s sexy dance number are not figures for emulation among those aspiring to prestige, unlike the unambiguously high-status and middle-class actor, Aravind Swami, whose *style* is anyway unaffordable to most labourers.

Let's now turn then to the question of which orientations towards consumption are widely taken up among Izhavas.

DIFFERENT CONSUMPTION STYLES

Attitudes to Austerity

As suggested in Chapter 2, labouring Izhavas are stigmatised within their community by reason of low-status occupation and putative lack of education and sophistication, placing them dangerously close to Pulayas. Their condition of poverty, commonly referred to euphemistically as *progress illa* (no progress), is further amply demonstrated by their inability to engage in prestige-oriented consumption, progress's commonest indicator. Poor Izhavas' houses are almost bare of furniture, the only wall decorations a picture of Narayana Guru and some old illustrated calendars. Men own just one white, durable, synthetic *mundu* and a couple of white shirts for special occasions, and a couple of patterned *lungis* for everyday wear. Women have a couple of synthetic *saris*, using blouse and *lungi* for daily wear, and own no gold jewellery other than the thin chain holding their *tali*. New clothes are rarely bought; children's clothes and women's blouses are stitched at home. With no permanent income source, these families rely on loan-sharks or patrons to make ends meet during lean periods.

Unlike Pulayas, who stand together and – justifiably – cite continuing severe discrimination, past slavery and overall low initial material status as reasons for failure of mobility, Izhava manual labourers are stigmatised within their own community. Their poverty is commonly and uncharitably imputed by others to causes other than un- or under-employment and attributed instead to a combination of ignorance and lack of restraint. 'They [poor Izhavas] want to be big', commented Satyan, a successful Izhava entrepreneur, 'They want to earn at least 200 rupees per day, and every night go to the toddy-shop and spend everything, like kings. Maybe the next day there is no work and no money, but they don't think of it.' Besides being denounced for heavy drinking, a practice associated (as we have seen) to low-status labouring classes and to the caste's degraded past, these Izhavas are also accused of misplaced consumption, or of not complying with Narayana Guru's exhortations to conduct a thrifty life, saving, investing in productive activities and stopping unnecessarily expensive expenditure, for example on life-cycle rituals. Like Pulayas, they are assumed to have an inability to plan, defer gratification and think strategically.[3]

On the other side, criticisms of 'irrational consumerism' are widely extended towards Gulf migrants. State government and policy planners expected that income generated by Gulf migration would yield not only obvious benefits to migrants and their families but would also induce wider economic development (cf. P.A. Kurien 1994: 759). This anticipated 'trickle down' effect has so far failed to materialise. Contrary to optimistic expectations, while Gulf migration did little to overcome economic stagnation (Isaac & Tharakan 1995: 11–12), it generated, among other things, inflationary rises in prices (for example, of land and building materials), salaries (for example, in the construction business) and the state's trade deficit (for example, via imports of expensive consumer goods from neighbouring states) (Nair 1989: 352ff). One popular view attributes Gulf migration's shortcomings to the alleged 'economic irrationality' and selfishness of migrants who, rather than invest remittances and savings in productive enterprises, indulge in expensive lifestyles, and whose extravagant *nouveau-riche* habits have transformed Kerala into a consuming rather than producing state. Against this, in Valiyagramam, as in other Gulf migrant communities in Pakistan (for example Shahnaz Kazi 1989; Addleton 1992), Bangladesh (for example Osmani 1986), Sri-Lanka (for example Eelens & Schampers 1992; Mook 1992; Brochmann 1992, 1993) and elsewhere in Kerala (for example Mathew & Nair 1978; Nair 1986; P.A. Kurien 1994; Nair & Pillai 1994), only a small portion of Gulf money is used for acquisition of luxury goods: the majority of migrants, having repaid debts, met social obligations and provided for basic needs, have little left to invest in major enterprises (cf. Nair 1986: 100).

By contrast, successful adoption of an austere endeavour is often presented as piecemeal explanation for the relative social and economic success of some sections of Izhavas. Sunderan, retired ferryman and solid SNDP supporter, asserted:

Izhavas are prepared to do any job: we are hard workers – that is why we came up. Nayars are lazy and want to sit the whole day at home doing nothing. They used to be rich, but spent all their money on drinking and big Onam feasts.

In similar tone Matthew, Christian ex-Gulf migrant and owner of a local cinema and a modern printing business, argued, 'Hindus squander money to maintain status; in the past they used lots of money to celebrate Onam. They would sell their land to do so, which was bought by Christians.' Matthew – practising Protestant – and Sunderan – drawing an opposition between modern reformed Izhava practices and the decadent and ultimately self-defeating past practices of the upper castes – remind us of popular colonial discourses conjuring pictures of Travancore as a feudal society ruled by despotic Rajahs and corrupt local rulers with no consideration for their subjects, interested solely in the immediate satisfactions of sensual pleasure and self-aggrandisement (cf. Price 1996).

On analysis, small businesses set up by ex-migrants belong either to those who profited from the first wave of migration in the 1970s, when opportunities were many, wages were good and possibilities of accumulation were genuinely high, or to those holding higher-paid highly skilled or professional employment. The mass of Izhava migrants are newcomers to migration and usually working in less well-paid and lower-skilled jobs. Those with sufficient economic resources who do invest choose to put their money into businesses in neighbouring states, claiming that profits are severely limited locally by high labour costs and lack of adequate infrastructures.

Satyan, an Izhava returned to Valiyagramam after 30 years in Muscat (Oman), is exceptional. When his father – a small shopkeeper – died, leaving the family in poverty, his mother went to work as a labourer while Satyan supported his studies by agricultural labour. In 1963, after passing matriculation, he went to Mumbai to work as apprentice engineer for a motor company. Nine years later, recruited by an English company, he went to Muscat.

At that time Muscat was only sand; I was the first Izhava from Valiyagramam to go to the Gulf. My manager, a Britisher, put me in charge of the diesel-maintenance workshop. After a few weeks I told him that we didn't have appropriate machinery to do the job properly; he said that there was no money to invest but I could use any extra profits I could make from the workshop to buy new equipment. I worked very hard doing lots of overtime and we became the best service station in west Asia. Although I was much liked and well paid, in 1990 I decided to return to Valiyagramam. I thought that I could take the risk; being qualified, I can always go back to the Gulf. So I imported an engineer's testing bench from Germany and started a diesel workshop. All my friends said I was a fool and would soon lose all my money, but I let them talk. I calculated things very well, like a bank investment, and I know the trade very well: I learnt it from the British and Germans. In Kerala there may be labour problems, but employers are part of the problem. If you pay well and treat workers well, they'll work sincerely. I work together with my employees; help them out, stay with them the whole time and always pay salaries on time. There are twelve diesel services in Kerala, but other owners only work as managers, turning up in the afternoon to give orders and go back home; every day I am the first one in the workshop.

Satyan is a remarkable example of the ethic of restraint and industry preached by Narayana Guru and later adopted by the SNDP as a necessary step to ensure the caste's economic progress. For many Izhavas, especially those wishing to maintain or increase respectability and prestige with limited economic resources, ethics of prudence are invoked to justify, without loss of face, hard labour and low consumption levels. However, this stance cannot be maintained as long-term strategy: after an initial phase of capital accumulation, *progress* should be demonstrated and publicly acknowledged by keeping up with levels and styles of consumption of those to whose status and prestige one aspires: the Nayar and Christian middle classes (cf. Lipset et al. 1994: 255–6). Since 1991, with implementation of economic liberalisation and subsequent introduction of bank consumer loans, pressure to conform has become even greater. Madhu – retired government clerk, Communist activist and active SNDP member – always took pride in his saving abilities, carefully recording in a diary every expense, planning future purchases in detail; he continually mocked the alleged spending excesses of the *nouveaux riches*. By 1995, however, he had spent Rs30,000 on a marble floor for his front room and doorstep. Apparently feeling that this unexpected change in attitude required justification, he told us:

What could I do? I come from a good family; as an ex-government employee and *social worker* I am respected by everyone around here; I also have a daughter to marry. Nowadays everyone has marble floors: I had to get one myself, otherwise people would think that I am poor (*pavam*) or stingy (*pisakkukku*).

Other recent acquisitions include a table fan and a black and white television. To support increased consumption demands, Madhu turned his back on retirement to become, aged 60, an LIC agent. Still his daughter complains that he has worked hard and long for very little, comparing the family's home with that of their migrant neighbours whose television is colour and whose marble flooring is of the costliest quality, imported from distant Rajasthan, not nearby Andhra – instantly recognisable. She declares that she will never marry a government employee like her father because these people are just little people, always worrying about money and penny-pinching. She hopes to marry a migrant.

Referents for Consumption

Activity in consumption arenas is not limited to those needing prestige. Local Brahmans have not felt the need to enter wider production arenas, searching for wealth and occupational prestige; they hold and are the villagers most oriented towards caste-based forms of status, relatively independent of income or occupational status. Brahmans' relative lack of interest in new forms of production is not mirrored by their attitudes towards consumption: village Brahmans own colour televisions, stereo cassettes and Honda kinetic scooters. Many of the items being widely bought – vehicles, clothing, entertainment equipment – conform to Appadurai's characterisation of 'luxury goods': restricted; complexity of acquisition; capacity to signify complex social messages; requiring specialised knowledge; a high degree of linkage to body, person and personality (1986: 38).

While Izhavas oriented towards SNDP or Leftist criticisms of consumption as an activity per se operate double standards commending thrift and modest living while spending, the majority – wealthy, mobile or even poor – criticise distribution of resources but do not see anything inherently problematic in consumption. For a community struggling to throw off the stigma of production-based caste roles as toddy-tappers and agricultural manual labourers, an increasing focus on consumption as source of identity is advantageous (Gilroy 1993; Miller 1987, 1995a, 1995b). At the same time, consumption offers the chance to make money work twice: cash purchases simultaneously display economic capital while converting it. When examining upwardly mobile Izhavas' current consumption practices several historical facts need to be kept in mind: first the presence in Travancore, up to the early twentieth century, of rigid and jealously enforced sumptuary laws. Certain styles of clothing, jewellery, housing and so on were forbidden to Izhavas, reserved for high-caste Hindus (Jeffrey 1993: 62; Mathew 1989: 76; Kooiman 1989: 148–54; cf. Bourdieu 1994: 121 on the codification of symbolic capital implied in sumptuary law). Past exclusion of large parts of the population from many significant areas of consumption regardless of economic status has led, then, to over-determination of present practice, seen at work in several areas. Previous restrictions on usage of gold and jewellery have contributed to their current lavish use, as those to whom these ornaments were formerly forbidden enthusiastically purchase and wear them: jewellery designs said to be 'traditionally Nayar' or 'Brahman' are especially popular. Similarly, it is not surprising that those to whom two-storeyed houses were previously prohibited as not fitting to their caste status should now, given the opportunity, save and spend to construct lavish mansions. A related fact is that of a special relationship between lavish consumption and nineteenth-century Hindu kings or petty chiefs, exaggerated through colonial accounts and in popular memory (cf. Rao et al. 1992; Price 1996).

Consumption is the main way of showing wealth, and has been for many years: *thamburanmar* had a lavish standard of living and gave gifts to their dependants, to whom they acted as employer, landlord and patron. Figures like the ancestor of the village's former *janmi* are renowned and remembered for the sumptuousness of their feasts, the extravagance of their gifts and the opulence of their lifestyle: in short, the scale of their spending. Members of titled Izhava families stressed to us that titles were available from the king on payment of large sums, emphasising that their status is rooted in (past) wealth and spending. Even Pulaya agricultural labourers told us that their headman (*valluvan*) at the turn of the century had ridden on a costly white horse. Where wealth and high-caste status, poverty and low status, went closely hand in hand and where the rule of *noblesse oblige* required ruling classes to spend heavily, consumption takes on a substantial status aspect. Meanwhile consumption is not simply expression of relative wealth but is a long-term investment in the family. Many areas of high spending, (such as health care, dowries, private education), are those in which the recipients' personal qualities are improved; it is here, in the bodies of persons who are embodiment and objectification of the casted family, that class shades off into status (cf. Pocock 1993: 336–7).

Turning to recent history, Izhavas' rejection of nineteenth-century status and adoption of a modernist future-oriented endeavour means that they are highly attuned both to class status – strongly oriented towards consumption – and more generally towards the actions of those identified with modernity. The early twentieth-century plantation owner K.V. Krishnan (Chapter 1) followed his European boss in buying a car; later others, like Advocate

Remini's father, followed suit. Satyan, trained with British and Germans, consciously models his lifestyle on Gulf-resident Europeans. Recently both Christian community and Gulf migrants have acted as innovators in production, taking up new employment opportunities and, in consumption, bringing new items and practices into the village.

Villagers – particularly those such as Izhavas and Christians for whom the past holds no glories and is relatively uninteresting as compared to Nayars and Brahmans – identify the modernity which they embrace with consumption and with the relatively wealthy Arabs, Europeans and North Americans who appear to be masters of it. Migrants are agents linking Valiyagramam to the modern consumption elites of these developed zones. The arrival in his ancestral village of a New York resident, video camera in hand, and the return via Dubai duty-free shop of a successful Gulf migrant are examples of ways in which consumption levels are accelerated and set with reference to a wider global economy. Meanwhile liberalisation has led to the growth of the consuming middle class within India itself. The increasing number of televisions in the village monitor these changes, as villagers learn about – and local shops begin to stock – minor items such as Sunsilk shampoo and Wrigley's gum, available in small sizes and as occasional purchases even to the less well-off. The Gulf remains the main referent for ideas about consumption; while the more sophisticated professional elite discusses the relative merits of Singapore or Malaysia for shopping, even villagers who have never been to the Gulf can recount with enthusiasm the range of goods available in Muscat or Sharjah.

Consumption practices offer opportunities to display knowledge, taste and discrimination. The colonial period saw mass-manufactured branded items becoming available; connotations of high-quality, prestigious foreign-ness, and goods' associations with the powerful colonialists made names like Cadbury's desirable and familiar (cf. Achaya 1994). Branding is becoming increasingly important since a wider range of goods have come into the village and advertising has focused villagers' attention. Class status is increasingly being shown by careful, knowing consumption, taking on an air of distinction (Bourdieu 1984). A small packet of Pomsy brand fried potato snacks, ready to eat and available at village bakeries for Rs5, carries more cachet than a plate of the same potato snacks fried at home, bought from the baker at Rs5 for a half-kilo unbranded packet providing six or more servings. Styles and tastes are hierarchically arranged, brand-names acting as markers of distinction: a Keltron (Kerala Electronics; a state enterprise) television confers less prestige than an Onida, Indian made, which, in turn, is not as good as a Sony made under licence in India, with maximum prestige attached to foreign-made, imported televisions. Global brand Nivea face-cream is more prestigious than Indian brand Himalaya Snow, while those really in the know prefer imported Nivea over locally bought, Indian-made versions of the product. Sometimes people leave the labels on consumer durables to emphasise their origins.

The latest fashion among 'modern' and wealthy villagers in 1996 was the Honda Kinetic scooter – highly costly at Rs34,000, but demonstrating wealth and prestige in a way that an Indian-branded Bajaj cannot. Bajaj's attempts to appeal to patriotism with their 'Hamara Bajaj' advertisements went unheeded in Valiyagramam, where even RSS activists are buying Honda Kinetics (although some re-spray them saffron). Hierarchies of consumption result, based around access to and knowledge of goods and services. Certain distinctive styles are apparent, oriented towards particular consumption circuits and referring to indigenous and foreign elites. Preferences for goods from afar, preferably foreign, like the recent increasing preference for marriages conducted outside the village suggests the advantage for those with mobility aspirations to the appropriation of prestige through literal, physical mobility and incorporation of the 'Outside' (cf. Friedman 1994; Rowland 1994; Wilk 1994; Miller 1994a,1994b). Family units seek to expand their prestige through expansion of the territories to which they are linked, and through appropriation of valued items (goods, languages, styles, brides, sons-in-law) coming from outside.

Styles and Circuits of Consumption

One type draws upon urban Indian style and is based upon items bought by indigenous middle classes. People spend in local markets, going at most to the cities to buy, for example, women's printed silk *saris* and men's ready-made shirts by Indian big names who advertise in the Malayalam and English press (for example Garden Vareli, Bombay Dyeing). Engineer Sadashivan, Advocate Remini and Prabhakaran teacher keep an eye on styles arriving from the Indian metropolises and available locally in shops such as Anjali Saris – a three-storeyed air-conditioned luxury showroom – and Making Time – a smart glass-fronted shop selling only watches and clocks from desirable brand names such as Titan; both businesses are newly opened in Krisnakara town. Within Indian-oriented styles, films are an important reference for both middle-class and popular fashions in clothing and hair. Manufacturers and local tailors produce many different versions of new fashion items, in various qualities and at varying costs. Kappa Parambil Maniamma's daughter, a dressmaker, told us that she is never out of work because each new film brings in a new style, which people want copied immediately. Female fashions are also heavily featured in colour articles in women's magazines such as *Vanitha*, permitting participation even to those prohibited from cinema-going; when Caroline admired Sulekha's new *churidar*, with patches splashed across it, Sulekha, (15), proudly pointed out both that it was *Mani Chitrayude Tazhe-style*, as worn by the heroine of the latest Malayalam film, and that it was a *ready-made* and not a cheap copy.

Increasingly, television is also becoming a source of information about styles, Malayalam and Hindi serials on Doordarshan having recently been supplemented by foreign *telenovelas* on satellite and cable, available locally since 1995. The effects of being able to see Arabic and Japanese Top Ten music videos, American-produced serials like *The Bold and the Beautiful* and *Santa Barbara*, Euro-soaps such as *Riviera*, shows dealing with (often remote) social issues like Oprah Winfrey's, and a never-ending supply of old Tamil movies, have yet to be felt: our experience in 1995 was that most households turned the television on for limited and specific periods to watch Malayalam films, serials and news and Top Ten film songs in Malayalam, Hindi and Tamil, but that other programmes were largely ignored (cf. Das 1995). At the same time, if global television styles become part of Indian metropolitan culture, they may then filter into the village in mediated form.

Another style is oriented towards the world of the *sahippu*, the white-skinned. This includes consumption practices associated with colonial and commonwealth styles and has become merged with styles drawn from migration to English-speaking countries. Examples are the use of Christmas cake, wine and Christmas cards (by Hindus as well as Christians), watching football on video or cable television and the wearing of jackets and waistcoats by men and short dresses instead of *pavada* by little girls. Experienced retailers such as Pushpa Department Stores in Krisnakara's Anglo-Indian neighbour-hood and Spencers in Thiruvananthapuram cantonment, catering for many years to a limited clientele composed mainly of Anglo-Indians and wealthy Christians, have recently experienced a boom in business as they expand their lines from Anglo exotics such as jelly crystals and gripe water to include recent arrivals such as Maggi instant noodles, Nescafé instant coffee and Gillette shaving cream in an aerosol. Even smaller general shops in Krisnakara and Chantakara now stock disposable nappies, anti-perspirant and chewing gum. Since members of the prestigious and wealthy CSI (Church of South India) congregation had closest associations with the colonial British, and since those families with members living in the UK, USA or Australia are mostly Christians, it is not surprising that members of these communities tend to be the most adept at and keen to embrace this style (cf. Luhrmann 1996). Meanwhile, participation remains limited to certain aspects: most villagers remain horrified by manifestations of this style in self-presentation commonly seen in Chennai and occasionally in Ernakulam city, such as Bermuda shorts for men or short hair for women. Those few Izhavas with relatives migrated to the English-speaking world confess that they find them a little too foreign on their visits to the village: their dress and behaviour embarrasses, while they complain about what they see as the village's lack of amenities and primitive facilities, something hard to understand for their non-migrant relatives, who, comparing Gulf-rich Valiyagramam to other parts of Kerala or India, cannot but think that the village is highly advanced.

These styles, referring to indigenous, colonial and foreign elites, obviously overlap; for example Indian metropolitan style partly draws upon colonial and USA/UK-derived fashions. These used to be pre-eminent for those with wealth and prestige, but are being increasingly challenged by a style oriented towards another centre of consumer power: the professional classes of west Asia. Again, the styles we are describing obviously shade into each other, so that 'Gulf style' cannot always be clearly distinguished: many of those working in the Gulf are from the English-speaking world; some items available there and popular in Valiyagramam – such as men's white training shoes – are global products not specific to the Gulf; the Gulf itself is subject to influences from Europe and the USA. As a global bazaar, in which goods from west and east are available and as the most important source of prestige goods and styles, the Gulf is becoming increasingly dominant as the pace-setter for innovation in consumption. Items popular during 1995, not only in Gulf households, but also (as gifts received) in many others, unavailable in local markets except as smuggled goods, included Nestlé tinned powdered orange juice, Vache-qui-Rit brand processed cheese, 555 cigarettes, Panasonic *two-in-ones* and fake Lacoste polo shirts. Gulf returnees have also brought new social practices with them, such as shopping at supermarkets and using leisure time to go on day trips or *tours*, not only for pilgrimage or to visit family but also for pleasure, visiting resorts like Ooty and famous cities like Mysore.

Recent changes in attitudes towards eating outside the home are an example of Gulf-derived innovation. In 1991 there were no respectable restaurants in the area, only a few tea-shops and meals hotels heavily frequented by labourers, lorry-drivers and so on, serving a handful of women clients in a screened-off area and avoided by most villagers. The restaurant in Krisnakara's recently built large hotel was usually empty, more often serving chilli chicken to parties of drunken men than meals to families: this hotel takes most of its trade from its air-conditioned bar. By 1995, Sun and Moon and Hotel Diana had opened in Krisnakara; these are both pleasant restaurants with table-cloths, vases of flowers on the tables, china plates, cutlery and popular film music. As well as standard Kerala rice meals, they serve novel items beyond the scope of most village women's cooking skills. At first, these establishments catered mostly to illicit *romancers* looking for a quiet hiding place and to Gulf-returnees (accustomed to the idea that families can eat out together for pleasure and that this can be evaluated as a high-status rather than shameful practice). Soon, the town's middle-class bank employees and shop assistants – men and women – were lunching in groups; families followed shortly after. Although most villagers still maintain that eating outside the house is a bad thing to do, or lament the cost of eating there as prohibitive (Rs28 for a set rice meal as opposed to Rs12 in an ordinary meals hotel), we have seen one or two Valiyagramam families there. While tomato soup, fried rice and noodles are widely popular, we have seen few eat hamburgers, and nobody going for the 'fish and chips' pictured on a coloured advertisement placed outside Sun and Moon. As Christians like to present themselves as innovators and as *modern*, and as they are uncon-cerned with caste pollution, it is not surprising that they have been prominent among these first families to break taboos on eating out. As more of them go to restaurants and set the trend, and as Nayar colleagues and neighbours join them, we expect that parts of the Izhava middle classes will also follow. Some families are testing the water by sending a servant or family man to buy a parcel of chicken fry or fried rice to take home.

Behind the idea of taking one's wife and children out to a restaurant lie images of leisure and the nuclear family. Skilled migrants in particular (who can afford to take their families with them) find themselves settled in relative isolation, thrown upon wives and children for company and socialising with other migrants in nuclear family units, with no older people around. In striking contrast to what Gardner reports as increased orthodoxy and desire to fit back in among Bangladeshi return migrants, Valiyagramam villagers return as self-consciously *modern* and innovators (Gardner 1995). They bring with them new habits of spending time together – watching videos, shopping or going for day-trips. One scandalised mother-in-law told us that her son, daughter-in-law and children – recently settled back after 20 years in Kuwait – liked to lie in bed late on Friday mornings, something which the latter told us that they, like everyone else, had always done in the Gulf. The returned migrant's wife, who had gone to Kuwait immediately after marriage at 21, and whose two children, now in their teens, had been born there, complained:

Here there's no holiday, every day is the same, always up and doing kitchen work before 7 a.m. The Arabs, they take one day off; in your place you have Sundays. Then the family can go out or do something together.

Returning male migrants also often bring ideas about their own role in the family which are at odds with current village thinking, which keeps father at a little distance from his wife and adult children; wives may also have higher expectations of satisfaction within marriage. Families returning to live with older relatives after long periods away are often unwilling or unable to *adjust* as other villagers expect them to, for example wives preferring to sit and eat in the living-room alongside their husbands and children, rather than staying in the kitchen to eat with other womenfolk. This rise in values of conjugality and nuclear domesticity is also reflected in television programmes such as Asianet's 'psychiatrist's advice' and in the recent explosion of Malayalam publications dealing with family life in popular Freudian terminology. Some magazines, such as *Doctor's Answers*, deal frankly with sexual matters as well as providing information on mental and physical health and development. Articles in popular women's magazines such as *Vanitha* and *Greha Laxmi* have a similar focus, with articles on home-making, marital happiness and child development. Such magazines are bought not only by migrants or middle-class villagers with aspirations towards a *modern* and sophisticated lifestyle, but also by many of those with a little spare cash, intrigued by the glamorous possibilities represented therein.

CASH AND THE REMITTANCE ECONOMY

Cash is prominent in many arenas of local life. At temple festival processions, cash donations collected around the neighbourhood go at the front of the procession, held aloft for all to see; festival days are marked by giving cash gifts; a popular necklace design is the *pavan-mala*, a string of gold sovereigns; fake paper US $100 notes are available in *stationery* shops; a large number of local families are dependent upon cash remittances sent by those working away. Money is commonly invested in itself: those with large amounts, notably Gulf migrants, often operate private loan companies. While money may be invested in small amounts as life assurance policies, bonds or other forms of financial capital, the bulk of a family's cash assets are usually kept relatively liquid in short-term fixed-deposit bank accounts. Historically, south India has been a major importer of silver for coinage, Malabar's famous spices being traded for the extra bullion required for a cash-hungry economy (for example Chaudhuri 1985: 215–18; Washbrook 1988: 59).[4] It is for its unique liquidity and ease of movement that cash is so valuable, making a large bank balance not only a sign of wealth but specifically a promise of cash richness (cf. Rao et al. 1992: 72ff; Price 1996: 100ff).

People keep large amounts of cash in the house, and move them around in complex loans and transactions. When Rs25,000 went missing from Usha's house one Sunday, a neighbour remarked that the thief could have been anybody, because we all knew that the key to the house safe was kept in the empty Quality Street tin on the glass wall-display unit. Beena came one day to her friend Anu's house to ask to borrow Rs5000 because she needed to pay her daughter's school fees that day. Anu, frowning, asked us if we had any cash in the house as she could only manage Rs1000. We did not have that much at home, but Anu's husband arrived and peeled Rs4000 from a roll in his shirt pocket. The entire amount was returned the next day when Beena had time to go to the bank. US and Singapore dollars, Riyals, Dinars and other foreign currencies are also kept in many houses and traded informally.

Preoccupation with cash and how to lay one's hands on large amounts of it are reflected in many money myths, like the one reproduced in Chapter 1 from Premadasan's impoverished father, in which a large number of gold coins are found by a man going to milk a cow: a true *Kamadhenu*. The basket of coins is a variation on a common Malayali theme of the *nidhi*, the crock of gold, often found under the foundations of a house but also turning up in other magical places. When a bolt of lightning struck a coconut tree in our (Izhava) next-door neighbours' house, setting fire to it, extinction of the fire was immediately followed by furious digging, since several onlookers had heard that *nidhis* could be found in exactly these rare circumstances. The wealth of those who make money quickly, typically migrants, is widely attributed to luck, through just such a find or more sinister means. Lenin, a young man who worked in Mumbai for several years before returning to Valiyagramam to open a bakery with his modest savings, was reputed to have made his money by becoming the lover of – and later murdering – a wealthy Mumbai widow. Stories of counterfeit notes forged in printing presses, typically in the house's basement, abound; our rented house, owned by wealthy Christians, was reputed to have had such a press.[5] These myths recognise the importance of luck or *chance* in making money, express scepticism about the possibilities for significant accumulation through normal employment or business, and throw the morality of great and sudden wealth into doubt (cf. Taussig 1980; Parry & Bloch 1989: 10). Professionals are often referred to as *minting money* or having a *licence* to print money; high-chargers such as doctors or lawyers may be referred to as *cash-pluckers*, the metaphors expressing the ease and naturalness with which these elite groups, still overwhelmingly excluding Izhavas, appear to procure money, in contrast to most workers, who labour long for lesser rewards.

One popular form of income for educated but unemployed young men who want to stay in the village is to run a *blade*.[6] Men as young as 22, like Ashok, (an Izhava), take gold jewellery as security deposits for loans, handling thousands of rupees. Ashok, who has a Bullet motorbike, a stereo cassette and a wardrobe of good clothes, is affable and easy-mannered. Like other *blade*-owners, he does not resemble the village moneylender of myth but is a smart youth from a respectable middle-class family, living with his retired military father, housewife mother, two brothers and house-servant in a neat six-roomed 1970s brick and plaster bungalow; his business is considered legitimate employment. Ashok runs his business discreetly from home; many *blades* have premises and signboards, in which case the owner dignifies his enterprise with the name *private bank*. Several shop-front village *blades* are run by ex-Gulf migrants who combine the business with some other small enterprise such as a travel agency, telephone booth or photocopier. Another means of raising cash is the *chitty fund*. In contrast to the cut-throat individual business of the *blade*, this is a cooperative group enterprise and is often run by women.

Holding land and owning property is important, but so too is command over cash. Wealthy men make large cash donations to temples and churches, names and amounts recorded on notice boards and in printed festival calendar booklets distributed to houses in the catchment area. When a group of men go drinking together, Rs100 notes are flashed and masculine prestige gained by paying for rounds; men with money in their hands will – and will be expected to – subsidise an entire evening's drinking and eating. The commonest way of celebrating is to give a *treat* or *party*: for women, distribution of sweets among women and children; for men, hosting an evening's drinking for male friends and relatives. The comparative cost of men's part in festivities is a function of masculine status: male sociality demands generous spending. Cash is a signifier not only of wealth and prestige, but of masculine status, notes reckoning the worth of a man. We have seen that young men's values are calculated in monetary terms on the marriage market; mature men's values are at least partly reckoned by their earning power, concretised in banknotes which may be left raw or converted into other forms of objectified personhood (cf. Carsten 1989). At weddings, the bride's brother or cousin takes pride of place as he arrives with a black briefcase stuffed full of wads of notes: the dowry. Since provision of dowry is officially a fraternal responsibility, the briefcase's contents speak directly of his status. Wedding gifts presented during the ceremony to the couple as they sit under the *mandapam*, are strictly gendered: women give ('traditionally') cooking pots or (more lately) household items (ornaments, tea-sets) to the bride; men give cash gifts to the groom. Women's gifts link women, via other women, to hearth and kitchen; men's cash gifts are not mere impersonal money but represent something more masculine passed from male guests to groom.

Malayalis working out of Kerala often comment on the lesser use of gold jewellery among women in other parts of India, noting with horror that in some places ornaments are made of silver, a substance considered by most as fit only for children's waist-chains or young girls' anklets, these items also increasingly being seen in gold. One Izhava young man who had lived in Nagaland defined people there as barely human on two counts: types of food eaten and that 'They don't know what gold is for, they don't use it.' Among many Brahman families gold remains limited to what is considered a decent and tasteful minimum, while Pentecostalist Christians renounce all ornamentation, but among the mainstream a woman's jewellery should be 22 ct gold (*swarnam*) and there should be plenty of it. An armful of gold bangles is not a mark of *nouveau-riche* status or lack of sophistication but an admired ornamentation; even at the poorest of marriages, a bride wears at least 24 grammes of gold. Women lend and borrow gold freely so that any woman with a wedding or public function to attend dresses to maximum effect; those who cannot borrow even a gold chain wear false (gold-plated) jewellery.

Gold is a special kind of consumption item, since it is almost cash. It can be converted instantly into a cash value or used at a local *blade* to raise immediate cash, and can be re-converted equally swiftly, serving as bangle one day, hospital fees the next and bangle again by the end of the week. As jewellery, its monetary equivalent can be (and is) calculated instantly by any onlooker; wedding guests guess with some accuracy the weight and hence value of gold exchanged between bride's and groom's families. Gold is sold and melted down with minimal loss of value, bought by applying weight to the day's price. Making-up charges at local jewellers' are either small or waived, profits being made upon the gold sale itself. There is little demand for hand-crafting or artisan workmanship which would have to be paid for: gold is usually machine manufactured and bought almost net of making-up charges.[7] If a continuum were drawn with cash at one end and inalienable cultural capital at the other, gold would exist at the first level of conversion near the cash end of the scale. Gold is simultaneously economic and symbolic capital, and converts instantly into pure economic capital (Washbrook 1988:

59, 'giving south-west India a completely different (gold) currency to the rest of the subcontinent'). Kerala's long-standing fascination for gold, like its keenness for cash, reflects its greater involvement with global flows of capital, labour and coin to its long history of interconnectedness to an international market commodity economy.

CONVERSION OF WEALTH AND INVESTMENT IN THE LONG-TERM

Consumer Goods

Things such as gold and fashion clothing, more or less accessible to any villager, fail to provide the exclusivity and solidity required of higher-level symbolic or cultural capital. As items used for decoration and improvement of the self, they refer only obliquely to the larger mobility unit of home and family. Long-term mobility strategies demand that cash be spent on goods and services which construct durable prestige, improve future life-chances and build up the quality and reputation not merely of the cash-earning person but of the entire household unit. A first level of spending by young householders or potential householders is directed towards consumer durables. Young men buy refrigerators, televisions and so on for their natal house, which they may eventually take with them when they make the later major investment of building their own house.

A clear opposition is drawn between what is produced locally (*nadan*) and what comes from outside (*vides*), the level of inclusion of these two categories being determined contextually (cf. Gardner 1993). The term 'local' might at times be restricted to include only the village, opposed to whatever is not from Valiyagramam, or it might be used to define whatever is produced in India as opposed to imported products. Villagers prefer to eat and drink what is local – rice and water in particular, but also fruits and vegetables. Products from one's own land and water from one's own well are considered superior and talked about as if they had quasi-therapeutic qualities, in contrast to the poor quality of what is consumed in restaurants or other people's houses, or purchased from shops. While we will turn later to consider relations between people, land and food, for the moment it is enough to say that to minimise risk, control is maintained over the origin of intimate stuff such as food (cf. Daniel 1984: 61ff).

Apart from food items, what has non-local origins is usually preferred, be it for reputed better quality, and/or rarity and novelty. At the centre of trade routes with the Far East and Western Asia, Kerala society has been exposed for centuries to a variety of foreign goods, technologies and styles, the main consumers being the upper-caste wealthy elite (C.T. Kurien 1994: 25). The advent of British colonialism did more than merely introduce new foreign goods and tastes. Development of a commercial/capitalist economy facilitated constitution of a new class of relatively wealthy consumers, those who made significant gains through involvement with the colonial economy.

New goods originated within colonial circuits; existing goods became unrestricted by abolition of sumptuary laws; all became available to a larger number of people. Consumption progressively lost connotations of being proportionally related to caste status. Izhavas K.V. Krishnan and Alummoottil, buying foreign imported cars and having colonial-style houses built, were enthusiastic participants in consumption of 'outside' and 'modern' styles.

In the post-independence period, consumption has become increasingly influenced if not driven by migration. Gulf migrants are at the forefront of consumption, being simultaneously the most conspicuous consumers and the main source through which new consumer goods and styles find their way into Valiyagramam, exercising an overall dominant influence over competing sources of goods, styles and tastes. An exciting development in 1996 was the opening (by outsiders) of a shop in Krisnakara specialising in selling imported items, a 'tax paid shop', instantly ironicised by villagers as 'the *smugglers' shop*'. Quality Street sweets, Nivea cold cream, Sony portables and popular novelty items such as 'touch-lamps' – table lamps which come on and off at the wave of a hand – are now available to villagers with cash. On inauguration day a stream of approving returned migrants visited the shop, greeted each other and passed on news; it seems that the shop will become a focal point for and further develop the already strong social links existing between many ex-migrants, *Gulfans*. One man remarked happily to us that the shop exactly reproduced a Gulf shop, while the manager confirmed, 'Everything you can get there, we now have on stock here, and if there's anything missing we can order it and get it immediately.'

Looking at the items which *Gulfans* buy, the house of our neighbours Vasudevan was quite typical and conforms to what is known of Asian Gulf migrants in general (for example Mathew & Nair 1978; Nair & Pillai 1994; P.A. Kurien 1994). He is a 32-year-old Izhava who has been working as a labourer in the building trade in Muscat for six years. In 1991, not yet married, he owned a thatched house which he shared with his younger brother's family. The house was like an electrical appliance shop: there was a television, VCR, *two-in-one*, fridge and a washing machine which – for lack of running water – lay unused in its original packaging. Vasudevan's marriage was fixed for the following year and he had started construction of a separate brick house where the goods would eventually be moved. While looking for a bride he returned at least once a year, each time bringing new electrical goods for himself and at least one *two-in-one*, VCR or camera to sell locally. 'When you arrive in the Gulf you buy a *two-in-one* or a colour television, being careful where you buy because there are lots of shops selling duplicates which break down within a couple of weeks', Vasudevan explained.

When you go Kerala you take the items you have bought and used during the year and sell them; when you go return to the Gulf you again buy new ones. If you need cash quickly you can sell as soon as you come out of the airport. Outside

Thiruvananthapuram airport there are Bhimapalli Muslims who ask if you have anything: they buy it cash. But they don't give a good price and it's better to wait and sell in the village to people you know. Very often I don't make any profit, just recoup costs, but I gain lots of *well-wishers*. There is always demand: some people ask in advance for what they want or write to me to bring it next time I come; they might want medicines or a foreign-made carburetteur for their Bullet motorbike.

Malicious neighbours commented that Vasudevan's real profits came from his activities as a small-scale smuggler of foreign currency and gold, a fact proved, according to them, by frequent night-time visits received as soon as he arrived in the village. The opening of Krisnakara's Tax Free Shop may well provide those like Vasudevan with an easier outlet for smuggled goods.

During first fieldwork (1989–91), the only non-migrants to own an amount and variety of consumer durables comparable to Vasudevan's were professionals, large traders, high government servants – that wealthiest section of village population among whom Izhavas are rare. Among non-migrants with income levels similar to Vasudevan – college lecturers, bank employees, medium-level government employees, factory workers and others earning Rs3000–4000 per month – consumer durables were much less common. These usually included less expensive and less prestigious Indian or Kerala-made radios, black and white televisions and small fridges. They did not usually have electrical kitchen equipment such as food-mixers or wet-grinders. Low-income villagers would have only a cheap radio, if that. In 1991, Japanese-made colour televisions and *two-in-one* radio casette players, invariably the first consumer durables to be brought back from the Gulf, were found in every migrant's household; VCRs and imported fridge-freezers remained relatively rare, found almost exclusively in the houses of those who had been in the Gulf for three or more years.

By 1995 the amount and variety of goods to be found in Valiyagramam houses had increased considerably. In Vasudevan's front room, in the new house where his wife and newly born child now live, stood a hi-fi tower system in a glass cabinet; Caroline was taken into the kitchen to admire a microwave oven, the latest acquisition. Vasudevan has also sold his old Indian-made Bullet motorbike, replaced by a Kinetic Honda scooter (stored in the spare bedroom when he is away). Houses of the many *Gulfans* who have (since 1991) permanently resettled in the village are even more remarkable. Sunny, whose Izhava grandfather converted to Christianity, is the son of a poor and landless duck-farmer. Sunny went to Muscat in the early 1970s to work as an air-conditioning engineer in a hospital; in 1983 he started a small drinking-water bottling unit. Over ten years he has become one of the wealthiest men in Valiyagramam: in Muscat he reputedly has ten lorries; three brothers, two brothers-in-law, and several other villagers are employed to work in his thriving business. Planning to return permanently he has bought prime roadside land in a Nayar-dominated area and built a spacious villa. Almost every piece of furniture is imported from Muscat, including a velvet-upholstered three-piece suite; a large rug; a metal and glass coffee table; a large wooden dining table; six straight-backed chairs; and air-conditioning for all bedrooms. He also brought a complete kitchen unit with gas-cooker. 'If you leave the Gulf for good, you are allowed to bring back your entire household effects free of duty, but they must be used. All this stuff', gestured Sunny, 'is new. I know someone working at Cochin port who *adjusted* the papers to show the furniture is second-hand. I am still waiting for a crate to arrive with another air-conditioning unit, curtains for every room and a ten-volume encyclopaedia for my children.'

Since their introduction in 1991, foreign electrical goods have appeared in local shops, bringing down the price of Indian brand-names, while banks have introduced or expanded existing 'consumer loans'. An integral part of the controversial policies of economic liberalisation introduced in 1991 by the Congress government, intended to encourage growth of an internal consumer-goods market, these loans enable those in permanent employment but with modest disposable incomes to borrow for the acquisition of consumer goods. Such loans have been enthusiastically taken up as the only means for many to enter the consuming classes; in 1996 local factory workers received around Rs1200 monthly and school-teachers in private schools between Rs500 and Rs800, making small regular payments preferable to lump sum outlays. The most dramatic consequence of the 'consumer loans' aggressively marketed on television and in every newspaper and magazine has been a sudden increase in the number of cars and motorbikes and, importantly, televisions. There are now televisions in about a quarter of non-labouring households; in 1991 this figure was about one house in ten. Low-income labourers, excluded from 'consumer loans' and whose purchasing power has been further eroded by high inflation, continue to watch television sitting outside the windows or on the doorsteps of middle-class houses, although the *panchayat* has recently installed one public open-air television in every *Harijan colony*.

As televisions spread to a larger number of households, their power of distinction has diminished, just as the symbolic capital afforded by a refrigerator decreased throughout the 1980s, refrigerators giving way to televisions as the 'must-have' item for the middle classes: in 1995, this role of scarce and maximally prestigious good had been taken by VCRs, connections to cable TV and cordless telephones (cf. Bourdieu 1984: 71, 249). By 1996, when the telephone exchange switched over to electronic signals, and many more home connections were being made, innovators were eagerly anticipating the introduction of mobiles.

While they remain an asset that can be sold in case of hardship, the prestige brought by consumer goods is as important as, sometimes exceeding, specific use or financial value. Sunny's modern kitchen is not much used apart from making coffee and tea for visitors, daily cooking being done by a servant on an open fire in a 'traditional' kitchen in a separate adjoining room (cf. Rowland 1994: 157ff; Wilk 1989). Display of goods remains a double-edged phenomenon: public shows of wealth leave holders open to mis-fortunes caused by evil eye or open to neighbours' jealousy, exactly as noted by Gell (1986: 114) among the Muria but in contrast to Stirrat's claim that consumer goods are actively used by Sri Lankan fishermen with the intention of arousing jealousy (1989: 107). Envy and jealousy are particularly feared as prime motives for resorting to *mantravadam* (cf. Pocock 1973). The successful Kuttiyil family (Chapters 1 and 3) are well aware of their Izhava neighbours' jealousy and try to take every possible preventive measure against *mantravadam*. All the women of the house go twice daily both to the *gurumandiram* and the nearby Siva temple; monthly Ganapati *homams* are performed in their house by a Brahman *pujari* for the family's advancement and *progress*; an astrologer is consulted regularly to detect possible sorcery. After Kuttiyil's foreign colour television from Muscat stopped functioning properly, it was moved from the front-room to one of the bedrooms where, when not in use, it remains covered by a cloth.

Limited in use as external indicators of wealth, consumer goods – as often as not hidden within the house – are an important means through which a household gets a sense of and evaluates its own *progress*. Owning the full range of electrical gadgets as bought and brought back by all Gulf migrants almost as a fixed set identifies a household, to itself and others, as a 'Gulf migrant house', similar in wealth, taste and style to other 'Gulf migrants'. This 'set' of goods incorporated, quoting Alfred Gell, 'into the personal and social identity of the consumer' (Gell 1986: 112), 'dialectically negate the conditions under which the ... wealth was actually obtained' (1986: 114) and 'objectify and transform' a productive career (1986: 115) which, in the case of Izhava Gulf migrants – mostly employed on short-term contracts as labourers – is likely to have involved considerable hard work, hardship and deprivation, sometimes living in segregated and closed sites and sleeping in rough temporary dormitory accommodation.

For Izhava families with mobility ambitions, hierarchies constructed around consumption promise to be status-neutral. Prestige consumption focuses upon purchase of items such as consumer durables completely removed from local arenas of production, appearing almost magically on television screens, from boots of taxis bringing home returning migrants and, increasingly, in local shops. The goods themselves, sleek and shining, objectify values far removed from the mud of the fields or the chaos of the building site. Meanwhile, the act of spending evokes masculine prestige, specifically the figures of the nineteenth-century *thamburan* and the Christian *planter*. In K.V. Krishnan's story we see the ghosts of both figures: in his actions – distributing largesse to the famine-ridden, riding the streets in his motor-car – K.V. Krishnan usurped the powers of local Brahman landlords and British plantation-owners alike. Even modest spending levels objectify a man's contribution to family *progress* and promote his status as respectable householder.

Investing in Future Generations

Longer-term consumption strategies are the necessary corollary of the pursuit of 'householder' status, while apparently offering opportunities for future family mobility. As the next generation of the mobility unit, efforts are made to provide children with the healthcare and education which help them climb the ladder further.

Education
Investment of considerable capital in children's education has two implications, one dictated by economic considerations and the other related to issues of prestige. Economic importance is attributed by Izhavas – as by all villagers – to education. Since the mid-nineteenth-century opening of the first missionary schools, 'Western' education (in particular English-medium) has been seen as the key to achievement of economic success. Among Hindu castes in particular this perception was fuelled by the growing success of Christians who, by reason of religious allegiance, had privileged access to missionary schools and could find employment and do business with British companies. At the turn of the century, among the programmes of the two most powerful caste organisations in the state (NSS and SNDP) construction of independent schools and colleges was given priority (Jeffrey 1993: 55ff; Tharakan 1984). In Valiyagramam, demand for schooling increased to the point where opening a school became a profitable economic investment, an aspect overshadowing other considerations such as providing a non-Christian-oriented education for Hindu youths. When, with independence and absorption of the Travancore-Cochin and British Malabar into the Indian Union, Malayalis (Nayars and Christians) found good employment opportunities outside the state, the economic benefits of education became even more apparent. Later, the obvious greater economic gains made by skilled/professional and/or English-speaking Gulf migrants, sealed in the villagers' minds the notion that education and economic success go together. In Valiyagramam (as in Kerala as a whole) large amounts of money are spent on fees for private schools and tutorial colleges which supplement the teaching given in government schools. All students are encouraged to go to university; only if they continually fail university entrance exams are they sent for vocational training in professional colleges.

Lack of education is also considered, especially among Izhavas, synonymous with 'backwardness' and consequently with low status. Dr Palpu and the poet Kumaran Asan, two university-educated SNDP founding fathers, were constantly put to us as examples of education's role in the caste's advancement. Education was the base of Narayana Guru's drive to reform Izhava social and religious practice; education is perceived not simply as a means to achieve economic prosperity, since nobody can fail to be aware of Kerala's high levels of unemployment, even among graduates, but is seen as a means to support claims for higher status: in the past, education was the sole prerogative of Brahmans and other upper-caste Hindus. Under the *gurukal* system, *savarna* children were taught in the compounds of Brahman and Nayar houses, which *avarna* children were forbidden even to approach. Kanians and Izhava *asans* provided rudimentary informal education for *avarna* children. Sending children to expensive private schools (which also necessitates buying specialised textbooks, drawing equipment and distinctive uniforms) and paying for autos or use of the universally recognisable school bus, is an obvious way to demonstrate family prestige. English-educated children who publicly call their parents 'mummy and daddy' instead of *amma* and *acchan*, and who are able to recite English nursery rhymes and songs, are evidence to outsiders of the parents' sophistication and *culture.*

Even less well-off manual labouring families find the necessary cash to enrol at least their sons, usually also their daughters, at pre-degree college. Boys' general lesser commitment to study is reflected in examination results and perhaps contributes to the liberality of village parents, who usually permit their daughters to study for as long as it can be financially supported. Established government-recognised colleges charge from Rs10,000 upwards for admission, but there are 'management quotas' allowing principals discretion to admit students for lower fees: there is massive competition for these places. The so-called 'parallel colleges' (see Nair & Ajit 1984) which are unrecognised, charge much less: an annual fee of around Rs1000 (cf. Jeffrey 1993: 55ff; 150ff). Our ethnography confirms arguments about the privileged place of education as a site of cultural capital, a place where cash is converted into very long-term and durable capital, changing the very habitus of the schooled and exposing them to the culture of the dominant, while also providing them with certificates, contacts, 'right behaviour' and so on which they can later 'trade in' (for example Harker 1990; Bourdieu 1984; DiMaggio 1994: 459). The Indian passion for private English-medium education is a particular instance of this phenomenon.

We have seen that Kuttiyil family (petty traders to Gulf migrants in one generation) send their children to private Church schools where they are taught in English and where a rigorous curriculum includes activities unavailable at state schools (music, dance, sport, a variety of arts and crafts). Engineer Sadashivan is considering investing in a private college providing high-quality teaching for pre-degree certificate, hoping that his son will then achieve the high grades necessary for admission to medicine or engineering. The eldest daughter of Babu, a successful Christian businessman, is sent to a costly and prestigious women's college in Thiruvananthapuram city (where she stays with relatives) for pre-degree studies. Education, which can make huge differences to children's future chances, is an area both highly developed in Kerala and subject to extreme stratification.

Although schooling in state-run schools is free up to 16, educational opportunities are not equally available. Students whose parents cannot pay for extra tutorial teaching tend either to fail SSLC or to obtain such low grades that they cannot get access to further education. Even if they achieve high marks, it is rare for these students to achieve such outstanding results as to qualify for admission to government universities which demand – given the competition – extraordinarily high marks. At the same time, these students' families do not have the money to pay capitation fees required to enrol students whose marks are not high enough. Although Valiyagramam (like Kerala as a whole) has reached total literacy, the lower strata continues to be excluded from higher education and from the benefits gained from it. As the population's poorer section is formed mainly by low-status villagers, it is the *avarna jatis* who, regardless of policies of positive discrimination in education, continue to be denied access to higher learning.

While Izhavas, like other ex-untouchable communities, place as great a value upon education as any other community, all children staying on to attempt SSLC at 16, material conditions for casual labouring families place great restraints upon young people's capacity for study. Better-off students have electricity, tables, chairs, good food, extra tuition, some quiet space in a proper house to study, no demanding family responsibilities and few worries: none of these advantages are available to the children of the poor, and failure and drop-out rates are correspondingly high, with very few making it to degree level. The small government grants given to Scheduled Castes, covering fees and basic textbooks only, are not available to Izhavas, as an OBC. The smart clothes, quality private tuition, supplementary textbooks, study tours and practically unlimited chances for examination re-takes which most others take for granted are dispensable luxuries for the children of labourers. While their parents hope for mobility and want to see their children better educated than themselves, this is rarely possible. These children take their chances at village government primary schools and the state-funded management-run Mahatma High School, usually dropping out or failing early. Table 4.1 gives an idea of the situation for poorer families, taking 10 labouring households containing 48 over-15s from our survey data. While this sample contains one degree student, there are as yet no degree-holders. Izhava graduates in the village are as yet few, known throughout the community.

Valiyagramam has twelve primary schools, all Malayalam-medium, nine government and three privately run[8] and two English-medium nursery schools, one run by Seventh-Day-Adventists and one by the management of the village high schools. A mixed UP (Upper Primary) school was originally set up in 1953 by a wealthy local Nayar family. In 1970 the school was upgraded to become a high school and in 1972 bifurcated into two single-sex establishments, Mahatma Boys' and Mahatma Girls', currently with around 1000 pupils and 40 teachers each. In 1995 the management committee set up an English-medium nursery school. Mahatma's status is somewhere between the government high school and the private fee-taking Christian and Hindu high schools, all in town: it is government grant-aided, which means that Kerala State pays the teachers' salaries but recruitment is in the hands of the management committee. The influential Nayar family who started the

Table 4.1 Educational Attainments in Labouring Households

Educational attainment	Number	%
SSLC fail	26	55
SSLC pass	14	29
Pre-degree certificate fail	6	12
Pre-degree certificate pass	1	2
Degree student	1	2
Total	48	100

school continues to be strongly represented on the management committee and has provided many of the present and former teachers and head-teachers. Almost all of the teachers at MG Girls' are Nayar and Christian, while those at MG Boys' are predominantly Brahman and Nayar. Some of the handful of unemployed Izhava graduates in the village, along with the one or two Pulaya graduates, work for very low pay as teachers in one of the 20 or so 'private tutorial colleges' around the village, thatched premises where children sit in rows reciting the contents of their textbooks; these would-be teachers know that, without connections, they have little hope of a bona-fide teaching post (cf. Sivanandan 1979; Carrier & Heyman 1997).

Families' priorities and commitment to future-oriented mobility strategies are reflected in the sacrifices made for children's sakes. We know an Izhava family of seven surviving on one Gulf wage providing monthly remittances of around Rs2000, who send the two smallest children to Sacred Heart English-medium primary school in Krisnakara. This family is not unusual, since private education is high on everybody's list of consumption priorities. Those who can afford it prefer to send children – at considerable cost – to prestigious fee-paying private schools from nursery onwards. Costs average around Rs3000–6000 for the initial registration fee (*donation*), monthly fees of Rs50–200, and monthly school bus costs of Rs75–100. Table 4.2 gives an idea of some approximate costs in the education sector. Many, unable to bear soaring costs of fees, uniforms, textbooks, trips and so on at secondary level, and mindful of Mahatma's good reputation, pull children out at age 10 to continue their education locally. Others with more cash to spare and who want the prestige which only a private school can provide choose between Christian- and Hindu-run private secondary schools, charging substantial fees. In contrast to the vast popularity of private primary education, we know very few families whose children attend private secondary schools – most of those are Christian and Nayar Gulf migrants. Almost everybody sends their children to Mahatma High, which is local, free and gets reasonable examination results: the SSLC pass rate is 57 percent, higher than state average and better than at some of the local private secondary schools.[9] There are usually around 5–10 distinctions a year (among children from

Table 4.2 Education Costs

Establishment	Fee	Covers
Management-run Technical Training College	Rs15,000	Admission for two-year course
Local (non-prestigious) Hindu College	Rs10,000	Admission to pre-degree course
NSS-run high school	Rs50,000	Normal admission
NSS-run high school	Rs20,000	Admission on discretionary 'management quota'
Christian-run prestigious lower primary school EM	Rs5000	Admission at reduced rate for Christian child
Christian-run prestigious lower primary school	Rs100	Monthly school bus fees
Christian-run prestigious lower primary school	Rs200	Monthly school fees
Christian-run prestigious upper primary school	Rs500	Annual book fees
Christian-run non-prestigious lower primary school	Rs20	Monthly fees
Town Christian prestigious college	Rs45,000	Admission to pre-degree course
Local non-prestigious tutorial college	Rs900	One-year's fees for general tuition towards SSLC
Local non-prestigious tutorial college	Rs250	Two months' pre-exam coaching for any SSLC subject

already-privileged families of Nayars, Brahmans and Christians). Mahatma School, which charges no *donation* and only a nominal fee of Rs10 per term, is felt to be good value by parents.

Health care

Another area of huge expenditure is private health care, divided between formal clinics or dispensaries and informal home-based practices whose numbers are difficult to ascertain. Valiyagramam is served by one Allopathic and one Ayurvedic free government primary health care centre (PHC). The allopathic PHC,[10] newly re-built in 1994, runs doctor's surgery, dispensary and family planning clinic, and undertakes health education, vaccination, mother and baby clinics, chlorination of wells, mass blood testing for malaria, monitoring of water supplies and so on. Almost nobody uses it when needing a doctor since – although consultation is free – medicines must be paid for, making it more expensive in the long run than visiting a private doctor. More popular private health care, used even by manual labourers, comprises two practising homeopaths; five allopathy practices/dispensaries; and eight formal Ayurvedic practices, including a branch of Kottackal Arya Vaidya Sala, a commercial Kerala-wide enterprise selling standardised Ayurvedic medicines. Apart from the Ayurvedic PHC, opened in 1994, we were aware of four *vaidyans* (Ayurvedic practitioners) practising from home, and three women offering post-natal care to mothers and babies, but there are certainly very many more. A more highly qualified surgeon-doctor is available in a village a bus-ride away (7 km), while several private hospitals and consultancies operate in town. The latest and most expensive private hospital, a three-storeyed brick and glass building owned by a consortium of Gulf and US returnees, has staff with qualifications and experience gained abroad, latest health technology, and levels of cleanliness and facilities considerably higher than those usually found. The SNDP is currently planning to open its own private hospital in Krisnakara.

While private doctors serve almost everybody from all communities and classes, going to hospital as an in-patient is an arena of extreme stratification with enormous variations in costs, facilities and prestige. For most people, their only experience of needing such facilities is related to childbirth. The extremes of the scale are set by the government hospital – a place avoided by all those who can afford to – and the new 'Gulf hospital' providing – at a price – a full range of ante-natal care, including ultra-sound scans. All births now take place in clinics and hospitals, agricultural labouring women using either the small government hospital in Chantakara or the larger government hospital in Krisnakara and almost everybody else finding the money to go to a private clinic, nursing home or hospital. A normal delivery with five-day post-natal hospital stay costs between Rs500 and Rs1200 at a private clinic; a caesarean section and ten-day post-natal stay costs around Rs2000–3000. At government clinics, costs come down to around Rs100–400. Variations largely depend upon which drugs are prescribed: for example antibiotics – routinely given after birth – costs vary enormously according to brand and quality. Differences in prices between government and private hospitals depend largely upon facilities; even the smallest nursing home has more staff per patient and better rooms than the government hospital's private wing.

It is a reflection of people's care and future hopes for their children that the village's only doctor qualified beyond general medicine is a children's specialist, and that all women register with a hospital as soon as pregnancy is suspected for ante-natal care and a hospital birth. Most villagers have become, for whatever reasons, committed to the ideal of a two-child family, those two children to be provided with every possible benefit to improve their lives. Most women have an IUD fitted in hospital immediately after the first birth, which is then kept for two to six years, after which it will be removed and the second child conceived; after the second birth post-partum sterilisation is widely practised. Whatever methods are used, village households, (apart from those of some Christian families opposing contraception) have almost uniformly seen a dramatic drop in birth rates since the 1960s (see Mahadevan & Sumangala 1987; Mari Bhat & Irudaya Rajan 1990; Nair 1994). Popularity of new ideals of family life goes hand in hand with increasing demands for cash as children are provisioned with high quality goods – books, clothing – and services – medical care, schooling, tuition – to be launched on to the job or marriage markets where parents again spend huge sums as *donations* or dowries to employers or affines. All these are payments for which parents hope to see both immediate and long-term mobility returns for the 'family', that abstraction of status and wealth embodied in those particular offspring who gain good employment or make advantageous alliances. Spending goes beyond conversion into prestige for the immediate benefit of the current household, towards investment in long-term improvement of the family oriented towards future generations. The two major items of investment are land and houses; arenas offering greater possibilities for enhancing prestige and presence and higher levels of durable symbolic capital than does spending on consumer goods or private service provision.

Houses and land as embodiment of self, status and family name
One of the most important areas of investment of migrants' remittances and employees' salaries is land for habitation (*parambu*; garden land) and cultivation (*punja*, single-crop paddy fields and *virippu*, double-crop land). Land continues to be an important form of symbolic capital: with current high prices, a concrete house in the centre of the village and a couple of acres of prime paddy land are an obvious indication of the wealth of the owner. In 1996, a newly built two-bedroomed house on a 20 cent roadside plot in Chantakara went for Rs9 lakhs.

As in the rest of Kerala, interest in land was reflected by a sharp rise in land prices – up to 2000 percent over the last 20 years – tailing off slightly since the decline of Gulf revenues (cf. Prakash 1978; Nair 1989: 352; Gardner 1993: 4). Table 4.3 gives an idea of increases in average prices per 1 cent of *punja* and *parambu*. The higher figures indicate the costs of more expensive land: i.e. *punja* nearer to the village and roads and *parambu* near tarmac roads and the village centre. Many recent buyers have invested savings in land in the knowledge that prices would continue to grow faster than bank interest rates.

While Christians building new houses prefer roadside plots, Izhavas – like other Hindus – consider not only location but also the 'status' of the land to be settled, often choosing land off the roadside but in the interior, as close as possible to village centres and to temples, traditionally zones inhabited by wealthy upper-caste villagers. Izhavas living in the village peripheries, near paddy land or in Izhava-dominated areas, always try to move into better

Table 4.3 Land Prices

Year	Cost of punja	Cost of parambu
1970	Rs35	Rs500
1980	Rs75–100	Rs1000–1500
1985	Rs150–200	Rs2000–3000
1990	Rs300–350	Rs2500–4000
1996	Rs500	Rs6000–9000

areas. While land for habitation is bought as soon as enough money for the purchase is available, to be followed later by the construction of a house, agricultural land is bought later, if at all. Interest in paddy land is strongly motivated by status considerations and the wish to be self-sufficient in rice, which brings us on to complex ideas about the composition of persons and bodily absorption of qualities.

An Izhava Gulf returnee who had recently bought paddy land explained, 'You can only trust rice from your own field. If I eat what [rice] they sell in shops I become ill; if I eat my own rice I stay healthy.' Rice sold in shops, especially government subsidised ration-shops, is generally felt to be of poor quality, second rate and full of stones: stomach troubles are attributed to eating it. These complaints are partly well-founded inasmuch as all local rice runs out during the last two months before the harvest and the only rice available in shops is either imported from outside Kerala or is of second quality. However, most of the time the rice sold in shops is produced locally and is of good quality – identical to that grown in one's own field. Rice is Kerala's staple crop, the 'body-builder' *par excellence*, the only food capable of standing metonymically for a full meal or the act of eating, and existing as a verb: '*Choru kazhicco?*' (Did you eat rice?) signifies 'Did you eat?'; '*Choranam*', future imperative, means 'I must eat', or 'I haven't yet eaten' (cf. Carsten 1989).

In common with other South Asians, villagers understand food as something undergoing transformation and refinement within the body, passing its own qualities and essences into the eater. Rice grown in one's own land contains the qualities of the person to whom it belongs, while people in turn are nourished by partaking the qualities of the land on which they live and cultivate. Exercising control over bodily intakes, minimising undesirable qualities and maximising desirable ones, endures as a defining feature of caste hierarchies, as villagers continue willingly to eat temple *prasadam* and to refuse food from those considered of lower status (cf. Obeyesekere 1976; Kakar 1986; Zimmermann 1987; Daniel 1984).

Before sowing, a handful of paddy mixed with earth from the compound of the landowner's own house is germinated there before being mixed with the rest of the paddy to be sown. In this way, paddy grown in the field is linked in to the land of the owner's house, imbued with its qualities. After harvest, a sheaf of paddy brought from the fields is placed over the threshold or the *ara*: this *nira* is Mahalakshmi, who will bring further prosperity. People, house, compound, rice and paddy fields are all drawn together, their qualities harmonised. Those who eat from their own paddy land, thereby knowing the exact provenance of the rice and eating grains compatible with their own qualities, imbued by the compound earth, can claim superiority over those having less control over the sources of what they put into their body, and which eventually becomes their bodily substance.

In the same way, eating the fruits and vegetables growing on garden land, one takes in qualities from that land. This garden land on which houses are built is also the residence of familial ancestors and spirits, with whom new residents will enter into intimate exchange. Qualities received from land include those ingested through the transformed substance of former residents buried or cremated there. To expand, Izhavas, (like other Hindus), bury or cremate family members in the house compound's south-west corner. Through a great many successive ritual transformations, taking place during successive rituals at increasing distances from the death-place, the parts of the person become less and less personalised, and more anonymous/ undifferentiated[11] (cf. Parry 1985; 1994). In Kerala, the final agent of transformation of persons is land. The component parts of the person which are broken through funerary rituals are many. First, elemental matter in combination is broken back down into its constituent *panchabhutas* (five elements, see for example Subbarayappa 1966) via prayers and actions done before the pyre is lit or the corpse interred, when the body is offered back to the elements whence it came. The pyre or burial itself effects a second transformation. After cremation some burnt ashes and bones are ritually washed and taken away, the remainder being left in the pyre pit, which is then filled in.[12]

Transformation begun through the agency of persons – the barber, a member of the Thandan caste, and male mourners – is continued by trees and ancestral garden land as the pyre pit or burial mound is planted with important fruit- and root-bearing plants. The Izhavati[13] agreed with other Izhava informants that a coconut tree is what should properly be planted at Izhava funerals. Izhavas are closely associated with coconuts, both through hereditary caste-specific identity and through origin myths (offered by themselves and others), identifying them as a population which came from Sri Lanka along with the coconut tree, a plant not indigenous to Kerala. The remains of buried or cremated family members then provide substance on the land to feed – that is to become the food of – or to be transformed by trees. Trees, in the Izhava case a coconut tree, feed family members, passing on qualities from persons buried in the land in what Uchiyamada (1995) calls a sort of 'endo-canibalism' (cf. C. Osella 1993; Malamoud 1975; Zimmermann 1987).[14]

Within the compound, the house is the long-lasting and concrete embodiment of a family and its worth and reputation: indicated in the identity between family and house names. It is widely understood as the objectification of the family's senior male, the householder, who provides cash to buy land and build the house. One young woman complained that her family, formerly of medium wealth and status, has lost its position (*stanam*), illustrating her argument by pointing to the new brick houses which have lately replaced the thatched huts surrounding her family's old teak three-roomed house, 'When this house was built [1950s], it was the grandest around here, now it's nothing. This house is exactly the same as it was when my father inherited it. He hasn't extended or improved it at all.' Her implication, as understood by her depressed father and worried mother, is that her father's life has been a failure: he has nothing to show. Her complaint also underlines the point that prestige, being relative, is an ever-shifting goal (cf. Price 1996: 135).

A man's first duty, after marrying and fathering children – taking on Hindu householder status – is to build or improve the family home, leaving behind (usually to his youngest son) something of value which speaks of a certain status. Buying, renovating or building a house is a priority for the mobile, replacing thatched or wooden huts. As considerable capital is required to build a new house (average Rs150,000–250,000 for a concrete three-bedroom house, excluding land costs) this is usually a very long-term goal planned and executed over many years; for migrants, it requires several periods of migration. Choice of building materials – concrete or less expensive bricks or breeze blocks – is in itself a prestige matter; concrete buildings cost around Rs100,000 more than brick houses, breeze block built houses standing somewhere in the middle. Bricks are also divided in price and prestige between locally made country and industrially manufactured bricks. Concrete houses indicate not only the owner's affluence but also his sophistication and taste. Villas are reminiscent of the luxury bungalows occupied by rich and Westernised characters in popular Malayali films. Some, instead of the usual family name on the plate outside, have self-chosen house names, often Hindi-ised or Sanskritised ('India Sadanam'), sometimes named after the householder's son and heir ('Murali Bhavan'), sometimes frankly ironic ('The Ritz'). We once saw a wooden dog-kennel outside a house whose owner had mischievously painted the kennel's name, 'Chikku Bhavan'.

Since concrete houses have become relatively common, built by many who are not even high earners or migrants but mere salaried employees, wealthy villagers maintain distinction by having new houses built either in 'ethnic' open brickwork style made fashionable in Kerala by English architect Laurie Baker (Bhatia 1991) or reconstructing *nalukettu* style. Others, already committed to opulent modern villas, make expensive additions to already grand mansions: air-conditioning; marbled verandahs; fitted kitchens; double garages; large sit-outs with wrought iron gates. As new items for house improvement become locally available in the village – the latest was a shop selling Rajasthani marble – those who are able buy them to make their houses 'grow' (cf. Carsten and Hugh-Jones 1995).

Sometimes these covetable newly constructed houses become the object of family disputes. Shaji, 34, has been in the Gulf for eight years. His mother was polyandrously married to two poor men, petty shopkeepers, but Shaji studied for a technical qualification and has a well-paid welding job in Saudi. He replaced his family's shabby wood and thatch house three years ago for a brick and concrete four-roomed bungalow with verandah, marble flooring, and glazed windows. The house cost over Rs150,000. Shortly after completion, Shaji married and again left for Saudi. His wife has begun to say that the house belongs to her husband since it was bought with his wages, and that she is therefore mistress of it. Soumya points out that no family member except her husband contributed anything to the considerable building costs. While she – a matriculate from a household of educated and working women including school-teachers – feels herself entitled to live in a good modern house, her in-laws, unsophisticated ex-labourers, feel entitled to claim shelter and support through the efforts of the son they have raised in poverty and through difficulties. Shaji's parents and divorced sister protest that the house was built before marriage and intended for them; he owns another plot of land in another part of the village where he should build a second house, where he, his wife and children can live. Soumya wondered to us why her husband should waste money building another family home when he has already worked hard to raise one: future wages could be better used to buy things to put in the home and on the education of the children, the first of whom is now 3. She is allegedly trying to bolster her arguments by treating the house as hers and her in-laws as unwelcome guests. Shaji's cousin complained to us, 'She won't let them use the inside bathroom, because she says that it's hers, it's in her house.' Here we again see new ideals of family life coming into conflict with older ones.

Houses are constructed over a period of years: placing a foundation stone is a vow (*nercha*), with the *asari* acting as priest and is a public commitment to build, made years before cash to continue work is raised. Side extensions, verandahs, extra storeys, may all be added long after the original house has been built. A house is a never-finished project: as a family's wealth, reputation, prestige and membership grows, houses will also grow. A house and its plot, explain Asaris, as laid down in *taccasastras*, is a living being composed of land-spirits (*Vastupurushanmar*), with its own birth-date, horoscope and luck, growing along with the family who live in and around it, living and dead members (C. Osella 1993: 459ff). The living household is not composed only of human members; house, paddy land and garden plot do not merely reflect the status of inhabitants but are, like them, the living objectification of the wider family group, its name and reputation, and a source and target of quality. Melinda Moore (1985) stresses the importance of understanding that old *tharavadus* were not simply matrilineages but units of house, land and people together: what she does not go on to say, but which is clear in Valiyagramam (as in Valentine Daniel's Tamil ethnography, 1984) is that land and houses, like people, are living beings imbued with particular qualities (*gunams*), and that some qualities are passed and exchanged between land, house and people living in intimate exchange with each other, always subject to each other's mutual influence (cf. Carsten & Hugh-Jones 1995; Daniel 1984: 79ff; Uchiyamada 1995).

Many Gulf migrants have been buying old *nalukettus* left vacant by their previous high-status occupants. To live in a *nalukettu* is an indicator not only of past wealth and pedigree but also of future well-being, since these houses are designed to take care of the families living within them. Encompassing deities and trapping benign forces while eliminating evil ones, a *nalukettu* is a microcosm: like the Hindu temple and the (male) human body, it is a perfect

structure enveloping, 'tying' and ordering space-time (cf. Beck 1976;
Moore 1990; Carsten and Hugh-Jones 1995). The wealthy who have no
*nalukettu*s to restore or who want the comforts of a modern house, along with
those who cannot afford to buy an abandoned *nalukettu*, often compromise
by making an old *ara*, salvaged from a demolished *nalukettu*, the heart of
their newly constructed house. We have seen several modern villas
constructed around an *ara* salvaged from an old house whose name and
family details can be recounted by the purchasers. Inflated prices are widely
paid for land, houses or parts of houses which formerly belonged to high-
status landowners. Visiting such houses, the new occupants are eager to
impress upon us the status of the old residents, whose family histories are
narrated in detail and with pride almost as though they had been their own
ancestors.

In many cases, along with a house, new occupants acquire the *pithrukkal*
and *rakshassu*s of previous owners; because ancestors do not like to move
away from their land, taking over a plot usually involves taking over the
kuriala and spirits there. If regular worship and ancestor sacrifices are not
performed, the new owner's family can expect to be visited with afflictions
just as they would be if they neglected their own ancestors. Neither the
inheritance of potentially dangerous supernatural beings nor the inflated
costs of these old houses diminish their worth in the eyes of the new
residents, who actually hope to become intimately linked to its deceased high-
caste residents. Land, houses and parts of houses are not easily alienable
from the people to whom they were previously attached. This intimacy of
relations between land and people is exemplified by procedures followed
during transferral of landlords' (*janmam*) rights. Transferral was sealed when
the original owner offered the buyer a glass containing grains of rice, flowers
and water taken from the land in question, with the words 'I give you the
water of such compound to drink' (Aiya 1989: 321). By drinking (or
washing his face and feet with) this water, i.e. by incorporating qualities
from the land, the buyer sealed his acquisition. These days, no procedure
exists which, recognising the relationship between residents and land, can
break or transfer it: villagers work on the premise that land retains something
of its former inhabitants. When Izhavas buy land from Nayars rather
than Christians, when families boast that their area was formerly inhabited
by Brahmans, or when migrants build around old *aras* on vacant *savarna*
plots, it is exactly this exciting possibility of transferral of qualities that is
significant.

CONCLUSIONS

Consumption is of especial importance to the mobile: it represents a display
of wealth, a first step towards capital conversion and, increasingly, a form of
asserting and re-fashioning identity. Izhavas buy consumer goods and
expensive private services for immediate objectification of prestige, keeping a

careful balance in order that strategies for mobility via consumption should not backfire: gifts and loans spread wealth, mitigating differences between individual families' progress and pledging allegiance to the solidarity and mobility of the wider group. Longer-term mobility plans are family oriented and involve channelling assets into objectifications – land, housing, children – which bolster householder status, convert cash into symbolic and cultural capital, and outlive the persons who provided the initial cash.

Some writers suggest that consumption may be more important for those at the peripheries of capitalism and modernity than for those at the centre (for example Classen 1996; Miller 1994a; Hannerz 1987). Unequal global relations of production, distribution and consumption must make concepts of centre–periphery unstable and perhaps of little use: relationships which were temporarily frozen and subsequently made to appear fixed and simple in the early twentieth century, such as that between Britain and India as coloniser and colonised, First and Third Worlders, appear once more complex, as under the pre-colonial situation, when, at the end of the twentieth century, capital, labour, information and profits once more flow along complex global channels, and as the Indian middle classes and elites swell (Appadurai 1990b; Chaudhuri 1985, 1990; Rudner 1994; Dirks 1992).

In contrast to middle-class villagers, whose future-oriented strategies allow them to extend personal consumption and identities to encompass progressively larger domains such as land, house and family, consumption practices of labouring villagers remain located within the realm of fashion, both transient and limited to the personal body and identity. Unable to afford shiny clothes and extreme hairstyles, they do not possess the economic resources necessary to move on to longer-term projects of mobility and self-realisation. Unlike Miller's Trinidad, where transience, style and fashion are valued as positive attributes of modernity and freedom, in Kerala transience is widely devalued (Miller 1994a; cf. Comaroff 1996: 21, Wilk 1994) where orientation towards the values of the householder are deemed to be appropriate for the non-Brahman majority and are especially dominant among the middle classes (Madan 1987). From this viewpoint, hyper-fashion and semi-durable consumption items are appropriate to early stages of life, to be replaced in maturity by a more future-oriented and durable lifestyle. The labouring poor – whose consumption remains severely limited – are mocked or pitied as remaining in a sort of permanent adolescence and caricatured as 'like children', unable to attain mature householder status. Labouring Izhavas who, as an intermediate caste with status mobility ambitions must retain distinction from Pulayas, cannot even permit themselves the consolation of withdrawal into the subcultures of fashion.

A distinction exists between what is internally consumed – rice, ancestral substance – widely preferred to be local, and what is added to the external self – consumer durables, fashion – unequivocally considered better when coming from Outside. While an increasing number of villagers are eager to incorporate some small degree of alterity in the form of Chinese noodles or hamburgers, they remain in a minority; all who buy land and build houses, consumption involving longer-term and deeper incorporation and absorption, have a keen eye to the caste status of the land and ancestors there. In general it seems that villagers, through consumption, are strategically constructing improved selves which, while externally participating in otherness *vides*, thereby extending the self and its linkages, remain internally and substantially local (*nadan*). In particular, the continuing importance of the status of land for Hindus as opposed to Christians suggests that caste status remains an important aspect of internal deep identity, in which the only type of otherness which can be countenanced is that of the high-caste and high-status (cf. Taussig 1993).

At the same time as families pursue class mobility through employment, marriage and consumption, battles for long-term caste mobility continue to be fought. An arena dominated by exactly the people – high-caste Hindus – who need to be impressed and convinced that Izhavas should not be considered low status is that of religion. Spending in religious arenas through temple donations, patronage of festivals and costly vows is also a highly effective method of conversion, offering long-term cultural capital and perhaps, if we follow Bourdieu (1990: 118), the most disguised form of 'hidden' capital. While consumption of goods and services is linked to social and economic relations and a world beyond the village, religion as a form of consumption remains firmly rooted within the village and in local social relations.

5   RELIGION AS A TOOL FOR MOBILITY

Religious practice is important for Izhava identity and mobility ambitions in three major ways: first, as a means by which the poor and low-status hope to improve their condition and by which those already doing well seek to maintain *progress*; second, for marking group or familial status and *culture*, and third – and importantly for currently upwardly mobile sections of the community – as a chance for wealth conversion. For families at the bottom of wealth and prestige hierarchies and for those with plenty of cash but little prestige as yet, religious behaviour itself appears as a form of consumption in which many practitioners are consulted and an eclectic selection of practices undertaken, the basis being potential effectiveness in addressing needs. Those with prestige in mind, be they of modest means and status, wishing to convert new wealth or long-standing community elite, can avail themselves of a far narrower range of practices and specialists. Religious practices have always offered hope of deities' blessings (*anugreham*) or escape from difficult circumstances, in particular the *dosam* which hinders well-being and impedes progress. Since Gulf migration began, the stakes have grown progressively larger while the number and variety of religious arenas for facilitating *progress* has grown rapidly. As in other fields, certain practices are associated with low castes, especially Izhavas and Pulayas, others with high castes, particularly Nayars. Meanwhile, that choices of religious practices and specialists are often determined by villagers' needs and commensurable to the gravity of their circumstances undermines analytic attempts to characterise or stratify particular practices.

Orthoprax Hinduism is a realm particularly associated with Brahmans; it also offers arenas of participation and performance deeply rooted in the local, unlike employment or consumption; it arguably offers the means *par excellence* of capital conversion. Just as employment is central in accumulation of economic capital, religion continues to remain a privileged site for the conversion or conservation of money into status and prestige, making it sometimes possible to present class mobility as status mobility. This goes beyond narrow processes of 'Sanskritisation' and into areas such as (re-)construction of family temples and shrines, where status is dominated by

154

models loosely associated to the Hindu *jajman*, the patron of life-giving/ regenerating sacrifices, hence practice is drawn from the community most closely associated with former landlords and *jajmans* – Nayars.

A gender division runs through the religious realm: participation is not compulsory for already wealthy men of prestige, who may instead effect capital conversion through *social work* or public service (*seva*) and who may even, on the educated Left, declare themselves *rationalists* or atheists. By contrast, women of whatever class and status are obliged to involve themselves in religion, holding the sacred duty of protecting their menfolk; conspicuous religious activity as part of generalised nurturant behaviour is another plank of female prestige. Since women are less involved in public life and have prestige constructed differently from menfolk, this also means – conveniently – that a high-status household can often take advantage of mobility opportunities available by using low-status religious specialists without loss of face by the simple expedient of sending its womenfolk to deal with the matter.

IZHAVAS AND RELIGIOUS REFORMS: NARAYANA GURU AND THE SNDP

The relation between religious practices and status was very much in the mind of Izhava reformers, self-consciously attempting to remove obstacles to caste mobility. At the turn of the twentieth century, Izhavas – branded untouchable – were excluded from *savarna* temples. At the same time, stereotypes common among higher-status communities and reproduced in colonial material such as gazetteers and missionaries' accounts, labelled Izhavas on the (mis-)understanding that castes were primarily defined in relation to occupation and religious practices. Mateer (1991a: 85) describes Izhavas' religion as 'demon worship' involving 'devil dancing' (1991a: 91); his lengthy description of hook-swinging and side-piercing (1991a: 92ff) is reproduced by Thurston (1906: 487ff; cf. Oddie 1995). The frontispiece of Mateer's 'Land of Charity' (1991a, original 1870) is an engraving of a 'Devil Dancer', an Izhava ritual specialist. Chapter 2 argued that a priority for Izhavas early this century was to shake off the label of 'toddy-tapper' through take-up of alternative employment: Izhavas similarly became increasingly concerned to renounce their assigned religious and cultural identities as enthusiastic practitioners of the forms of Hinduism considered in reform discourses as most barbarous and superstitious: hook-swinging; blood sacrifice; *mantravadam*; possession by and worship of fierce local deities. Narayana Guru himself called lower-caste temples 'places of filth and superstition', opposing the worship of such popular deities as Chattan and Madan (evil spirits in dominant Brahmanic discourse);[1] he also replaced offerings of toddy and blood with fruit and flowers (Heimsath 1978: 27; Lemercinier 1994: 198). Izhava temples were replaced by shrines; *asrams*; after the 1936 Temple Entry Act by attendance at public temples; and – after the death and deification of Narayana Guru – *gurumandirams*.

Narayana Guru's famous installation of a Siva temple at Aruvippuram outside Thiruvananthapuram formed part of his attempt to provide Izhavas access to Sanskritic deities and Sanskritised forms of worship hitherto forbidden. This story is given in all published works on the Guru and was recounted to us many times. On Sivaratri 1888, having called a large and curious crowd in the dead of night, Narayana Guru prepared to consecrate a Sivalingam. Some accounts claim that he dived into a pool or river and emerged after 30 minutes, clasping the stone which became the *lingam*. To high-caste criticism that an Izhava, as *avarna*, had no right to worship – let alone to consecrate – a Siva, Narayana Guru is famously reputed to have replied that he had consecrated an Izhava Siva and made no presumption to have consecrated a Brahman Siva (see for example Parmeswaran 1979: 57). In 1897 the Guru composed his noted textbook: *atmopadesha-satakam* (100 verses of self-instruction), making the principles of *vedanta* available to the masses; in 1923, he founded a Dharma Sangha order of *sannyasins*.[2] He went on to found other temples and *asrams*, all with Izhava priests officiating, notably the Jaganath temple at Thalasseri (1908), the Sarada Sivagiri Temple (1912) and the Advaita Asram at Alwaye (1913), where a 1921 conference on World Brotherhood was held: by 1909 he had established 21 such temples (Jeffrey 1993: 52).

While many Izhavas and much written material on the SNDP like to present Narayana Guru as autochthonous – uniquely and divinely inspired – he is clearly a figure of his times and some historical antecedents can be traced. We have already mentioned the Nayar Chattampi Swamikal, who became Narayana Guru's guru around 1882 and whose reinterpretation of *advaita vedanta* in anti-casteist terms Narayana Guru continued. Meanwhile, the philosophies of modernist and neo-Hindu rationalist reform movements led mainly by (often European-educated) high-caste men like Rammohan Roy, Aurobindo Ghose and Swami Vivekananda were well known in early twentieth-century Travancore, as were organisations like the Arya Samaj, concerned with reforming Hinduism in general from its alleged decadence and ossification (Jeffrey 1974; Hardgrave 1969). Narayana Guru's appropriation of knowledge and rituals held to be the prerogative of Brahmans, though commonly claimed to have been the first daring act in breaking Travancore *savarna* monopoly on high-status deities, is both foreshadowed in spirit by the fifteenth-century low-caste devotional (*bhakti*) poet Thunchath Ezhuthachan and anticipated in practice by a less known Izhava Siva temple, founded at Mangalam (a coastal village) in 1854 by Kalasseril Velayuthan Panikker (1825–74).

We visited Velayuthan Panikker's house in Mangalam, a traditional teak-wood *nalukettu* indistinguishable from a Nayar house, and went to the nearby public temple which he – long before the time of Narayana Guru – had built, and where he had installed a Sivalingam in 1854, 34 years before Narayana

Guru installed his 'Izhava Siva' in Aruvippuram. Panikker is described approvingly as a 'super-hero and super-*kallan*', a trickster figure; most Valiyagramam Izhavas have heard of him. A potted biography had even been published in the local high school magazine and stories like the following about him were readily forthcoming. He had been 7 feet tall, muscular, very fair-skinned and had personally flouted caste prohibitions and restrictions, requiring Izhavas who lived in his area under his protection to do likewise, for example by using public roads. At the time of the 1850s breast-cloth controversies, he had commanded all Izhava women in his area to defy the royal prohibition upon covering the upper body and had bought and distributed upper cloths to all *avarna* women at Kayamkulam market (cf. Kooiman 1989: 148ff). When some high-status men later intimidated covered Izhava women, tearing breast-cloths away, Panikker 'killed them with his sword'. On another occasion, dressed as a Brahman, he had gone to Guruvayoor, (even now the most orthodox temple in Kerala, famed in the 1990s for refusing admission to young women wearing *churidar-kurta* instead of *sari* or *pavada*); there Panikker had spent ten days learning about *puja* and installation of deities. When his Izhava identity was uncovered by a horrified and furious Brahman, he threw a bag of gold onto the table, saying, 'Yes, I am Panikker: take this gold for your services.' He ran off, chased as far as Shertallai (but not caught) by irate *savarna* temple officials.

Panikker's heroic actions, linking struggles against untouchability and caste restrictions to the appropriation of high culture and Sanskritic religion, appear little different in approach – albeit more militant – from those later initiated by the caste elite and since made mainstream. From the very beginnings of organised Izhava protests at the end of the nineteenth century, access to high-caste temples became a cornerstone and a prominent symbol of campaigns against untouchability and caste discrimination. In 1919, a meeting of 5000 Izhavas called for temple entry, while in 1921 Izhava Congress member and SNDP secretary T.K. Madhavan, member of the prominent Alummoottil family, raised the temple entry issue in the Popular Assembly, introducing in 1923 a resolution to Congress stating temple entry as a universal Hindu birthright. In 1924, an anti-untouchability committee formed within the Kerala Congress (KPCC) and by March 1924 the multi-community Vaikkom *satyagraha* had begun demanding not temple entry itself but the rights of untouchables to use public roads surrounding temples. The SNDP was the only *avarna* association to back the *satyagraha*; even so, many Izhavas kept away from it and there were rumours that Narayana Guru was not happy with the manner in which the struggle had been defined and co-opted by Congress and by Nayars seeking full temple privileges for themselves (Panikkar 1995: 114; Menon 1994: 105–6). A commission was constituted and the Temple Entry Committee made its report to the government in 1934. Impatient with the intractability of government and the Rajah, in January 1936 many prominent Izhavas publicly approached the Church of India regarding mass conversion; while the Anglican Bishop spurned them, the Mar Thoma Syrian Protestant church began serious evangelising and conversion. Many Valiyagramam families converted during this period; although – unlike Pulaya converts – they are now fully integrated into the Mar Thoma community, they are occasionally reminded by fellow congregationalists or by Syrian Catholics of their 'low-caste' origin and recent conversion.

From Thiruvananthapuram, C.V. Kunjaraman called from the columns of *Kerala Kaumadi*, the weekly paper founded and edited by him, for mass conversions to Islam or Christianity as the only way to escape caste discrimination. The newspaper's current editor, Mr M.S. Mani, C.V. Kunjaraman's grandson, told us that some of his grand-uncles had in fact converted, this being the easiest method at that time out of untouchability and caste restrictions. Pointing out that there was no coherent philosophy to challenge *chaturvarnya* under the Rajah's rule, Mr Mani commented that threats to Hinduism started within Hinduism itself: the threat to the lower castes by the higher castes. C.V. Kunjaraman himself had met the Rajah to tell him that people were converting because of the real freedoms gained by 'putting crosses on their chests' – to use public roads; not to hide away; to cover their bodies: he had hinted that mass conversions might follow. The Rajah had said, 'Go and tell the people to come back to Hinduism' and had made the Temple Entry Proclamation, (1936), but of those who had already converted few returned. In May 1936, a deputation was sent to the Rajah from the all-Kerala Temple Entry Conference. A petition of 50,522 caste Hindu signatures was presented to the *Dewan* on 3 November 1936; the Royal Proclamation declaring universal temple entry came on the Rajah's birthday, 12 November (Ouwerkerk 1994; Menon 1994: 80ff; Rajendran 1974). Right up to the present, full participation in mainstream temple worship and activities, central particularly to Nayar social and religious life, retains tremendous symbolic and political importance for Izhavas.

Religious Reforms in the Village: *Asrams* and *Gurumandirams*

Older people in Valiyagramam told us that from the 1920s onwards, responding to Narayana Guru's calls, many Izhava shrines had been destroyed, deities' images smashed. Physical destruction of shrines was a plank of missionary and SNDP activity alike: photograph 8 in Kooiman (1989) shows a group of Nadars (then known as Shanars, a Tamil caste of palmyra palm-tappers associated to Izhavas) grouped around the smashed ruins of their temple, presided over by a European missionary in pith helmet, his hand resting proprietorially and authoritatively upon the broken wall. We have seen many Izhava family shrines in which the main deity, made of stone and previously known as a fierce autochthonous form, had been re-named as '*appuppan*', '*Yogiswaran*' (ancestor spirits) or suchlike and relegated to subsidiary status at the edge of a newly constructed family temple under a Sanskritic main deity, most commonly Bhadrakali or Durga as in Nayar family temples. Blood sacrifices – later forbidden by law throughout Travancore – were widely abandoned, while the oracular institution of the *velichappadu* began to fade (Tarabout 1986: 276ff; Seth 1995). Refused a ritual role on a par with Nayars and unable to insist upon their new Sanskritised religious endeavour with the upper castes, Izhavas withdrew for a time from local temple festivals in which they were usually expected, along with Pulayas, to worship and represent lower, blood-thirsty deities (cf. Gough 1970; Menon 1994; Tarabout 1986; Mosse1994). During this period local Izhava religious life focused instead on one of the newly-established 'prayer halls'. Here community leaders spread the Guru's message and read and explained Hindu religious texts while encouraging the adoption of 'reformed' religious practice such as evening prayers and *bhajana*-singing in the home (cf. O'Hanlon 1985: 301).

The first representative of this reform to arrive in Valiyagramam in the 1930s was Dharmananda Swami, a member of the lowly unapproachable Parayan caste (see Uchiyamada 1995) who had spent several years in Sivagiri as disciple of Narayana Guru. He was initially beaten and chased out by Izhavas when he came to set up an *asram* in Sasthamuri's mixed Nayar and Izhava residential area. Izhavas recount – some with embarrassment, some in amusement – that the disciple was forced to return to Sivagiri to obtain a letter from Narayana Guru requesting the community to accept this humble representative of the Guru's teachings. Even then, many Izhavas refused and a rival *asram* was started by a local Izhava *swami*, the 'Parayan *swami*' retreating to Kappa Parambil's neighbourhood.

From the 1940s, newly formed SNDP *karayogams* took up the task of articulating Izhava demands for unrestricted access to public temples and for equality of worship alongside high castes. *Karayogams* have also promoted ritual independence and self-sufficiency, particularly with the construction of *gurumandirams*, shrines dedicated to Narayana Guru in his form as deified saint Gurudevan. When a *gurumandiram* is built, a statue of Gurudevan is installed with full *tantric* ritual exactly as for a temple deity. Thereafter an Izhava *pujari*, sometimes Sivagiri trained, performs daily *pujas*. At dawn and dusk he purifies the shrine with holy water and having recited *mantram*s and offered flowers, does *deeparadhana*, giving *basmam* as *prasadam* to the devotees present. Every month the *nakshatram* of Gurudevan is celebrated with special *pujas*, as are his *jayanthi* and *sammadhi*.[3] At the *mandiram*, the Izhava *pujari* celebrates the auspicious ceremonies of marriages and first feedings in front of the image of Gurudevan.

Many of Valiyagramam's *gurumandirams* have a movable image (*bimbam*) of Gurudevan which is taken during the temple festival season around the neighbourhood for a *parakku' ezhunellattu*. This is a ceremony commonly performed annually by larger local public temples in which the deity is offered measures of paddy, formerly by high-caste families only, nowadays by any local devotee. Gurudevan's *bimbam*, mounted on a yellow[4] decorated palanquin (*jivitham*) carried by two yellow-clad assistants and preceded by the *kuttuvilakku* and *chenda* is taken to every Izhava house in a procession exactly akin to those of full-fledged temple deities. Families set pictures of Gurudevan on their doorsteps; *vilakku* and paddy offerings are placed on a plantain leaf in front of it as when Siva or the goddess call to collect their offerings. When the procession arrives, the *mandiram pujari* receives offerings of paddy, camphor, flowers and money which he offers to Gurudevan, returning part of the offerings as *prasadam*. The amounts of paddy and cash offered are recorded with the name of the donor in a register by the SNDP branch secretary. After collection, paddy is sold at public auction.

The promoters of the collection in Sasthamuri, the SNDP local committee, explained to us in pragmatic mood the main purpose of paddy collection as providing extra income for the *mandiram*, proudly stressing its success as a demonstration of community prosperity. But for most Izhavas the paddy given is not a donation to the SNDP but an offering to a deity who returns blessing, removing *dosam* and misery from the house and furthering prosperity and well-being; it is no different from the measures of paddy given to Bhadrakali or Siva. Differing evaluations of the significance of this paddy collection and of what Narayana Guru represents, indicating a deeper diversity of styles, orientations and interests within the community, become most apparent during the annual *gurumandiram* festival.

Gurudevan: Social Reformer or Deified Saint? The Sasthamuri *Gurumandiram* Festival

An annual *mahotsavam* is conducted on the astrological anniversary of Gurudevan's installation in the *mandiram*; we saw it well celebrated in 1990 and 1991. Three days before the festival, the *gurumandiram* was carefully cleaned, repainted and decorated with flower garlands, coloured lights and yellow banners. Special *pujas* were conducted at dawn and dusk; throughout the day *bhajans* in honour of Gurudevan were sung. Just before dusk on festival night, a picture of Gurudevan mounted on a hand-cart, amidst flowers and decorations, was (like a temple deity's *bimbam*) pulled by youths to nearby Sivamuri Siva temple, to receive blessing and *darshan* and receive *prasadam* (*chandanam* and *bhasmam*) from the Brahman *pujari*. From this main temple the procession then began, preceded by girls with jasmine-garlanded hair pulled into side top-knots, holding auspicious *talapoli* and all dressed in *kassava-mundu*. A boisterous crowd of youths and men singing praises and shouting the name of Gurudevan pulled the cart through the neighbourhood to the *gurumandiram*. On arrival, the *talapolis* were placed in front of the shrine and the *mandiram* priest offered *puja* and *deeparadhana* to both of Gurudevan's images; this was done amidst a shower of flowers and auspicious shouts of *arppuvili* from men and *kuruva* ululations from women.

Outside the *mandiram* was the usual atmosphere characterising any successful, well-attended temple festival. Girls and women dressed in their best clothes flocked around temporary stalls selling *ladies' items* and children's toys. Seated on the ground surrounded by their wares two men sold calendars and posters of Hindu deities, Christian saints and political figures. Further away, under petromax lamps, card and dice gambling was going on. A temporary tea-shop had been set up. Groups of young unmarried men swaggered around showing off their fashionable clothes and trying to flirt with girls. Many men, including several of the local SNDP committee members, were by this point rather drunk, breaking into choruses of *vallam pattu* (cf. Tarabout 1986; Menon 1994).

In both 1990 and 1991, the large crowd accompanying the procession finally assembled in a nearby field before a temporary stage to watch a *cultural programme*. As the crowd waited, community leaders seated upon the stage made speeches. The line-up of speakers on both occasions included: a representative of SNDP state leadership; a member of SNDP District Committee; a lecturer from an SNDP college; the *panchayat* president, at that time an Izhava; a *sannyasi* from Sivagiri;[5] a *sannyasi* from Dharmananda *asram*; a Christian priest from Mar Thoma church, which has many Izhava converts; a Mosque preacher; President and Secretary of the local SNDP *Yogam*. The panel thus constituted tried not only to express that sense of religious harmony and ultimate unity contained in Narayana Guru's famous maxim 'One caste, one religion, one god for mankind', but also to represent the range of political orientations within the community. While the state SNDP representative and the *panchayat* president were Congress (I) supporters, the District member and the college lecturer were well known local CPI(M) activists.

Unlike *puranic* deities, Narayana Guru – worshipped as Gurudevan only among Izhavas – is the most prominent and powerful symbol of 'Izhava-ness' and evokes Izhava social and religious transformations (cf. Gath 1998); this can make the festival a politically charged affair. In the light of the backlash of violent protest fomented by upper castes in north India at prospective implementation of the Mandal Commission Report on caste reservations, every SNDP speaker took an unconditional stand in favour of positive discrimination for lower castes and promised support to the then V.P. Singh government and its policy of reservations. For several hours successive orators, their message carried throughout the village by loudspeakers, pledged the determination of themselves and the caste to fight, if necessary through militant action, casteism and inequality.

Izhava unity and solidarity – grounds according to SNDP orthodoxy and rhetoric for success of past and present status mobility ambitions – is itself carefully and ritually constructed during such festivals. Speakers drew direct correlations between the poverty, lack of access to education and discrimination faced in other parts of India by lower castes and their lack of organisation as *jatis*. They reiterated that only militancy and solidary organisation had brought Izhavas any progress. Restatement of the SNDP's role in representing and organising Izhavas offered political legitimation to its local leadership.

Gurumandiram Festival as Site for Construction of Caste Unity?

The festivals lend themselves easily to 'straight' Durkheimian readings, in which the community celebrates itself, affirming and re-creating social solidarity by coming together around the reified charismatic essence of 'Izhava-ness', Gurudevan. Solidarity is cemented by the conjuring – through fireworks, flowers, perfumes, music, lights, speeches and sleeplessness – of a festival atmosphere. That this is a hierarchical social body is clear, from the presence of leaders seated high upon a stage and accorded the prestige-enhancing accoutrements of flower garlands, microphones and lengthy introductions. The festival can also be read as a self-conscious performance of unity and identity directed outwards and enacted in the presence of others, notably the dominant and high-prestige communities, Christians and Nayars (cf. for example Baumann 1996). It is also an occasion on which, through displaying numerical and financial strength, pride, determination and unity, Izhavas (re-)negotiate relationships with upper castes. For example, the choice of Sivamuri Mahadevar temple as the procession's starting point was partly motivated by the fact of its having been for several years the site of bitter conflict and violent exchanges between Sasthamuri Izhavas and a section of the local Nayar community. In starting out from Sivamuri, Izhavas asserted the right of themselves and their deity to a relationship with this neighbourhood temple, and engineered a public recognition of Gurudevan's status by its Brahman priest.

Focusing upon stratification within the community, and particularly upon that between leaders seated on stage and the masses beneath, obliged to listen politely and applaud enthusiastically until the *drama* starts, we turn to Scott's remarks upon the formal ceremonies organised by dominant groups to 'celebrate and dramatise their rule' (1990: 58). While we can in no way suggest that a caste association annual festival bears close comparison with Scott's example – the empty parades of Stalinist states – we can find some resonances with the SNDP's theatrical, highly organised and disciplined 'display of cohesion and power', which 'no one comes to see ... [a] show all actors and no audience' (1990: 59). Local Nayars and Christians are – via loudspeakers – forced to some degree to participate, but they do not venture out on to the streets during the festival. Scott's analysis, that 'the actors are the audience' (1990: 59), and that such displays serve to remind local participants of their links with a wider group (in this case horizontal ties to Izhavas state-wide and nationally to other OBC communities) also seems useful, remembering that these masses may be called upon by their leaders as militant defenders of OBC dignity.

We can also understand these events as mimetic performance in which the styles of various high-status 'others' are appropriated; the SNDP has tried to fuse reformed Hinduism and modernist rationalism with what its leadership see as the best of Nayar and Christian religious practices (cf. Hardiman 1987: 157 ff). While the procession faithfully replicates that of a full-fledged temple festival, complete with girls in upper-caste dress, exactly as seen among Nayars at *their* festivals, the presence of a disciplined body sitting listening to their leaders speak evokes a Christian congregation. Hindus often attribute the economic and cultural *progress* of the Christian community to discipline, unity and organisation, seen as derived from the institutions of church and priest.[6] One committee member suggested that Gurudevan had always maintained that festivals and meetings must have an educational function. Community leaders should provide speeches and programmes aimed at people's general uplifting: economic sense, education, morality and so on. The point was that 'people should not go to festivals and pilgrimages merely for entertainment: education is crucial'. Moreover, festival-goers should be well-dressed, washed and groomed in order to get outsiders' respect.

Narayana Guru is seen among SNDP leadership foremost as a social reformer, whose teachings and spiritual leadership helped the community rid itself of superstitions and *backward*, low-status practices, while encouraging adoption of those 'Sanskritised' religious practices allowing Izhavas as a group to lay foundations to claims for raised status. Supporters of this position – SNDP officials and educated Izhava middle classes – often reminded us that later in life Narayana Guru began to preach that divinity is within oneself and that devotees needed neither temple deities nor ritual specialists to approach the divine. In line with austere and rationalist brands of modern Hinduism, the Guru began to install mirrors instead of deities, encouraging his followers to do likewise. By seeing their own reflection, instead of a deity's image, devotees would be reminded that God is within, and not outside the self. While this practice did not catch on, it had some effects: all Izhavas know about it and many explained the logic behind it to us, approving of the general sentiment that everyone should – all humans containing a spark of divinity – have respect for self and others. While this idea, common at the time, surfaced in Tamil Nadu in the guise of an atheistic self-respect movement (see for example Pandian 1995), in Kerala it was re-worked in terms of dominant *tantric* Hinduism: many frame it in terms of a person's individual *sakti*, fragments of universal undifferentiated *adiparasakti*. The principle of actually worshipping the divinity within remains unappealing to most, who continue to draw sharp lines between themselves and deities: living persons who are not saints or *siddhan*s have no divinity. Those Brahmans whose spiritual practices centre around awakening *kundalini sakti* appear to be the only group to feel quite comfortable with the idea of self-worship.

For many Izhavas, especially those struggling daily to make ends meet, political and didactic dimensions of occasions like the *gurumandiram* festival are of little concern, as are the philosophical speculations of Narayana Guru's *advaita vedanta*. Those whose economic situation forces them into devalued manual work, often in the paddy fields shoulder to shoulder with Pulaya labourers, have status and prestige too obviously low to aspire to modification by public displays of ritual worth. They participate in *gurumandiram* activities primarily to benefit from Gurudevan's power (*sakti*) and blessings. The large crowds attending *gurumandiram* festivals bear testimony to popular devotion for Gurudevan, considered no mere saint, but an *avatar* of Siva (cf. Babb 1987: 62 ff; Fuller 1992: 174–5; O'Hanlon 1985: 143 ff). In many houses the Guru's picture stands alongside other popular deities (such as Aiyyappan, Siva and Bhadrakali) in the *puja* corner, where a lamp is lit daily. Considered a direct and practical source of help in everyday life, Gurudevan's intervention removes obstacles hindering progress. 'After all, he was an Izhava', argued one older Izhava woman:

The *devanmar* are too busy with other things to take an interest in our lives. If you need help and you go directly to see the Prime Minister, he will say 'Who is this person?, don't disturb me!' and throw you out. But if you go to your *panchayat member* who knows you, he will use his contacts to get what you want.

Many Izhavas then consider themselves to have direct access to Gurudevan who – far from being a disinterested and caste-less *sannyasi* – retains a special relationship with his caste-fellows (cf. Parry 1974).

1994 Gurumandiram Festival Incident and 1995 Non-festival

At the start of the twentieth century the Izhava middle classes had found Narayana Guru's insistence on self-purification and anti-casteist re-interpretation of *vedanta* the strategies most likely to pay off in mobility struggles. An often-quoted story about the SNDP's foundation has the modernist Dr Palpu (Chapter 2) seeking advice from Swami Vivekananda on the way forward. Vivekananda's advice was that the Izhava movement would fail without some sort of saint or holy man at its helm. Narayana Guru was therefore pressed into service: the movement succeeded. Proud of their saint, flattered to be united and associated in one organisation with high-status Izhavas and eager to partake of the new identity offered under the SNDP umbrella, the Izhava masses gathered around elite leaders and the charismatic figure of Narayana Guru in the truly common cause of fighting untouchability. These differing orientations are usually smoothed over during *gurumandiram* festivals, but at times community fragmentation becomes apparent. Possible tensions between those who see Narayana Guru as a reformer and those who worship him as divinity, partly expressing a broadly class-based split within the community, have been continually neutralised by SNDP leaders through references to the Gurudevan's godliness and through fanning flames of fear of backlash from other communities, making a compelling appeal to the paramount need for displays of unity. The effect is that dissenting voices have become muted, their existence relegated to the register of gossip. In recent years, as a result of widening gaps between wealthier and poorer villagers, it has become increasingly difficult to reconcile conflicting interests and maintain public affirmations of community and unity. The 'problem' of the non-mobile labouring poor, simply an embarrassment in the fields of employment, marriage and consumption, becomes sharply relevant on occasions demanding caste unity.

Returning to Valiyagramam in January 1995 after three years' absence, we happily anticipated attending Sasthamuri's *gurumandiram* festival. But immediately we noticed that the *gurumandiram* was in disrepair; passing at dusk, nobody seemed to be lighting the lamp. Mentioning this, one or two people agreed that 'there was not much activity'. When we saw by chance all the local SNDP branch office-bearers together one day they confirmed that the festival was due soon. They had just now called a meeting on how to consult the community about plans. The meeting had decided that the community had no interest: young people in particular were not interested, and there would probably be no festival.

Surprised, we called in on Soman Pilla, a retired headmaster who has many times been SNDP president, for more information. He began by confirming that 1995's festival would be a small day-time programme only, with no late night speeches, no procession, no stage and no *cultural programme*. He added, 'All this needs money and organisation: we don't have the volunteers. You have to go house to house to collect donations. It needs work, time and money.' He hesitated. His son took over, to tell us bluntly that in 1994 people had shouted out abuse during a speech by Dr Lokanathan and the police had been called, commenting: 'Those people are ignorant; they have no education; they were drunk.' Dr Lokanathan is a respectable professional, a community figurehead: BAMS qualified Ayurvedic practitioner, CPI(M) activist and long-time regional SNDP official, currently *taluk* secretary. He contested (unsuccessfully), as a Left front candidate in the 1996 state assembly elections. Soman Pilla mused, 'These people are always drinking, because they can get cheap drink; they drink anything, whatever's available ... they just want to come and laugh and watch a low-brow *drama.*' On the issue of Gurudevan's status as reformer or deity, he concluded, 'The particularity of Hinduism is that you can set up anything as a temple – a stick, a rock, your grandfather a year after his death – and then call people to worship.' Not only was this not necessary but positively undesirable: 'We can pray in our house ... but people like to go to temple. In Hinduism anybody can set up anything as God.' Over tea, we were told: 'Don't write that there's a split here, it's just one person behaving badly', 'There's really no problem, we ignore them and they ignore us', 'The thing is that education is crucial – until people get it, nothing will change.'

The next day, we dropped in on Paramu: retired schoolteacher, CPI(M) activist, teetotaller and ex-president of the Communist Farmers' Association. He also minimised the incident, identifying the 'main troublemaker' as one isolated individual, Murali, a labourer living in Sasthamuri. Murali – drunk – had been quickly overpowered and taken away, summoned the next day in front of the SNDP *Yogam* committee. They had warned that it is very bad to behave like this on public occasions: 'Other communities – Christians and

Nayars – are both well-behaved and are watching the behaviour of Izhavas.'
Paramu concluded thoughtfully that 'such people' are always drunk and
looking for fights, badly insulting other people. 'They work very hard, but
spend half of it every night on drink'. While Paramu as a Left Party activist is
forced – as respecter and supporter of labourers – to take a more generous
perspective, both he and Soman Pilla (educated, left-wing, rational, pragmatic) exemplify the gap between the community's leadership and its poorest
members, increasingly stigmatised or disowned, written off as 'ignorant' and
'drunk', othered as 'these people'.

The terms in which Soman Pilla and Paramu speak of 'uneducated
drunkards' and the focus of both on drinking recall almost exactly the terms
of denigration commonly used by outsiders to speak of Izhavas as a whole.
Worried about the caste's public image, Soman Pilla and Paramu gloss over
the fact that intoxication is generally part and parcel of temple festivals. On
many occasions, non-Brahman male devotees consume liquor to gather
physical strength for performing exhausting feats and to raise courage and
power, necessary for close contact with powerful and/or fierce deities.
Festivals are commonly the occasion of 'carnival-like' and even 'market-
place-like' atmospheres (following Bakhtin, quoted in Scott 1990: 122, 175),
characterised by drinking and a general loosening of restraints, at least
among men (cf. for example Marriott 1968b). Recently, the RSS has been
mounting campaigns against drunkenness at festivals in almost all village
temples, arguing that it defiles purity and brings a bad reputation to the
Hindu community. We will return later to examine this interesting gap
between popular practices and public images, and the processes of repudiation of self and other involved in identity shifts.

Conflicts arising from differing interpretations of what Narayana Guru
represents cannot be located in simple oppositions between middle-class
elites and a more heterogeneous base, although at the level of the village they
often take this form. Over the years, Narayana Guru's legacy – essentially
religious but containing strong social elements aimed at wider reform – has
been the hotbed of several acrimonious confrontations between different
factions of state-level Izhava leadership within wider political struggles to
define Izhava self and public image. The first occurred within a few years of
the Guru's death, giving rise to a formal split between those emphasising the
movement's universalist and spiritual aspects, claiming themselves heirs to
Narayana Guru's heritage, and the mainstream, who stressed the continuing
need for an Izhava caste association devoted to pursuing social reform and
fighting for representation. Recently, conflict exploded in 1995 following
election of a new committee to administer Sivagiri *Math*. Two opposing
factions emerged. The first, holding a majority (including allegedly VHP/
RSS-oriented members of SNDP leadership), argued that as Narayana Guru's
teachings fell within the wider fold of Hinduism, Sivagiri *Math* should be
considered a Hindu shrine, have other Hindu deities installed and become like
any other Hindu temple. The minority faction, led by the *Math's* former

leader, Swami Sashtikananda, claimed that Narayana Guru's vision went far beyond traditional boundaries of 'Hinduism' and, insisting upon maintaining Sivagiri as a predominantly Izhava institution, refused to accept the changes advocated by the majority. Swami Sashtikananda and his followers resigned from the committee, leaving it without the necessary quorum to operate, and organised a sit-in protest in the *Math*. The embittered majority began legal proceedings to remove the protesters which, following a High Court injunction, led to police intervention and a day of violent clashes with the protesters. Over the following months, Swami Sashtikananda's faction, with the support of many organisations and political parties, organised several demonstrations and strikes throughout Kerala. What is at stake here is not only control of the SNDP's considerable assets but questions of defining Izhava identity and the relationship which *avarna* OBCs have with dominant Hinduism, a question which becomes ever more pressing at a national level with the rise of the Hindu nationalist BJP.

STYLES OF WORSHIP

Religious practices are by no means exhausted by the cult of Gurudevan as Izhavas, like other communities, use a range of practices which they hope will enhance or maintain family fortunes, from magic to expenditure of huge sums in lavish display. A strong gender division runs through religious activity: while it is generally women who are responsible for family welfare and therefore most frequently undertake vows and visits to religious specialists, light the house lamp daily, read the *bhaghavatham* aloud at home, it is mostly men who become involved in arenas where religious activity shades off into accumulation of cultural capital or political involvement.

The principal concern of a large number is help in everyday problems, and relief from frequent periodic crises caused by poverty, underemployment, illness, family quarrels and so on. In local terms, they seek in their relation with the divine to alleviate the *dosam* afflicting them, hindering hopes of *progress* and threatening well-being. *Dosam* implies a blockage, impeding flow of benign and malign forces which should circulate evenly through society, bringing luck or *chances*, good and bad things, to all in turn. Obvious symptoms of blockage are poverty, illness, bad luck; success and fortune are unmistakable indicators of blessing (*anugreham*). Increasing economic differentiation has led to proliferation among every community of agents dealing with *dosam*. Many small Pentecostal churches are dotted around the village, their adherents mostly poorer Christians. A monthly charismatic meeting run by Potta Mission (Vincentian Catholics) serves a huge crowd of Marthomite and Jacobite Orthodox Christians, many drawn from the aspirant lower middle classes, and unwilling to be associated with low-prestige Pentecostalism or to renounce their own community religious affiliation. Temples – notably those dedicated to Durga – are blossoming, offering wide ranges of vows and services all specifically dedicated to the problems of the would-be mobile, which range from failure to find suitable employment to dissipation of family funds by men's drinking and gambling habits (cf. Fuller 1996a, 1996b).

The existence of this eager 'consumer market' is facilitating the introduction at an increasingly fast pace of new rituals and offerings as well as revivals of old practices. In 1996, while newspapers reported the re-introduction of a *velichappadu* at a Bhadrakali temple some 30 km away, at the nearby Devimangalam Siva temple, for the first time in at least 100 years, a ten-day long *mrtiyanjaya homam* (a Vedic-inspired sacrifice) was performed, claiming to ensure 'victory over death'. Organisers told us that with tickets at Rs25 each and between 750 to 1000 people visiting daily they expected to clear around Rs300,000. One Valiyagramam Durga temple has witnessed a ten-fold increase in the number of women offering *naranga vilakku* during the annual festival, a practice totally unknown in 1991 (cf. Fuller 1996b: 16); it has increased annual income so much as to be able to present the deity with one (in 1996 two) *lakshamdeepams*, the simultaneous illumination of 100,000 small oil lamps mounted on a temporary wooden frame. Professional video crews make films of the spectacle to sell to those unable to attend. In 1995 one local Brahman, taking stock of increasing demand for specialised rituals, resigned from his job as priest in a village temple, bought a plot of land and built a shed where he now conducts daily round-the-clock *agni homams* with the help of his son-in-law who is learning astrology. Within a year this Brahman was able to begin construction of a two-room extension to his house and to buy a colour TV and VCR. The re-introduction of non-reform practices is not as haphazard as these examples might suggest. There are at least two clear trends: the first (already identified by Fuller 1996b), suggests extensive territorial expansion of popular inexpensive practices, such as *naranga vilakku*; the second, more localised, is Brahman-driven and entails adoption of expensive '*vedic*' rituals. The latter represent a different order, since Brahmans and anything framed as '*vedic*' are associated with significant cultural capital.

Poor and newly wealthy alike are closely concerned with the forces hindering or easing *progress*: the former as those whose only hope of escape appears to rely upon a *chance* coming along, and the latter as those who through a *chance* such as migration or business luck have escaped their former condition and must now avoid 'falling back' through *dosam*. The newly wealthy are generally grateful for success, acknowledge that luck and the gods play a part in it, and fearful lest luck should change or the gods withdraw their help. 'People want to get money easily, so they do *pujas* and *nerchas*', argued Appukuttan, a 70-year-old Communist activist: 'the Gulf has exacerbated this tendency. Since Gulf migration there is too much money; people don't know what to do with it. It is frightening to make so much money so quickly, so people give away large amounts as *danam* to temples' (cf. Parry 1986, 1989). We have already seen that not all who try to improve their fortunes are able to do so, while even those with a *chance* do not always profit from it. Many, like Satyan, the Gulf-returned Izhava owner of a thriving diesel workshop, reminded us that, 'God is great' and that life's outcomes do not depend totally upon our own efforts. '*Bhagati nammal, bhagati daivam*', 'half our doing and half God's', is a common proverb. Another Gulf-returned businessman, running a print workshop, thought that success or failure came 10 percent from our efforts and 90 percent from God. Households whose fortunes improve suddenly, leaving neighbours and other family members behind, live – justifiably – in fear of envy; increasing disparities in wealth provide obvious motives for resort to *mantravadam*.

While poorer Izhavas frequently visit local temples and *gurumandirams* to make small coin donations and occasional vows, and while the recently wealthy make large cash donations to local *gurumandirams* and temples, both groups find that Narayana Guru's *advaita vedanta* and SNDP rationalism are neither satisfying nor ring true with their experience and understanding of power as something located outside of themselves. Going to a reformed Izhava temple and looking into a mirror, they see only themselves: small, powerless and either poor or rescued from poverty through the actions of something greater and more mysterious than seems to be reflected in the mirror. What these two groups seek is a direct and personalised relationship with a deity endowed with enough power to help them to achieve or maintain success. The twin planks of their religious practices are devotionalism and magic, both pursued with indifference to considerations of the status of the deity or its officiants. The personalised helping relationship which these groups need may also be sought via a deity's intermediary: the local area abounds in holy mothers and fathers, *gurus* and *swamis* at *asrams* or small temples. Such people include those like Swami Shubhananda (see p. 171) who operate within Narayana Guru's reformist framework, and those like Tenganoor Amma (see p. 172) who patently do not. Meanwhile, possession, a means by which the powerless take power into themselves, happens more and more rarely among Izhavas, mostly limited to frightening and uncontrolled experiences of possession by demonic or human spirits: experiences to be avoided, but occasionally occurring among young women. Early twentieth-century reforms which stopped Izhava participation in physical austerities such as hook-swinging are perhaps one reason why village Izhavas are rarely to be found among those (mostly Pulaya and low-prestige Nayars) who practise the controlled and willed divine possession of *kavadi attam* on Sivaratri or Tai Pooyam, devotion and power demonstrated not only by trance-dancing, but especially by bodily mutilation, commonly insertion of skewers into the face (Oddie 1995; Tanaka 1991; Collins 1997; Osella & Osella 2000).

Families in search of blessings also participate enthusiastically in pilgrimage, not only to the non-communal Sabarimala Aiyappan temple in the hills, a pilgrimage performed by Malayali men of all faiths, income groups and statuses (see Daniel 1984; Sekar 1992; Gath 1998) but also going to further-off places such as Palani in neighbouring Tamil Nadu. They also make special trips to temples reputed to be powerful. These could be mainstream temples, visited also by the wealthy, the respectable, and the high-status, in which powerful forms of the goddess sit. One such is nearby Puthenkulangara – favoured by Nayars – where Bhadrakali is given regular mock blood sacrifices (*kurudi*), and occasional genuine ones (such as the *kuttiyottam* mentioned below) while her power is augmented by the huge number of devotees who visit her. At the more distant Kairalipuzha, situated high in the hill-forest full of raw power, live cockerels are dedicated to a Kali whose reputation as fierce (*ugra*) and powerful is strong. Families may also visit local 'Pulaya temples' where officiants and most devotees come from Scheduled Castes and where non-Puranic deities receive daily offerings of arrack and regular *kozhivettu* (cockerel sacrifice).

The wealthy show devotion and give thanks by making far greater and more costly vows than their poorer caste-fellows; this takes them into arenas in which they are then also able to convert capital and compete directly with wealthy Nayars. Sacrificial logic also facilitates familial status improvement, not only because a devotee returns from a vow – always also a self-sacrifice – improved, but also because s/he publicly takes on the role of *jajman*, wealthy and powerful sponsor of the sacrifice (Biardeau 1976, 1989; Fuller 1992; Tarabout 1986). While the wealthy and status-conscious section of the Izhava community finds a greater affinity to religious practices and specialists associated with Nayars and tries as much as possible to distance itself from lower castes, most would not hesitate if the need arose to visit a Pulaya temple or a powerful low-caste *mantravadi*. As a face-saving compromise, discreet early morning visits by a household's womenfolk are an option.

Economically secure Izhava families also have enough resources to take proper care of family deities and ancestors (*pithrukkal*). In this way they neutralise the risk of *dosam* arising from neglect while enjoying the status brought by running a family temple – a practice associated with Nayars. Izhavas who are primarily oriented towards status – the established middle class and the elite – eschew low-status practices and take part in prestige-capital accumulation through vows at respectable temples, use of high-status ritual specialists (such as members of Warrier and Nambutiri castes) and through increasing celebration and elaboration of the *kutumbam*, the wider family group. This is usually constituted around a 'house and land and family temple unit' which mimics the Nayar *tharavad* (cf. Fuller 1976a: 51–3; Moore 1985). Smaller players, who may not be living on original family land where ancestors are cremated and hence have no ancestor shrines to convert into temples, tend to provide functionaries for the SNDP and local Izhava temple committees; larger players, who tend to reside if not in an original family house at least in an older plot – which may even have a *kavu* – tend to withdraw entirely from 'Izhava' arenas, and to 'move along with Nayars'. Given the vast number and range of practices here we can focus on just a few forms to analyse their styles and implications.

Shubhananda Swami

Shubhananda Swami (d.1994), was a young local school-teacher who became a follower of Dharmananda Swami (Gurudevan's first follower to arrive in Valiyagramam, mentioned above) and – aged 25 – left Valiyagramam for Sivagiri. He told us that after his spell in Sivagiri he had gone 'into the forest to do *tapas*'. His devotion was rewarded when Gurudevan eventually appeared to him, giving him his blessing and *sakti*.[7] Shubhananda returned to Valiyagramam and, having argued with and split from (the Parayan) Dharmananda Swami, started holding prayer meetings in a thatched hut in Sasthamuri. He was one of the founders (in 1941) of the first local SNDP *karayogam* and was later elected SNDP *taluk* secretary. Eventually he built an *asram* where he lived together with some of his followers. Since his death in 1994, devotees have begun to claim that he was an *avatar* of Narayana Guru.

Every Sunday morning, between 50 and 70 devotees – two-thirds of them women, almost entirely local Izhavas, with a few Nayars and Christians, almost all from the labouring classes – gather at the *asram*. Before the session starts, whoever has come with a particular affliction approaches Swami's attendants, giving their name and details of their problem; they leave a donation (*daksina*) of not more than 10 rupees, often far less. The session begins with one of Swami's yellow-clad *sannyasi* explaining some aspects of Gurudevan's religious and social teachings, showing continuity between Gurudevan and Swami. Holy water having been sprinkled towards the congregation and towards an image of Gurudevan, Swami would arrive, helped by two attendants, to lead the congregation in prayers to Gurudevan and to Siva. Lighting a lamp to Gurudevan, Swami would recount episodes during which he had directly experienced Gurudevan's *sakti* and the truth of his teachings. Since Swami's *sammadhi* in 1994, his disciples continue to run both *asram* and Sunday public gatherings. The gathering chants a prayer in which Siva, Gurudevan – and since 1994 Swami himself – are asked to remove '*dusta sakti, sarpam dosam, bhavana dosam* and *sudram sakti*' (power for evil, problems or illnesses caused by snake deities, problems or illnesses caused by problems in the house and the power of sorcery). An attendant reads some 20 names (some not present, some of whom are migrants) who seek Swami's intercession to remove troubles, followed by more loud prayer at which point some women usually start to weep openly, and healing and exorcism begins. The process is comparable with descriptions from similar settings (for example Kakar 1982: 104–5; Parry 1994: 233ff; Fuller 1992: 231ff).

One Sunday a woman fell at Swami's feet in a state of possession. She had been staying in the *asram* for more than three months, a widow who had been sent there by her family after four relatives (including her husband) had died. A *sannyasi* told us that she was possessed by 47 spirits. Swami put his foot on her head and asked, 'Who are you? Tell me your name you dog, you rascal! If you don't tell me I will beat you!' The woman at his feet, in convulsions, shouted abuse to Swami, screaming, 'I will destroy you and this *asram*, you motherfucker.' Swami commanded: 'Go and burn in the flame!!' and lit some camphor to the lamp in front of Gurudevan. Other afflicted people followed, and the entire session lasted more than two hours. After final prayers, Swami retired to his room to receive those seeking private advice and special blessing; finally, all were given a vegetarian meal cooked in the *asram* and served by the *sannyasis*.

At Swami Shubhananda's *asram*, *dosam* and *mantravadam* are removed from the poor without compromising Narayana Guru's tenets and resorting either to the use of magic or the help of fierce deities, in an eclectic style combining references to Narayana Guru as social reformer, deified saint and incarnation of Siva. Swami's popularity does not and did not depend only on his reputed *sakti* but also on the quality and affordability of his help: while the Swami is not directly approached for fulfilment of material wishes, his intervention removes obstacles to well-being without recourse to other expensive rituals or *nercha* to deities.

Tenganoor Amma

Some 2 km away lives Tenganoor Amma, whose reputation is no less than Swami's and whose clientele is wider-ranging. While neither the respectable reformed nor the status-conscious come to her, she serves those many Christians, Nayars and Izhavas, poor or wealthy, who need immediate relief. Izhavas whose preoccupations with *chance* and *dosam* are not satisfied within SNDP orthodoxy come here. Amma, through possession trance, is able to offer Bhadrakali's direct intervention and the gratification of personal interaction with a deity. Amma's history begins when a young man returned from receiving religious instruction at Sivagiri to marry and settle. During meditation, Bhadrakali appeared and her *sakti* entered him. She offered him the power of helping other people; he asked the goddess to give her *sakti* to his wife. In the face of hostility from fellow-villagers, who accuse them of encroaching public land and printing *black money*, the couple built a temple with attached Ayurvedic pharmacy and began to work.

The main shrine (Siva and Parvati) is flanked by Durga and Bhadrakali, Nagaraja and Nagayekshi. Amma arrives each afternoon in red blouse and red *sari*, her hair loose. Going to the main shrine, she stamps her feet and waves the goddess's sword in outstretched hand. Eyes rolled up, tongue thrust out and arms flailing, she whirls and stoops, tossing her head so that her hair flies around, all the time stamping. Regular devotees at the side of the shrine softly sing the refrain, 'Om, Sakti! Om, Parasakti!'. Amma then brings Bhadrakali's *pidam* from the shrine and sits on it under the *mandapam*. Knees apart and feet firmly planted on the floor, Amma speaks – sometimes abruptly, sometimes girlishly, giggling and rolling her eyes. She is of course possessed: addressing her, devotees are in direct communication with Bhadrakali (cf. Tarabout 1999).

On one afternoon we visited, she saw seven clients in less than two hours: to a woman complaining of evil magic (*sudram*) against her, Amma confirmed her doubts, giving a blessed metal figurine (*rupam*). Another client complained that her husband was not returning from the Gulf. Her family had promised a dowry of Rs100,000 but had paid only a quarter; mother-in-law was telling her son not to come home on leave, because she knew that he would forgive his wife and waive the dowry. Amma advised that she could bring the husband home, but only with costly rituals. Meanwhile, Amma advised the family to pay more dowry; otherwise more troubles would ensue. The woman left after receiving a *rupam* to be placed near the picture of her husband. Two clients – one allegedly showing signs of *lunacy* and another with a skin complaint (diagnosed as *sarpam dosam*) – were given prescriptions for Ayurvedic medicine from Amma's shop. An obviously poor man whose wife was having an affair and giving money to her lover, was given a knotted black thread (*tadika*) blessed by Amma to make his wife wear, to keep the other man away. A man asking for help with eviction was advised to bring Amma the court order; she would put a spell on it and would also tell the name of a court clerk who could be bribed. Although devotees' *daksina* is relatively small (usually around Rs10–20), Amma, unlike Swami, often prescribes performance of particular rituals and/or Ayurvedic remedies bought from her shop. But beside differences in technique and specialisation, relationships with their respective devotees are similar – they act as intermediaries between devotee and divine. Through such personalised, albeit mediated, relations with deities, devotees draw attention to their plight and hope for direct intervention. Unlike Swami, Amma makes only occasional and cursory references to Narayana Guru.

Hanuman Tantri

All but the highest Izhavas call upon Hanuman Tantri, a very different style of ritual specialist, offering the same services to Izhavas and in Izhava temples as are offered by Brahman *tantris* in public and higher-status temples. From a titled Izhava family, he claims to have learned his trade from a local Brahman *tantri*. Like his Brahman counterparts, he does not claim any sort of supernatural powers; his *sakti*, he asserts, derives solely from knowledge and control gained over the years. Now in his late sixties, he lives in an old *nalukettu* receiving clients – almost all Izhavas – in a brick shed a few yards east of the house. Wearing only a white *mundu*, he sits behind a small table on which stand a couple of almanacs and a small bag containing cowrie shells for astrological prediction. He has a good reputation and receives visits from locals and those from neighbouring villages, seeing every day around 20–30 people. The services he provides are exactly akin to those of Brahman *Tantris*: he combines astrology with divination, performance of special *pujas* and *homams*, installation of temple deities and so on. Like Brahmans, he claims no involvement in *duskarmam*.

Part of his job is straightforward astrology. Clients come to ascertain a *muhurtam* to start an action, to draw up astrological charts for newborn babies, to match horoscopes for would-be spouses and so on. Many also visit for relief from specific afflictions. According to Tantri, predicaments are of two types: 'genuine' ones caused by temporary or permanent negative astrological configurations and others, caused by divine beings. Like other local specialists, Tantri claims that evil eye and *mantravadam* are on the increase. Increasing economic development and differentiation has led to more resentment and conflict within families and between neighbours (cf. Pocock 1973: 25–40). He diagnoses many cases as envy-motivated *mantravadam*. The action advised is not only appropriate to the problem but also dependent upon a client's financial condition. Tantri charges no fee, receiving (like Brahmans) only *daksina*, but can predict by appearances how much a client will give and how much they can afford to spend to redress *dosam*. For wealthier clients, diagnosis is a lengthy 30 minutes questioning with answers matched against circumstances. Tantri diagnosed one client's skin disease as *sarpam dosam*, recommended an Ayurvedic doctor and suggested an expensive *sarpam puja* lasting several days and requiring the presence of the Tantri himself. Difficulties at home might require an equally expensive Ganapathi *homam*; possession or troubles from evil spirits might necessitate construction of a new shrine. If clients are obviously poor, a consultation with Tantri lasts no more than 5 minutes. Their *nakshatram* is checked against current planetary configurations. The remedy consists of a *mantram* half-heartedly murmured by Tantri while tying knots in a black *tadika* thread which the afflicted is to wear. Sometimes clients are advised to pray at particular temples. Both Tantri and his poorer clients know that these are inadequate remedies which offer only limited help and protection: still, they are better than nothing. At the other end of the scale, a properly performed *homam* can easily result in a job in the Gulf.

Hanuman Tantri, like Velayuthan Panikker and Narayana Guru, embodies Izhava aspirations to appropriate Brahmanical practices while simultaneously asserting community religious self-sufficiency. While Shubhananda Swami, Tenganoor Amma and Hanuman Tantri have a steady and numerous clientele, they are seldom publicly visited by the status-conscious, wealthy section of the Izhava community. By contrast, one religious practice which does run right across the board is that of making a vow to a deity directly, sometimes without first recourse to specialist diagnosis. The largest of these vows, at prestigious temples, offer opportunities for public demonstrations of wealth, claims to status and conversion of substantial capital.

Sacrificial Offerings at Temples: *Kuttiyottam* and *Anpoli*

Favoured among those of wealth and status are vows (*nercha*s) to sponsor parts of festivals at major public temples. A *nercha* out of reach to almost all villagers is *kuttiyottam*, performed at a popular Bhadrakali temple where many Nayars worship. Puthenkulangara is a large public temple around 250 years old which has grown up this century to become a regional pilgrimage centre and one of Kerala's wealthiest temples. *Kuttiyottam* there is a symbolic human sacrifice consisting of the offering of some drops of blood drawn from one or two pre-pubescent boys. For nine days prior to the sacrifice, coinciding with the main festival day, the boys – purposely 'adopted' from poor low caste families – are kept in the sponsor's house and every evening are taught four particular dance steps which they will perform on the tenth day at the temple. These dance steps, accompanied by songs praising Bhadrakali, are taught by semi-professional performing groups[8] hired by the sponsor who also provides vegetarian food to whoever attends the nine evenings of preparation.

Kuttiyottam, literally meaning 'running and stabbing', was 'traditionally' (i.e. in the nineteenth century) offered by Nayars; Izhavas, excluded from it, are said to have performed *tukkam tullal* (hook-swinging; see Oddie 1995) on the following day, under the sponsorship of the prominent Alummoottil family. While some Izhavas claimed ignorance of *tukkam tullal* or denied that it had ever been practised, others said that in the 1930s when Alummoottil family led Izhava protests for full temple access, in line with Narayana Guru's exhortations, the whole community withdrew from *tukkam tullal*. Post temple-entry, Alummoottil are said to have been the first *avarna* family to sponsor a *kuttiyottam*: recent patrons (1980s and 1990s) have included a Christian businessman and several wealthy Izhavas. Following this festival over several years, we have seen increasing escalation in scale and cost to the point where, in 1995, eight of eleven *kuttiyottam* sponsors were employed outside Kerala (mostly Gulf), at high levels such as engineer or computer programmer. Minimum expenditure for successful sponsorship has risen to Rs200,000, from Rs100,000 when we first saw the festival in 1990.

From being a relatively small-scale affair involving inhabitants of four villages surrounding the temple, *kuttiyottam* has expanded to include not only the 13 local villages now officially recognised as under the protection of Puthenkulangara Amma, but also outlying areas. In Valiyagramam, falling outside of the official 'catchment area', the first *kuttiyottam* was performed in 1993, followed by others in 1994 and 1995 respectively, all three sponsored by well known wealthy Nayar families. We feel it likely that within the next five years a Valiyagramam Izhava family will sponsor a *kuttiyottam*. Many village festivals, including Sasthamuri *gurumandiram* and several Izhava family temples, now include in their programmes performances by *kuttiyottam* singing and dancing troupes,[9] while *kuttiyottam* songs are routinely played on local temples' loudspeakers. While the newly rich generally offer this lavish vow as a sign of extreme gratitude and devotion to the powerful Devi who facilitates capital accumulation, *kuttiyottam* – involving the sponsor leading a huge procession to the temple where crowds of several thousands are gathered – is a very public statement of wealth and prestige. The humble idiom of *bhakti* is transformed into an occasion both for capital conversion and for status claims.

For those with lesser amounts at their disposal and no huge amounts of capital to be converted, smaller sponsorship vows are available locally. One of the most prestigious, performed at Valiyagramam's popular Kottakara Devi temple, is *anpoli*, an offering to Durga promoting the donor's prosperity and well-being. *Anpoli* involves offering five measures (*paras*), each containing a different item: *paccari* (raw rice), *nellu* (paddy), *pazhangal* (bananas), *aval* (dried and beaten rice flakes) and *malar* (parched rice). The right to make this offering was originally strictly limited: two high-status old Nayar families, one living to the east of the temple and one to the west, held exclusive hereditary rights (*avagasham*) to sponsor offerings on behalf of all those in their neighbourhood. In contrast to inexpensive and innovative popular vows such as the lime-lamp mentioned earlier, *anpoli* (like *kuttiyottam*) has the cachet of an exclusive, elaborate and costly offering to a powerful and Sanskritic deity, sanctioned by long tradition. When we first saw it in 1990, *anpoli* had been officially taken over by two NSS *karayogam*s at east and west, for which they received a grant from the temple administration. Although *anpoli* is made by the NSS, taking over rights from families who relinquished traditional rights (*avagashangal*), in practice powerful individuals within the association tend to ascribe to themselves and to their family alone the honour derived from the offerings.

Izhavas have been compensating for their exclusion by caste from this main *anpoli* on the festival's last day by innovating, making similar offerings during Durga's visits to their neighbourhood for paddy collection. Izhava families in Kottakara used Sivamuri temple committee to organise *anpoli* on behalf of the whole *kara* when Kottakara Devi visited Sivamuri temple in 1991; another *anpoli* was offered by the SNDP *yogam*. As more and more individual households now offer a measure of paddy during *parakka' ezhunelattu*, an 'offering inflation' has taken place, in which distinction demands that those wishing to assert high status must do something more: *anpoli* provides an opportunity. By 1993, individual families (almost all Nayars) were offering *anpoli* in place of the more modest and usual *para* when Durga visited their neighbourhood for her annual offerings. In this way, three levels of participation and prestige have been established: the labouring poor – who have hardly enough paddy to feed themselves – may offer a small measure (*idanghezhi*) of paddy or none at all; the vast majority of households will offer a full 5 litre measure (*para*); and a few will offer *anpoli*. Such innovations as '*triple anpoli*' are now being used to maintain differentials between the wealthiest Nayars and the rest.

In 1995, for the first time, an Izhava family (belonging to the *naluvittumar*: father a retired policeman, son a government employee in the state capital) offered individual household *anpoli*. This was done at the 'core' family house, where two small ancestor shrines had been in 1991, but where by 1995 a small family temple stood, newly renovated and extended with Gulf monies sent by the household's eldest son. Family and neighbours crowded into the compound to be part of the excitement of seeing Kottakara Devi take *anpoli* from an Izhava house. The offering was seen by some as a clear bid by the sponsoring household to reconstitute *naluvittumar* families as a high-status unit acting on behalf of all neighbourhood Izhavas, as it was in the nineteenth century, analogous to the right-holding dominant Nayar families of Kottakara east and west. By offering *anpoli*, this household then furthered the status both of the caste and of their own *kutumbam*.

Renovation of Family Temples

It is not unusual that one priority of this *naluvittumar* family, when Gulf monies began to arrive, was to renovate a neglected shrine into a proper temple, a practice started in the 1980s by wealthy Nayars: to construct or reconstruct a family temple is a common means of conversion, family temples representing substantial cultural capital. Family temples of poorer Izhavas, like those of other ex-untouchables, often consist of a small *kavu* with a few blackened stones dedicated to ancestors and minor deities. In many cases these *kavus* are left unattended and no offerings beside an occasional oil lamp are given. Wealthier Izhavas, like Nayars, have 'proper' family shrines which might have been neglected at the height of the SNDP's reform campaign but which are now renovated whenever a family reaches a degree of economic prosperity, with monthly *pujas* performed and an annual festival conducted. Those with resources for taking proper care of family deities and *pithrukkal* neutralise the risk of *dosam* arising from neglect, which would damage a family's general welfare and well-being. They can also assert status and (re-)construct a public identity as people who have position (*sthanam*): house, land, ancestors and temple, and in some cases a serpent's *kavu*, are held together by the living, as they 'should' be.

Usually in an Izhava family shrine, besides a *kuriala* (ancestors' shrine) there are two classes of deities. The first is one with whom the whole *kutumbam* has had a long-standing relation, usually a form of the goddess. Owners often assert that the goddess comes from some well-known temple, attracted to the family shrine by a spiritually powerful ancestor. This means that at some stage in the recent past the family has consulted an astrologer who, after *devaprasanam*, has clarified that their old family deity (often a simple stone) was in reality not a bloodthirsty and violent goddess but a higher deity from a well known temple. A new image (in more proper and orthodox representation) is installed, replacing the old stone which becomes transformed into a subsidiary helper (lower form) of the newly installed goddess. This in turn allows for transformation of the anonymous *pithrukkal* grouped in the ancestor shrine. One is reconstructed as an *appuppan*, publicly a powerful *Yogiswaran* – sometimes privately an expert *mantravadi* – who had the power and devotion necessary to bring the high deity to the family. The renamed ancestor is physically separated from the others in the *kuriala*, and set in a new shrine (cf. Tarabout 1990). The second category of deities in Izhava family temples are autochthonous land spirits, all potentially dangerous if left to roam free and unattended but helpful to the family if fixed in a particular place and propitiated. Archetypical autochthonous deities are Nagas (snake gods and goddesses): the first beings to populate Kerala after it arose from the water, thus the original inhabitants to whom the entire land rightfully belongs. Some temples simply consist of a *kavu*, a patch of land dedicated to Nagas, left untouched and 'wild' and on which serpents are said to live (cf. Uchiyamada 1995).

One wealthy and powerful Izhava family near Kottakara, former holders of the *avagasham* to hold cock-fights and now comprising more than ten households (including many migrants to north India and the Gulf), founded a *gurumandiram* and SNDP branch in its neighbourhood. The family head, long-time secretary of the SNDP *karayogam*, also concerns himself with running the family temple. The main deity (as divined by Hanuman *tantri*) is Bhadrakali, brought from a temple in Chennur (10 km south) by a Yogiswaran. Minor deities are Nagas and Malaimurti (a mountain deity). While elders speak of the shrine as dedicated to Chattan (a mischievous, sometimes malevolent deity), younger family members deny this (cf. Tarabout 1992, 1997). *Kozhivettu* was stopped ten years ago at renovation and only surrogate *kurudi* (using turmeric and lime) is performed: the goddess, who used to be very *ugra*, has therefore become calmer. The family maintain – against common belief – that the goddess does not resent this change in offerings and has not lost her *sakti*. Since renovation, the *velichappadu* is possessed by Yogiswaran far less frequently: just twice a year, when *kurudi* is performed. He explained that nowadays people do not listen to his advice, do not wish to vent their problems publicly and cannot wait for an occasional *tullal* to get counsel, preferring immediate and private consultation with other ritual specialists when the occasion arises. Since renovation, at considerable expense, the family has altered rather than severed links with the *gurumandiram*: a full-fledged annual festival has been started at the family temple, whose procession starts out from the *gurumandiram*.

Another temple belongs to Engineer Sadashivan's titled and wealthy Izhava family. This temple's secretary and president, both SNDP office bearers, are respectively a *vaidyan* (Bachelor of Ayurvedic Medicine qualified) and a *travel agent*. In 1989, the temple was renovated under the instruction of Hanuman Tantri, constructing two main shrines for Yogiswaran and Bhuvaneswari and smaller shrines for Brahmarakshassu and Naga. Slightly apart from this main complex stand the smaller older shrines: the original *pithrukkal* with, on the south-west corner, one old stone dedicated to *peyvaliyacchan*, a 'demon grandfather' who takes toddy as his main offering. Since 1989 there is no *velichappadu* and no blood sacrifices are performed, not even surrogate ones. The fact that *kozhivettu* was previously regularly performed suggests that before installation of Bhuvaneswari, another goddess, more fierce and violent, sat there (cf. Tarabout 1992). In 1991 the annual festival was a small family affair; by 1995, thanks to substantial donations from a wealthy family member based in Bombay, a large programme – including musicians, singers and dancers – had begun, and small crowds attended nightly. This appears to be in the process of becoming a neighbourhood festival competing with the *gurumandiram*.

The process of transformation of family deities and adoption of Sanskritic ritual has not yet reached the dimensions found in the western coastal belt, where *puja* is performed regularly by Brahmans, something still unheard of in Valiyagramam. Renovation of family shrines and temples is widely promoted by sections of families who have made significant economic gains. They adopt the constitution of a 'family association' to look after the temple and the festival. As among Nayars, these associations are seen as rebuilding family strength and unity which was lost when the *tharavadu* system disintegrated, although the unified matrilineage reconstructed thus may be only occasional and fictitious. Apart from a few families continuing to reside locally, a large proportion of the members of these 'family' associations live scattered across Kerala, India or even abroad, meeting only once a year on the occasion of the annual festival (cf. Bloch 1994; Mascarenhas-Keyes 1986). We came across several such family committees (among both Izhavas and Nayars) which have registered themselves as investment societies, placing money collected from family members into schemes such as joint ownership plantations or the thriving Kochi stock exchange; profits are used to maintain the family temple and in other activities promoting family prestige, including offering scholarships to the children of impoverished family households.

While high-status professional village Izhavas may not have the resources to perform *kuttiyottam* or similar extremely costly vows, and may only occasionally hire a Brahman – to perform Ganapati *homam* in the house – they are mostly able to 'move along with Nayars' locally, and their religious lives hardly differ from those of Nayars. They renovate family temples, ignore the SNDP altogether or take part in its activities only at leadership level, shun *gurus* and *ammas* and attend prestigious *savarna*-dominated public temples. The most ambitious section of the community has one particular avenue for consolidating and asserting prestige: becoming directly involved in activities at the main village temples.

CONTESTING AND CONSOLIDATING STATUS: PUBLIC TEMPLES

A few Izhavas with the economic means and/or influence necessary to go further than visiting temples or making paddy offerings seek election on to the committees which run public activities, the high-profile annual festival being a particularly important arena. 'When you have made money, you make large donations to the temple and go there every day', explained Balachandran. 'Your name will keep appearing in temple programmes. If you make a large donation for construction of a marriage hall, your name will be written outside on a plaque. After a while, you try to get elected to a committee.' Endowments are a means of publicly and concretely advertising and converting wealth, and an entry into Nayar-dominated circles (cf. Price 1996: 106ff). At the same time, while the Nayars who run the committees and festivals of public temples might allow one or two token 'respectable' Izhavas into their circle, they continue to resist full-scale participation of Izhavas as a group in temple life.

The Struggle for Access

Izhavas involved in temple committees are typically older men, permanently settled in Valiyagramam, who hold or have recently retired from government servant posts; they belong to respected, widely connected (possibly titled) old families. As men of influence and prestige within their own community, they frequently hold executive positions on management committees of local SNDP *karayogams*. This is an extremely important pre-condition: by promoting caste unity through SNDP activities and Gurudevan's cult, they build militant caste-bases which can easily be mobilised to support bids for access to temple committees. Individual quests for prestige here become merged and linked with the wider status mobility strategies of the caste as a whole whose interests, as community leaders, such men claim to represent. Individual successes are presented as successes for the community at large; at the same time, these Izhavas provide a focus for the status ambitions of the whole community and are sometimes the catalyst for mass challenges to caste hierarchy.

Divagaran is one of few Izhavas to have reached positions of power in one of Valiyagramam's three main *Devaswam* Board public temples. He is an affable, relaxed man, living in a 1960s two-roomed brick house with wife, daughter-in-law, two daughters and aged widowed mother, polyandrously married to two brothers. A third daughter lives away with her husband, an army *jawan*. Two sons-in-law work, along with Divagaran's ITC-qualified son, in Dubai, 'in a *company*'. Divagaran studied only up to fourth standard, enjoys a drink and a smoke, and does not speak English. In this he differs from those Izhava leaders who emerge from the abstemious educated Left, often school-teachers. While belonging to the *naluvittumar*, his family are not of particularly high prestige; mother's husbands were casual labourers and landless small cultivators. That the new Gulf connection is rapidly improving family fortunes is evidenced by the full sets of gold anklets, waist-chains, bracelets, rings and neck-chains worn by all three babies in the house. As the Dinar remittances come in, the family are on the verge of take-off and will probably start substantially extending and reconstructing the small brick house within the next few years.

Until retirement in 1995, Divagaran worked as a *peon* in the town sub-registrar's office, registering land documents. While this is not a high-salary post, he received regular cash gifts for ensuring smooth registration of – sometimes fraudulent – land transfers. Because of his job, according to neighbours he has, 'many Nayars in his pocket; he knows so many secrets'. This fact, as well as the status enjoyed by virtue of a *government job* and by being son and grandson of SNDP founding members have all enabled him to stand several times as SNDP President or Secretary, and to build a reputation as a big-man and community leader. He successfully used this weight as an Izhava leader and his close contacts with Nayars to facilitate election on to the committee of the well-attended public *Devaswam* Sivamuri Siva temple, later becoming secretary. Election as temple secretary was an important personal and community achievement: he was the first Izhava – first non-*savarna* – to be elected to this committee. However, the progressive involvement of Izhavas in Sivamuri temple has not gone unopposed.

Sivamuri Siva Temple

The temple, dedicated to Mahadevar, used to be the private temple of a powerful Nayar family, Wariampallil *tharavadu*. This was one of the four biggest landowning families in Valiyagramam, employing many Sasthamuri Izhavas as sub-tenants and/or agricultural labourers. Looking for new economic opportunities at the turn of the nineteenth century, the then *karanavan* joined with other wealthy Nayars to build Mahatma School where many Wariampallil members have since worked. By the 1950s, the family had lost much of its wealth after a series of bitter partitions. Unable to afford maintenance, Wariampallil passed the family temple properties on to the *Devaswam* Board, who agreed to give the local NSS *karayogam* – composed mostly of Wariampallil members – an annual grant for celebration of *Mahotsavam* at Sivaratri.[10] In this way the temple was opened to all neighbourhood residents, while the main public activity – the annual festival – remained under Nayar control, via the local NSS.

   With time, Sasthamuri Izhavas began to complain that since the temple had become public its festival should also belong to everybody and not merely to the NSS. They petitioned the *Devaswam* Board which, in 1981, set guidelines for constitution of a new committee inclusive of representatives from all neighbourhood Hindu communities. However, the Sivaratri festival continued to be associated primarily with Nayars who, through the NSS, claimed 'traditional rights' (*avagashangal*) over it. In 1988, a section of the committee resenting NSS dominance, led by local Izhavas, proposed a new festival: a *saptaham vayana* (seven-day reading of the Bhagavad Gita). They proposed that this should coincide with *Mandala Puja*, the 41-day season of special religious observance for the popular Sabarimala pilgrimage and a period when temple attendance is high. This proposal gathered support from one impoverished but senior section of Wariampallil family Nayars, anxious to curb the rising power of a junior branch, called Puthen Pallil, recently enriched through Gulf migration. Although Puthen Pallil had begun to devote more time and money to the development of their own family temple, they continued to participate in the Sivamuri committee and had acquired prominence within the NSS *karayogam*.

Puthen Pallil Nayars immediately opposed the new festival. A *saptaham* usually ends with an *arat* procession including collection of paddy and money from the neighbourhood. The day proposed for the *arat* coincided with the annual festival procession of Puthen Pallil family's newly refurbished temple. Puthen Pallil members, supported by the RSS, argued that Sivaratri should properly and by tradition be the only major festival at Sivamuri and insisted that a new celebration was unnecessary, adding that a festival was already conducted on that date at their own family temple, to which all local people were welcome. This position was obviously unacceptable to other Sivamuri temple committee members and supporters. For Izhavas, it would have meant publicly accepting the superiority and spiritual patronage of Nayars; for Nayars, it would have meant validating and accepting claims to precedence from a '*nouveau-riche*' junior family branch. Since neither faction was prepared to give in, the Sivamuri committee split: on one side, Puthen Pallil sponsored formation of the *Sivamuri Kshetra Samrakshana Sammiddhi* (Sivamuri Temple Protection Committee) with a local NSS leader, a Puthen Pallil member, as president, and – to pre-empt claims of high-caste bias – a Scheduled Caste (Vira Saiva) *Devaswam* Board employee as secretary. On the other, the proposers of the new *saptaham* festival formed the multi-community *Sivamuri Kshetra Samrakshana Ayudhava Sammiddhi* (Sivamuri Temple Militant Protection Committee), with a Nayar from the disgruntled senior branch of Wariampallil as president, a Pulaya as vice-president and Divagaran – Izhava – as secretary. Growing tension between the two committees came to a head in 1989. At the end of the *saptaham*, the *arat* took place as planned: on the same day, Puthen Pallil held its own family temple's festival. The two processions ended up crossing each other's path that night, near Sivamuri temple. Both groups claimed precedence: in no time, fighting started between Puthen Pallil Nayars on one side and Sasthamuri Izhavas on the other. Puthen Pallil – supported by RSS militants – caught the other procession unprepared, smashed the windows of the decorated lorry leading Sivamuri's procession, and managed to pass first.

In 1990 the committee sponsoring the *saptaham*, under pressure from Izhava members, prepared its retaliation. During the first part of the procession, on its way to the river for the deity's holy bath, Izhava houses and the *gurumandiram* prepared large *receptions* for Sivamuri Mahadevar and made a point of accompanying their offerings with fireworks and loud *bhajana*. In the evening the returning procession attracted a large crowd, among whom Izhavas and Pulayas were conspicuous for their number. The procession was led by SNDP members and Izhava youths pointedly singing devotional songs dedicated to Aiyappan of Sabarimala, a deity whose pilgrimage attracts not only low- and high-caste Hindus alike but also Muslims and Christians, and who is popularly argued to symbolise unity and harmony (Gath 1998; Sekar

1992; Daniel 1984). They were followed by a hand-cart carrying two 4 metre high *kala* prepared by the local Pulaya association and a group of eight Pulayas performing *kambavakali* (usually relegated in multi-caste processions to the back; cf. Gough 1970; Beck 1981; Tarabout 1986). Next came a Pulaya *bhajana* group and two lines of about 50 young girls (mostly Izhavas and Nayars) holding *talapoli*. They were followed by temple drummers; temple committee members; the temple *pujari* carrying the *bimbam* and finally by a caparisoned elephant carrying a garlanded picture of Krishna. Along the way, many families offered paddy while the local Pulaya association, which had set up a temporary shrine with pictures of Siva, Krishna and Ayyan Kali (a Pulaya reformer), gave a *reception* of songs and fireworks.

In striking contrast, the Puthen Pallil procession included only Nayars – mostly from Puthen Pallil with a few from Wariampallil, the original root family. It was opened by about 150 girls in two lines carrying *talapoli*, followed by a professional troupe of *kazhakamtullal* dancers, by hired musicians and a decorated lorry carrying a large PA system playing songs for, and carrying a picture of, Bhadrakali. Significantly, Bhadrakali has a martial aspect and is especially effective in gaining victory over enemies; she is also the protector of *dharma* – the moral order – and she is especially associated with the Nayar community, some of whom keep her sword in their *puja* rooms. To make their claims for precedence even more explicit, the Puthen Pallil procession started from the Durga temple inside the abandoned Velathumpadi Palace, former residence of the area's Brahman *janmi*, Edapalli Rajah.

When the two processions met, there was immediate tension: Izhavas and Pulayas accompanying the Sivamuri procession tried to push forward; the RSS and Puthen Pallil men, outnumbered by the other group, had to step back. The presence of the police and of all *panchayat* members prevented the breaking out of an outright fight, as had happened the year before. After lengthy negotiations, the Puthen Pallil procession was let through first, preserving Nayar precedence and pride. The next day, Izhavas claimed to have scored a significant victory: their procession had been larger and had included villagers from all local communities, supporting the claim that the other committee was totally unrepresentative of the village mood and that it was nothing but a tool in the hands of Puthen Pallil, the NSS and the RSS. At the same time, Izhavas privately exhibited the ambivalence typical of castes in their position, speaking with pride about having been able to head up a procession marching alongside neighbourhood Nayars.[11] The delicate issue of precedence between the two processions, relegated to an issue of mere 'traffic control', was not discussed.

By the time we returned in 1995, clashes between Izhavas and Puthen Pallil Nayars had become a permanent feature of the *arat* procession, while the split between the two Sivamuri temple committees had taken on overtly political overtones, with the RSS and the Left Parties openly declaring support for opposing factions. In the meantime, the Puthen Pallil-RSS committee has continued to claim Sivaratri as the only legitimate festival of Sivamuri temple, making it an increasingly large occasion. Local RSS leaders and supporters are appealing to discourses of tradition and *dharma* and appealing to the rights (*avagashangal*) held by Nayars to prevent Izhavas from gaining prominence in this festival. The cover of the 1995 Sivaratri festival programme featured artwork showing a 'traditional' and hierarchically organised orderly procession, representatives of each caste in their 'rightful' places. This has been accompanied by public campaigning against drunkenness during processions, a feature common to all festivals and usually passing unremarked as part of a celebratory atmosphere but here explicitly attributed to Izhavas. When we visited him in 1995, Divagaran complained bitterly of having become the object of a particularly vicious defamatory campaign, with Nayars openly accusing him of stealing temple funds to buy drink. He will shortly retire from government service; undeterred, he told us that he has recently given up SNDP activities and is looking forward to having more free time, to concentrate further upon Sivamuri temple activities.

Festivals as Sites of Struggle

Temples have often been a privileged site of conflicts, usually revolving around the definition of the position of families/individuals or castes within an order constituted around the deity, ultimately creating and legitimising status and power (Dirks 1991). Struggle and conflict are embedded in many temple village rituals, particularly annual festivals. In Valiyagramam, as in the rest of Kerala and other parts of south India, festivals occur at a time of cosmic crisis, of chaos and decay, often said to be represented by crowds of drunken, disorderly devotees (for example Tarabout 1986, 1993; Beck 1981; Biardeau 1984; see also Fuller 1992: Ch. 6). Through the intervention of a deity the demonic crowd (*asuras*) – the forces of disorder (*adharma*) – are finally defeated; through their sacrifice,[12] socio-cosmic order is recreated and restored.[13] The deity is thus re-established as 'ruler' at the centre of an ordered microcosmic universe constituted around the temple (cf. Inden 1978: 58–9; Tarabout 1986: 301). Strong competition takes place around the assignation of rights (*avagashangal*) to perform ritual tasks during festivals. Particularly fierce is competition to attain pre-eminence as major protector-devotee of (sacrificer to) the deity and the temple, reproducing at the local level a role which was the prerogative of Hindu kings. Such conflicts, often formalised during festivals as competitive ritual display between opposed neighbourhoods (such as the east–west *anpoli* above) were formerly limited to upper-caste villagers – the traditional holders of these rights – ambiguously defined as 'the neighbourhood people', *karakkar*. While RSS and NSS traditionalists insist upon sticking to narrow definitions, Izhavas are struggling to widen the meaning of '*karakkar*'.

Temple festivals are one major public arena where claims of individual Izhavas and of the caste are put to annual test. During festivals, the caste's ritual worth is projected outwards to the entire village. Actively participating in major festivals by honouring deities and offering paddy in *para* donations or *anpoli* publicly demonstrates both that Izhavas have enough surplus wealth to make offerings and that their status is high enough to make offerings acceptable to the deity. Claims to have 'reformed' religious endeavour have been used to justify Izhavas' appeals for a place in major festivals on equal footing with the Nayars. The relative success achieved in this direction depends equally upon Izhava caste militancy, the support of a sympathetic *Devaswam* Board and fragmentation of the upper castes. If the leadership of a few prominent Izhavas has been instrumental in the caste's partial success in asserting its presence in village festivals, it is also true that the support of the caste has been determinant for the personal success of ambitious Izhavas.

Izhavas sometimes become victims of their own strength, determination and militancy. As they try to gain prominence in festivals, the opposition of upper castes – Nayars in particular – grows stronger. The case of Sivamuri temple is not unique: the committees of Valiyagramam's other two main public temples are also split along exactly similar lines and festivals there have also been occasions of open confrontation between Nayars and Izhavas. In two other incidents occurring between 1989 and 1991, a section of upper castes tried to bar Izhavas and Pulayas from participating in celebrations, clashes being limited in both cases to an exchange of insults and a few punches, thanks to the quick intervention of *panchayat* members and police. In the effort to contain what they perceive as a threat from the lower castes, Nayars appear to have made temples their 'last stand' for the maintenance and assertion of caste distinction, an arena for preservation of monopoly cultural capital. Izhavas who have struggled for prominence in public temples without the support and push of fellow-caste members have been more successful, their efforts going relatively unopposed. These are mostly Izhavas from high-status families, holding professional jobs, who maintain a distance from caste-mates, preferring to mix socially with Christians and Nayars of similar class standing. These are Izhavas who find the SNDP and Gurudevan's cult a straitjacket which, by stressing 'Izhava-ness', effectively fixes upper limits, grounded in the overall status of the caste, to the mobility of individuals and families. Accordingly, they seldom take part in activities of the SNDP or of *gurumandiram*.

Sadashivan, an executive engineer in the Electricity Board, is typical of this small group, which also includes people like Advocate Remini and her husband (Chapter 1). Sadashivan lives near the temple of Kottakara Durgadevi, of whom he is an ardent devotee. The main deity is Vana Durga and is said to contain *saktis* of Bhuvaneswari and Bhadrakali. The temple was founded, according to familiar myth, by a Brahman from a nearby town, with the help of 'local people' (*karakkar*). This Brahman, having 'stolen' the top half of an image from a local Bhadrakali temple, stopped to rest at Kottakara. Trying to resume his journey, he could not lift the image: he understood that the goddess's will was to remain on this site. Calling local Nayar residents to help, he built a temple around the goddess's rooted image (cf. Tarabout 1990). The Brahman rewarded these families by giving each of them special *avagashangal* during festivals. While most Nayar families have retained these *avagashangal*, the NSS has replaced those few who have forfeited their rights by moving out of the village. After the *Devaswam* Board – to whom the temple had been entrusted since the 1950s – recognised the validity of Nayar festival rights, Engineer Sadashivan and some non-right-holding Nayars started a new festival, a *navaham*; a committee was formed with Sadashivan elected as secretary. This *navaham* has been an outstanding success: daily crowds of less than 100 devotees in 1990 had by 1995 swollen to several hundreds. The final day's *lakshamdeepam* attracts thousands from all neighbouring areas. Each year new and fashionable rituals such as daily *homams* and new types of offerings such as *naranga bali* are introduced. The committee records the nine-day event on videotapes for Durga's many local devotees working in the Gulf.[14]

For Sadashivan, undisputed leader of the *navaham* committee, reasons for success are two-fold:

First, I established a good accounts system, recording every rupee received; each year, based on income, we decide upon a budget for the following festival. We don't go house to house to solicit donations; people come here to offer money: they trust us, know we are *sincere*. Second, there is a particular atmosphere during *navaham*. When people come they feel like helping out, doing even menial tasks. Nobody gives orders, there are no arguments and everyone simply gets on: we are all devotees of Durgadevi, we do this with her blessing.

By appealing to the ethos of *bhakti*, Sadashivan neatly side-steps and neutralises the issue of caste, while his focus on 'good book-keeping' highlights his professional status over caste identity.

Sadashivan's personal success is clearly attributable to his position as a well-respected, affluent, management-wise, government-employed engineer. Rooting his bid for leadership on his known and sincere personal devotion to Durga rather than upon collective caste-based ambitions, in other words by insisting upon his identity as 'devotee', he has managed progressively to win over and maintain support from many Nayars, unlike Divagaran, who stands at Sivamuri unambiguously as an Izhava, opposed to NSS and RSS dominance and militantly supported by his caste-fellows, drawing on to himself and his caste continuous opposition and threats. Sadashivan's professional status and two-storeyed house also remind us, as is apparent from his demeanour, that he is in a different social class from Divagaran and therefore more likely to see prestige ambitions succeed. At the same time, Sadashivan is divorced from his caste-fellows and does not enjoy their unqualified support. Those Pulayas who mock Hanuman Tantri as a 'junior Brahman' might well mock Sadashivan as a 'junior Nayar' (see Bourdieu

1984: 109ff and Mahar et al. 1990: 20 on the dilemma of the *parvenu*). Many of those Nayars who publicly accord him great respect continue in private – as he is well aware – to consider him as inferior. 'Nayars might be friendly to you', Sadashivan bitterly reminded us, ' but behind your back they despise you. In their mind they still have very strong caste prejudices.'

CONCLUSIONS

Narayana Guru insisted that the search for the socioeconomic progress of the community as a whole should be underpinned by and could not be divorced from adoption of Sankritised, Brahmanical-oriented practices. To the progressive essentialisation of Izhava identity over the late nineteenth century by reference to stigmatised religious practices, Narayana Guru answered with an opposite essentialist project whereby the community was to abandon practices rooted in popular Hinduism and adopt a reformed endeavour constructed around the Guru's austere interpretation of *advaita vedanta*. With the caste's new identity becoming inseparably associated with Narayana Guru himself, the SNDP has used Gurudevan's charismatic figure to narrowly define a religious orthopraxis around his cult. Local incidents at Sasthamuri *gurumandiram* and state-wide factional conflicts at Sivagiri *Math* underline the limits and contradictions of this project, revealing a plurality of interpretations which accord Narayana Guru the status of universalist social reformer, saint particular to the Izhava community, local Hindu deity or *avatar* of Siva. Emphasising different facets of Izhava identity, and therefore the prospect of a diverse range of possible wider alliances, politicisation of these conflicts is inevitable.

Attempts to delimit Izhava religious practices within the narrow confines of the cult of Gurudevan run against the ambitions of those members of the middle classes who, desirous of 'moving along with Nayars', strive to distance themselves from strong public association with that 'Izhava-ness' of which Narayana Guru has become the central symbol. While both Swami's *asram* and *gurumandirams* fully follow Sanskritic rituals and eschew the use of magic, blood sacrifices and so on, they remain irredeemably low-status, stigmatised by their associations with poverty and especially with 'Izhava-ness'. Referents for prestigious religious practice remain *savarna* Hindu and mainstream arenas such as public temples. Essentialist projects are also challenged by prevailing practice within popular Hinduism which allows for continuous proliferation and adoption of new rituals and practitioners way beyond any simple Sanskritic/non-Sanskritic dualism (Fuller 1992). The majority of villagers choose contextually among an eclectic series of practices, specialists and temples, selecting according to their needs or by reason of reputation and power. At the same time, different styles can express a plurality of social positions within the caste.

With the escalation of costly vows like *anpoli* and *kuttiyottam*, wealthy Izhavas increasingly come into direct competition with Nayars. This movement is seen most clearly in annual festivals and the running of public temples, opened since 1936 to *avarna jatis* and arenas in which politics and religion become closely entangled. In the next chapter we will turn to focus more directly upon village Izhavas' involvement in politics, an arena which dramatically highlights villagers' multiple identities, the fact that personal and familial mobility interests often run counter to those of the group, and which forces out an issue underlying the central dilemma not only of people like Engineer Sadashivan but more generally of all his caste-fellows and of all those intermediate ex-untouchable castes in the position of the Izhavas: who to stand with.

6   MOBILITY AND POWER

Achievement of power is important for Izhava status ambitions in two major ways: as a means to exert pressure for mobility claims and as a prestige-enhancing end in itself (Bourdieu 1990 suggests power might be the most disguised form of capital). Since the start of the twentieth century, Izhavas have attempted to become publicly and self-consciously unified, both as a single caste under the SNDP and within political parties and pressure groups, whether as members of wider social classes or as an interest group in alliance with other communities; they have on many occasions and in many arenas acted as a group to press caste mobility claims. They exert agency through democratic means, offering support to political parties or representatives in return for policies favouring the interests of various sections of the caste; through extra-parliamentary activities – for example standing together as a communal pressure group; through militant mobilisation asserting presence, as during temple festivals. Mobility strategies often lead ideological issues to be subordinated to pragmatic considerations, whether oriented towards immediate short-term gain or to longer-term prestige plans: alliances, whether formal-structural or informal-personal, are often issue-based and short-lived.

Formation of the SNDP created conditions for unification within a state-wide caste of hitherto endogamous regional groups such as Izhavas, Chovans and Tiyyas, but also for the articulation and projection of an essentialised collective identity, albeit moulded in the image and aspirations of the Izhava elite. SNDP activities, whether centred around Gurudevan's cult or militant actions in defence of Izhava 'rights', are public arenas through which attempts are made to construct (internally) as dominant and to project (externally) a collective caste identity embodied in the orthopraxis of community leaders. These efforts are undermined not only by occasional eruptions of plurality but by the SNDP's inability to represent the conflicting political interests of an increasingly economically stratified community. With the growth of Izhava middle classes and intensifying politicisation of Izhava labourers, economic disparities – initially addressed at the turn of the nineteenth century within the general problem of caste disabilities – led to emergence of class-conscious identities and alliances with larger social groups cutting across castes, partly objectified through allegiance to trade unions and political parties.

Power is also important for families' mobility ambitions which may, as we have argued throughout, run counter to the mobility of the caste as a group. Here power, which may be more or less structured and formalised, is commonly expressed through highly personalised patron–client relations, an important aspect of formal and informal local politics. Family mobility ambitions may be furthered through acting as patrons accumulating prestige and 'name', or as clients receiving concrete benefits from a patron. Patronage is a means through which *manam* (family or individual) is continuously constituted and affirmed, either positively or negatively. Family, caste, class and political party affiliation are not mere external structures of group affiliation enabling intra-group alliances, but are all sources of personal identity allowing the forging of wider communities and identities. Alliances and conflicts are always available to multiple interpretations and can be disguised or manipulated, as when alliance within a political party is presented as alliance based on class or/and caste, or when inter-caste violence is presented as party political violence. Group affiliations and alliances have serious status implications: alliance with Nayars under the banner of 'Hindu' identity carries more prestige than alliance with Pulayas under the rubric of 'ex-untouchable castes'.

THE STRUGGLE FOR REPRESENTATION

Old Political Relations: *Janmis* and *Naluvittumar*

Questions about the old political order in Valiyagramam received similar answers: 'Valiyagramam was ruled by Koickal Kaimal's family: they were *janmis*, collected taxes for the Rajah and had right of life and death over everyone.' According to the account of Koickal Pillai, the now destitute descendant of this high-status Nayar family:

The family moved into the locality from south Kerala, following defeat by Chola kings, bringing with them 300 Nayars and 500 Harijans. This place was under the control of Edapalli Rajah, who gave us tax-free land and the power to rule in exchange for allegiance. He gave us the title 'Kaimal'. Later, Edappalli Rajah came to agreement with Kayamkulam Rajah and this land went under Kayamkulam's control. When we arrived here there were no temples: my family donated land and had them built. We had power over all *karas*.

The Edapalli Rajah referred to by Koickal Pillai as the owner of all village land was a Nambutiri Brahman, the Illangallur (Edangallur) Rajah of Trikkakara (Kochi). He controlled an important Kerala temple dedicated to Vamana, *avatar* of Visnu who defeated Mahabali, mythical demon-king of Kerala (Menon 1993: 68ff.; Osella & Osella n.d.). By reason of privileged ritual status, through donations made to his temple's deity and through *sambandham* relations with the Kochi Rajah, Edapalli Rajah accumulated vast tracts of land throughout central and southern Kerala. In Valiyagramam alone he controlled more than 300 acres of *punja* and another 190 acres held by local temples which he owned (Sreedhara Menon 1965: 104–5, 170ff; Kurup 1977: 102–3; Tarabout 1986: 444–7; Sivan 1977). Through local retainers, Edapalli Rajah maintained authority inside temples as well as over large holdings of *Brahmaswam*, while Koickal Kaimal's family exercised power over the village as a whole. Records show many occasions of conflict in which each tried to usurp the other's sphere of authority. In 1709, for example, the annual festival of an Edapalli temple started without Koickal Kaimal's authorisation; as reprisal, Kaimal's supporters killed the temple elephant-keeper. Edapalli fined Koickal 120 *fanams* but the latter escaped payment by direct appeal to Kayamkulam Rajah (cf. Price 1996)

With the 1753 defeat of Kayamkulam Rajah by Martanda Varma, Valiyagramam was annexed to Travancore. While Edapalli's land remained untouched, Koickal Kaimal's family – allied to Kayamkulam Rajah – was divested of land rights and political power.[1] Local political structures were further altered by settlement of a new *janmi* – a supporter of Travancore royal family – who acquired authority over Valiyagramam's southern half. According to Unni Saar, retired Brahman school master and descendant of this *janmi*, '*jajmana* rights and land were given by the Rajah to my ancestors as a gift in recognition for services. We sorted out disputes and brought artisans (*viswakarmakkar*) to the area.'[2]

During this period, each neighbourhood had an Izhava headman assisted by the *naluvittumar* in representing the Izhava community in front of upper-caste *janmi*s. Thurston wrote:

[there is] a class of secondary dignitaries known as Kottilpattukkar or Naluvit-tumar. In every village there are four families, invested with this authority in olden times by the rulers of the State on payment of fifty-nine *fanams* to the royal treasury. They are believed to hold a fourth of the authority that pertains to the chieftain. (Thurston and Rangachari 1909, vol. 2: 409)

The headman and the *naluvittumar* enforced caste rules among *karakkar*, arbitrated in conflicts and collected levies for paying service castes. Authorisation and presence of headman and *naluvittumar* was necessary for performance of any life-cycle ritual and for Izhava festivals (Mathur 1977). As we have seen, still now *naluvittumar* families are identifiable, try to claim higher status than 'ordinary' local Izhavas and have provided many SNDP officials and community leaders.

Political Representation and Democracy: The Izhava Memorial

Policies of progressive centralisation of state powers and disempowerment of landed elite and local rulers such as Koickal Kaimal, initiated by Martanda Varma, continued throughout the nineteenth century, now sponsored by successive British Political Residents. Colonel Munro (*Dewan* and Resident 1810–19) established a central secretariat and judicial system centred around *zillah* courts and a court of appeal. He introduced well-defined administrative divisions, gradation of administrative officers, and separation of military and judicial duties from revenue officers. The state took over more than 2000 temples bringing extensive previously tax-free landed properties (*devaswams*) under Revenue Department administration. Under Malby's Residency (1860 onwards) British civil and criminal codes were introduced in Travancore. With introduction of centralised political structures, access to state apparatus and power-wielding government jobs became the focus for protests of those communities excluded and unrepresented in the new system. One particular development common in southern states were anti-Brahman movements against Brahman dominance in general, and in particular their near-monopolisation of government employment. In Travancore this movement had a twist because Brahmans in government employ were mostly immigrant Marathis and Tamils. Of 232 Bachelor's degree holders at Maharajah's college up to 1891, 67 were Nayars and 112 non-Malayali Brahmans (Jeffrey 1994: 148). Nayars (who had *sambandham* alliances with Malayali Brahmans) therefore took up the cause not as anti-Brahmanism but as protest at 'outsider' domination, presenting the Malayali Memorial, a request for 'sons of the soil' reservations, to the Rajah in 1891.

While influenced by and generally supportive of both anti-Brahman movements and the localist arguments of Nayars, Izhavas were part of that 30 percent of the population (*avarna* Hindus), to whom government service and political power were in any case denied: they accordingly understood their main problem to be *savarna* caste domination. The first Legislative Council (1888) and the 1904 Sri Mulam Thirunal popular assembly, a debating forum with little real power, both largely excluded Izhavas and were monopolised by Nayars, the largest payers of land tax. Issues of political representation, framed as a central part of wider demands for an end to caste discrimination, were highlighted in the first Ezhava Memorial, presented to the *Dewan* in 1895 by Dr Palpu. No reply was received; Palpu came in 1896 to meet the *Dewan* in Thiruvananthapuram. On 3 September 1896, a mass petition signed by 13,176 Izhavas reiterated the memorial, requesting the Rajah to confer upon Hindu Izhavas the same privileges and rights enjoyed by caste-fellows who had converted to Christianity. These included rights to education, to use public roads and for women to cover the bosom. While couched in traditional terms of feudal dissent,[3] the Izhava Memorial (reproduced in Rajendran 1974: Appendix I) hints at transformation towards new frames of reference: modernist ones of rationality, accountability, representation, democracy and meritocracy. When these modest petitions failed to produce significant results, Izhavas were forced to join together in more openly conflictual methods of protest. As one Izhava leader argued, 'This was our first big human rights movement ... the government was beating the backward classes and they were bowing low, but the more they bowed, the more they got beaten.'

Construction of the Caste around a Caste Association as Mass Movement

Against this turn of the century background of massive social change in many spheres, accompanied by an intractable state prepared to offer only crumbs, prominent Izhavas debated their goals and the best means to achieve them. Under the influence of the caste's newly emergent middle class several Izhava social reform movements blossomed throughout the 1920s and 1930s, while a range of potential leaders vied to analyse the community's problems and offer solutions. According to Isaac, by 1930 seven important Izhava caste organisations existed in the Alapuzha-Chertalla region alone (1985: note 68).

The SNDP was founded in 1903 with Narayana Guru as life-president. The well-known poet Kumaran Asan, editor of the monthly newspaper *Vivekodayam*, acted as secretary for many years (1903–19) and became president in 1922; Dr Palpu was the first vice-president. These co-founders of the SNDP embodied through their life practices already existing but as yet unarticulated middle-class ideals and the drive towards accumulation of symbolic and cultural capital (Bourdieu 1990: 123, 130; cf. Hardiman 1987: 163). Dr Palpu personified rationality, English education and new employment patterns; Kumaran Asan high culture, refined sensibilities and aesthetics, hitherto prerogatives of the upper castes; Narayana Guru himself stood for mimetic appropriation of high-caste religious styles. These three strands coalesce in the SNDP, eventually to become the community's official mouthpiece, assisted by T.K. Madhavan (1885–1930) from the powerful Alummoottil family, who as secretary helped it become a mass organisation. While a Weberian interpretation would identitify these individuals, particularly Narayana Guru, as charismatic, Bourdieu argues that 'charisma' is nothing but fetishised power, the misrecognition of symbolic capital (Bourdieu 1990: 141, 1992). The new economic, political and cultural power amassed by sections of Izhavas throughout nineteenth-century socioeconomic changes settled on the shoulders of these exemplary persons chosen as leaders.

The SNDP grew out of Narayana Guru's Aruvippuram Siva temple's 1900 eleven-member management committee. Its headquarters moved to Thiruvananthapuram in 1904, to Sivagiri in 1915 and finally to Kollam, where it remains today. Membership was originally very low, the annual subscription rate then being Rs100. In 1927, T.K. Madhavan used National Congress Party activist experience to organise a recruitment drive turning the SNDP into a mass-based organisation. Within 18 months of cutting subscription rates and organising public meetings and door-to-door collections, membership increased from 4200 to 50,000 (Jeffrey 1974; Rajendran 1974; Rudolph & Rudolph 1967; Srinivas 1988: 95ff). One prominent descendent of T.K. Madhavan told us that the latter originally travelled alongside Narayana Guru making speeches, but that Izhavas had been afraid to join because of upper-caste reprisals. When the total Izhava population stood at 100,000, SNDP membership consisted of a mere 7000 members drawn from wealthy families. Dr Palpu, T.K. Madhavan and Kumaran Asan went before the *Dewan* as representatives of Izhavas to point out that the community was the highest tax-payer but went unrepresented. When the *Dewan* retorted that an organisation of 7000 members did not speak for the caste as a whole, T.K. Madhavan's organisational skills were called upon, and he began to travel throughout Travancore starting local branches.

In Valiyagramam, although already highly active in the area, the first SNDP branch (*karayogam*) was not set up until 1941, taking over some of the *naluvittumar's* political and ritual roles (cf. Rudolph & Rudolph 1967: 34). One innovation was legal registration of all Izhava marriages; the *karayogam* also took charge of centralising commerce of coconuts and derived products, acting as a lending bank to break ties with high-caste landlords. Later, it organized Izhava tenants' land claims. *Karayogam* internal structure reflected the old socio-political order: *naluvittumar* families were usually founders and administrators of local branches. The president of the first village *karayogam* was the *kara* Izhava headman; other administrative posts were – and have been since – divided among *naluvittumar*. Today the post of president is no longer held automatically by any group but by whoever can muster enough support in leadership bids: most presidents continue in fact to come from *naluvittumar* families.

Agitation for Representation

While the Legislative Council was reformed in 1919 and in 1921, broadening the franchise to include university graduates and those paying Rs5 tax, Izhavas did not gain rights to representation until the 1930s. In 1928, via the SNDP, Izhavas submitted a memo to the Simon Commission for representation and enfranchisement. In 1932 the Assembly was dissolved and the legislature made bicameral with enhanced powers. Izhavas joined with other 'backward groups', Muslims and Latin Christians (many of the latter converted fisherfolk), in the All-Travancore Joint Political Congress, protesting against lack of representation. A memorandum was submitted to the *Dewan* demanding abolition of property qualifications, universal adult franchise and reserved seats. When the state refused to cede, amidst mounting tension the *Nivarttana* (Abstention) Movement was started; in 1933 the SNDP voted (alongside Muslims and Latin Christians) to boycott elections. During the Abstention Movement, SNDP General Secretary C. Kesavan was jailed for sedition for two years. Finally, in 1935 the government extended the franchise to all those paying Rs1 minimum tax (raising enfranchisement from 3 percent to 10 percent), recognised the principle of reserved seats in the legislature for backward communities and set aside ten seats. In the 1937 elections, Izhavas contested and won eight seats in the lower house and two in the upper, where the Joint Political Congress took the majority. (Chirayankandath 1993; Ouwerkerk 1994; Rajendran 1974; Kumar 1994; Mathew 1989).

After victories obtained during Joint Political Congress (JPC) years – 1935 job reservation in lower grades of public service; 1936 Temple Entry proclamation; 1935's limited extension of the franchise – the SNDP leadership took a more conciliatory stand towards the *Dewan* (C.P. Ramaswami Aiyar), the Rajah and the upper castes.[4] The SNDP was less than lukewarm towards the Travancore State Congress (TSC), a new political formation loosely based upon Gandhism, in contact with the National Congress and emerging in 1938 to draw broad support among all communities. The SNDP's programme – wider than that of the JPC – demanded both protection of the interests of lower castes and minorities and establishment of 'responsible government' (Mathew 1989: 94ff; Ouwerkerk 1994: 111ff). While a few Izhava leaders were among TSC founders and supporters, the SNDP *Yogam* 36th Congress (1939) passed a resolution stating 'members of the [SNDP] shall not be members of the working committee of the State Congress' (in Kaimal 1994: 23).

In contrast to high-caste nationalist movements but in common with low-caste movements in other parts of India, broad opinion among Izhavas was that British rule had – in some aspects – benefited them and provided a spur for social change. We have argued that economic and social changes growing out of colonialism permitted a rise in class status for some Izhavas and encouraged modern social reform: widening of educational opportunities; relaxation of sumptuary laws; limited political representation. While Isaac & Tharakan (1986: 25) label as 'conservative ... developed into reactionary' those Izhava streams which cooperated with or even welcomed British rule, one SNDP national official reminded us:

Even Gandhiji was in favour of the caste system ... he was a Vaishya, in favour of disparity ... they wanted us as illiterates and slaves ... the British gave some small rights and humanity, like the right to go to school ... the SNDP was not in favour [of independence]: today's local kings will be tomorrow's rulers and we'll be in hell under *chaturvarna*.

Kumaran Asan, echoing these sentiments, wrote in his famous poem '*Oru Thiyyakuttiyude Vicharam*' ('Thoughts of a Tiyya [Izhava] boy'), to which many villagers referred us:

Why should you cry, mother India? Your slavery is your destiny. Your sons, blinded by caste prejudice, clash among themselves and die fighting. For what purpose, then, is *swaraj*? [home rule, the rallying cry of the nationalists, led by Gandhi]

A newspaper editor echoed to us the fear which prospects of independence provoked among *avarnas*, 'There was no rule at that time, no law: it was Maharajah's rule.' By virtue of their structural position within caste hierarchies, Izhavas were forced into ambivalence on the issue of national independence, and foresaw the bleak post-independence outcome of a meshing of high caste and nationalist sentiments.

Consequences of the SNDP's Consolidation

Despite Narayana Guru's continuing and increasing protests that he was not an Izhava and that the SNDP was never intended to be an Izhava caste association, it inevitably gradually became so (witness the Valiyagramam Izhavas' refusal to accept Dharmananda, the Guru's low-caste Parayan follower sent to found an *asram*). As is common among ex-untouchable but mobile castes, the Guru's fundamental teaching, 'One caste, one religion, one god for all humanity', was (and still is) commonly appealed to in argument against anti-Izhava discrimination but ignored when Izhavas look towards Scheduled Castes. Izhava unwillingness to compromise chances of prestige through alliance with *avarna* groups considered lower-status further favoured co-option of the potentially universalist SNDP by Izhavas. Other *avarnas* grouped separately: Pulayas in the the Sadhu Jana Paripalana Yogam, founded in 1907 by Ayyankali; fisherfolk in the Vala Samudaya Parishkara Sabha, founded by K.P. Karuppan in 1910.

The SNDP endeavoured to hold all Izhavas together while addressing the problem of material disadvantage, but the appointment of a saint as figurehead led to privileging of cultural and symbolic – specifically religious – change while recruitment on a caste basis and the SNDP's eventual constitution as a caste association contributed to under-estimation of class factors. On the question of whether caste associations genuinely represented group aspirations and interests or merely those of a self-interested elite, we believe that the early proliferation of groups and ideological positions on 'the way forward' confirms a genuinely widespread impetus for change at the turn of the century (Isaac & Tharakan 1986a). Elite and masses allied to fight issues – untouchability, representation – relevant to all caste members and where some benefits were gained by all (cf. Pandian 1995). That benefits such as reserved employment places were later spread unevenly, while class differences within the group were not fully addressed, came as a result of early identification of 'the main problem' as stemming from caste discrimination rather than class inequalities, and subsequent decisions to struggle as a caste-based group. For the elite, the turn of the century problem was one of caste – not class – inequality; the masses, eager for mobility, felt that they had more to lose than to gain by such strategies as alliance-making with Pulayas, or 'labourers'. Eventually, a pragmatic working within the existing system was favoured over attempts to fight it wholesale and revolutionary options were dropped; middle-class dominance in the early movements led to adoption of essentially conservative approaches towards action. As Fernandes (1997) points out, it is the use in everyday life and in analysis of static and sterile categories such as 'caste' and 'class', and the desire to differentiate them, which predispose to a failure to address satisfactorily issues of inequality.

Failed Attempts to Create an All-Izhava Party

Efforts by the Izhava elite to constitute an all-Izhava party, the Socialist Republican Party (founded in 1974 as an offshoot of the SNDP), proved unable to represent the interests of the entire class-divided Izhava community (Nair 1994: 94–5). Dissatisfaction with the Left recently led to the creation of what is effectively another 'Izhava party'. K.R. Gowri (known affectionately among Izhavas as Gowriamma) long-time CPI(M) party member and an architect of land reforms, is a prominent Izhava Communist leader who has been state minister but never chief minister (Jeffrey 1993: 214). In 1994, allegedly with support from the Izhava elite, she formed the JSS (Janadipatia Samrakshana Samidhi; Committee for the Protection of Democracy), dissatisfied with CPI(M)'s failure to recognise the principle of caste reservations and accusing the Party leadership of remaining in the hands of upper castes, blocking lower-caste members from leadership. Many Izhava Communists around Valiyagramam expressed support for Gowriamma, although they were unwilling to leave the CPI(M), doubting JSS chances in election. Along the coastal belt and other Izhava-dominated areas – traditionally Left strongholds – the JSS gathered support: many candidates won in 1995 *panchayat* elections although most voters returned to the Left for state assembly elections months later. In an interesting continuation of his grandfather C.V. Kunjaraman's pragmatic policy of secession in the face of failure of representation (calling in the 1930s for mass conversions), Mr Mani expressed support in 1995 *Kerala Kaumadi* editorials for the breakaway JSS. Valiyagramam Izhavas admired his championing of 'Gowriamma'.

We have suggested throughout that Izhavas are – and know themselves to be – divided by socioeconomic criteria into at least four major groupings: the poor small-tenants and labourers preoccupied with making a living and educating their children out of degraded and badly paid manual work; the educated employed, many belonging to the reformist Left, who pursue mobility on all fronts within bourgeois frameworks of 'respectability'; a high-status elite, mostly urban professionals, concerned as at the turn of the century with throwing off 'Izhava-ness' altogether; and the heterogeneous middle classes, pursuing upward mobility but, being at different stages in the processes of accumulation, with divided interests. The SNDP – an all-Izhava association – like the SRP – an Izhava party – have been unable to address the problems of and represent all Izhavas; any new grouping may expect similar failure.

Izhavas, then, generally see their best hopes for mobility in alliances with other communities, constituted through mainstream broad-based political parties. While some have joined Congress parties, often hoping at local level for the benefits of patronage, the community at large has been a major supporter of the Communist parties (cf. Rajendran 1974; K.S. Nair 1984; Nossiter 1982). Congress has long been considered to represent the interests of Nayars, wealthy Christians and the Izhava elite; some high-status Izhavas have become Congress leaders and state ministers. The successfully mobile – for example Gulf migrants – have been shifting their political allegiance towards Congress. 'In the 1950s and 1960s we voted for the Left parties because they had good social policies and land reforms', explained Ramakrisnan, retired Izhava shopkeeper with a son in the Gulf, 'When the Communists said that they would take money from the rich and give it to Pulayas we voted Congress.' Congress inter-caste/inter-class ideology is proving more appealing to many in the 1990s than the Communists' class-conscious endeavour, as aspirantly mobile Izhavas reject parties which, leadership notwithstanding, have never ceased to be identified with their 'poor' and/or 'low-caste' supporters. As *avarnas*, Izhavas are suspicious of the BJP and it hardly figures in the community political landscape.

From Caste Association to Left Parties and Trade Unions

While SNDP leadership, primarily representing the interests of the elite and bourgeoisie, moved throughout the 1930s and 1940s towards policies of restraint and moderation, a considerable section of the community became attracted first to trade unions and later to the Communist Party. Areas with large Izhava populations (for example Alapuzha, Shertallai) were centres of development of a commercial/capitalist economy in Travancore. Alapuzha's Izhava coir workers and toddy-tappers and bidi-workers throughout Kerala were among the first to unionise: their militancy soon became well known (Isaac 1985; Kaimal 1994: 75ff). Chellappan, who joined the Party in the early 1940s told us:

I was born in 1924; at 15 I went off around Kerala and Tamil Nadu working as a woodcutter. During the Second World War I wanted to join the army but my father wouldn't let me, so I went to work making wooden ammunition boxes for the British Army. All the coir and factory workers there in Kollam – all Izhavas – were against the Dewan C.P. Ramaswamy, although the SNDP supported him. I had already joined the Party before of the 1946 Punnapra-Vayalar massacre (see Kaimal 1994) ... Why did I join the Party? Because I am a *tozhilali* (worker) and the Communist Party is a workers' party. Even though I'm an uneducated man I could understand that they wanted a better life for the workers: better wages and land reforms.

Communist parties claimed continuity with those radical strands in the early Izhava reform movement silenced in the name of caste unity and absorbed by the SNDP. Early reform leaders like K. Sahodaran Aiyyappan (1889–1968) are recognised as having sown the seeds of class consciousness, socialist sentiments and militancy among Alaphuza's (predominantly Izhava) coir workers (Isaac & Tharakan 1986a: 21ff). An early legislative assembly member, Aiyappan had close contacts with co-members Kumaran Asan (the famed Izhava poet who became an SNDP founder-member) and with Ayyan Kali (1866–1941), founder of the Pulaya community organisation. In 1917 he founded and led the 'Brotherhood Movement', editing a newspaper *Sahodaran* (brother). Aiyappan analysed the problem facing Izhavas as one common to – hence requiring unity of – all lower castes, campaigning for inter-dining with lower castes and for inter-caste marriages: in 1918 one 5000-person multi-caste meal took place. All this initially won him out-casteing and the nickname of 'Pulaya Aiyyappan', which he declared a compliment. Aiyappan, described variously as profound *advaitin* to convinced atheist, was an admirer of Russia: in 1919 he was encouraging Izhava coir workers to follow the Soviets' lead and to take militant action against *savarna* castes and – if necessary – the royal family. In 1945 he presented a Declaration of the Rights of Izhavas to the Cochin branch of the SNDP, and altered the reformists' famous maxim, 'One caste, one religion, one god' into the more radical slogan 'No caste, no religion, no god' (Isaac & Tharakan 1986a: 10, 21ff; cf. Periyar E.V. Ramasamy in Tamil Nadu, Pandian 1995: 387).

As Rao points out, in 'village economies' where landlord tends to mean higher caste and labourer lower caste, it is easy to identify caste as the problem: this was the case in 1950s Travancore (Rao 1987; cf. for example Kumar 1994: 70). That caste and class tended to coincide made the growth of caste-based protests into class struggles almost inevitable.[5] Values such as education, rationalism, enterprise and self-help were central to SNDP and Communist parties alike: Communists shared with the Izhava reform movement a broad commitment to modernism, albeit within a different ideological framework. Members of educated, reformed, Left-leaning sections were (and still are) often heavily involved in both SNDP and Left parties.

Contrasting with both the militant industrial coastal belt and Kuttanad's paddy-cultivating zone, unions and the Communist Party flourished in Valiyagramam only from the late 1940s. First to join the Party were wealthy upper-caste Hindu and 'High' Christian college students, already sympathisers with Gandhian ideals and the 'Quit India' movement and politically active in Travancore State Congress-led agitation for 'responsible government'. For many the Punnapra-Vayalar massacre represented a political turning point. As one wealthy Christian, *panchayat* member and long-time CPI member recounted:

Initially, we were all for Congress. We went to college with Gandhi caps and *khadi* and were often suspended for it. When news of the massacre reached Valiyagramam I took my bicycle and went with two friends – a Nayar and a Thamburan – to see. Lorries were taking away the bodies of those killed by the army; the coconut trees were riddled with bullets: *Dewan* C.P. Ramaswamy had ordered this carnage. On the way home we all decided to join the Communists. From then onwards we met in the house of Thamburan, who became our leader. His family were very strict: they hadn't before allowed Christians or Nayars inside the house; he used to go accompanied by two Nayars; he never ate or drank anything outside the palace. But over the following months many Party leaders came to Valiyagramam to hide from the police; several stayed in the palace. Because we were all educated and from well-respected families, we could go around the paddy fields to talk to labourers and they would trust and listen to us.

Encouraged by young men from influential landowning families, political agitation among agricultural labourers took hold (cf. Menon 1992: 2707, 1994: 131ff).

Izhavas joined the Agricultural Labourers' Union, which initially had recruited almost exclusively among Pulayas, only in the late 1950s. Between 1969 and 1972 Izhava labourers took part in the 'land-grab' movement, supporting landless villagers' enclosure of small plots where their huts stood (cf. Oommen 1985: 124ff). Izhava tenant cultivators also joined the movement, attracted by a programme of land redistribution tilted in their favour and, as in other parts of Kuttanadu, this met with violent reaction from landowners and police (Mencher 1980; Herring 1980, 1983, 1989; Krishnaji 1979; Radhakrishnan 1989). Political struggles brought by and accompanying land reforms accelerated processes of class organisation (cf. Beteille 1974: 161ff). From shared opposition to Communism, labour militancy and land reforms, landowners forgot community differences to act together as a political force. Effects of this alliance are still remembered: Koccappan, retired Izhava agricultural labourer, recounted:

As the [Labourers'] Union grew, the landowners formed an association against us. Between 1954 and 1974 they fought a war against us. The worst was 'Niranam Baby'. He organised an army: landowners and *goondas*, Christians and Nayars. They dressed in a vest and an areca leaf cap and went around with sticks, killing labourers and trade unionists. Previously, Nayars and Christians distrusted each other, but then they joined against us. (cf. Alexander 1980: 77)

At state level, this alliance materialised in a campaign against the 1957 Communist government education policies, resulting in the latter's fall (cf. Jeffrey 1994: 153–6).

PATRON–CLIENT RELATIONS AND BIG-MANSHIP

While Izhavas have acted as a group to wrest some power from dominant elites, individual households continue to jostle for position in local con- figurations where power and prestige become inseparable. Patronage, a personalised relationship of mutual support between powerful and powerless, strong and weak – a vertical alliance – is a basic template for relations of power between people and families (cf. Harriss 1982: 238; Breman 1985: 264–6; Herring 1989: 95). Since these are relationships (not fixed statuses) people commonly play client to certain villagers and patron to others. In this way, villagers are linked together and eventually to state and national agencies through hierarchical chains. Involvement in such relationships aims to enhance mobility for both parties: a patron or sponsor's prestige partly rests upon number and status of clients, while a client expects to receive concrete benefits – job recommendations, introductions to government officials, allocation of scarce resources (for example telephone or gas connections). While clientship generally implies loss of status, accepting the position of petitioner within a hierarchical dyad, this is mitigated through hierarchies among clients: to be client to a wealthy, powerful, high-caste older man can actually augment prestige and is in any case better than being client to a less-respected man. Smooth-running of patronage relations and mitigation of clients' status-loss are facilitated by high degrees of personalisation and ambiguity in the relationship. Specifically, clients are often treated as and may act as valuable friends or even as quasi-family members, while both patrons and clients make use of familial discourses about *sneham*, loving care, to humanise, soften and disguise their relationship (cf. Kondo 1990a: 119ff; Freeman 1979: 144ff; Osella & Osella 1996). When clients accept gifts and help from their patrons, they are able to do so because the relationship has been constructed within the kinship idiom.

Sneham describes the emotion appropriate to the relations between people who, through kinship ties, sharing food, living on the same land, being in close physical contact with each other, share and pass substance. It develops over time via contact and through sincere performance of mutual responsibilities from both partners in a relationship; it exists only when embodied and enacted. By virtue of intimate connection, clients claim to share something of the patron. Intimate connections create 'flows' between givers and recipients, binding them to each other; for those who regularly 'get into the house' or share meals with their patron this process is intensified. By being identified as the trusted long-term 'friend' of an important man, a client will be granted a degree of respect by others (cf. Freeman 1979; Uchiyamada 1995), suggesting to the client and to outsiders that the relationship is of a higher order than mere mutual convenience.

Becoming a Patron: Gifts and Loans

Patron–client relations have classically been seen as dyadic, individual. Since family status is strongly linked to its senior men, and because of the use of the *sneham* idiom, patronage actually connects households. Circuits of patronage run within two linked families: if one man approaches another for help in finding his son employment, his wife approaches the eldest woman in the patron's house to ask for help with her daughter's dowry; his daughter may approach the patron's daughter to ask for cast-off clothes. The nineteenth-century practice of patrons naming client's children – future workers and clients – has long died out, but agricultural labouring families still take family and house names from their landowning employers. In a familiar movement, the two families appear as unequal but intimately linked opposites, one the negative reflection of the other and each necessary for the other's existence, in the same way that Bhagavati, (house goddess of prosperity and cleanliness) depends upon the existence of her twin sister, Chettabhagavati/Jyestha (house goddess of dirt, disorder and poverty) (cf. Smith 1988; Moore 1988: 261; Osella & Osella 1996: n9). Uchiyamada (1995) explores some processes by which high-status patrons improve their fortunes via links with the low-status (cf. Raheja 1988): senior men with serious status ambitions *must* aspire towards patronship.

Gulf migrants especially commonly have substantial wealth to convert and invest in a bid, on permanent return to Valiyagramam, for position as patron. Gulf migration has a few significant cases of rapid rise of hitherto poor villagers who, on the strength of newly acquired wealth, have altered power relations within their own community and the village as a whole. Opportunities for gift-giving opened up to Gulf migrants can be used instrumentally to create new and transform existing social relationships. Given to people of higher status gifts can be establish relations of goodwill; gifts are said to *soap* the recipient, opening up a road for future return favours. Savings can also be utilized to create networks of clients. Upwardly mobile migrants may try this strategy with the close circle, i.e. to represent kinship obligations as the voluntary open-hearted largesse of a patron. Recipients not in a financial position to resist being assimilated as clients publicly continue to receive gifts as just *sneham* dues from a kinsman or close friend. The fact that a new relationship is tacitly understood is demonstrated by a migrant's increased demands for assistance and services going far beyond normal kinship obligations, by non-reciprocation of such services, and by the gift-receiver's meek compliance.

Cash loans, devoid of the gift's possible ambiguities, are even more powerful weapons for binding clients to patrons. Solicited by and given within the same circle as 'rightful' gift-receivers (relatives, friends, close neighbours) loans range from a few hundred rupees to cover unexpected medical expenses and repaid within a few days to several thousands of rupees to make up the cost of a ticket to the Gulf or raise dowry, returned over a longer period of months. As these are loans given on trust without securities or interest – unlike those from private financiers – lenders are in a position to demand, beyond repayment, the debtor's long term cooperation and support. *Gulfanmar*, having easier access than anyone else to relatively large amounts of cash, are the obvious people to whom villagers first turn when in need of a loan; returnees often end up setting up as professional money-lenders. Baby Chacko is one who has done so successfully.

Baby started life poor – son of a landless Izhava ploughman (convert to Marthoma) – but a good agriculturalist. Baby got a lucky break when land reform gave him land he worked for absentee landlords. By judicious trading in paddy, Baby built up capital to get to Bahrain where he worked as a mechanic for seven years. He now owns twelve acres of paddy land; a lorry; a car; a motorbike; two *blades;* and lives in comfortable architect-designed roadside two-storey house with garage and surrounding coconut garden.

Asked the reasons for his success, Baby candidly replied:

> Major expenses are labourers' salaries but I only employ my relatives. I pay them less than other labourers, they work with *sincerity* and never cause any trouble. They are all poor; I always helped and lent them money when they needed it. They can't refuse now.

Emergence of low-caste *nouveaux-riches* as patrons is invariably accompanied by attempts to discredit them: Baby is often described as dishonest (*kallan*) or a hoodlum (*goonda*). Like other *Gulfanmar*, he is widely believed to have made his earnings *on the black*, smuggling gold and dollars; several people told us that he owned a printing press for turning out counterfeit notes. Baby's reputation as money-lender is equally tarnished: people gossip that he demands sexual favours from the wives and daughters of defaulters.

Big-men

Established and respected patrons build up networks of clients forming potential power-bases for political ambitions and permitting bids for higher status. Such people (like Divagaran, Chapter 5) are 'big-men' or 'little-big-men'. They are mostly male; just as women teachers, government officials and professionals are referred to and addressed as '*Saar*', '*Doctor*' and so on, 'big-manship' is a role in which a few older high-prestige women may be found. Women acting as patrons outside women-only arenas are acting – as older women sometimes do – as gender-neutral people in a predominantly male arena. Mines & Gourishankar identified a form of leadership widespread across south India and constituted around 'institutional big-men'. Distinguished from their Melanesian counterparts whose prominence depends solely upon personal charisma, south Indian 'big-men': (1) are quintessentially hierarchical and individual, unique and eminent persons; (2) are able, through personal qualities and ingenuity, to attract supporters; (3) are central to a constituency, self-defined through redistributive strategies; (4) are apparently altruistic benefactors whose favours are actually instrumental, status-seeking, but which also circumscribe personal liberty to the common good; (5) enact leadership through a variety of institutions, to gain both social credit as generous and trustworthy and the public fame and honour which further distinguish and individualise them (1990: 761–3). Raman, described in the next section, like other patrons discussed later, fully fits into this characterisation of a south Indian 'institutional big-man' more recently elaborated by Mines (1994).

A Village Little-Big-Man

Raman's nickname, 'Chicken Biryani', invokes both his financial *sound*-ness and his wide-ranging sociability, twin pillars supporting his reputation and popularity. The nickname refers to his famed prodigious appetite for the fragrant luxury which is a speciality of Muslim and Christian communities. Occasionally in his younger days, rather than eat the usual toddy-shop (chilli chicken, fish fry, boiled tapioca) or roadside stall (chilli omelette, *dosa)* fare, he would persuade his friends after a few drinks to accompany him to a Christian meals hotel where he treated everybody to his favourite dish. Family responsibilities have long since put paid to *treats* in town, but Raman's work as Agricultural Cooperative Society clerk brings him into contact with many people, meaning many wedding invitations. Non-Hindu friends never hesitate to invite him, knowing that he will be a good guest; after two or even three helpings of *biryani* he will praise the wedding for weeks to the many customers coming to him for seeds, fertilisers or pesticides, thereby adding to his hosts' reputation.

Raman, short and stocky, sports a bushy white handlebar moustache curling satisfactorily upwards at the oiled tips, huge even by military standards (although he has never been in the army). He favours a somewhat loud dress style for a man of his age and employment, eschewing the usual clerk's *mundu* and white shirt for brightly patterned *lungis* in vivid hues carefully matched with polyester sports shirts in complementary shades. He has a large tattoo of the god Aiyappan on his right forearm. Raman is usually seen wheeling rather than riding his old black bicycle; he stops to talk to almost everybody he meets along the road. When he is in a hurry and must cycle, he still always waves as he passes and yells, 'What's the news?', it not mattering that the answer, 'Oh, nothing, no news', gets lost as he speeds by, question and answer being customary Malayalam greetings. At 62, Raman still enjoys joking; age permits him to flirt safely with almost all village women, from ten to eighty. He confines himself to those who he knows will not take offence and with the rest maintains extreme respect and distance or an avuncular manner. Raman is a gregarious, generous and open-hearted man, especially admired within his own community for not having cut himself off from poorer relatives and friends after making good. He belongs to a large well-known family widely related to other Izhava families in the neighbourhood and with a considerable affinal network throughout the district. Raman's father was an illiterate boatman; even now most of the family remain poor labourers, but they know that they need never starve since Raman will always lend money when needed, and will be generous in his help when it comes to marrying their daughters. His own sister is married to a Pune factory-worker, an enviable situation achieved almost single-handedly by Raman, who both contributed handsomely to the dowry and was able to find and fix the match by means of his far-reaching contact networks.

We first met Raman at the market, where he stands for an hour or so every evening disseminating gossip gleaned that day at the Co-op, gathering more to pass on via customers the next day and waiting for dusk to fall so that he can take a discreet drink in the toddy-shop. He rarely gets home to dinner before nine: there is always somebody wanting advice on anything from a boundary dispute with neighbours to illness within the family, while Raman enjoys his role as trouble-shooter. He is a small-time member of that unofficial army of political party and SNDP activists, school-teachers and clerks who, by virtue of education, status and contacts, give general advice, assist in marriage arrangements, help with college, job or pension applications, mediate in disputes and generally keep tabs on all that goes on. These *social workers* help Valiyagramam life run smoothly, mediating between their caste and others and between villagers and such external agencies as education or health officials, ensuring that undesirable interference in village affairs by such forces of the 'outside' as police or state government is minimal. Police are called in only when every other possible intra-village means of settling a dispute or dealing with trouble has been exhausted by the local big-men.

Raman first introduced himself to us in 1989 as the cousin of our next-door neighbour. In this role, he ingenuously asked the usual questions about our purpose, finances, family backgrounds, religious and dietary habits and so on, slipping in a few extra questions designed to check exactly how we intended to conduct ourselves and where our allegiances would lie. Finally, satisfied that we were neither in league with outside agencies nor allied to any particular local factions, he re-introduced himself: 'I am the Agricultural Co-op Society secretary, so I know everybody around here and most things that go on. If you need to know anything or get into trouble, come to me and I'll try to help you.' Raman it was then, who introduced us to local shopkeepers, passed word round that we were not missionaries but researchers and warned travelling fish-vendors not to cheat 'our foreigners'. By 1995, we had inevitably become drawn into village politics through friendships with certain families. We were close to one family distantly related to Raman with whom he has now broken relations, following 1992's local political violence when the two households took different sides – our friends for CPI(M) and Raman's household for RSS. Raman's relative with whom he is on hostile terms is a rival local little-big-man, CPI(M) activist for over 30 years. Familial and personal rivalry between these two men, whose potential power bases among relatives and neighbours overlap, is sharpened by fierce political rivalry between the Left and the RSS. Our relationship with Raman is now limited to civil greetings along the road (until such time as relations may thaw between hostile factions); at the same time, the two households acknowledge kinship, which tempers mutual hostility and Raman's attitude towards us.

Clients can be drawn to sponsors through personal or occupational status or as representative of a powerful group (most commonly a political party, farmers' or labourers' union, or caste association). There are levels of big-ness among big-men, and different arenas of patronage. Local contractors may, for example, be patrons to many villagers – offering work and subcontracts and acting as go-between with wealthy people – but a client 'outside', petitioning politicians and government officials for award of valuable contracts. The Izhava elite have local representatives of political parties and village little-big-men as clients; lower-status and less wealthy Izhavas have the same people as patrons. Village big-men are intermediaries between levels acting with variable relative status in different arenas, linking spheres and smoothing social and political relations (cf. Tambiah 1985).

Big-Men and Political Parties

Let's look at a fairly typical case of dispute mediation undertaken in the name of a political party (in which all protagonists are Izhavas). Leaving home one morning, Paramu – CPI(M) activist, Communist Farmers' Union representative, retired school-teacher and local little-big-man – was approached by Babu – caste-fellow, ex-Congress Party worker – for urgent help in unravelling a complicated situation. Babu's relative, who lives away, owns a substantial house which had been standing empty and which he wanted to rent out. The only would-be tenant was the cook at the market toddy-shop, a non-local. Having argued with the toddy-shop owner, the cook directly approached the licence-granting liquor contractor for a sub-licence to set up and run his own toddy-shop; he planned to rent a house and run the business directly from home. Babu, acting as mediator between house-owner and cook, had agreed to take a portion of profits as payment for persuading his relative to rent out his house. This house-owner, mistrusting the cook but wanting rent monies, agreed to let for a trial period of two months for a deposit of Rs900 and a monthly rent of Rs300, payable in advance. Over these two months the house-toddy-shop made Rs10,000 profit, becoming a clandestine drinking place for the gang of young RSS supporters living in the immediate neighbourhood. When the house-owner sold the property, he asked Babu, as mediator, to tell the cook to leave. The toddy-shop clientele urged the cook to stay, offering support. When Babu and the house-owner visited they found the cook claiming that a one-year lease had been agreed, supported by belligerent youths. At this point, Babu – out of his depth as a very small would-be little-big-man – turned to Paramu, a bigger big-man with the backing of a political party behind him. That this party is the CPI(M) and not Babu's party (Congress), posed no problem to anybody: the situation demanded recourse to the neighbourhood man most likely to handle it. From Paramu's point of view, the situation's promise of confrontation with RSS militants only added relish.

Paramu went alone early next morning to speak to the cook, subtly extracting during conversation the latter's native village, house name and so on. Returning at lunch-time with the house-owner, Babu and a senior Comrade, Paramu found the cook again in belligerent mood: a crowd gathered to watch the fun. After much argument and threats on both sides, Babu handed over the deposit to Paramu, who passed it to the cook with advice that as his full personal details were known he should take the cash and leave without making further trouble if he did not want comeback. The cook took the deposit but barred himself into the house with a few RSS young men, shouting that the lease should be extended. Paramu turned to his Comrade with a loud voice: 'Quick, Chellappan!! Go to Kottakara and call the comrades waiting there!!' The cook pushed out of the house and immediately left Valiyagramam. Later, the story provoked much mirth among Paramu's friends, who knew very well that there had been no band of comrades at Kottakara. This incident added to Paramu's reputation as a trouble-shooter, put both house-owner and Babu in favourable mood towards those who had come to their aid, and provided good publicity for the efficaciousness of the Party's help. While participation in power relations commonly comes like this, through involvement with an organisation, leaders (such as branch secretaries) and (to a lesser extent) activists commonly also act as patrons on an individual basis. They therefore require status appropriate for patronage and are commonly already 'little-big-men' before entry into formal politics. As a result, not all who are politically active can aspire to become big-men.

Two members of Kappa Parambil family who are long-time CPI(M) members and activists are Chellappan and Gopalan. Chellappan, 72, a retired woodcutter, lives modestly on remittances sent by his children. Despite more than 50 years' Party membership he cannot hope to move out of the small arena represented by the local committee: in the incident above, he acted as Paramu's helper, his muscular form the implicit threat. Similarly, when the CPI(M) won *panchayat* elections, Gopalan – as most senior local committee member – should rightfully have become *panchayat* president. However, *panchayat* presidents must attend functions and mix with people like Members of the Local Assembly (MLAs). As a near-illiterate and un-sophisticated retired boatman, Gopalan was felt not to be up to the job, which went to a younger man – more educated and wealthy with far less Party service.

The husband of Maniamma, a widow of 54 from Kappa Parambil, was a ferryman who became seriously ill in 1993. The doctor recommended hospitalisation; the family were unwilling; a senior local Party member came to the house to persuade them. It was in any case too late: Maniamma's husband was brought home to die. In 1994, Maniamma and her children moved into a newly built two-roomed brick house with the Party's help. She has long been a solid CPI(M) supporter and activist (*party-worker*) and has often been grateful for the Party's help, as have other family members: the Party has a strong power-base among sections of Kappa Parambil. While Maniamma is one of two women on the Party's branch committee and while the party relies upon Kappa Parambil support, she has never held and will never hold higher office: as a barely literate agricultural labouring widow she does not command the respect or prestige necessary for acceptance into an office-bearing position. Nor, although her ward was selected as a *panchayat* reserved seat for women, could she be selected because, according to another Party activist, 'She's a good speaker, but can't read and write.'

The female candidate chosen was a young Nayar advocate, resident in Thiruvananthapuram but whose parents live locally.

Political Parties as Patrons

Activists and leaders use their position to build village power-bases, augment status as little-big-men and obtain favours from higher-level officials. Political parties and the SNDP need many 'little-big-men' in every locality to gather support which can later be called in by higher-level leaders. Supporters are involved in long chains of patronage, acting as clients not only to those who help them directly but also – indirectly – to SNDP or Party or state agents from which favours and benefits downwards (cf. Tambiah 1985: 252ff).

Kunjappan was a very poor Sasthamuri man, with a neighbourhood reputation as a cheat and thief. He worked part-time in a Christian-owned ration-shop while his wife sat at a makeshift stall selling loose cigarettes and tea. Supplementary remittances from a son in the military dried up after the son's marriage and left the household in penury. One evening a neighbour noticed a gold chain missing; she asked around at several places including Kunjappan's house, but nobody found it. Her father consulted an astrologer who confirmed common suspicion that Kunjappan had found the chain and kept it. That night, Kunjappan got very drunk at the toddy-shop before coming around all the houses in the street saying, 'I am not a thief; I didn't take the chain. Come and search my house.' Nobody went, saying that he had probably already sold it. In the morning, his mother found him hanging dead in his roadside tea-stall. His body hung for several hours before anybody could be persuaded to cut it down and deal with the funerary and legal arrangements, although Kunjappan's family were staunch Congress members and clients of a local wealthy Christian family: nobody from either group was willing to get involved in the scandal. Eventually a CPI *panchayat* member from another neighbourhood visited the house to deal with the police report, the death certificate, the funeral arrangements and payment of an insurance claim. Kunjappan's mother, widow and the entire family now owe allegiance both personally to the man who helped them and – through him – to the CPI.

Panchayat Politics

Village little-big-men who achieve election on to the *panchayat* get involved in a range of issues: allotting new concrete latrines or house-building loans; allocating contracts for re-surfacing roads; approving construction of new shops. They mobilise connections to speed up installation of telephone lines or procurement of gas cylinders; letters of recommendation from *panchayat* members help obtain admission to colleges and issue of passports. It is of enormous benefit to family, community or neighbourhood to have its particular patron elected; *panchayat* members also considerably augment prestige and mobility opportunities. Following implementation of Rajiv Gandhi's '*panchayat raj*' scheme, in which power (to administer, for example, roads, health care and lighting) has been devolved, stakes in local political arenas have grown considerably and the power and reputations of *panchayat* members with it.

Kappa Parambil family, a potential vote-base of over 100 adults, has several CPI(M) activists and a handful of Congress workers. Family votes generally used to split 75 percent/25 percent in favour of the Communists but at the 1988 *panchayat* elections a family member – a woman school-teacher – had stood as Congress candidate. Some argued that, as a family member, she should be supported; the family vote split 50/50 between Congress and the CPI(M). In 1995 elections another family member, a retired military man and local SNDP branch secretary, was elected *panchayat* member representing the CPI(M), for which he has long been an activist and where most family members' sympathies continue to lie. Internal family feuds and political differences put aside, Congress supporters and personal enemies voted for this man: concrete benefits associated with a family member on the *panchayat* are too great to ignore; the whole family's status is enhanced by having provided a *member*.

The help which *panchayat* members offer as mediators between villagers and various institutions provides great leverage over potential clients who are then expected to support their patron and/or his party. At the same time, needy villagers try to maximise their chances by remaining on good terms with activists from both Left and Congress parties. Ultimately, the votes *panchayat members* receive are directly proportional to their capacity to 'deliver the goods': once a *member* fails, support quickly wanes. Negative assessments of *member's* abilities depend not only on personal shortfalls but also on the position of parties at state level. A *panchayat* candidate whose party is in power – or likely to assume it – in the State Assembly is regarded by voters as in a better position to attend to needs and therefore has more chances of election.

In 1988 Soman Pilla (the austere local SNDP leader from Chapter 5) decided to stand as Sasthamuri *panchayat* candidate. Educated, economically comfortable and member of a high-status family which in the nineteenth century provided caste headmen, he believed he could rally the Izhava vote. In a neighbourhood with a large Izhava population this would mean a good chance of election. His popularity increased just before elections when he led protests against the local NSS, who forcibly tried to prevent Izhavas from using the communal water-tank. He filed his papers as an Independent Left-candidate but, to his shocked disbelief was not only not elected, but received hardly any votes. Caste-fellows eventually preferred a Nayar Congress candidate, distant relative and supporter of a powerful Congress MP, thereby unbeatably well-connected.

While voting behaviour is dominated at *panchayat* level by such pragmatic considerations, party affiliations come into play more strongly at district, state or national level, while floating voters are influenced by wider political issues. The 1991 District elections took place amidst agitations around the Mandal Commission Report (on reservations). Most Izhavas voted for Left Front candidates because Left parties, although opposed to caste-based reservation, supported V.P. Singh's government. National elections two months later, in the wake of Rajiv Gandhi's assassination, provided a landslide Congress victory. Voting behaviour, then, reflects Izhava experiences over the century, which has proved that the most effective means of pursuing change is to band together in temporary pressure blocs. The question of on what basis those blocs should be formed, like the wider issue of political representation, remains unresolved.

THE BREAKING DOWN OF POLITICAL ALLIANCES

Class-based alliances within all parties frequently break down as a result of different communal interests (cf. V.K.S. Nair 1966; K.S. Nair 1984: 193ff; Mathew 1989: 142ff). One Communist activist, commenting on K.R. Gowri's criticism of the CPI(M) and formation of the JSS, argued that she was correct to insist that caste is an issue which must be addressed:

> It's difficult to destroy castes because people always think of it first. They want to show who they are: everybody keeps caste in the forefront of their mind. After Gandhiji, Ambedkar, Narayana Guru and the Communists, castes are still here. Even with mixed marriages, people's minds don't change: everyone feels *jati*.

Among the Izhava poor the symbolic capital represented by caste status is one of the few things families have to hold on to; far from favouring class alliances, increasing economic differentiation, which leaves many Izhavas behind, may actually bolster determination to maintain distinction from Pulayas and related castes, leading Izhavas to identify themselves primarily with their own successful caste-fellows with whom they hope to make advantageous vertical alliances of patronage. Meanwhile, members of the upper strata – advocates, doctors and engineers – try extremely hard to ignore caste. These Izhavas hope to be treated as co-professionals alongside Nayars and Christians among whom they work and socialise, but generally find that outside of public spaces pragmatically defined as caste-neutral they are still not welcome.

Middle-class Alliances Break along Caste Lines

The issue of reservation is perhaps the greatest block to middle-class alliances. Izhavas, like Muslims and Latin Catholics, are officially classified as OBCs (Other Backward Communities): a group of communities subject to discrimination, albeit to a lesser extent than those designated SC (Scheduled Caste): ex-untouchables such as Pulayas and Parayans. In 1919 Christians,

Muslims and Izhavas (49 percent of the population, but debarred from government service) joined to form the Civic Rights League, for the right to public service. A Public Service Commission (PSC) was constituted in 1935 (amended 1957, 1967) allotting reservation of 14 percent of posts for Izhavas. As OBCs, Izhavas would also be eligible under central government proposals dating back to the 1980s, based upon recommendations of the – so far unimplemented – constitution and Mandal Commission Report, for reserved places in central services and public sector undertakings. Since 1991's attempts by V.P. Singh's government to implement Mandal's recommendations, and ensuing anti-Mandal riots in many parts of north India (cf. Radhakrishnan 1993: 11ff), the issue of reservation has returned to the forefront of Kerala politics. Forward communities have been demanding total abolition of caste reservations or reservation for their own communities' poorer sections. The SNDP, most vociferous among Kerala OBC organisations, arguing that PSC implementation of reservations is routinely avoided, particularly in high-level positions, by failure to report vacancies, so that the 14 percent quota (still less than the Izhava percentage of population) remained (in 1995) unfilled, demands not only full implementation but also increased reservation quotas commensurate with community numbers. Congress and CPI(M), albeit from different perspectives, were favourable to introduction of economic criteria to exclude the OBC wealthy, the 'creamy layer' (cf. Mathew 1989: 164; Radhakrishnan 1993: 17–18). Opposition to this 'creamy layer' principle was running high in 1995 among Izhavas; attempts by state government to conduct a socioeconomic census to determine OBC economic conditions were halted under massive protest after less than a week.

Middle-class and elite Izhavas, educated and urbane, certainly hope to benefit from reservation legislation: posts in government employment exist at lower grades, but at middle and higher grades the so-called 'creamy layer' of the community plays at a disadvantage against Nayars and Christians for the high stakes of prestigious, secure, decently paid pensionable employment – a valuable rarity in high-unemployment Kerala. SNDP State President Advocate K. Gopinathan put his case to us: discrimination was and is experienced by and exercised against the community as a whole on the basis of caste status, regardless of other factors; reservations should also be on a caste basis, regardless of other factors. Dr Palpu's considerable wealth and education did not prevent him from being barred from government service and mocked as fit only for tree-climbing; as much as present caste discrimination, it is this historical imbalance which has led to Izhava exclusion and Nayar and Christian dominance in public service which caste-based reservations seek to redress (cf. Radhakrishnan 1995). Radhakrishnan points out that '(I)n India, exclusion is mostly historically accumulated and not ... thrown up by economic restructuring' (1995: col. 12).

Working-class Alliances Break along Caste Lines

Caste is also a barrier to alliance within the working class. Valiyagramam Izhavas, unlike those in Izhava-dominated occupations (coir industry, toddy-tapping) and/or in Izhava-dominated areas (Alapuzha to Kochi coastal belt) did not immediately join the Unions and the agrarian struggle. Izhavas, considering Agricultural Unions as predominantly Pulaya organisations, were unwilling to stand shoulder to shoulder with lower-status labourers.[6] While initial reservations were overcome by Upper Kuttunad's agricultural movement's growing strength, and by the gains it won, considerations of caste status often continue to outweigh class consciousness and class solidarity. Examples are legion: on a daily level, caste's persistence is signified by Izhavas (including Left party militants) continuing maintenance of some sort of untouchability towards lower castes. During union disputes, Izhavas are often accused by Pulayas of falling too easily to employers' offers, preferring quick – albeit less favourable – settlement over public militant action alongside Pulayas. Within Left parties and unions, there exists de facto separation between castes. As Izhavas progressively withdraw from agricultural labour, Agricultural Union members tend to be mostly Pulayas; the few Izhava members are already considered by others as lower status by virtue of the tasks they perform and through association with Pulayas. Head-load workers' union members are predominantly Izhavas and Christians; the Farmers' Union includes Nayars as well as Izhavas and Christians. Because Pulaya households are concentrated in (formal) '*Harijan colonies*' or (informal) '*Harijan zones*' where others are reluctant to live, the Communist parties' territorial organisation creates practical segregation.

Some occasions require public display of Party solidarity and allegiance to anti-casteism. Refusal to accept food at a Pulaya fellow-Party member's wedding would be unacceptable. Sometimes, Pulaya Communist activist hosts employ Nayar cooks. Still Izhava and other non-Pulaya guests eat with extreme apprehension: in the following days many complain of stomach pains and diarrhoea, ascribed to the quality of the water drunk at the wedding. On occasions of public protest or demonstrations, Pulaya support and presence is not only accepted but required, firmly relegated to the role of followers. Since 1991, resenting continuous marginalisation and tired of being taken for granted with little benefit, many Valiyagramam Pulayas have withdrawn support from mainstream parties – turning towards the Dalit Panthers,[7] newly emerging locally; at the same time they are being actively canvassed by the RSS with promises to treat them as 'Hindus', an encompassing category making no reference to *jati*. Effects have been mainly felt by the Communist parties.

While many Left Izhavas stand in complicity with high castes, continuing to believe and argue that no Pulaya has as yet reached required levels of qualification, sophistication or *culture* for leadership, their own community's long-standing and expanding professional section precludes application or acceptance of similar arguments against them. Izhavas point out bitterly that the Left's anti-caste and egalitarian arguments – nationally and locally – lack sincerity. Although several Izhavas (for example Achutanandan, Susheela Gopalan and T.K. Ramakrishnan) can be counted among CPI(M) state and national governing bodies, villagers point to splits between leadership – commonly *savarna* – and followers – overwhelmingly *avarna*. This split has historical roots, Communist parties being strongly associated with founding figures such as E.M.S. Namboodiripad (extremely high-ranking Brahman) and A.K. Gopalan (high-status Nayar). Jokes that the Left was founded (as indeed in Valiyagramam) by disgruntled and rebellious younger sons of Nambutiri or Nayar families, excluded from power and inheritance within the traditional joint families, ring true to many; beneficiaries of policies such as land reforms (middle-tenants, many of whom were Nayars, rather than the landless, mostly *avarnas*) also suggest to many villagers that *savarna* interests dominate (cf. Jeffrey 1978; Menon 1994: 131ff). K.R. Gowri's split was precipitated, it is rumoured, by refusal of her demand that it was 'her turn' to become Chief Minister, the position going to Nayanar (high-status Nayar).

Solidarity within Left Parties Breaks Internally along Class Lines

Left alliances also break along class lines, notably between manual labourers and others. Increasingly, incidents occur highlighting dissatisfaction with both the SNDP and the Communist Left. Locally, one man has been involved in several recent incidents; consideration of the differences between him and those caste-fellows claiming to represent his interests underlines the widening gulf between manual labourers and the rest of society, specifically the sense of exclusion experienced by those left behind in recent Gulf and liberalisation consumer booms.

Remember that the Sasthamuri *gurumandiram* festival, held in great style and with widespread community support in 1990 and 1991, was hardly celebrated in 1995. While ostensible reasons included lack of funds and manpower, a central contributory reason was fear of putting community splits on public display, as had happened in 1994, when Warriattu Murali catcalled the speech of one SNDP official and CPI(M) leader, Dr Lokanathan, a wealthy, educated professional, socially far distant from Murali. Murali was again in trouble with community leaders during 1995 harvest, when his behaviour towards a fellow-Izhava and local CPI(M) representative led to reprimands and discipline from the Party theoretically representing his interests (as manual labourer and head-load worker's union member)

Vijayan – retired Izhava school-teacher, CPI(M) activist, ex-president of the Communist Farmers' Association – farms 90 cents of paddy land and is an active Block Member. He employs Pulaya labourers and a Pulaya *nokkakaran* to organise cultivation, but frequently visits his fields to supervise the supervisor, enjoying his prestigious status as *farmer*. Vijayan was part of the group of representatives from Communist Farmers' and Workers' Unions which formulated the 1995 harvest agreement and published a joint leaflet for general distribution:

This is a very bad year for farmers: government subsidies have been cut; prices have gone up; farmers are selling gold and using cash assets in order to farm. This year threshing must be done within three days of harvest, otherwise the farmer will call others to do it.

Vijayan commented, laughing, 'These laments and threats are our farmers' tricks'. It continued: 'Head-load will now be paid as agricultural work, falling within the agricultural agreement. It will therefore be paid in the fields in advance of transportation.' Head-load work had never before been seen as 'agricultural work'. Redefining it not only paves the way for future negotiations on less equitable bases; it also associates those impoverished Christian, Izhava and (rare) Nayars who do it to 'agricultural workers', a category indissolubly associated with Pulayas.

Previously, head-load gangs visited households for payment long after harvest; there would be negotiation or disputes on how much paddy had been transported, what had been the agreed rate, and so on. One CPI(M) activist and her father, member of the Communist Farmers' Union, explained that if paddy was first brought to the house and workers then paid later in the year when they called to collect their share, they had then been paid to carry what was their own rice. This was known as '*kulinde kuli*', wages on the wages. Our arguments – that paddy was carried not to the worker's own home but to that of the landowner, workers still carrying their own paddy (unpaid) home, likely (especially for Pulayas) to be some distance away, near the very paddy fields from which it had originally been brought – had no impact. Communist farming families also complained of being pressurised to pay more: one woman from a staunch CPI(M) family, whose own sister and husband work as agricultural labourers, complained, 'They came to *our houses* to put pressure on us, making a *vazhakku*.' We recognise again here the symbolic significance of the house, as objectification of the householder and family; and as protective exoskeleton for the family, most especially for womenfolk. Here (Communist) farmers and their families are simultaneously disallowing chances for further negotiation over wage rates, contractualising arrangements by excising delay, and increasing social exclusion, loosening ties between farming and labouring families.

Vijayan complained that since the 1995 leaflet came out there was 'big tension' around the village. Murali, identified by Vijayan as 'The man who yelled 'cooo, cooo' at the *gurumandiram* festival – he's a drinking man', usually transported Vijayan's paddy. Since the leaflet, he had been passing insults whenever he saw Vijayan in the street, which was often, since the two are neighbours. Vijayan went to Babu, leader of Murali's 12-strong head-load gang, asking him to work without Murali, otherwise Vijayan would not use that gang. Babu duly split the gang, Murali's half carrying someone else's paddy. Vijayan lamented, 'When Murali sees me in the street, he abuses me and says I'm not on the side of the workers but of the farmers; he says, 'You are a farmer now: you only look after the interests of the farmers.'

Towards the end of harvest, when Murali and fellow-workers had transported almost all the paddy – having been paid the new, lower rate in the fields – Vijayan was one day cycling through Vallamkuttom Bridge, a Pulaya area. Murali, there with friends, asked loudly, 'What's a dog doing riding a bike?' Vijayan stopped, dismounted and asked, 'What did you say?' Murali repeated it, sniggering. Vijayan reflected, 'Because of harvest there were many Party workers in the field who'd have supported me in a fight, but I thought – it's been a good harvest, the atmosphere is like a festival, why spoil things? I let it go.' Later, however, when Murali's gang was unloading straw in the alley leading to Vijayan's house, Vijayan reported the incident to gang-leader Babu. Murali, listening from the top of the lorry, shouted down insults to which Vijayan – now on home territory – responded, 'Come down and I'll beat you up.' As Murali climbed down, cursing, Vijayan accused him, 'I know you're an RSS man – that's why you do this; your two brothers are RSS rowdies.' Murali angrily retorted that he was a Congress man and denied any RSS connections or motivations. Vijayan's son Rejish later gathered some 'DYFI comrades' ('young Communist' friends), and went to threaten Murali, telling him not to insult Vijayan again. As Rejish left, Murali again called out, 'I'm not RSS, I'm a Congress man.' Vijayan concluded, 'At tomorrow's Party committee meeting we'll discuss this. There'll be a reprisal – nothing too strong, just a warning should do.'

Murali chips at facades of unity presented to outsiders and within Party and community. At an SNDP festival, he – an Izhava – catcalled and insulted an Izhava SNDP official, supposed representative of Izhavas as a whole; during the harvest, he – a manual worker – insulted and threatened a Communist activist, supposed supporter and representative of labourers, and again a fellow-caste member. Talking about the festival incidents, Soman Pilla and his son stressed lack of education and *culture* and drunkenness, taking pains to stress that this was not peculiar to Izhavas. After making specific criticism of Izhavas in Murali's area, they ended stressing unity and minimising the incident, blaming 'just one person behaving badly'. Vijayan similarly stressed Murali's drunkenness, describing him as 'always drinking'. For these Izhava and Leftist activists – teetotal family men – this serves not only to frame incidents in a certain way – meaningless behaviour not to be taken seriously, by somebody out of their senses – but also to frame Murali: drunkard, a man lacking *culture* and a proper sense of family and community responsibility – in short, the antithesis of themselves. While Vijayan's genuine respect for labour leads him towards a more generous perspective on Murali, whom he acknowledges as 'a hard worker', finally the latter's lavish toddy-shop expenditure weighs the balance against him. Both men use SNDP and Party power to censure and silence Murali, with Vijayan refusing to listen to Murali's accusation that he 'only looks after the interests of farmers' and writing off Murali's animosity as motivated by Party factionalism.

Murali appears before reformed Izhavas as an unwelcome *revenant*; a ghostly figure consigned to a disavowed history and denied voice in the present. Manual labourer, drinker and friend of Pulayas, he embodies the Izhava-ness of a bygone era. Those active in the SNDP and the Party need men like Murali united behind them as the power-base for their own political ambitions, whose fulfilment they will present as successes for the whole community. Some differences exist: Soman Pilla, long-time middle class and high status, from the headman's family, privately despises fellow-caste members as uncouth; Vijayan, also titled and high status but more recently and precariously middle class in his modest newly built house, must (as committed Communist) respect labour, but finds himself dismayed and disappointed by caste-fellows. Leaders like Divagaran, the militant temple activist encountered in Chapter 5, whose private personas and habits do not live up to SNDP public style, maintain a careful double-face of private empathy and public disavowal.

Scott (1990: 202ff) wonders what enables people to make the 'symbolic declaration of war' (1990: 203) which is the first public declaration of the hitherto hidden transcript (1990: 142). Eventually, he leaves it at a 'quite particular matter of individual temperament, anger, and bravado' (1990: 210). While this may partially account for Murali's behaviour, as may his drinking (the explanation commonly offered), we must also pay close consideration to the stark difference between his circumstances, as a hut-dwelling casual labourer, and the circumstances of those around him. There are significant differences, clearly identifiable as differences in capital accumulation and – it must be said – in habitus, between him and those who claim to represent him. In his drunken outbursts, Murali tries, somehow, to assert presence and voice dissent against his inauthentic representatives. They silence his voice, avoid listening to him and deny him presence, ignoring or dismissing him as 'drunk', 'uneducated' and 'rowdy, troublemaker', or as 'political adversary, RSS supporter'; while he strongly resists the last label, he is currently powerless to resist the others (cf. Scott 1990: 206). As Bourdieu continually points out, the power to name, classify and label is the form of symbolic power or symbolic violence *par excellence* (Bourdieu & Wacquant 1992: 14; Mahar et al. 1990: 14; Duncan 1990: 182).

ALTERNATIVE ALLIANCES

Class divisions within the Izhava caste, already noted by Aiyappan (1965: 165)[8] are not the only reasons for a drop in SNDP popularity. Paradoxically, some problems result from the organisation's success. Commensurate with SNDP successes in improving Izhava image (if not yet entirely status), those who have benefited most from such changes have re-focused their ambitions, taking on more and more the styles and aspirations of *savarna* castes. This is so not only among middle class and elite, but also generally among educated Izhava youths who have never experienced directly the severest caste discriminations of the past and have grown up mixing – especially in schools – with their contemporaries from every community. For these aspiring sections of the population, involvement in the SNDP has an undesirable side effect: a too-close association with an all-Izhava institution and hence with 'Izhava-ness' itself. The identification of 'SNDP' with 'Izhava' reinforces the group's 'Izhava-ness'; connotations of this 'over-Izhavaness', in so far as it continues to connect community members with a past in which they were untouchables, makes obstacles to redefinition of group identity as non-*avarna*.

The increasing popularity of the RSS among young Izhavas is one result of uneasiness with caste-based identities. This is an apparent paradox, because Valiyagramam RSS activists are among the most orthodox, traditionalist and caste-conscious members of the upper castes. However, RSS ideology contains a strong pan-Hinduist rhetoric particularly attractive to Izhava youths: caste considerations are said to be secondary to membership of a wider community of 'Hindus', sharing traditions, culture and motherland (Basu et al. 1993; Andersen & Damle 1987; Van der Veer 1994). RSS-promoted activities, festivals and camps represent rare opportunities for Izhava youths to socialise intimately with upper-caste youths resulting in cross-caste 'friendship'. Moreover, the RSS encourages physical and mental fitness through training in yoga and martial arts. Mastery of these skills, formerly upper-caste prerogatives, fosters the belief among young Izhavas that they are becoming integrated into a world from which they were formerly excluded. RSS training camps are seen by many young men as modern heirs to Kerala's *kalarickal* system, evoking the chivalric martial past especially associated with Nayars. Izhava youths also hope through RSS drill to refine and make superior their embodied selves, refining their *gunams*[9] (cf. Zarrilli 1979, 1989, 1999).

Sometimes Izhavas refuse co-option and stand alongside other ex-untouchables, taking an anti-*savarna* perspective. This tendency, in its more conservative form of an alliance limited to same-status (OBC) communities is represented state-wide by the 1990s revival and extension of the 1920s' 'triple alliance' (Latin Christians, Muslims and Izhavas) under the umbrella of 39 organisations forming the Backward Classes Liberation Front. Valiyagramam has no Muslims and its Latin Christians live in a segregated fishing colony on the village borders; while many express interest in the idea (supported by the SNDP) of this 'third pole' standing between *savarna* and 'untouchable' there is as yet no local body representing such an alliance. In 1995, high-ranking SNDP architects of a proposed front watched with interest political developments in Bihar, where a Dalit/OBC coalition swept the polls. One failed attempt to create a 'third pole' emerged before 1996 state assembly elections, when the JSS, the mostly Muslim PDP (People's Democratic Party) and several small OBC parties tried to constitute a united front on a common platform. Following internal disagreements, an alliance failed to materialise, leaving the JSS to reach agreement with the Congress Party and the PDP standing alone.

Other Izhavas appear ready to turn toward more radical action, splitting Hindu communities into two blocs in which Izhavas should stand alongside Muslims and ex-untouchables in a generalised 'alliance of the downtrodden' against the oppressors, identified as 'forward communities'. In 1995, some young Izhavas were discreetly passing around cassettes of speeches made in 1992 in Malappuram by fiery PDP leader Abdul Madani; they wanted us to listen and arranged a hearing, warning that it was 'dangerous' and 'secret' material. Calling for Dalit – Muslim – Izhava unity, Abdul Madani recounted many incendiary stories of *savarna* Hindu villainy and atrocities, reiterating each time that the perpetrators were neither Muslims, nor Dalits, nor Izhavas, but '22-carat cow-worshippers'.[10] He ran through statistics proving the dominance of *savarnas* in the state. Listening with us, one long-time CPI(M) activist referred to police brutalities and inactivity during the Ayodhya incidents and reluctantly admitted 'Madani's analysis is correct.' Such unity among all classified as non-*savarna* currently has no local stable concrete form, being limited to post hoc reaction to *savarna* violence. The presence of the Christian community, who might stand with *avarnas* against *savarna* Hindu dominance or with wealthy *savarnas* against *avarna* labour, is another complicating factor, adding to the complexity of local power configurations. Minor confrontations often occur: drunken groups of Nayars cause disturbances outside or minor damage to *gurumandirams*; they try to bar *avarnas* from temples, festivals or public ponds. Reaction is immediate: following incidents, strikes are called and roadblocks set up, while demonstrations crossing the village force shops to close, calling for revenge against '*savarna* attacks'.

The Left's inability or reluctance to allow reality to 'caste' or to face caste/community issues beyond tactical allocation of seats – evidenced in its uneasy attitude towards reservations and its dismissal of community-based organisations like the Muslim League as mere 'communal organisations' – means that this fertile ground lies fallow apart from episodic violence, or gets usurped by non-radical populist organisations like the PDP.

CONCLUSIONS

Oommen (1990: 188ff & 245ff) suggests that Indians have multiple identities which cross-cut and prevent stable one-dimensional solidarity. Fernandes (1997) goes further to highlight the artificial nature of the categories used to separate identity strands. Because of continuous shifts from caste, to class, to party identities, conflicts arising in any sphere easily spill over into or become represented as part of another. Murali's case suggests that identities couched in terms of caste, class or party affiliation are in turn internally fragmented, open to continuous redefinition and conflicting interpretations, embedded in the social practices of different sections of the community. This internal fragmentation or fluidity enables subjects continually to re-position themselves according to the perception they have of their own social condition (Bourdieu & Wacquant 1992: 133). While we resist the temptation of labelling particular discourses as hegemonic, incidents at festivals and during paddy harvest indicate that within political struggles over discursive constitutions of identities, all voices do not carry the same weight, nor does everyone have equal power to resist – in particular negative – identifications.

Given the existence of a plurality of context-specific and internally fragmented identities, allowing subjects to recognise themselves and to participate in several social groups, it is not surprising to find that attempts in the context of wider political bodies to essentialise and/or fix particular identities or social relations to the exclusion of other possibilities continually fail. The success of local leaders like Raman and Paramu rests on their ability to gather support by playing out, according to context, different aspects of their and their interlocutor's social identity. Paramu's sophisticated personal tactics for 1996's electoral campaign offer a telling example. As he explained:

When I go to an Izhava house it is straightforward. Our [CPI(M)] candidate is an Izhava, so I just say 'He is *our* candidate, *our* man: vote for him' and people readily agree. With Nayars it is different: I remind them that Congress Prime Minister (Narasimha Rao) insulted all Nayars by not removing his shoes while visiting the Mannattu Padmanabhan Nair (NSS) memorial. I also argue that Congress is anti-Hindu, appeasing Muslims with schools, jobs and factories, while 'we Hindus' receive no help at all. In a Christian house, I show pamphlets comparing prices from 1991 to 1996 and I say, 'Mr Varghese, we want to give our children a good future, but how can we ordinary people find money to pay the fees for a decent school?' I also warn that if the BJP comes to power they will start demolishing churches.

Turning finally towards what we may term 'micro-politics' will shed more light upon the dilemmas Izhavas face and the various loyalties and aspirations which, pulling them in one direction and then in another, contribute to their multiple consciousness or 'janus-face' (Nagaraj 1993). This focus will also enable closer examination of both essentialised and relativised aspects of caste and an understanding of some processes through which caste identity is constructed and assigned.

7 MICRO-POLITICS, OR THE POLITICAL IN THE PERSONAL

Izhavas, as families and as a group, have achieved considerable class mobility, pursuing goals set at the start of the twentieth century for accumulation of wealth and prestige. They have also apparently achieved mobility within caste hierarchies: considered at the turn of the century as unapproachable, hence banned from public and sacred spaces, they now participate in public and mainstream Hindu religious life. This is not to say that caste has disappeared; rather, the idioms in which it is articulated have changed, and the areas of public life in which it operates have been reduced. Caste meanwhile continues to be marked within the body: while physical contact is still a highly charged event, discourses which developed in Kerala over the nineteenth and twentieth centuries refer to characteristics such as inherited 'natures' and 'cultures' or hierarchies of qualities, at once physical, mental and moral: codes for 'caste' (Dumont 1970: 226ff; Barnett 1977; Searle-Chatterjee & Sharma 1994: 19–20; Fuller 1996c: 11–12; Parish 1996; Osella & Osella forthcoming). Interpersonal interaction – touch, food-transactions – remains at the heart of much ontological experience of caste. In the present as in the past, conservative solutions – Sanskritisation, 'passing' – hold sway (cf. Berreman 1979: 211).

While Izhavas claim that the SNDP and Left parties work as motivators for caste's weakening, evidence from other parts of India suggest that caste's mutation is a widespread phenomenon (for example Fuller et al. 1996c; Searle-Chatterjee & Sharma 1994). Unlike village ethnographers of the 1950s and 1960s, we know in the 1990s – thanks largely to the work of historians – that caste in pre-colonial times was not the rigid 'caste system', based upon occupational or religious status, presented to us in colonial literatures (see for example Cohn 1987; Dirks 1987, 1992; Charsley 1996; Muralidharan 1996). While caste's nature and content – past and present – may be disputed, this needs to be separated out analytically from wider issues regarding the prevalence of hierarchy as an organising principle of social life, and specific questions about the cognitive status of this hierarchic principle.

In certain areas of social life the principle of hierarchy, certainly a bulwark of and widely assumed to be *the* central ordering principle of caste, claimed (following Dumont) to be an over-determining principle of social organisation in India, is challenged, reversed, discarded or openly toyed with. This happens among everyday categories of friends, lovers, the young and comrades; and in states and conditions which are highly temporary, limited and idealised. Everyday reality remains suffused with values and manifestations of hierarchy, of which caste is but one. The principle is in evidence, for example, in the existence and continuing resilience of formal rules of respect in address and manner which pertain between young and old, men and women. Ethnography of everyday interactions and of public demonstrations will help us to argue that the principle of hierarchy, even if it be pervasive and cognitively grounded, is not the only thing to notice in Indian social interaction (cf. for example Dumont 1980a: Appendix A; Parry 1974; Kolenda 1990: 127; Parish 1996). Hierarchy does not appear to be inescapable: in public demonstrations called by the Left parties, people show themselves capable of an alternative vision of the social body, as non-hierarchical. That this vision, like the everyday denials of the fixity of hierarchy apparent in young people's friendship and romance, is not then translated into wider practice does not lead us to pose a monolithic hierarchical 'India' or 'East' in opposition to an equally monolithic egalitarian 'Europe' or 'West' (Dumont 1970; Said 1978). Rather, as well as the easily observable value of hierarchy, less commented upon but equally observable values of ambiguity, indeterminacy or ambivalence also provide highly important principles of everyday Indian social life, which may both mitigate hierarchy and themselves act as independent sources of aesthetic and moral value.

SOCIAL DISTANCE AND HIERARCHY LITERALISED: COMMUNAL RELATIONS AND GROUPS

In nineteenth-century Travancore, social distance and hierarchies were literalised and corporealised, acted out for example in gestures such as covering the mouth with the hand by low castes in front of superiors or in clothing styles (for example low-caste people of either sex were permitted to wear only a waist-cloth). Pollution was held to be passed through the air from low to high caste: untouchability became, in Hindu-dominated Travancore, unapproachability. This was the rationale for exclusion of lower castes from public places (schools, temples) and for the extreme avoidance of high castes which untouchables were enjoined to practise, on pain of violence (see for example Jeffrey 1993; Rao 1987: 27ff). High-ranking Nambutiri Brahmans at the very top of caste's hierarchy used servants from the *savarna* martial Nayar caste to police the boundaries; older villagers still remember how the latter were required to walk ahead of their masters, shouting warning to all to clear the paths. Non-Brahmans would hastily dive into gutters or bushes as Brahman 'lords' passed by. Obsessive enforcement of untouchability and pollution practices famously made Swami Vivekananda declare that 'These

Malabaris are all lunatics, their homes so many lunatic asylums, and they are to be treated with derision by every race in India until they mend their manners and know better' (in Parmeswaran 1976: 16–17). While locals paint this picture of nineteenth- and early twentieth-century Valiyagramam, villagers also point out that, in practice, Christians were used as absorbers or neutralisers of caste pollution. Nayars over the age of 50 remembered their parents being handed items from Pulayas and Izhavas via the hands of a Christian (cf. Fuller 1976b:). Many local oil-pressing families are Christians, transmitting no caste pollution to the highly absorbent substance. People use high levels of creativity in daily practice to circumvent cumbersome 'rules'.

At the same time, that we still often see, in the 1990s, people born in the 1960s using gestures like mouth-covering in front of 'superiors' suggests the degree to which such practices form part of a habitus: as Bourdieu remarks, hierarchy is inscribed upon the body (1990: 69ff; cf. Taylor 1995: 561: 'la déférence que je vous dois est inscrite ... dans la manière que je me tiens en votre présence'). As Bourdieu defines the habitus, it is 'embodied history', a generative structure which exists in mind and body alike, born of accumulated knowledge and practice and contributing to the production of practices including a 'bodily hexis' located within an identifiable social milieu (for example Bourdieu 1990: 52ff, 69ff; Wilkes 1990: 116ff; Bouveresse 1995). The habitus, then, far from being a purely mental mind-set or ideology, is inscribed within the body and within transmitted practice. Some practices, such as the requirement that a man uncover his head but cover his knees in the presence of a superior, have been partly subverted by modern styles (in this case the use of bare head and trousers in place of head-cloth and waist-cloth). But it is noticeable that when waist-cloth or head-cloth are worn, as among manual labourers, the wearers still commonly whip off their head-cloth apparently automatically in the presence of a 'superior', for example when the landlord approaches, while men of all communities lower their waist-cloth in the presence of 'superiors'. A Christian man of 60 demonstrated to us the formal greeting required when meeting a *thamburan*, or twice-born master: 'ripping and tearing' (*valichukeeri thozhukka*), consisting of a symbolic tearing open of the shirt or breast three times. While he had not performed the gesture for many years, it still came easily to him – an example of the 'respect economy' which requires the gift of things which are 'more personal, and therefore more precious than goods or money' (Bourdieu 1990: 128). Hierarchy, then, in many aspects has to do with the body, be this through self-presentation and adornment, disciplining and control, or ideas about physical pollution. Hierarchy's embodiment in its most extreme cases takes the form of violence, exerted episodically by putative superiors upon inferiors.

After the SNDP organised an agricultural and industrial exhibition at Kollam in 1904, Izhava men were seen around Punjapad dressed European-style in long black coats, their women wearing upper-cloths. Local Nayars, affronted at this presumption of dignity by untouchables, tore the clothing from Izhava women, assaulted and raped them. Izhavas going to school were beaten for refusing to maintain unapproachability distances; houses were ransacked; printing presses at Kollam were set ablaze. Punjapad was said to be a 'hotbed of Nayar-Izhava conflicts': the clashes which began in January 1905 intensified over the next two months. Local Izhavas stood together united and defiant under the SNDP, whose leaders, including Kumaran Asan, came to Punjapad urging Izhavas to resist caste Hindu violence unto death. Finally, in March, a meeting was held in Kollam for reconciliation (Mathew 1989: 76; cf. Kumar 1994: 91).

In 1982, the wife of one leading Valiyagramam Nayar landlord (their son a prominent Congress politician) physically attacked an Izhava girl bathing in Mahadevar temple pond prior to going on Sabarimala pilgrimage. The following day, three Pulaya devotees were attacked and beaten by *savarnas* as they left Mahadevar after worship. Feelings among lower castes, already running high after the pond episode, exploded. Mahadevar temple premises had come to be used as a training ground for RSS militants: members of lower castes stormed a training session and two RSS activists were killed as they failed to escape. The police intervened and mass arrests were made among the Pulaya community. According to Pulayas themselves, only the Left parties actively campaigned in their favour, support from Izhavas quickly withering away. Over the following months, an RSS-mounted campaign of violence against Communist and trade union activists in the village culminated in the murder of a prominent local Nayar Communist leader.

During temple festivals RSS supporters, mostly Nayars, have often clashed with Pulayas and Izhavas; only swift intervention by *panchayat* members and police generally limits ensuing clashes to exchanges of insults and a few punches. But sometimes bad feelings cannot be contained. During one 1992 festival – ironically at Valiyagramam's only public temple dedicated to Aiyappan, the caste-less and community-less deity presiding over the Sabarimala pilgrimage, symbol of Kerala's anti-communal spirit – Koccappan, a Pulaya, went to a tea-shop outside the temple for tea and snacks. He complained that prices were unreasonably high. The Izhava tea-shop owner, an RSS sympathiser, insulted and abused Koccappan, accused him of drunkenness and ejected him. Usually a quiet man, Koccappan went to call relatives and friends from the temple; shouting and threats ensued. A few days later, one of Koccappan's relatives was jumped by RSS youths while returning home from the paddy fields and stabbed to death. The Left parties refused to intervene on the grounds that the murdered man had not been a Party supporter.

While only a minority take part in such violence or attempts to enforce pollution rules, many more people privately support it, while the majority continue to maintain some degree of untouchability with caste 'inferiors'. Some battles have been won this century, but many are still left to win: Izhavas are militant and organised, always fighting discrimination and trying to push against boundaries of caste prejudice against them; yet higher-caste dominance is still a fact in multi-caste rural areas. And it is still as casted persons – people whose identities contain elements of 'Izhavaness' – that Izhavas meet with other persons, themselves 'casted', and assumed to be of higher or lower status. Their structural position within a hierarchy accounts for Izhavas' apparent double consciousness: as casted persons, they act as aggressors towards Pulayas, while themselves suffering aggression from Nayars. Pulayas sometimes say that Izhavas 'Stand with the Nayars by day and with us by night' (cf. Nagaraj 1993). While 1980s' temple violence, like the 1992 murder, presents itself as motivated by political rivalry between RSS and opponents, villagers recount these stories in terms which make it clear that for them the underlying 'real' issue was that of caste and the policing of its boundaries.

UNIVERSALISM LOST

Over the twentieth century, many Izhavas fought to replace the hierarchical social body of caste and to resist discourses (common in orthodox Hinduism) making correspondences between the macrocosm (the moral universe, encompassing society) and the microcosm, taken as the (Brahmanic, male) human body (for example Subbayarappa 1966; Shulman 1980: 90; Zimmermann 1987: 164, 221; Beck 1976; Obeyesekere 1984a: 40ff). Narayana Guru's most famous maxim runs in full:

One caste, one religion, one god for humankind
Of the same blood and form, there is no difference;
Animals of the same caste alone procreate;
Viewed thus all humanity belongs to one caste.

The content of this slogan is something which, in various forms of universalism and monotheism, had already come into common currency in other parts of India (for example O'Hanlon 1985: 98–9). What was novel in early twentieth-century Kerala was Narayana Guru's re-interpretation of *jati* as biological species[1] and his appeal to rational scientific empiricism, using modernist frames of discourse which were becoming widespread through new forms of education and the huge expansion of print media. The Guru's encounter with Gandhi was often recounted to us: he stood firm against Gandhi's defence of *chaturvarna*, the system dividing Hindus into four ranked meta-classes – envisaging a social body with Brahmans as head, Sudra labourers as feet and *avarnas* excluded altogether. 'Gandhi visited Narayana Guru at Sivagiri in 1925. He pointed to a mango tree, saying:

'See that tree: the leaves are alike in colour but diverse in shape: some are long, some large, some small. Like that there is disparity in humans'. Narayana Guru took three varying mango leaves, broke them open and showed Gandhi that the sap was the same, saying, 'They appear different, but in quality they are the same.'

As one SNDP official put the Guru's argument, semen from a human man in the womb of an elephant will have no result, but semen from a Chandala (untouchable) man in the womb of a Brahman female will cause pregnancy: that semen from any human male can impregnate any human female proves that 'human' (*manushyajati*) is a species or *jati*.

Such universalist demands for caste's total eradication were revolutionary calls common during the early days, when reformers like Dr Ambedkar proposed an undifferentiated segmentary social body in which all would be the same. K. 'Sahodaran' Aiyappan of the Brotherhood Movement likewise analysed the problem as one requiring unity of all castes for abolition. While few we spoke to volunteered Sahodaran's name, most had heard of him; he was widely dismissed as having been a dangerous extremist or laughable marginal who, by mixing with Pulayas, had failed to understand the realpolitik of social mobility.

Amidst a plurality of approaches and movements at the turn of the century, pragmatic needs of consolidation and unity in the face of opposition favoured adoption of one organisation as the community's public voice. The question 'which community?' hardly existed by the 1920s: campaigning had begun over problems of sumptuary restrictions and unapproachability, hence focusing upon obvious 'caste' rather than 'class' issues. The Communist parties were still to come into existence: no mass organisation analogous to the SNDP fought inequalities specifically in 'class' arenas. Inequalities within caste were temporarily put aside as the bourgeois experiential problem of anomalies between high-class and low-caste statuses (as mythologised in K.V. Krishnan's elephant story from Chapter 1) was addressed. Villagers draw parallels – in talking both of the start of the twentieth century and its end – between caste hierarchies suffered within the village and racial and class hierarchies suffered outside it, comparing the old agrarian economy, colonial plantations and Gulf 'labour camps'. Subjective experiences of hierarchy appear as analogous in many ways for those suffering discrimination, marked, for example, by a shared trope – the vehicle whose use was forbidden by 'superior' – in the 'elephant' and 'car' stories. These continuities, parallels and links were not picked up by the SNDP whose attention, under its bourgeois leadership, remained fixed upon caste.

While material disadvantage was a large part of the problem of the caste's lower and middle sections, the first goal set was removal of disabilities arising from untouchability: access to better and wider employment opportunities would, it was assumed, follow on from this, while new opportunities in factories and plantations would, it was confidently predicted, take no account of caste, an assumption prevalent in the early twentieth century and held on to even in the face of evidence against it (Klass 1978). That modernism and urbanism would totally displace caste, a purely superstructural feature belonging to a bygone feudal past and incompatible with the modern factory, was assumed by – among others – Nehru and Ambedkar (Chakrabarty 1989; Nagaraj 1993; Chandravarkar 1994; Fernandes 1997; cf. for example Pandian 1995 on Tamil Nadu's self-conscious embracing of modernism under Periyar's self-respect movement). Meanwhile, material disadvantage would be dealt with through SNDP programmes of education, training schemes, promotion of industry and self-employment, and so on. Appointment of Narayana Guru – a *sannyasi* – as SNDP figurehead paved the way for later deification as Gurudevan and consequent elaboration of the reform movement's cultish and sectarian aspects, while appointment of Izhavas to leadership positions and the post-1920s mass recruitment drive ensured that SNDP came to be closely identified with 'Izhava', re-configured by Izhavas and outsiders alike as an Izhava caste association.

Twentieth-century substantialisation and ethnicisation of caste favour public discourses based not upon modernity's rhetorics of sameness but on principles of equality in difference: the SNDP vision by the end of the twentieth century is of a differentiated but non-hierarchical social body composed of many communities (*samudayangal*). This supersedes earlier universalist visions of those like Dr Ambedkar and Sahodaran Aiyappan, who proposed an undifferentiated social body in which all would be the same. At the same time, modernist rhetorics of egalitarianism are counterpointed by the insistent prevalence of hierarchy in value and practice in daily life. Through examination of some particular points of articulation within this social body – personal interactions – we can try to understand something of the general mechanisms of hierarchy and of challenges to it.

Izhavas pragmatically rejected Sahodaran Aiyappan's revolutionary message and do not generally feel able to risk gains made this century by acting upon Narayana Guru's universalism. Izhavas display what Nagaraj laments as the 'Janus-faced collaborative tendencies' of non-Dalit ex-untouchable castes, tendencies which (it is recognised) are 'an integral part of their mobility' (1993: 5–6). This is evident in continuing and increasing practice of forms of distinction between themselves and other ex-untouchable castes, notably Pulayas, and tendencies to limit alliances to the forging of horizontal links with other similarly placed 'backward classes', such as Muslims and Latin Christians. We have argued that caste, and indeed hierarchy, are embodied and enduring: now we can turn to think about aspects of 'hierarchy embodied'

WAYS OF RELATING: HIERARCHY, INTIMACY, EQUALITY

Embodied Ways of Relating

Possibilities of relating to others are expressed through gestures which people may use: significant for what they say about relative status of greeter and greeted, whether they make or break hierarchy, and for the possibilities they offer of physical contact.

Fuller (1992: 1) rightly gives prominent place to the *namaskaram* gesture as a powerful and India-wide recognised greeting. Unlike greetings common in Arab and European cultures (stylised kisses, hugs or handshakes) *namaskaram* involves no touch: it implies respect, but physical and social distance. Absence of contact protects those greeting from a danger which – the most frank of villagers admit – remains in many people's minds: taking on something 'dirty' and unwanted through contact with a caste inferior (cf. Fuller 1976a: 48). *Namaskaram* also – like the literalisation and embodiment of distance through untouchability – implies detachment, is inimical to intimacy.

Common gestures involving touch – foot-touching and blessing by head-touching – imply no mutuality. They are non-reciprocal, action on one side being met by acceptance and reaction on the other; the touch itself is strictly hierarchical, giving physical expression to extreme status inequality between a pair. In foot touching, an inferior demonstrates voluntary submission to his status by grasping the lowest part of the other's body (cf. Babb 1983); in blessing, the higher is unprotestingly allowed to touch the *uchi* (the fontanelle, considered to remain open to the outside), the most sacred and vulnerable part of the body (Osella & Osella 2000). Bodily contact acts as a function of relative status, in which inferior partners can only make humble overtures to the lowest part of the other, whereas superiors can unbidden put themselves into the other's most valued and intimate space (cf. Brown & Levinson 1987; Scott 1990: 31).

In a culture in which discrimination was given concrete form in literal enforcement of something widely known as 'untouchability', the act of touching holds a potency lost on nobody, least of all upon ex-untouchables themselves. Breaching 'no-touching' rules or asserting their meaningless-ness requires not mere touch but mutual and reciprocal entering of intimate space. An Izhava party man needing to demonstrate good faith towards a Pulaya comrade or an Izhava trade unionist testing a Nayar comrade seek reciprocal touch. At the extreme end of the scale, men from spatially segregated *Harijan colonies* may initially require potential friends from 'outside' to demonstrate total disregard for scruples about purity and pollu-tion by sharing cigarettes passed from mouth to mouth.[2] Perhaps the commonest way in which all men, whatever their status, who want to show good faith, equal mutual respect, closeness and non-hierarchy demonstrate this to themselves and to observers is by hand-holding.

While women have a particular relationship to touch and to intimacy, able sometimes to be physically close with each other in ways that menfolk cannot, and while they commonly hand-hold as young unmarried girls, mature women hold hands far less than do men. As youths, men are far more physically close with their friends than are girls, going beyond hand-holding to close embracing, and later limit rather than stop entirely same-sex physical closeness. Men of 40 and 50 greeting each other in the street stop to talk and take each other's hands, twisting each other's rings, interlacing fingers, stroking each other's palms with the fingertips. Men's far more elaborate range of hand-holding behaviour and higher degree of same-sex intimacy is indicative of deep political and moral significance. Women hardly circulate in non-familial arenas: they may 'go outside' for education or paid employment but are not found in the streets playing status games or keeping up 'face' (*manam*). The very social and physical distances which mature men commonly put between themselves in public and use as indicators of status become chasms to be bridged in encounters between two men denying competitiveness or hierarchy between them. Yet in their youth it will have been a different story ...

YOUNG MEN'S FRIENDSHIPS: DENYING HIERARCHY?

Young men often appear to subvert or escape caste and indeed hierarchy in their relationships with each other. Free from the domestic chores and relative seclusion which fall to their teenage sisters, 'boys' up to the age of marriage (*payyanmar*) are given great freedom, managing to cajole small amounts of money from indulgent elders with which to visit the cinema, keep up with fashion, treat friends to snacks at tea-shops and buy popular magazines and music cassettes. Strictly segregated from girls and socialising in all-male gangs, boys share in what is sometimes in Kerala called *college culture*. This is something of a misnomer, having less to do with college-going than with position in the life-cycle, and participation is not limited to students; school or college merely permit boys space away from home, time and pocket money which need not be accounted for.

Boys share cash, clothes, cassettes, cologne and other goods freely within their gangs, using almost forcible methods of redistribution, and do a lot of tough joking and testing: all widespread practices long familiar within anthropological literature as methods of reinforcing egalitarian relations (for example Taussig 1993: 90ff; Kent 1993; Miller 1994a: 228). When a gang decides to go to the cinema, whoever has cash on that day will pay and no accounts are kept; if one boy has a new and fashionable shirt, others demand and get their chance to borrow it, sometimes even before the original owner has had a chance to wear it himself. Within gangs, intense physical contact and sharing affirm egalitarian principles, breaking down social distance and posing a perceived threat to the hierarchical and ordered values of wider society.

One middle-aged Izhava man commented sourly, 'When I saw those boys [four young men aged 19 to 25] who had opened the new video studio at the market, I knew they weren't *serious*: these are the type who are always sitting with their arms around each other.' While his remark appears opaque, he is referring to deeper meanings of the boys' profound physical closeness. Their intense involvement in distance-negating intimacy, like their disregard for private property or accumulation, marks them in mainstream society as not yet adult or *serious*, not yet prepared to take on their full – casted – social identities and the persona required by mature males pursuing respect and prestige. Focused upon accumulating and consolidating capital for the family group, mature men generally remain distant and formal with 'outsiders', limiting public same-sex physical contact to hand-holding with a selected few men, those of equal status or those with whom distance must be denied for political reasons.

We have shown elsewhere (Osella & Osella 1998) how both the general principle of hierarchy and its specific manifestations in the form of gender, age and caste hierarchies are not simply over-ruled but are played with – to great effect – in young people's pre-marriage cross-gender relationships: throughout the course of *romance*, hierarchy is exaggerated, reversed, confused and abandoned. An initial phase – aggressive sexual joking – moves into the risky play of flirting (*tuning*) and adoption of a pose of romantic hero, staking out arenas in which young men compete, are judged by their peers, and form themselves into hierarchies around masculine performance (cf. Herzfeld 1985; Miller 1994a: 172ff; Yelvington 1996: 325). As boys move out of single-sex masculine performance arenas and into the cross-sex world of flirting and *romance* proper, two aspects of *love* and indeed of masculinity – assertive aggression and supplicant tenderness – mark boys as ambiguous creatures, and place them at opposite ends of two different hierarchical dyads with girls. Girls are equally ambivalent: during *tuning* and making a *line* (i.e. developing a regular flirting relationship), they may relate in turn to a boy as superior, erotic mature woman, or as inferior submissive younger sister.[3] As *romance* progresses, opposing roles and dyads fuse and collapse into each other, hierarchies founded upon difference being reversed and undermined, finally revealed as arbitrary.

Eventually, however, as most young people abandon *romance* (sometimes only after several years) and accede to arranged stranger-marriage in the interests of familial and personal reputation and mobility, 'normal' rules of hierarchy are reasserted: family above person, elder people above younger, but also – in the unspoken and naturalised doxic requirement of caste endogamy – our caste above others, and other castes above us (Bourdieu 1990: 68). While cross-community friendships, egalitarian sharing and distance-breaking physical contact all blossom on the street among men, and while *romance* and *love* cross community boundaries and stake out arenas in which hierarchy is 'played', transgressed and reversed, within the spheres of the home and family, conventional hierarchies of caste and gender are still widely strictly maintained.[4]

While the old *tindal jati* classification, used in the nineteenth century to label Izhavas and others as unapproachable, has been outlawed, Izhavas are still unequivocally and uncontroversially considered *avarna*, defined as hierarchically inferior to *savarna jati*s and as outside *chaturvarna*'s social body. Members of *savarna* castes commonly still feel uneasy about admitting Izhavas to their homes and about going into Izhava homes, while taking food or drink from an Izhava house appears to remain unthinkable for all *savarna*s. While we have seen Christians entering Izhava houses and comfortably eating cooked food there, and Nayars entering and eating in Christian homes (in both cases, mostly young men), we have never seen a Nayar voluntarily

eat from an Izhava house.⁵ While adult men sit together sharing drinks in
public spaces (toddy-shop, hotel bar), enjoying public sociality based upon
class and gender solidarity and alcohol consumption, they do not commonly
visit each other's homes, much less share meals. For a Nayar man to hold
hands with his Izhava friend on the street requires only external contact, and
that too in a neutral, public space; consumption – a symbolic taking into
oneself of the other – implies internal contact, and assimilation of alien
substance; entry into a caste inferior's home would imply intimacy and one's
own assimilation into or encompassment by the other. When entry into an
'inferior's' home is unavoidable, refusal of intimacy is signalled by refusal to
take food and – often – more brutal signs such as failure to remove footwear.

Satyapalan (Izhava) and Rajasekharan (Nayar) had long been friends.
That they, along with their friend Sunny (Christian), referred to themselves
jokingly and ironically as 'RSS' (their initials), demonstrates both their
closeness, such as to make them a unit, and their avowed disregard for caste
orthodoxy, represented prototypically by the RSS. After college, they visited
hotels in town to chat over tea and snacks; whoever had cash would pay, with
no accounts kept. They often visited the cinema together, borrowing each
other's shirts to extend their 'dressed-up' wardrobes. They belonged, in short,
to that category of young men dismissed by status-conscious elders as 'not
serious': always seen close together and with their arms slung casually
around each other's shoulders.

One day Rajasekharan's motor-scooter ran out of petrol right near
Satyapalan's house. Luckily Satyapalan was at home, and elder brother's
motorbike stood outside. Rajasekharan siphoned off enough petrol to get
home and spat vigorously several times to get rid of the taste, wiping his
mouth with his handkerchief. Satyapalan invited him, 'Come inside and have
some lime-water to rinse the petrol out of your mouth.' As Rajasekharan –
who had never called at Satyapalan's house before – hesitated, Satyapalan's
expression changed. He entered the house and returned with a glass of lime-
water which he held out, in view of (Izhava neighbour) onlookers, to
Rajasekharan: 'You have petrol in your mouth, take it.' Rajasekharan,
embarrassed and flustered, tried to cover himself. 'No, really, it's alright now:
I can't taste anything.' Satyapalan held the glass challengingly in
outstretched hand. Rajasekharan took it and quickly swigged off less than
half, grimacing, before handing it back saying, 'That's enough thanks, it's
okay now.' The friendship tailed off after this ambiguity-breaking incident:
the egalitarianism implied in physical proximity, meal-sharing and clothes-
swapping was negated, and the meaning of the pair's relative caste
relationship fixed, by Rajasekharan's reluctance to take lime-water from
Satyapalan's house, a space coded 'Izhava'.

That many Izhavas (young and old) make cross-community friendships
with Christians is testament to the comparative ease of relationships
when strict considerations of caste do not enter into them: Christians judge
and rank others according to wealth, prestige, manners, *culture* and so on,

and may ignore low-caste status if family status is otherwise high. That Christians were historically considered immune to caste pollution might help here. While they often share the prejudices of high-caste society towards Izhavas as a group, Christian qualms about food-sharing or physical contact tend to be based upon a particular evaluation of a person as fit or not fit to be accorded intimacy. That many local Izhavas converted to Christianity (especially Marthomite) further eases relations. By contrast, relations between Nayars and Izhavas remain extraordinarily charged. The extreme hostility which often breaks out between Nayar and Izhava must be seen in the light of the fact that these two castes form the immediate boundaries of the *savarna/avarna* divide. Nayar insistence upon orthodoxy must then also be understood in terms of their continuing role – derived from their unique structural position – as those responsible even now for policing this boundary on behalf of *savarnas* as a whole. Just as early twentieth-century Brahmans walked fearlessly around the village, unbothered by maintaining the distances they held necessary because Nayar servants could be relied upon to warn low-castes to jump off the road, so nowadays Brahmans are able to remain aloof from and apparently uninvolved with violent clashes between Nayars and *avarnas*: Nayars do the work of the border police.[6]

LOCAL ESSENTIALISM: QUALITIES AND NATURES

We are suggesting that caste appears to be an enduring habitus and doxa, a 'pre-verbal taking-for-granted of the world that flows from practical sense' (Bourdieu 1990: 68): we will pursue this point to argue that whatever changes in content have taken place over the century, structural positions remain as they were. When talking about persons, villagers draw upon the concept of *swabhavam* (nature, disposition). *Swabhavam* comprises a particular combination of qualities (*gunams*), importantly birth qualities (*janniccu gunam*) and environmental qualities (*samsa gunam*).[7] These qualities have physical, mental and behavioural effects upon one's nature and have social values attached to them. The degree of dynamism and mutual influence in the qualities' relationship is such that it is difficult to separate them: for example, Pulayas are widely held to be 'hot' not simply by virtue of birth community, nor because of having hot jobs and hot behaviour, but also because they live in hot outside regions and are continually exposed to each other's hot company (Osella & Osella 1996; C. Osella & F. Osella forthcoming).

In the short term, at the level of person or group, fluidity is relatively stressed: the very existence of *samsa gunam* assigns a strong role to environmental and behavioural factors. *Samsa*, as environment, is extremely broad, covering air, water, food, deities, people, animals: everything and everybody around the person; it is also accorded great power.[8] *Janniccu gunam*, meanwhile, is a gradual crystallisation into fixed form of a combination of qualities transmitted to the foetal environment during the gestation period, made up of substances/qualities passed on by parents and by others (for example mother's brother) which act before birth on the foetus.

The effect of *samsa gunam*, while considerable, is limited. There seems to be consensus that ethnicity, community affiliation, *jati*, lodge in *janniccu gunam* and hence resist change. Very few would agree with the revolutionary possibility expressed by one Asari family (carpenters by *jati* and by trade) that *jati* is not determined by birth. This family stressed behavioural aspects of *jati*-ness, 'doing' rather than 'being', claiming that *jati* as a means of classifying types of people was primarily concerned with division of labour (cf. Good 1982). Thankappan Asari claimed that especially 'in these times', when few followed caste occupation, birth *jati* no longer indicated true *jati*. When this family are commissioned to build houses according to *taccasastram*, they consider the householder's occupation and lifestyle. 'If, for example, an Izhava lives a good life and is working as a school-teacher, he is Brahman-type, and should have his house built as though for a Brahman.' There are several possible rationales for this: first is the commonly accepted principle that one who teaches becomes *guru*, one who studies Ayurveda becomes *vaidyan*; a second, for which we find no evidence but much counter-evidence, would be that *jati*-ness is purely a matter of *samsa gunam*, and hence easily changed; a third that the 'species' aspect of *jati*-ness can be delinked from or made subordinate to its occupational aspect; a fourth, implicit in the possibility of astrological interpretation of and corrective prescriptions for individual destinies, that the *janniccu gunam*, containing *jati*-ness, is itself mutable to a degree. While a few informants had doubts, pointing out that in old age Narayana Guru seemed like a Brahman or Nayar, for most informants *jati* is lodged in the *janniccu gunam* which, it is widely agreed, can only radically change through *janmam*, a process of gestation and birth: be it in this life (for example Brahman initiation) or the next. Reincarnation is a doctrine rejected outright by most non-Brahmans, who see *janniccu gunam* created anew in each foetus along with a unique individual soul (*jivatmavu*), and ceasing to exist at death.

Janmam is understood neither as a one-off nor as 'natural' process: persons change and refine *janniccu gunam* through rebirths (during future lives or present incarnations). Brahman initiation is another form of birth, altering the initiand's *janniccu gunam* from Sudra to Brahman quality, the gestation and birth symbolism very explicit and clear in textual accounts (Kaelber 1976: 358, 1978: 57; Smith 1986: 70); Malayali Brahman informants described the *samavartanam* or 'bringing to life' ceremony at the end of their initiatory *brahmacharya* period as a 'second birth', with the male guru standing both as 'second father' and ritual birther, superseding the human mother. Since Martanda Varma, Travancore's Sudra rulers were reborn Ksatriyas through Hiranyagarbham rituals (the Rajavu symbolically crawls out through the womb of a life-sized golden cow, see Bayly 1984: 190; Rao et al. 1992).

Janniccu and *samsa* are not impermeable to each other, but may have profound mutual effects, especially over long periods of time. Although a large part of the Valiyagramam Christian community consists of recent (two to three generations back) Izhava converts, those Izhavas (and Nayars) who converted to Christianity in the 1880s are by now carefully integrated into the Marthoma or Jacoba communities. They and everyone else have forgotten or affect to forget their past status, which we were able to ascertain only with extreme difficulty, through land records, missionary and church records and careful enquiry.[9] There are families in Valiyagramam having both Christian and Hindu branches who refuse to acknowledge any mutual relationship, and who consider themselves to have completely different natures (*swabhavangal*) and qualities (*gunangal*).[10] Three generations after conversion, children born to such families have a high degree of Christian *gunam*s, and are not considered to have any Hindu *gunam*s at all. How has this been possible within 100 years? First, Christian baptism appears to be a rite of passage akin to Brahman or kingly initiation, a ritual change which acts upon the body and effects transformation of the *janniccu gunam*, a rebirth: an interpretation in line with what missionaries and priests would tell converts. At the same time, converted Izhavas (and Nayars) are indistinguishable in habit and practice from older converts, unlike converted Pulayas, who are continually accused of being 'shirt-piece Christians', of not following a Christian lifestyle, and of 'sticking' to Hinduism: baptism alone, then, is not enough. *Janniccu gunam* must be reinforced by *samsa gunam*.

Most villagers agree that *janniccu gunam* can be slightly modified over long time periods and at the level of the group: Izhavas as a whole have this century somewhat improved and altered their qualities (*gunam*s) and nature (*swabhavam*). But radical changes are difficult to sustain and strongly contestable, even at group level: Izhavas, while not identified as '*Harijans*', are still held by Brahmans and many Nayars to be associated to *tamogunam* and are still acknowledged by all – including themselves – as *avarna*. On the question of changes, villagers take a different view depending upon whether they are talking about themselves or others, and whether they want to draw out possibilities for mobility (most commonly in relation to their own group) or whether they are trying to 'fix' the natures of others. Some orthodox *savarna* Hindus maintain that people should always stick closely to birth *gunam*: these people criticise migrants for leaving their ancestral homes, Nayars for becoming factory workers, and Pulayas for wanting to go to college; many villagers reject these conservative arguments.

When talking about possibilities of mobility for *jatis* held lower than one's own (particularly Pulayas) villagers exclude altogether the likelihood of even minimal positive changes resulting from alterations in environment or habits (*samsa gunam*). Some even deny that *Harijans* can modify their *samsa gunam*. Conversely, the same villagers, while discussing themselves in relation to 'higher' communities, tend to stress possibilities of change and mobility offered through interaction of environment with *samsa gunam*, suggesting either that improved *samsa gunam* modifies *janniccu gunam* or under-playing altogether the latter's role. Fluidity and permeability of the person, insofar as they allow for assimilation of superior qualities (buying 'Nayar' or 'Brahman' land and houses; eating rice from a known paddy field) are positively valued – regarded necessary for achievement and consolidation of status mobility.

Given that people are open to unwanted and dangerous modifications of bio-moral qualities, attention is devoted to the interface between person and environment (Parry 1989: 513–14). Discourses about 'compatibility', common among Brahmans and used by many to talk about their position in relation to lower communities, become assertions of distinction, fixity and hierarchy. People should avoid possible dangers of transactions and interactions outside of caste by sticking to their own way of life, marrying within caste and so on (cf. Marriott 1968a, 1976; Appadurai 1981; Rao 1986). Here, the person's relative fluidity and permeability, entailed in *samsa gunams'* vulnerability to external environment and its knock-on effects on *janniccu gunam*, become ideological props for the caste system.

Finally, discourses on qualities have taken on a wider political relevance this century, following the development of caste associations. Associated to notions of 'race', aspects of *gunams* are becoming transformed into fixed qualities (entailing physical traits, cultures, characters and attitudes) which differentiate people in substantial ways (cf. Dumont 1970: 270; Barnett 1977; Jeffrey 1978; Mayer 1996; Fuller 1996c: 20). While in Kerala racial arguments have as yet found no coherent political articulation, they have been instrumental in development of representations of castes as bounded, racially defined communities with characteristic configurations of *gunams*. For many Pulayas, Pulaya-ness means being an indigenous Malayali by birth, as opposed to Izhavas (Sri Lankan immigrants), Nayars (Tamil immigrants) and Brahmans (north Indian immigrants). Claiming to be the only true *Dravidian* 'sons of the soil', having *bandham* with the local *punja*, Pulayas also make sharp distinctions between themselves and *Tribals*, only and always hill people. Brahmans generally present themselves as *Aryans* from north India, all *Harijanmar* (SCs) as *Tribals* and intermediate middle communities as *Dravidians*. While some Nayars follow this, they sometimes include them-selves with Brahmans as *Aryans* or *Mediterraneans* and often subscribe to theories that Izhavas came from Sri Lanka. Popular among Izhavas is the argument that Brahmans are northern outsiders but that everybody else in Kerala, including *Tribals*, is *Dravidian*; some also subscribe to theories linking themselves with Sri Lanka.

When we told him we were writing a book about the Izhava community, Krishnan Kutty, a Nayar RSS sympathiser, told us elliptically, 'The coconut plant comes by itself, by water, floating. It flourishes in other people's land. Rubber was brought here, but the coconut came alone. It floats.' As well as expressing unease about Izhava flexibility and adaptability – 'floating' – Krishnan's statement highlights possible dangers for Izhavas of associations with Sri Lankan (i.e. foreign) origins and with the coconut tree, insinuating and spreading itself uninvited wherever it floats until it comes to dominate indigenous species. The ubiquitous and uniquely useful coconut tree has become a symbol of Kerala: coconut oil is Kerala's most widespread cooking medium; flaked or grated coconut is essential to many Kerala dishes; coir provides ropes, string and mats; coconut fronds roof houses and burn in cooking hearths; coconut toddy remains a popular drink and an important ingredient in staple food items like *appam*; tender-coconut water is valued as a pure drink which can be given to or accepted from persons of any caste and is also renowned for medicinal properties (rich in vitamins and amino-acids, and is always offered to invalids); coconut flowers are essential in Hindu temple rituals and marriages. The Izhava putative affinity (*bandham*) with coconut, so central to Kerala life, could conceivably be re-worked to the caste's advantage.

Summarising, discourses about 'qualities' and 'natures' can be used to present different *jatis* not as interdependent, hierarchically ranked groups within a caste system but as independent and tendentially equal 'communities' (*samudayangal*) competing for power and wealth within society. The problem for Izhavas – as for Pulayas and other ex-untouchable castes – becomes that of contesting what is held to be their community's particular essential and unique configuration of qualities: in this case, what is at the core of 'Izhava-ness'.

The Izhava Spirit

When Beena (Christian) heard the news that Vasu (Izhava) was secretly *romancing* an Asari girl, she remarked, 'He is a genuine *kotti*, isn't he?' When we did not understand the word, Beena explained that it meant 'Izhava', but in a derogatory way: it implied lying, cheating, bad character and so on, and we should never use the word to an Izhava's face. She warned that '*kotti*' was far worse than the common epithet 'Chovan', used in nineteenth-century missionary reports and gazetteers as the caste's name, replaced over this century by the more respectful 'Izhava'. The dictionary told us that '*kotti*' refers to the act of toddy-tapping and to the animal bone used in the process: both features strongly associated with untouchability (Gundert 1989: 304–5). We have already focused on the extent to which Izhava caste identity has been – and continues to be – over-determined by the figure of the toddy-tapper: derogatory names for Izhavas such as 'Chetty' and 'Air-Force' commonly refer to liquor while carrying additional connotations of flashiness and deceit. In stereotype, 'Izhava', 'toddy-tapper', 'untouchable' and 'dishonest person' have come to be elided. Izhavas themselves, trying to conform to dominant culture and suffering from stigmatised assigned identity, appear sometimes to suffer under a form of double consciousness in which other communities' negative judgements form part of their own self-assessment (cf. Fanon 1986).

One evening, tired and hungry, we made several moves to leave Karthikeyan's; finally, we bade farewell as he and his daughter stood on the doorstep. Suddenly he re-started the conversation, telling us some forgotten piece of information about a large local Izhava family and asking about our plans were for the next day, a complicated question requiring long explanation. Karthikeyan's daughter, a 23-year-old college-student, exasperatedly snapped at her father, 'Leave them alone! Can't you see they want to leave?' She apologised to us, adding, 'He's a real 22-carat Izhava'; her father looked abashed and bid us goodnight. We never asked Rija what she had meant by this remark: she may have been referring to his exhaustive knowledge of and propensity to discuss all things Izhava; or to his 'rough manners' in detaining us in conversation on the doorstep; or to his 'rudeness' in asking us directly about our plans. While we always enjoyed Karthikeyan's warm informality, Rija often found herself embarrassed by her father, pleading with him to behave according to the mainstream bourgeois norms to which she, a graduate, aspired.

We mentioned to educated Left Izhava friends that we had been to visit Parayavelapadi's colony, allegedly involved in illicit distilling, and that we had met with several families, who had been guarded but friendly. This prompted talk about various households involved in illicit production or sale of liquor. Suja, 22, mentioned that one mutual neighbour often called to borrow Rs10 on his way to buy drink, and that he was really quite fun when he called in again on his way home after four or five glasses, telling stories and jokes. She mused that people like that are the real Izhavas, they have the 'real Izhava spirit'.

Asking about the 'Izhava spirit', we were offered another Izhava distillers' colony as an example. During the pilgrimage season, when all Izhavas are enjoined to visit Sivagiri, almost no Valiyagramam Izhavas had, as usual, participated. If association with Narayana Guru and the SNDP is avoided as being 'too Izhava', then the Sivagiri pilgrimage, its participants clad in bright yellow (the 'Izhava' colour) is a vulgar public demonstration of Izhava-ness (cf. Gath 1998). A group of outside Izhavas had arrived in the village on foot, *en route* to Sivagiri. The colony families had been the only people to go to greet the pilgrims, and had walked alongside them through the village. Suja expanded:

Those people are so sincere. They're all very attached to Narayana Guru, to the SNDP, to *gurumandirams* ... it's funny, because they all have Narayana Guru's picture in the house and yet they do distil liquor. But they've got the genuine Izhava spirit; us here, these houses, we're not that attached to the SNDP or to Narayana Guru, not like them: they're really sincere. They believe Narayana Guru is a god; we say he's a social reformer.

Suja's family, educated and respectably employed or studying, reformed in their religious and social practices, see themselves not only as less faithful to their community association but also as less authentically 'Izhava' than those in the distillers' colony, who are firmly attached to both of the (only apparently) antithetical nineteenth- and twentieth-century Izhava 'traditions': alcohol and the SNDP.

AVOIDING IZHAVA-NESS: FAMILY OR CLASS PRESTIGE AND 'PASSING'

Kerala's 'first professional journalist' C.V. Kunjaraman, editor and founder of *Kerala Kaumadi* newspaper, reputedly was a brilliant man. We described earlier how he campaigned against untouchability, negotiating possible mass conversions to Christianity. His grandson told us that after the Izhava Memorial, C.V. had written three editorials simultaneously: for a 'moderate' Nayar paper; for an extremist nationalist paper; and for *Kerala Kaumadi*. Each editorial had taken a different slant, presenting arguments tailored to the newspaper's particular readership: C.V. Kunjaraman always maintained that opinions should be neither an iron cage nor brittle, and was accordingly able to slip himself as necessary into the antithetical positions of extremist nationalist or supporter of the British.

Velayuthan Pannikker, the Izhava hero encountered earlier, was one day travelling from Ernakulam to Kayamkulam by boat. On that day Travancore's Rajah was due to travel the same river route. People lined the banks in a grand reception with firecrackers, flowers and music. There was a block on the river to prevent other boats from travelling that day, but Pannikker said, 'Damn this, I'm going on my boat.' As he passed along the river the people – expecting the Rajah – let off firecrackers and threw flowers; when the real Rajah arrived later, all the crowds had gone home and there was nobody or nothing to greet him.

For seriously mobile Izhavas, working towards ambiguity in public self-presentation serves to distance themselves from the 'Izhava-ness' holding them back. A certain flexibility in self-presentation and ambiguity in the self is, for Izhavas, a positive attribute; in many situations, Izhavas decide that the only way to get by and achieve public respect is by 'passing'. While Pulayas and Parayans continue *en masse* to suffer severe economic and cultural disadvantage and discrimination, members of the Izhava community – 'top' among ex-untouchables – often draw upon their more ambiguous, intermediate status and upon the very principle of indeterminacy (a source of aesthetic value in mainstream social life: C. Osella and F. Osella 1998, F. Osella & C. Osella 1996; Trawick 1992: 37–43, 242–58, 265–8; cf. Rosaldo 1993: 92ff, 109ff).

While caste and class are no longer coterminous as under the nineteenth-century colonial agrarian village economy, there is still significant overlap. While the nineteenth-century agrarian economy transparently favoured Nayar and Brahman dominance, community and class remain significantly entwined within the twentieth-century economy of paid employment and migration; most graduates and professionals are Nayar or Christian, as are most of those who can speak English, the prestige language, confidently. The importance within class hierarchies of markers such as dress-style and speech further blurs lines between class and caste, both presumed, through qualities (*gunams*), to involve questions of *culture*.

Vasumati, a school-teacher, showed Caroline her *tali*, a small gold leaf, saying, 'I wear a Nayar *tali*; people looking at this would think I was a Nayar lady.' She also always wears a *sari* at home, never changing into the more comfortable but low-prestige *lungi* and blouse associated with *avarna* Hindus (just as white waist-cloths (*mundus*) are associated with *savarna* Hindus). Vasumati's son, 27, favours trousers and is indistinguishable from his Christian friends. To his mother's criticisms he justifies himself, 'You have to lower a *mundu* [in respect] all the time: with trousers, we're equal.'

When we first met the head of Kottakara Devi temple's festival committee, we 'read' him as a Nayar. His two-storeyed roadside house is near to the temple, where many orthodox and high-status old Nayar families live. He was introduced to us as 'Sadashivan Engineer, committee president', and looked every inch a person of high status, wearing ready-made trousers and shirt and a good watch; temple devotees deferred to him and greeted him with conspicuous respect. Only after several meetings did we realise that he was elder brother of the Izhava *vaidyan* living next door and that his original family house stood on the other side of the village in an Izhava-dominated interior area. Like Advocate Remini, whose family story began this book, Sadashivan engineer's professional status and self-presentation as a person of high class – wealthy and cultured – make it easy for him to 'pass'. People often say that he 'moves with Nayars'; the similarities between his house (location, decor), family, lifestyle – in short his habitus – and the styles of his Nayar neighbours is remarkable. A common proverb makes the point that even the most impervious objects can be affected by even the most delicate: 'If a rock lies next to a jasmine bush it will also smell of jasmine.' Sadashivan's hope that by living surrounded by Nayars, he and his family will assimilate their qualities, has then been partly answered.

Some, appealing to the high degrees of culture or distinction present in class hierarchies (see for example Fuller 1996c: 28) argue that examples such as this are simply questions of ignoring caste and foregrounding family or professional status, or asserting Sanskritised or otherwise improved status for one's own caste. Yet recent work (for example Fernandes 1997) confirms for us the impossibility of disentangling 'caste' from 'class', such that Fuller's 'professional stuatus' or Beteille's 'family status' (Beteille 1991) will always hold connotations of caste or community. In Valiyagramam, 'professional' carries overtones of 'Nayar' or 'Christian'. While early sociological work held categories – race, sex, class – as separate and tended to see different statuses as operative in different arenas (see for example the work of Myrdal cited in Warner et al. 1994), and while later work acknowledged an intersection or interaction between categories, the most recent – post-1980s – research suggests that categories actively participate in and shape each other, such that, as Stuart Hall has argued, 'race is ... the modality in which class is "lived" ' (Hall 1980, cited in Bradley 1996: 126). As Fernandes writes, 'The question ... is how to ... move beyond an "interaction" or "interplay" between discrete identities, terms that continue to suggest static distinctions between categories of social analysis' (1997: 6).

And while it is also true that Izhavas have, as a twentieth-century 'community', come a long way, their structural position remains the same as under nineteenth-century caste hierarchy – poised mid-way between the unambiguously *savarna* Nayars and the *avarna* Pulayas (cf. Bourdieu & Wacquant 1992: 133). The choosing of risky 'passing' as a strategy and the unpleasant consequences upon unmasking confirm the resistance of caste hierarchies, and the lengths to which people will go to try to escape them. We have seen strategies of deliberately concealing caste status openly used on many occasions by Izhava individuals or families outside of areas where they are known – which in densely populated Kerala can be as little as 2 km away.

The closest friends of Madhu – Izhava – were a Nayar and a Christian; together the three, all in their twenties, waited outside the Siva temple on Friday evenings to *tune* with the girls coming out. Madhu had a regular *line* with a Varma girl (very high-status Ksatriya); she confided in us after the *line* had broken that she had imagined Madhu to be an aristocratic Nayar. He also flirted with another girl: educated and wealthy, but of low-caste status (Velan), this girl was herself an expert in 'passing' and mixed mostly with Christians. She and her family were surprised to find out that Madhu, who had visited their house many times, was not a Christian. Yet another of Madhu's *lines*, a Nayar girl, had taken him seriously enough to ask her mother to find out about his background with a view to marriage. Mother and daughter were horrified and astounded when they discovered that Madhu was not, as they had thought, of their caste. While Madhu never lied about his caste identity, we several times saw him ably performing impression management to encourage his interlocutor into mis-attributing Christian or Nayar status. On the rare occasions when a persistent questioner discovered his identity the ensuing problems convinced us that Madhu had good reason to try to hide it.

Once,[11] we called in Madhu's company upon a Brahman friend of ours; unusually, he did not usher us into the house, but detained us upon the verandah while he tried in several of the standard roundabout ways (father's name, house name, location of mother's house in the village) to check his suspicions about Madhu. When he could not determine Madhu's caste identity without an outright rude question (almost never resorted to), he led us into the living room, presumably having attributed non-untouchable status to the polite and well-dressed young man who had told him – truthfully – that he had studied at an English-medium school and a prestigious Christian-run college in the city and who worked as a bank clerk. As we left, Madhu expressed great relief; we had all been in danger of an unpleasant and humiliating scene had the Brahman realised Madhu's true identity. Just such a scene did actually occur when we went, again with Madhu, to a Nayar family temple festival. All went well initially as Madhu, dressed in gold-bordered white mundu and clean shirt, speaking confident English, answered questions about his studies and employment. Suddenly, audible shocked whispers ran around the group: 'Only our own people' (*nammude aal matram*); 'No outsiders'; 'Who is he?'; 'He looks like a Pulaya'; 'I've seen him with Pulayas.' Word had been passed around by somebody who had recognised that Madhu was not a Nayar; direct questioning which proved that he was not, after all, a Pulaya, but 'only' an Izhava did not improve the atmosphere; we all left the festival immediately, in great humiliation and indignation. This time, Madhu's attempts at passing had failed.

While nineteenth-century forms of pollution distance have disappeared or diminished, considerations of caste and status as well as untouchability persist and are part of everyday life.[12] This takes two forms: a private one practised by those who, for a variety of reasons, publicly deny its existence; and another – public, violent and episodic – exercised by a minority. In its 'mild' form, caste discrimination continues to be expressed by the near-total absence among adults of private inter-caste interaction and intimacy such as dining, visiting, friendships and marriages, and by the contempt in which Pulayas are held, and the distance at which they and other ex-untouchables continue to be kept by the rest of the population, preventing them from overcoming their social and physical marginality. Inter-caste relations remain largely contained in the public sphere where they cannot be avoided. In working places, especially in government institutions and public corporations where reservation policies in favour of the lower castes are implemented, villagers are forced to interact with people with whom they would not otherwise entertain any close relation. Similar situations occur in political parties' activities and in temple committees.

In some rare cases, due to Kerala state's reservation policies, ex-untouchables in managerial posts supervise upper-caste employees. In one of Valiyagramam's two village offices, the village officer is a Pulaya while two of his junior clerks are Nayars and a third is a Namboodiri Brahman. This situation is almost unique: very seldom do Pulayas reach such prestigious positions. In the *Harijan colony* (140 households) where we undertook a census, only one person was employed as a 'government servant': a police constable – likely according to informants to remain at this rank for his entire career because of discrimination. More commonly it is Christians, Nayars and Izhavas who are brought together in the workplace. In these circumstances, all involved know that other forms of interaction on the same footing are impossible. Izhavas do not usually try to socialise with upper-caste colleagues outside work, knowing that solicitations in that direction would bring embarrassment for both parties, forcing into the open and making explicit tacitly acknowledged caste barriers. This embarrassment is occasionally exploited by the boldest to force colleagues from upper castes to accept food. One Izhava school-teacher formally invited all his colleagues to a meal in his house on the occasion of his retirement. The fact that the invitation was made publicly and well in advance coerced the other teachers into – reluctant – attendance. While his colleagues regarded his invitation ill-mannered and uncouth, this did not deter him from trying to get maximum 'prestige-mileage' from the occasion, including arranging a commemorative photograph.

Some social occasions, notably weddings, are semi-public but entail consumption of food, an activity otherwise limited to the intimate family group. Particular arrangements are made to enable some form of participation by guests of higher caste or superior prestige: we mentioned the practice, common among the poor and low-status, of holding a *tea party* at which only *bakery items* (i.e. purchased food not cooked in the house) are served. In this way, friends, neighbours and patrons of high prestige can attend some part of the wedding functions and take some food without damage to their reputation. Sometimes, high-status guests attend a wedding ceremony but leave before food is served: transparently feeble excuses of other urgent engagements which force them to leave before the meal are never challenged by hosts, and leavers are never forced into the ambiguity-breaking position of having explicitly to refuse the food offered. Such deliberately fostered indirectness generally maintains the social balance.

When upper castes try directly to enforce untouchability or caste privileges, the results are almost inevitably violent confrontations. These explosions of violence take place because power relations in the village have changed over the century. The political, economic and ideological authority of upper castes (Nayars and Brahmans), which in the past legitimised their actions and allowed them impunity, has diminished considerably. At the same time, the objects of discriminatory practices, particularly Izhavas, have acquired political consciousness and reached within their own community a high degree of caste solidarity and organisation. In confrontations over caste the stakes are always high: failure to respond to an open infringement of what a group believes to be its own rights and status does not merely entail a public loss of face; more importantly, it legitimises the other side's claims and actions. Caste is continually enacted and theatricalised, asserted and refuted, in public spheres.

UNIVERSALISM REGAINED? POLITICAL VISIONS

Reversed Service versus Human Chains

Local politicians often seek to flatter lower castes or announce their indifference to caste hierarchies by strategies of reversed service. This was practised for example at the village inauguration of Kerala's state-wide literacy campaign. A meal was cooked and served in a village school by *panchayat* officials and local dignitaries, many of them Congress Party members, many of them high caste, to literacy campaign volunteer teachers, many of them Communist Party members, many of them low caste. By humbly serving volunteers, especially those from the lower castes, the officials reversed the usual hierarchies.

If we wish to take these actions at face value, as enlightened denial of status differences, we are faced immediately with several difficulties. First, humbling oneself by serving food to guests is commonly experienced during weddings: as such, it is part of everyday experience but strictly restricted to a ritual context; outside of a wedding feast where he played host and patron, no Nayar would stoop to serve food to his Izhava or Pulaya neighbour. Reversed service is then clearly understood as something which may happen on certain demarcated ritual occasions, and which carries no ramifications outside of that special context. A second problem is posed by the atmosphere of such events: the literacy campaign lunch was taken by all parties in a spirit of fun, like the Saturnalian traditions attached to British Christmas, in which school-teachers serve a ritual meal to their pupils or hospital doctors wait upon nurses and porters. Clearly marked – by joking, mock servility and mock commands – as a mere transgression, the act of reversed service carries no weight in the outside world. Scott (1990) returns to similar reversals, wondering whether those anthropologists who analysed such rituals as mere safety valves or as actual preservers of the status quo overlooked the potential for real protest and challenge to be slipped in. Certainly, those being served on such occasions delight in humbling the mighty: calling upon their temporary servants demanding more rice, another *papadam* and faster service. The tone in which all this is done makes clear that everybody understands it to be a temporary and transgressive state: the server is not really in fear of the person commanding, nor does the commander hold any real sanction.

Aside from empirical issues of the content and style of the event are issues of structure: a straightforward reversal of hierarchy is not a denial of hierarchy. Scott points out that images of resistance commonly take the form of a 'world turned upside down'; while such imaginings may offer strength and comfort to those on the wrong side of hierarchies, it is clear that reversal provides no blueprint for change. Whatever covert resistance may be practised during occasions of reversed service, the central problem – lack of equality – is not addressed. This suggests that we should take another look at anthropological analyses of such reversals as actually working to strengthen structures of inequality. Bourdieu makes the point that upper classes choose symbolic transgression as a form which combines well with political neutrality (1977: 50); Haraway (1992: 306) is among those who argue that transgression, being an exercise in boundary-crossing, relies in the first place upon the notion that there are firm boundaries to be crossed. We have suggested elsewhere that the exhilaration and thrill of *romance* is predicated at least partly upon the existence of gender and caste hierarchies, and that transgressing boundaries and rules of hierarchy plays a large part in the shaping of *love* as an extraordinary and disorienting (temporary) experience (C. Osella & F. Osella 1998). Comparison with another common local political strategy further highlights just how far from daring reversed service is.

Kerala-wide human chains, in which thousands of people link hands across the state, are organised by the Left parties from time to time as public demonstrations of intercommunity solidarity; in recent years, villagers have taken part in human chains after the Mandal disturbances, the Ayodhya incidents and the Bombay riots, all exceptional large-scale incidents of public violence in which communal caste and religious identities were high-lighted.[13] While participants in a human chain may stick closely with family or neighbours, so that the effect – like that of *panchayat* feasts – is of political theatre manipulated by the politicians in charge, the underlying concept and spirit of a chain is not at all like that of reversed service. A chain addresses and challenges the problem of hierarchies, drawing its power and effective-ness for participants and onlookers from the potent emotional resonances and political implications of cross-community mutual touch. In contrast to *namaskaram*, which involves no dangerous touch; head- and foot-touching, presupposing a clearly hierarchical intimacy; reversed service, which leaves hierarchy untouched and is transparently ironic; hand-holding suggests that equality and intimacy can after all be combined, as the identical, middle parts of bodies – arms, hands – are physically joined.

While a reversal of hierarchy is far too strong a statement to be taken seriously by most, and would in any case replicate an undesirable situation, an assertion of equality may possibly be countenanced by the forward thinking and progressive. A reversal of service says, 'I, the *panchayat* president – male, Nayar, in middle age, a school headmaster – humble myself before you – a junior teacher, Izhava, female, in your twenties': such an assertion can never be taken seriously by participants or observers, hence the lighthearted jokes and delight at the thrill of transgression. As a political gesture, reversed service shows only the goodwill and open-heartedness of superiors, and threatens nothing. A human chain by contrast asserts, 'We are equal and intimate', a statement which may at times be countenanced seriously by participants and observers, and which is backed up by the potent force of physical contact.

The organic metaphor of society appears over and over and in many places: in Hindu *chaturvarna* theory, in the Christian Bible, in the secular writings of liberal modern social scientists such as Weber and Durkheim, all of which stress potentialities for social cohesion through differentiation. By synechdocal logic, the organism commonly taken as source for this metaphor is the assumed unit of society – the human being – giving us the human body as a model for the social body. This human body, differentiated and hier-archically ordered, vertical and symmetrical, is ruled by its head, receptacle of the most privileged organs of perception – the brain and the eye.[14] While the human body has proved a convenient and attractive metaphor, it is not helpful to those seeking equality (Haraway 1992). Massive state-wide displays of non-hierarchical intimacy made in human chains offer an alternative vision of the social body. This metaphorical body social is not anthropocentric: more like Haraway's internally undifferentiated segment-ary earthworm than an internally hierarchically differentiated mammal, it does not stand upright with head in the heavens and feet in the mud, but spreads along the ground, moving and expanding horizontally. While twentieth-century mutations of castes into communities have patently not managed to shake off either values of hierarchy or the logics of purity and pollution, the very possibility of the vision of the human chain suggests that segmentary logic is not lost or alien to India (cf. Kelly 1993: 475 on segmentation as 'a form of social differentiation that is egalitarian in character'). Many writers point out that the caste system before colonial systematisation and ossification had many features associated with classic segmentary systems (for example Stein 1980; Price 1996; Quigley 1993). Whether this be an enduring pre-colonial feature or a new a-modern vision, its appearance here confirms both that segmentary logic is by no means alien to late twentieth-century Indian thought and practice, and that the radical universalism of the India's early twentieth-century movements for social change is not irretrievably lost.

CONCLUSIONS

Over the twentieth century, village Christians have struggled for capital accumulation and conservation in competition with Nayars, taking on 'Nayarised' practices, while Nayars have taken on 'Christianised' practice, a familiar phenomenon among those who live side by side (Nagaraj 1993; cf. Bourdieu 1992: 97). Christians have attempted to convert wealth into prestige through practices heavily reliant upon Hindu ideas about status (patronage, political centrality, gift-giving, taking the role of sponsor, maintaining social distance). Meanwhile, Nayars have attempted to regain ground lost early in the twentieth century by boosting class status, following Christians into English-medium education, technical and professional occupations, migration within India and overseas, and high consumption. While these two dominant communities are often at loggerheads as groups, they mix fairly freely as individuals, and many adult Christian and Nayar men have friendships. As this middle-class middle-status block grows and as knowledges are standardised, Nayar and Christian discourses on hierarchy draw closer. Ideas about caste are now commonly expressed in terms of community (*samudayam*), qualities (*gunams*) and natures (*swabhavams*), not specific to Hindus. In places like Valiyagramam, where Izhavas live alongside Nayars and Christians, community identity becomes acutely self-conscious and strongly oriented towards the mainstream. Izhavas – especially in mixed areas like Sasthamuri – aspire towards the status represented by Nayars and Christians, both 'communities' envisaged as unequivocally middle class and in possession of both wealth and prestige. However, whatever Izhavas do as a group to improve 'Izhava-ness' or Izhava qualities, their inherited group nature remains Izhava *swabhavam*, the *gunams* of individual Izhavas being Izhava-like, not Nayar-like or Christian-like. Qualities attributed as particularly Izhava are still overwhelmingly negative, whether old (fondness for alcohol) or new (deceitful).

Considerations of status and hierarchy are then intrinsic to various component parts of social knowledge – *trigunams, swabhavam* – used to talk about types of person, castes and communities: not externally imposed. This latter assumption was Gandhi's error, in envisioning the possibility of *jati* without hierarchy, based on the *varna* system and a division of equally respected labour; Vivekananda side-stepped this same difficulty in his teachings on the variability of social responsibilities (*dharma*); Narayana Guru disagreed with them both, understanding that fact and value are inseparably joined (cf. Bourdieu 1994: 20ff) but the Guru's early universalist anti-caste message, leaning more towards Dr Ambedkar than Gandhi, could not be carried through. Izhavas in the early twentieth century, impatient for mobility for themselves, were constrained to work within wider society in which dominant values remain oriented towards hierarchy, values of egalitarianism being relegated to informal and lowly valued spaces inhabited by women and the young. Reform seemed the only option.

Examination of several aspects of social life confirms that hierarchy *does* seem to be embodied and literalised in much social interaction and that the social body envisioned in Kerala is commonly a differentiated and hierarchical one. When the principle of hierarchy is challenged, we find: that playing with and reversing hierarchy is understood as taking place in temporary or extraordinary circumstances, the very acts of playing and of reversal themselves symptomatic of transgression and extraordinariness; that substantial denial or transgression of hierarchy is limited to a section of the population, the young, whose voice counts for little and who will in any case 'grow out' of such non-comformist behaviour with maturity; that apparent subversion may take place within frameworks of ambiguity which leave principles of ranking tacit or unexamined.

That both hierarchy and its masking within ambiguity continue to provide important principles which act also as sources of aesthetic value, appears clear. Against apparent trends which see caste and hierarchy – relational values intimately connected with values of purity and pollution – as withering in the face of substantialisation, our ethnography suggests that dismissal of Dumont's claim that substantialisation is secondary to the overarching principle of hierarchy is premature (Dumont 1970: 226ff; Barnett 1975; Searle-Chatterjee & Sharma 1994: 19–20; Fuller 1996c: 11–12). Whether social groups are viewed as castes or as *communities*, quasi-ethnic groups, separateness and distinction of groups are not separated from hierarchical evaluation: as Dumont asserted in his criticism of Needham; as Bourdieu reminds us in relation to class markers (1984; 1994: 20ff); as Fernandes' recent ethnography makes clear; and as Narayana Guru tried to persuade Gandhi, 'facts' tend not to be separated from 'values'. As P.R. Radhakrishnan puts it, 'all classifications are based on social distinctions, and virtually all social distinction means exclusion of some kind' (1995: col. 1). Given then the resilience of hierarchy, the easiest solution for individual members of ex-untouchable castes has become 'passing': a strategy which works only for certain people and only in certain arenas.

Looking at one particularly charged and relevant arena of Kerala social life – political demonstrations – suggests at the same time that this principle of hierarchy, even if it be pervasive and cognitively grounded, is not inescapable. In public demonstrations called by the Left parties, people show themselves capable of an alternative vision of the social body as non-hierarchical. The principle of hierarchy, while arguably dominant, is not the only generative structure.

While Dumont has sometimes been caricatured as setting up an untenable orientalist dualism between egalitarian 'West' and hierarchical 'East', the prevalence of the hierarchical over the egalitarian vision confirms the existence of continuing inequality and domination: that Dumont overstated egalitarianism in Europe and constructed an untenable dualism need not lead us to turn his argument on its head or reject all parts of it. Like the islands of anti-hierarchy within a hierarchical system (see for example Dumont 1980a: 184ff; Parry 1974; Kolenda 1990: 127), broad-based egalitarian visions have yet to be translated into wider practice. Yet, as well as the easily observable value of hierarchy, equally observable values of ambiguity, indeterminacy or ambivalence also provide highly important principles of everyday Indian social life, which may both mitigate hierarchy and themselves act as independent sources of aesthetic and moral value. Toren (for example 1994, 1996) has argued that, in Fiji, values of hierarchy are complemented and often contested in everyday life by values of equality; theoretical bias and a tendency to see hierarchy everywhere, while missing egalitarianism, has led to failure to recognise these instances of equality. Parish (1996), attempting to explore the problem in Nepalese caste society, makes a similar argument. While these alternative values may be more easily observable among the young, they do persist into later life in informal arenas such as same-sex friendships involving physical intimacy and cross-sex flirting and joking relationships.

8   CONCLUSIONS

This book has taken us through lives lived over the last 100 or so years. It has therefore necessarily been about modernity and has, through its focus on a determinedly modern self-fashioning and reflexive community, also necessarily been about mobility. Mobility has a time-span and a history, a trajectory through social space which can be mapped on to two other time-trajectories: that of the human life-cycle and that of historical linear time. We have, following Bourdieu, used these trajectories as a starting point for analysis, arguing for example that over the twentieth century, the cultural figure of the Hindu householder has become merged with the bourgeois paterfamilias and revitalised as the consuming man of substance. Such changes, wrought in both the human life-cycle and in historical linear time, have been subsumed within this century's totalising time-span narrative of 'progress'. Members of low castes opted into this narrative at the turn of the century and had faith in its promise of the future, which would bring continued improvement and continuous change for the better. At the end of the century, we no longer have such confidence in 'progress' or the faith that things will easily change. The forging of modernity has not led to a crumbling of caste or class hierarchies and discriminations, nor have such hierarchies shown themselves to be mere 'superstructures' (Aiyappan 1944, 1965). In fact, modernity itself is increasingly coming under pressure as both project and as analytic concept. Insofar as modernity, as a set of empirically observable practices, produces and is experienced through ambivalence, fragmentation, contradiction and discontinuity everywhere, then we are all modern. But if we confront practices with (Western) self-representations of modernity such as those found in classical sociology, we have to recognise, following Bruno Latour (1993), that we have never been modern because we have never abandoned our past. However, while 'modernity' corresponding perfectly to classical theory might never exist anywhere, ideas (concepts and ideals) of something called 'modernity' certainly do exist and are continually appealed to in people's economic endeavours, political projects and identity crafting.

While social scientists question modernity, as a concept or pragmatic orientation towards the world it is then still very much alive. At the moment of modernity, a new self-consciousness appears, along with a predilection for dividing the world up into a 'traditional past' opposed to a future-oriented present. Izhavas attempted to turn their back on their nineteenth-century caste identity and embrace modernity, for example by taking up reformed Hinduism and English-medium education. The future-oriented mobility ambitions resulting from these processes are extremely long-term, fulfilment of desire projected long into the future so that families willingly undergo much deprivation for the sake of saving to launch children or grandchildren into employment or marriage markets. Modern identities are also reflexive and carefully monitored, while mobility entails constant performance, directed both towards the self and outwards to others, with special performances taking place at certain highlighted occasions: families at weddings; the caste at public temple festivals. As Izhavas have carefully converted newly made cash into power, menfolk have come into competition with Nayars and Christians as potential patrons and big-men. While most remain content to move within their own caste, acting as patron and leader to caste-fellows, the most ambitious move into the wider public sphere where they directly compete with the established middle classes. At the same time, at the group level new opportunities for the exercise of power represented by democracy and the operation of communally based pressure groups have benefited the caste.

The SNDP's early ideals of thrift and hard work, useful at the beginning of the century, are now loosening as consumption becomes an increasingly important arena to play in, and as families who have accumulated modest capital begin to channel it into the next generations. Consumption and distinction, which played such an important part in both nineteenth-century caste hierarchies, where they were jealously bolstered by sumptuary laws, and in twentieth-century imperialism, where they were manipulated by plantation and colonial law, re-emerge in the postcolony with a new importance in every sphere of life, from health care to religion, as people more and more appear to be judged by an overall 'lifestyle'. Parallel processes of bourgeoisification have led Izhavas over the course of the century to move away not only from nineteenth-century practices such as spirit possession but also from their twentieth-century reform body, the SNDP, now becoming inescapably associated with the constraining 'Izhava' identity and with ethics of thrift, hard work and modest life which are at odds with mobility ambitions demanding high spending on children, disdain for labour and the pursuit of leisure. This comes about because Izhavas do not live in a social vacuum; they watch and are watched by Nayars and Christians. '*The real is the relational*: what exists in the social world are relations ... which exist 'independently of individual consciousness or will', as Marx said' (Bourdieu 1992: 97).

Nayars and Christians have similar class interests and sometimes form alliances: they perform a similar range of jobs and together form the bedrock of Congress Party support. They are also often in competition with each other: for employment, places at university and class prestige. Culturally they are often quite different, and tend to define themselves by schismogenetic opposition (Bateson 1958: 271 and cf. Strathern 1988: 334ff), stressing and playing up their differences, and behaving with open hostility towards each other. Christians are stereotypically taken by others as – and promote themselves as – proponents of and adherents to rational modernity and innovation – hard work, thrift, material success; Nayars then stereotypically define themselves and are defined in opposition, as adherents to 'tradition' and the maintenance of the good things of the past – 'culture', religious observance, *dharma*. (This despite the pioneering roles of many Nayars in forming the Left parties and fighting for social reforms within their own community.) Izhavas get caught in the middle of all this, because they want what both groups have and often get wrong-footed by those whom they wish to impress, in whose gaze they live, because they appear to embrace tradition and modernity together and hence to be either confused about their own cultural identity, or not to have one at all. Middle-class and aspirantly mobile Izhavas find themselves continuously struggling to keep up with the practices and styles set by the dominant Nayar and Christian communities. The 'modern' identity embraced this century by Izhavas, and in the pursuit of which they often look towards Christians, is self-consciously opposed to a 'backward' one (education and reformed religious practices as opposed to illiteracy and hook-swinging), but Izhavas find themselves in a double-bind, since too much 'modernity' (working women, love marriages) undermines a 'Hindu' identity, the pursuit of which is a necessary part of claims for caste mobility. Much of the criticism levelled at Kappa Parambil springs from the family's leaning towards pragmatism rather than prestige.

Unlike Dalits who, paradoxically aided by separation from the mainstream, manage to forge autonomous identities and solidarity and find their own virtuosity in cultural arenas such as fashion and popular music, poorer Izhavas remain constrained to keep apart from Dalits and from arenas which would affirm or celebrate the labouring identity. During the mobility game, the goal-posts keep being shifted such that Izhavas experience a continual time-lag in their attempts to keep up (cf. Bourdieu 1984). As Izhavas attain employment in lower-level teaching and clerical jobs, make a little money through migration, and raise the cash and get the chance to buy up old *nalukettus* or build two-storey houses in prime village sites, the children of last generation's Christian and Nayar teachers and clerks have by now become professionals and have moved out of the village into the cities, where they are buying up prestigious modern apartments in serviced blocks. As Izhavas begin to get voted on to the committees of public temples, Nayars are withdrawing from public temple life and retreating into reconstruction of matrilineal *tharavadus*, complete with private family temple – a movement which can only be palely imitated by Izhavas, whose past roots entitle them not to lineage deities like Bhadrakali or to wooden *nalukettus* on prime land, but to now-demolished huts at the village margins and simple shrines to bloodthirsty autochthonous deities. Izhavas seem doomed to remain forever *parvenus*.

Izhava history and ethnography offer interesting comparisons with other similarly placed groups and are exemplary of some processes widespread in India; such groups of 'backward' castes, forming the backbone of much of the Indian countryside, have become increasingly powerful and assertive this century as they have turned numerical strength into political and social influence. At the same time, even the apparently most mobile and successful of such ex-untouchable groups continue to suffer the effects of the past: even among Kerala's urban middle-class intelligentsia, the picture is very different from that being painted for north India by writers such as Beteille (1996). We offer an anecdote urging caution upon those who are tempted to announce the irrelevance of caste among urban elites. The following incident concerns some of the most urbanised, sophisticated and cosmopolitan of Malayalis: NRI medical doctors trained in India's metropolises and now living and practising in the UK. We mentioned one such NRI doctor to another, both friends of ours who, it transpired, had trained alongside each other. We commented to one on how well the other was doing: working in a large UK teaching hospital, he was publishing research which seemed highly interesting and likely to propel him towards consultancy in record time. And yet, we mused, this man was extremely friendly and approachable; he didn't carry a massive 'head-weight'. Our friend listened carefully, nodding agreement but then, leaning towards us conspiratorially and dropping his voice, said, 'This might not be true, so don't repeat it, but I've heard – well, they used to say at college – that he's actually a ... you know, a ... an untouchable.' The other doctor belongs (as we well knew) to an OBC.

Modernity has seen Izhavas, like other communities, subject to processes of increasing bourgeoisification and a certain degree of common culture has grown up, especially among the middle-class sections of Nayars, Christians and Izhavas. Symptoms are practices such as monogamous marriage and the competitive struggle for formal qualifications and salaried employment. In public arenas this sameness is stressed, papering over the differences and rivalries between different groups within the middle class. The increasing public/private divide which bourgeoisification has enabled permits careful retention and policing of caste difference through protection and defence of the self and family, bulwarked in the now-private house, safe against unwelcome visits.[1] Meanwhile, attitudes and practices within the arenas of land, housing, food, marriage all indicate the impossibility of modernity's universalistic dreams. Caste remains strong, and, reinforcing Dr Ambedkar's point, Hinduism remains linked to caste, indicated for example by the heightening of caste identity, hierarchy and conflicts at temple festival times and by the appearance of the RSS – both thoroughly modern and thoroughly Hindu – in episodes of caste violence. Caste, in its various guises, is deep and is embodied, forming a habitus which continues to be reproduced; caste is finally reproduced through the family, which continues to maintain and defend its borders.

We must also acknowledge that not all members of ex-untouchable groups have benefited equally over this century, making hostile declarations about the lack of need for caste-based reservations appear somewhat premature: if our friend had been a member of an SC rather than an OBC it is highly unlikely – almost impossible – that he would find himself practising medicine in the UK. Even if several households from one Scheduled Caste family manage to build up some capital, that family will still find it difficult to participate fully in those arenas which convert wealth into symbolic and cultural capital, finding its members effectively debarred from admission to certain private schools, or from participating in village politics; an SC family will never find itself, unlike Advocate Remini's family, admitted into the village class elite where members make further useful contacts or, by dint of altering family culture, accepted to 'move among Nayars'. Izhavas, as an *avarna* group, share some characteristics with Pulayas, Parayans and related 'ex-untouchable' castes, but the fact that they, as a Backward Class, have been able to secure some degree of mobility this century, while members of the SCs remain overwhelmingly tied to the extremely vicious circle of untouchability and manual labour, alerts us against assuming too close parallels between *avarna* groups.

An important aspect of status asymmetry relates to the issue of power. Those who enjoy positive 'capital balances', in caste and/or class arenas, the *savarna* Hindus and the wealthy, are also often able to exercise substantial power as individuals or as families. From these groups tend to come those (mostly mature men) who run for public office, sitting on *panchayats*, school boards, temple management committees; those who act as patrons to less wealthy clients; those whose intervention and mediation is always sought by the less powerful when dealing with outside agencies, the village big-men who are connected outside the village to other big-men. At the other end of the continuum, among those who have no or 'negative capital', power can generally be exercised safely and openly only as a member of a group: as individuals, day-labourers and Dalits exercise only hidden or symbolic forms of secondary power, such as pilfering, cursing or magic (cf. Uchiyamada 1995). Within the village, individual assertions of empowerment by Dalits such as riding a motor-cycle or resisting being treated as untouchable are generally subject to (often violent) reprisals. To act in the public sphere usually requires the capital-less joining together in a trade union or caste association, or their acting as representative of their whole group, as when a Pulaya obtains a seat on the *panchayat* by virtue of reservations for Scheduled Castes. As Radhakrishnan points out, '[I]n India, exclusion is mostly historically accumulated and not ... thrown up by economic restructuring' (1995: col. 12) and it is this accumulation of exclusions exercised indiscriminately against a group which the SNDP continues to fight. The increasing impatience of the Izhava middle classes with their caste association and with political parties is linked to the growing number of senior wealthy men, like Engineer Sadashivan, who are now able to exercise power as individuals, reminding us of Bourdieu's point that the individual exists and is valorised among elite and bourgeois groups, whose ideological preference is to underplay the significance of groups in social life (for example 1990: 42ff; Bouveresse 1995: 577; Bourdieu 1984: 254ff).

While the SNDP has done much to unify the Izhava caste, internal stratification remains: within the caste, those permitted to use a title, those belonging to 'known' families or with particular prestige (the ex-headman's family; the *naluvittumar*) claim distinct status for themselves, while those stigmatised by the mainstream (home distillers) are kept separate. Modernity sees difference and hierarchy emerge strongly, rooted in wealth, employment, female seclusion, education and 'culture', the latter spanning a range of factors from attitude towards public drinking to marriage arrangements. It would seem that the category 'Izhava' is about to disappear under the weight of all these schisms, but it reconstitutes itself strongly in opposition to other communities, be this in episodic violence – temple struggles with Nayars, aggression against Pulayas; in the political arena – unification around the Mandal issue, block voting; or in the stereotyped attribution of a distinctive 'Izhava-ness'. Middle-class and elite Izhavas evoke Izhava-ness when convenient: calling poor caste-fellows to work, unpaid, at weddings; rallying the caste around issues such as reservations; canvassing support for local political ambitions. When not immediately convenient they prefer to ignore caste status, repudiating links to toddy-tapping and agricultural labouring caste-mates.

Izhavas have many ghosts following them: the *vellichappadu* – no 'devil-dancer' but the oracle of the fierce goddess – is one; the toddy-tapper is another; a third is the family head who recklessly authorises lavish spending and spectacle, running up debts, for life-cycle ceremonies. These ghostly aspects of Izhava identity, symbolically killed at the turn of the century during the early days of reform, are now re-emerging: shrines are being rebuilt, not always as imitations of Nayar-style 'family temples', but as centres of magical power; families forced to the economic margins seek refuge in illegal distilling; dowries and marriage expenses are escalating out of control. In Chapter 7 we saw violence leading to murder growing out of an initial accusation of drunkenness at a temple festival made by an Izhava towards a Pulaya: exactly the same charge as is made over and over again by outsiders and bourgeois community leaders alike against the mass of labouring Izhavas (Chapters 2, 4 and 6). This figure of the drunkard is one which Izhavas try to kill, over and over again: sign of 'backwardness', he also evokes the toddy-tapper stereotype which so enrages and thwarts the upwardly mobile. Community elite and bourgeoisie join to suppress these most unwelcome spectres, embodied in those dissenters among the labouring and drinking classes like Murali (Chapter 5) and Gopalakrishnan (Chapter 6).

The latter, failing to see the likelihood of benefit for themselves, refuse to pay lip-service to or to be drawn into the wider mobility project. The poor emerge as stigmatised in every social arena we have examined, an exclusion which appears to be increasing, leading them to be seen not only by the mainstream as failed householders but by their own caste-fellows as 'failed' Izhavas, those who have not lived up to mobility ambitions. Toddy-tappers and manual labourers are increasingly marginalised; those who contract love, local or cross-cousin marriages and who fail to reach the exorbitant levels of dowry and spectacular spending set by the mainstream are sidelined; the poor provide party followers but not leaders and often find that leaders do not represent their interests while demanding their support; their religious practices are spurned as 'backward' even as they are unable to compete in the high-prestige arenas of temple committees and patrons of sacrifices.

Taking stock of this century, we see that in many ways Valiyagramam life remains 'the same as it ever was': we find a small professional elite enjoying command of substantial economic, symbolic and cultural capital which they will manage to transmit on to their offspring; a large middle class, struggling to improve cash and/or culture holdings, consolidating or conserving enough to pass on; and a substantial mass of the poor, whose hold on any sort of capital is highly tenuous and limited. There has indeed been 'progress', but this century's relative improvements in certain arenas of life (such as educational opportunities) have been enjoyed at all levels of society so that the children of the poor, while now literate and attending school – better-off than their grandparents – are still overall relatively less qualified and educated than the children of the elite. While some development theorists have claimed (following Franke & Chasin 1994) that 'life is a little better', we argue that Izhavas have enjoyed some limited absolute progress coupled with relative immobility. Caste pride constrains poor Izhavas from building class solidarity with poor Pulayas, just as poor Christians' community loyalties constrain them from entering into wider class-based alliances: this division of the poor, which effectively worsens the positions of all of them, is a very old story indeed.

While there is often tension between family and caste identity, and while family mobility is often constrained by caste identity, caste continues to be reproduced through the family, via maintenance of private spaces coded as casted, via fortification of boundaries between the family – casted – self and inferior others, increasingly kept out of the private spaces which are to be kept pure, and via the arrangement of marriages within the caste. Food and marriage remain at the heart of caste reproduction and boundaries on exchange of intimate substance through food or marriage are still vigilantly policed from the top down, Nayars maintaining distance from Izhavas as Izhavas maintain it from Pulayas. This boundary appears to be weakening hardly at all: a Pulaya affine remains unthinkable for an Izhavas, and it is still distasteful for a Nayar to take food from an Izhava. While it is true, as Fuller (1996c: 3) points out in his introduction to a recent edited volume on caste,

that 'what caste is and what it means are now in a patent state of flux',
ethnography suggests that, after Dumont and following Christina Toren's
work in Fiji, the general principle of hierarchy between groups remains
pervasive and may be cognitively grounded (Toren 1990, 1993). As Barnes &
De Coppet (1990: 1) point out, hierarchy itself is a value, a generative
principle *certainly not unique to India*, points which Fuller himself appears to
acknowledge (cf. Fuller 1992: 253, 1996c: 11).2 If, as Toren (1990, 1993,
1996) suggests, the general principle of hierarchy is cognitively grounded (by
which she means also embodied and socially rooted) and acts as a generative
principle, then the nature and content of a group as a category of people may
alter over time without affecting the principle: Izhavas, be they 'toddy-
tappers' and 'devil-dancers' or 'SNDP folk' and 'Air-Force' remain in the same
structural position in relation to other Hindu communities, and continue to
be stigmatised. Bourdieu correctly insists that there can be no fact without
value and that groups can only be understood in their relations with each
other within a social structure: a structure which is deeply hierarchical is
likely to remain unchanged regardless of changes in the content of its
component categories.

Aiyappan (1944: 30ff) identified three main blocs of castes, which he
labelled 'A' 'B' and 'C':[3] these three groupings and the boundaries between
them remain unshaken. While Izhavas' allegiances may waver or vary –
voting Congress with Nayars and Christians; making a horizontal alliance
with other OBC classes; or looking to Dalits for intensification of *savarna/
avarna* struggles – their structural position remains the same, within a caste
hierarchy which remains unchanged since Aiyappan's first monograph,
regardless of any mitigations within pollution practices or degrees of class
mobility. Izhavas still clearly belong to 'bloc B'; Brahmans and Nayars,
savarna Hindu, still form 'bloc A', while Pulayas, Parayans and so on remain
unequivocally considered as the lowest castes, 'bloc C'. Even within the
crudest class hierarchy, Chapter 2 confirms again that the group as a whole,
like the other groups, has remained in the same place: the mass of Izhavas
stand clearly above the mass of Pulayas in terms of employment status and
below the mass of Brahmans, Nayars and Christians. This is reflected in the
brute fact of percentages of each major community working as unskilled
manual labourers: 23.3 percent of Izhavas; 50.5 percent of Pulayas; 0
percent of Brahmans; 7 percent of Nayars and 7.1 percent of Christians.

In their cultural practices, Izhavas have recourse to a mixture of styles
which unsurprisingly reflect this structural middle position, as part of bloc
'B'. At weddings, the overall form and style of marriage is like that of Nayars
but cash gifts may – as among Pulayas – be solicited and openly counted. The
range of commonest Izhava employment (military, migration, labouring)
covers jobs held by and especially associated with Nayars (military) Pulayas
(labouring) and Christians (migration). It is this structural middle position
which leads to the 'adaptable' habitus, analagous to that of the similarly
placed 'escapees' from London's East End described by Dick Hobbs, for whom,

'everything is negotiable' (1996: 180). Izhavas' extreme flexibility, willingness to negotiate and cultivation of the ambiguity or indeterminacy which eases social life is often criticised by others, as when the RSS activist (Chapter 7) enigmatically accuses them of 'floating'; when political leaders despair of their ever-shifting voting alliances; when the high-caste mock their religious and cultural eclecticism; when the low-caste accuse them of standing in one place by day and another at night. However, stories about the community hero Velayuthan Pannikker – consistently mistaken for someone other than who he is – and the example of the 'passing' Madhu (Chapter 7) show that it is exactly this Izhava talent for mixing things up and living dangerously, 'passing' and bluffing their way through, changing face to suit the circumstances, moving in the interstices of social structures, which has helped them survive and make the most of opportunities, easing their search for mobility (cf. Marriott on 'mixing', for example 1990: 18ff, and Hobbs on the 'Ultimate East End Entrepreneurial Story', 1988: 181).

Renato Rosaldo has written about the ambiguities involved in negotiating everyday life (1993: 92ff). In his view, 'optionality, variability and unpredictability produce positive qualities of social being', qualities which facilitate communication and cooperation (1993: 112), while 'open-endedness ... encourages a social capacity to improvise and respond creatively to life's contingencies' (1993: 120). This theme is by now a familiar one in Caribbean ethnographies (for example Miller 1994a: 34 on 'liming'); what we are suggesting is that it needs to be picked up in other, perhaps unexpected, places. Trawick's Tamil ethnography deals extensively with the means by which children are actively socialised into a flexible and ambiguous world, taught to take nothing as certainty and to learn adaptability (1992; cf. Toren 1996: 34-5 on similar processes in Fiji). The aesthetic of romance, and its reluctance to move towards closure is another example of a lesson in personal flexibility, as is young men's submission to the peer group's teasing and sharing (C. Osella & F. Osella 1998). Within the interstices of everyday social life we find an embracing of values antithetical to rigidity and to hierarchy, which resonate with similar values found in many other societies. Izhavas are virtuosi in flexibility, schooled in the values of indeterminacy. Ethnicisation and community-isation of caste increase rigidity, as it becomes possible for Izhavas and others to make assertions about essentialised and inescapable natures, 'Izhavas are like this'. As many have argued that modernity initially rigidified caste (for example Dirks 1987), it seems that the continuing processes of modernisation go on turning crystalline something which was once, in the days of localised lineages and kingly titles, fluid. Izhava indeterminacy and fluidity can then be read as a form of resistance to this fixity and essentialism, their shifting nature an attempt at defence against attribution by others and against being assigned a once-and-for-all identity and place.

Kelly suggests that 'social inequality can be minimally defined as social differentiation accompanied by differential moral evaluation' (cf. Kelly 1993:

473ff). While 'Brahman' (and to a great extent, 'Nayar'), continues to mean 'cultured person', 'Izhava' is taken to mean 'toddy-tapper' and 'low person', regardless of actual Izhava practice. The continuing linking of differentiation with evaluation illustrates the futility of modernist quests to solve this problem by disconnecting fact from value, as does the tenacity of class markers and racial stereotyping in modern industrialised democratic societies, supposedly made up of identical individual citizens (Bourdieu 1984). Fernandes (1997) takes this up in earnest to push further away from the split which insists upon caste or religious identity as pre-capitalist, feudal or non-modern and class as the necessarily pre-eminent pole of a modern identity. She points out that while Chakrabarty (1989) criticises the ahistorical and homogenised nature of modernisation theory's assumed worker, he still characterises identities formed through ties of religion, language or community as 'narrow' in contrast to the identity of worker, eventually thereby reproducing earlier privileging of European notions of what a modern individual is. Turning to sociological work on the long-time and heavily industrialised USA which tells us that is fact, there is a continuing importance in this undoubtedly most modern of societies of gender and racial identities, with a comparatively lesser importance given to class among workers, Fernandes aims to heal the split and bring South Asia and the West back into the same analytical space. Post-1980s research suggests that categories actively participate in and shape each other, such that, for example, as Stuart Hall has argued, 'race is ... the modality in which class is "lived" ' (Hall 1980 cited in Bradley 1996: 126). In the present, as in the recent past, while Izhavas have made significant gains, they remain subject to an *avarna* and ex-untouchable label: 'Izhava-ness' cannot be neutral any more than can 'Brahman-ness' or 'Pulaya-ness', and caste remains the modality through which class, in the modern Indian context, is lived.

Growing realisation of this may account for the rising popularity among Valiyagramam's young people of arguments which address the community's problems in terms of caste, rejecting as unrealisable the rationalist universalism of the early twentieth-century propagated by Narayana Guru and the SNDP and taken up by the Left parties. Having pursued goals of progress and mobility for a century by means of reform, class mobility and assimilation and through attempted redefinition of 'Izhava', some are considering the benefits of embracing the caste status which they are anyway unable to shake off (cf. Parry 1970). Such movements turn in three directions. The first, represented by the JSS, is a return to Izhava militancy; in Valiyagramam, where the 'Izhava spirit' is felt to be weak, the JSS has few supporters. The other two options rest upon redefining caste in terms of broader blocs of communities: within this scheme, Izhavas may pursue dreams of mobility by standing alongside Nayars and *savarna* Hindus against the 'real' untouchables – Pulayas and associated castes; or they may stand alongside other ex-untouchables to take an anti-*savarna* perspective. The first tendency is represented by Izhavas who participate in the RSS and in anti-Pulaya violence; the second in its more conservative form by the 'third pole' (OBCs only) proposed by the SNDP and in its more radical interpretation as a broadly based coalition of Muslims, Dalits and OBCs.

We have argued throughout that Izhavas are a modern community. We need now to reflect for a moment on how we envisage them as modern and what we understand modernity to mean in this context. Mainstream debates on Indian modernity have been informed by classic sociological writings, from Marx and Weber through Tonnies, assuming a unilineal and universal process of modernisation; a radical shift between community and society; a consequent withering away of 'traditional' forms of identity and practices based on ethnicity, community or caste. On the strength of these intellectual premises the existence or persistence of 'pre-modern' forms – in industry as well as agriculture, in cities as well as villages – constitute a contradiction requiring explanation. Different attempts, embedded in sociological master-narratives of modernity, however, are highly problematic. Here it is commonly assumed that modernity, and thus potential for progress and development, are not merely external to Indian tradition, but will eventually follow a unilinear path, in line with its unfolding in the 'old world'. The Indian experience of modernity thereby appears incomplete and defective: blocked or still in transition – clinging to the remnants of a feudal past; or somehow fundamentally 'other' and beyond the scope of modernisation theory; or schizoid, split between different arenas of experience – modern at work and pre-modern at home.[4]

To move away from analyses pathologising Indian modernity we turn to two related bodies of work: the first problematises western modernity itself; the second relativises modernity at large. A radical attempt to problematise essentialist (self-)representations of western modernity – in social science as well as institutional discourse – can be found in the work of contemporary social theorists such as Bauman and Wagner, among others.

Bauman argues that while modernity strives to create order from chaos and to eliminate ambivalence, efforts to generate classificatory order cannot but lead to more ambivalence and indeterminacy, which in turn call for greater and more refined ordering practices (Bauman 1991; cf. Latour 1993: 34). Where 'the other of modern intellect is polysemy, cognitive dissonance, polyvalent definitions, contingency' (1991: 9), the abhorrence of ambivalence is 'the natural inclination of modern practice' (1991: 8). Here dictatorial regimes and attempts to exterminate those hybrids or 'strangers' who defy neat classifications – such as the European Jews – are not aberrations or deviations from liberal ideals of modernity (cf. Habermas 1987), but the inevitable consequence of modernity's ordering practices. Meanwhile, Wagner (1994), proposing a periodisation of modernity and its representation in the social sciences, locates an inherent tension within the project of western modernity between 'liberty' – liberal notions of individual freedom and autonomy – and 'discipline' – continuous institutional efforts to restrict radical liberalism; a tension clearly illustrated in classical debates on the relationship between individual and society. Wagner (1999) also highlights the contextual nature of representations: while European imagination represents the United States as the only site of 'true modernity', at the same time it critically evaluates the triumph of unrestricted – and substantially amoral – instrumental rationality in America against a more ethical European modernity embedded in 'traditions', 'culture' and 'morality'. These analyses alert us to the unevenness of modernity as a project even in its so-called centres. Europe might be not yet modern, the programme unfulfilled; it might be seen as modern in similarly imperfect ways to its ex-colonies; it might be seen as never modern, the very project of modernity an impossibility which then itself gives rise to self-doubt and anxieties about identity (Latour 1993).

In a parallel move coming from postcolonial trends in anthropology and history, a singular classical master-narrative is replaced by a plurality of narratives, modernity is located in specific historical-cultural nexuses (cf. Rofel 1999; Piot 1999). Many qualities assumed within classical theory to be exemplary of modernity are then revealed as not necessarily universal: Piot argues that the 'maximising, self-interested, property-seeking' bourgeois individual is not the only form of modern person (1999: 20); Ong (1999) explores Asian modalities of modernity – perfectly compatible with capitalism and modern markets – which are based on assumptions about person and society quite different from those promoted within North American contexts (cf. Kahn 1997). Historians such as Chakrabarty, Chatterjee and Prakash have attempted to locate Indian modernity within specific historical processes.

Discussing working-class consciousness in Calcutta jute mills, Chakrabarty points out that theoretical problems in discussions of industrial labour relations in India arise from initial assumptions that 'workers all over the world, irrespective of their specific cultural pasts, experience "capitalist production" in the same way' (1989: 223). Chakrabarty suggests that modernisation theories have generally been built upon the historically specific and geographically limited cases of early modernisation in Europe, in particular theories of Britain's Industrial Revolution. Chakrabarty offers the possibility of pluralising our theories of modernity to recognise that industrialisation, capital–labour relationships and worker identity might all take different forms in different arenas of industrialisation and modernisation. Chatterjee and Prakash suggest that Indian modernity is not simply a replica of a western, or specifically British model, but is substantially 'Indian'. Looking at the development of Indian nationalism (Chatterjee 1993) and its relationship with technology and science (Prakash 1996, 1999) they identify a double process of criticism and recovery: of colonialist domination, while retaining universalist ideals of freedom, justice and progress brought by colonialism itself; of local 'backward' practices, while embedding modernity in a reconstructed body of traditions. Agents of this reflexive engagement with both modernity and tradition are those ambivalent 'strangers' (Bauman 1991) or hybrids (Latour 1993), the products of western modernity – the western-educated Indian elites – who rework and 'traditionalise' modernity for a home audience. Thus, Gyan Prakash writes that 'Indian modernity emerges as Janus-faced; crafted in the image of Europe, it is also ineluctably different; founded on the capital community opposition [sic], it is also the undoing of that polarity' (1999: 234).

While these two bodies of work go a long way in de-essentialising modernity, a series of problems remain. Critical social theorists bring to our attention the tension that exists between self-representations of modernity in public discourses and the practices generated by the same. A major difficulty here is that in these analyses modernity is a specifically western, or European, affair: the possibility that the project of modernity might unfold, maintain and define itself by continually producing otherness and ambivalence not just within the confines of Europe, but more importantly, in relation to those societies brought within the fold of European discourse through colonialism, remains significantly unexplored. At the same time, postcolonial critiques continue to deny the coevalness of Indian modernity: modernity remains an external, substantially western phenomenon, albeit eventually adapted, transformed and made 'Indian'. Importantly, while these authors recognise – contra earlier subalternist reification – that current traditions might be socially (re)constructed – in particular purged – in an effort to 'traditionalise' modernity, they do not consider that 'tradition' – together with a generalised condition of 'pre-modernity' – might be a category historically generated by modernity itself (Comaroff & Comaroff 1993; Latour 1993; Friedman 1990). In both cases we end up in a similar place, which is with a pluralisation of modernity, either by identifying contradictions, inconsistencies, ambivalences and fragmentations within the project of modernity itself – whereby Indian modernity ceases to be a pathology – or by relativising and hence identifying local trajectories to processes of modernisation – whereby Indian modernity is simply one of many possible different modernities.

We suggest that in order answer some of these questions and to make sense of the Izhava engagement with modernity we have then to move some steps further. First, we must insist upon the co-creation of a global modern world by European and non-European communities, recognising, as Prakash suggests, that for 'the formation of western modernity ... the benefit of empire was crucial; its identity and authority was forged on the stage of imperial and colonial domination' (1999: 12; cf. Comaroff & Comaroff 1993; Piot 1999; Stoler 1995). Despite modernity's claims to universalism, the construction of 'others' – so apparent in plantations and Gulf boom-towns – has been identified by analysts as central to the development of modernity – and not merely an epiphenomenon of it: modern western identities emerge as constructed in opposition to significant 'others', in terms of class, gender and race (Said 1978; Pandian 1995; Kondo 1990;

Jayawardena 1995; Nandy 1983; Sinha 1995; cf. Mudimbe 1988; Appiah 1992). Here the colonies and the colonised are the epitome of alterity, an obvious privileged ground for the elaboration of wider oppositions between modernity and tradition; between rationality and irrationality; between self and other (see for example Dumont 1980).[5] At the same time, the colonies are laboratories for testing and developing modern forms of knowledge and government, often developed first in the colonies and then used at home against populations of undesirables such as the insane, the criminal, the indigent, redeployed in an effort to control or 'reform' the emerging British working class (Comaroff & Comaroff 1993; Grewal 1996).[6] But modernity is not just constituted through colonialism at the level of discourse: while surplus extracted from the colonies constituted the basis for the development of modern western capitalism (see for example Habib 1995; Wallerstein 1979; Mintz 1985; Wolf 1982; Gilroy 1993), the colonial economy – plantations in particular – was the testing ground for the development of 'rational' and 'scientific' modes of exploitation (see Daniel et al. 1992; Breman 1989, 1991; Baak 1997; Kale 1995; Kelly 1991).

By recognising that we live in 'one world' and that we occupy the same analytical space, we are trying to move away from or break the continuous process of othering entailed in modernity and reproduced in much sociological analysis. The problem then is how to analyse difference within modernity without turning it into otherness. This brings us to the second step: we must acknowledge that modernity is local in its globality (or plural in its singularity) in that it is elaborated, made sense of and experienced everywhere in a continual dialogue with local ideas and practices.[7] Crucially, we believe that modernity is not taken on and adapted, but forged and developed in a specific location out of local material. Beteille (1983), Parry (1974) Mines (1994) and Parish (1996) have successfully argued that ideas of equality and individualism cannot be used to construct an opposition between India and the West, having as they do a long, specific local history. We have recently argued that popular Indian criticisms of public corruption might be embedded in long-standing local notions of natural justice, based on ideas of 'sincerity', as well as by reference to notions of bureaucratic efficiency.[8]

The Izhava reformer Sri Narayana Guru appealed to Indian ideas about equality in order to forge his modernist slogan: in the process of making modernity, pre-existing local discourses on egalitarianism were bolstered by discourses appealing to Science. For Narayana Guru, the scientifically identifiable *jati* was *manushyajati*, the species of humankind, and no human being could be 'other' to another. What we want to suggest here is that Indian modern practices based upon universalistic notions of justice, equality and individual agency are neither 'western imports' nor 'traditional', but arise instead through a series of debates and engagements between local and external universalist ideals. That the local pole of this relationship might be erased or go unrecognised in master-narratives of modernity (in western social sciences, as well as in institutional narratives of colonial and postcolonial states) might not come as a surprise: recognition would undermine the project of modernity itself, always needing as it does to be opposed to something else which is 'not modern' in order to justify its existence. When we begin to break through the type of dualistic categories generated by modernity itself, not only do we recognise that the 'other' cannot be treated as external to modernity, but also that modernity cannot be seen as a discrete western project totally external to the 'other'.

Third, our ethnography suggests that we must allow agency not only to the 'hybridised' elites who come into direct contact with European ideas and practices, but also to the illiterate labourers, blue-collar workers or unskilled migrants who, just as much as, *if not more than* their elite fellow-citizens, practice and experience modernity in all its ambivalences and contradictions. Indeed, if we move away from intellectualism and bring practice and embodiment to the centre of our analyses, then the factory worker, the migrant or the consumer of popular film is a far more important player than the Indian high-caste intellectual. But in doing so we also note from our ethnographic evidence – and unspoken in much of the more abstract theory – that the crucial difference between various styles and arenas of modernity is not the level of commitment or the degree of penetration but the extent to which the players are on the winning or losing side of a process which appears in its bottom line as inextricably tied up with production and consumption. Without returning to debates about class, perhaps we can hold on to the insight that modernity is about freedom and progress, but also about domination and impoverishment. And almost nobody anywhere feels themselves to be securely and happily modern: 'modernity is always in the next village' (Comaroff & Comaroff 1993), never present here right now. We insist in short, upon locating Izhavas within a global modern context and on the possibility – the necessity – of eventual comparison of disparate cases.

Izhavas have been at the centre of processes of modernity – working in plantations, forming social movements – since its earliest days, and continue to be deeply involved in it, via globalisation – as foreign migrants, as consumers – now. Their experience is one facet of a wider picture: what we see happening within the community, for example, with regard to the labouring poor – stigmatisation, increasing deprivation – is a mirror for what is happening globally, where the under- or unemployed classes face similar prospects of both poverty and exclusion. Globalisation is not only an economic and cultural phenomenon, but also a political one. As elites continue to connect and make alliances, the poor and dominated remain largely excluded, by virtue of relative immobility and exclusion from communications technologies, from the possibility of making equivalent counter-alliances.

Returning to Chapter 1, where we first noted our personal affinities among Izhavas, considering briefly our own families' histories over the course of this century, we remain struck by the many similarities between our respective groups' experiences. Caroline's grandparents, in the 1920s, worked as manual and domestic labourers; in the 1950s, some of the next generation moved into technical and skilled manual work, escaping relations of patronage and ties involved in domestic service; by the 1970s, some family members were making substantial amounts of cash, sometimes through migration; a few were even beginning to consider possibilities of higher education. Filippo's father spent most of his life away from home as a migrant worker in the construction industry, sending home remittances in valuable foreign currency. Increasing bourgeoisification is again in evidence – the grandparental generation sometimes revels in vulgarity to a degree shocking to members of the youngest generation. Also apparent are ever-escalating levels of consumption and tendencies of 'floating' and indeterminacy – for example in voting behaviour. Among lower-middle groups, who can choose whether to define themselves and stand with the working class/poor or with the lower-middle class/aspiring mobile, many people 'float', choosing to look downwards in solidarity with those below them in times of trouble and upwards towards those above them when things are going well. Values of egalitarianism and mutual aid are carefully preserved within the group, while flexibility and ambiguity aid one's passage outside it, navigating through a hierarchical world. The big difference, the thing that makes the experience of our particular – white – families and the Izhava families we know ultimately almost incommensurable is that membership of a negatively evaluated community remains, for Izhavas and others like them – i.e. those who live on the wrong side of carefully constructed and anxiously maintained ethnicised and essentialised hierarchies – for the moment apparently inescapable.

NOTES

CHAPTER 1 INTRODUCTION

1. Contrast with van der Veer (1998: 292) who suggests that all modern identities are forged in opposition to 'traditional', 'backward' ones – i.e. Friedman shows that 'authenticity' itself is a modern response. But van der Veer is right to identify 'tradition' as a category as forged from modernity.
2. Moore hints (1994: 79) that since social status and identity are multiple, formed and played out in many different arenas, the idea of multiple habitus may be useful; the idea of habitus as we understand it already embraces the possibility of multiplicity within, born out of a person's experience in multiple social arenas and fields and a life trajectory which takes him/her through many social spaces and circumstances, all of which make their mark (see for example Bourdieu 1994: 78–9).
3. What makes a particular habitus is not its content (for example a preference for carnatic music over ghazals), since content and also the habitus itself will alter over time (see for example Bourdieu & Wacquant 1992: 133), but its general form, as a 'system of dispositions' (for example a tendency towards hyper-conformity), the latter born out of early primary social experiences and subsequent social relations within fields: this is, importantly, a generalising theory (for example Bourdieu & Wacquant 1992: 131; Wilkes 1990: 120ff).
4. Grusky (1994a: 4) delineates eight bases of inequality: economic, political, cultural, social, honorific, civil and human.
5. Bourdieu (1990: 125ff) reminds us of the need to pay close attention to local representations.
6. These might include: an ideology of self-respect; the practice of thrift in the early part of the century, giving way lately to a focus upon consumption; mobilisation into groups and associationism.
7. Kuttanad itself forms a rough square with four towns at its corners: Krisnakara (south-east), Punjapad (south-west), Changannacheri (north-east) and Alapuzha (north-west), the district capital.
8. Unlike Izhava converts who have become integrated into the mainstream. Pulaya Hindus and Pulaya Christians freely intermarry and can be deemed one community.
9. During 1996, the Congress state government, under the leadership of A. Anthony, banned arrack and increased by 300 percent the duty on IMFL (spirits).

263

10. Informants characterised *Malayalam Manorama* as for Christians and Congress-oriented; *Desa Bhimani* for Communists; *Kerala Kaumadi* – popularly known as the *Izhava Kaumadi* – for Izhavas. The most popular paper, *Mathra Bhumi*, appealed to several Hindu communities and to many Christians.

11. At the International School for Dravidian Linguistics, Veli Thumba, to whose staff we remain grateful.

12. University of Kerala, Kariavattom; Centre for Development Studies, Ulloor.

13. During first fieldwork, a city-educated Izhava young man (Sahadevan P.R.), temporarily resident in Valiyagramam while working locally as a medical representative, also began to take an interest in our fieldwork. Sahadevan, a sociology graduate, came on a few interviews with us and also translated some documents. He has now migrated to the USA.

14. *Madamma* is a somewhat less prestigious social identity, stereotypically associated with television actresses and scantily clad unchaperoned tourists, than that of *sahippu*.

15. As people from social backgrounds different from those of most mainstream academics (in Bourdieu's terms, we have arrived at our current social position via trajectories 'different from the modal trajectory', 1984: 110), we also suspect that our experience of fieldwork may have been different from that of many of our colleagues. We have not pursued here what we think the consequences may be for our work, but want to affirm our conviction that anthropology urgently needs to continue and intensify the broadening of its church. Talking about our fieldwork with working-class British Asian friends makes clear that theirs are perspectives, for example, which would have many interesting and new things to say about South Asian ethnography.

CHAPTER 2 WORKING FOR PROGRESS

1. What sort of behaviour and style is understood as 'nurturing' should not be pre-judged; specifically, Malayali nurturing and motherliness differ considerably from US and UK styles, resembling descriptions given by Trawick (1990) for Tamil Nadu and by Kurtz (1992) for several societies.

2. In 1684 the Company received a grant from the Rani of Attingal (a small kingdom north of Venad) and established a factory in Anjengo; later similar agreements were reached with the Rajah of Venad (later Travancore) and factories were started at Eadawa, Kovalam, Vizhinjam.

3. Kannan Devan Hills Produce Co., for example, established in 1878, acquired an area of 215 square miles at the assessment of half a British Rupee per acre: by 1945 it held 100,000 acres (Ravi Raman 1991: 245; see also Kooiman 1989: 115ff).

4. Introduction of land tax on tenants of government land in 1802 was copied by private landlords who introduced similar measures for tenants. The result was that defaulting tenants, unlike their counterparts on goverment land who had more secure tenancies, could be expelled from the land (Lemercinier 1974: 160ff).

5. That the Alummoottil's fame extends beyond the Travancore Izhava community is witnessed by the 1994 Malayalam film hit, *Mani Chitra Tazhé*, purporting to tell the story of tragedies within this notable family, and by serialisation in *Kala*

Kaumadi magazine of the autobiography of the family's oldest surviving member, Mr Udayabhanu.

6. Information was collected from various family members, from Udayabhanu's autobiography, as well as from Izhava villagers. We also note the parallel rise of equivalent sections among related communities in other states; for example, Radhakrishnan (1995: col. 4) refers to Karnataka Chief Minister Bangarappa as belonging to the 'Idiga community (traditionally tappers) ... with a rich and influential liquor lobby at his command'.

7. Koccu Kunja Channar was assassinated by his sister's sons (his rightful heirs under the traditional matrilineal system), because he was allegedly planning to leave the greater part of his wealth to his wife and children.

8. See for example Beteille (1974: Ch. 4), Mencher (1974), Athreya (1987), Athreya et al. (1990: Ch. 6).

9. Data for 1910 were taken from the 1910 Land Settlement Survey, while those for 1959 and 1990 were drawn from agricultural subsidies registers in the the village office.

10. Because they spend most of their working life outside of the village, and share cultural space (by virtue of, for example, sophistication, having learnt a second language) with migrants, we include military and police personnel among the wider category of 'migrants'.

11. For these authors, the occupation of toddy-tapping not only defines the community's overall status but also associates Izhavas to the Tiyyas of Malabar and to other otherwise linguistically and culturally different neighbouring groups such as the Shanars/Nadars of southern Tamil Nadu (at that time partly under Travancore rule) and the Billavas of South Kanara.

12. This compares to the experiences of Dr Ambedkar (1891–1956): 'Despite ... an education which only a few ... could attain then ... caste-Hindus did not allow him to continue in office' (Radhakrishnan 1991: col. 1).

13. Similar jokes told among Pulayas are used in a different way, to mock occupational caste hierarchies and high-caste use of dowry to 'buy' good grooms.

14. The term for toddy-shop, *sharppu*, captures two notions: the English-derived shop and notions of sharpness, cutting, and so on, all of which make euphemistic reference to tapping (the knife, the cutting process). The ambiguity of the term is played upon by men, who often stop for a quick drink while out of the house on the pretext of marketing and joke about going *sharppu-ing*.

15. This difference in wages is reversed in nearby areas (cf. Herring 1984 (Kerala), Kapadia 1993a (Tamil Nadu)).

16. The first ploughing has been done by tractor instead of bullock teams since 1992.

17. The Northern Ballads (*Vadakkan Patthukkal*) tell the lives of those chivalric heroes and heroines who lived during the sixteenth-century golden age of the gymnasium system (*kalari*), martial arts (*kalaripayattu*) and blood feuds. The stories of the songs are universally known, taught at home and school, and have been been made into popular musical films. One group of ballads deals with a matrilineal family of brother, sister and sister's son, said to have been Tiyyas (Malabari caste unified with Izhavas during formation of the SNDP).

18. In 1995 there were eight phone booths and ten beauty parlours within a 3 km radius of the village.

19. A vivid account of the difficult life of the Christians who migrated from Travancore to the hills and high ranges of Malabar is found in S.K. Pottekat's

novel *Vishakanyaka* (1980). See also Tharakan (1978) and K.K.N. Kurup (1988).
20. Many times during interviews, a child of the household threatened to reveal the
    truth when we asked, 'What is x doing in Madras?' An adult would swiftly remove
    and reprimand the child and tell us firmly 'He has a job in a company!'
23. There are only rough, and often contradictory, estimates on the total number of
    Indian migrants in the Gulf; for example Nayyar (1989), Nair (1986) and Gulati
    (1983) estimate their number in 1983 as around 1 million.
22. Significantly, young men over-estimate Gulf riches: an apprentice fitter, 23,
    guessed that in the Gulf he would earn around Rs 40,000 per month when
    qualified, as opposed to his current salary of Rs 800.

CHAPTER 3 MARRIAGE AND MOBILITY

1. Consider two women, both in their early thirties: a widow, mother of two
   teenaged children, one a son, who had lost her husband in a violent road accident;
   and a long-married but childless woman. The first woman's status as mother
   mitigates the extent to which she is considered *asubbha* (inauspicious), while the
   married status of the second does not make her *sumangali*, nor does it prevent her
   from being considered *asubbha* as a result of her childlessness. Talking about the
   politician K.R. Gowri, one woman remarked that she was a 'bad woman'
   (*cittapennu*) and had never married; when we contested this, the speaker clarified,
   'Yes, but she didn't have any children, I mean'; this was considered to make her
   married status bogus.
2. Men were allowed to pass on to their wife and children only self-acquired property,
   while at their death rights of use on lineal properties were relinquished to
   matrilineal descendants.
3. The Anglo-Indian colonies of Tallassery in Malabar, where the first East India
   Company factory was opened at the close of the seventeenth century and of
   Pettah, outside Thiruvananthapuram, are both situated in Izhava-dominated
   areas, suggesting Izhava origins for many Anglo-Indians.
4. Since the demise of *sambandham* unions, the same applies also to Nayars and
   other castes who used to have liaisons with superior *jatis*.
5. For want of a satisfactory term, this refers to the category of those who hold two
   significant forms of prestige capital: white skin and the ability to speak English.
6. Arabs, the other 'foreign' group most commonly experienced as superiors, while
   often accorded high status are not usually considered suitable marriage partners.
   This is partly because they are not perceived as 'white-skinned' or 'English-
   speaking', and largely because they are Muslims, a group increasingly considered
   as highly unsuitable for Hindu intermarriage.
7. Fuller (1976a: 77–8) discusses some problems with classifying Malayalam
   kinship terminology as straightforwardly Dravidian.
8. In the Malayalam Dravidan kinship terminology, both cross-cousins are referred
   to as *murapennu/muracherukan*, despite a preference for matrilateral cross-cousin
   marriage.
9. It is not unusual for 'careless' families to find out, after the marriage of a son or a
   daughter, that in-laws are unable to fulfil the promises made before the wedding.
10. Literally MB and MBW. The terms *maman* and *mami* are used in modern slang to
    mean both marriage broker and a prostitute's protector/pimp. A *maman/mami* is
    then a man/woman who procures sexual partners.

11. The bridegroom and his friends call upon the girl a few days before the wedding to ask details of sizes, colour preferences and so on, and to take away one of the girl's *sari* blouses as a model for stitching the wedding blouse.

12. Scheduled Caste families in Valiyagramam remain as yet without exception excluded from the middle-class category, almost all being agricultural or manual labourers. Brahmans, who practice a Sanskritic form of 'true' *kanyadanam* marriage, performed via Vedic rituals completely unlike those of other Hindu castes, participate in an extremely narrow marriage market in which 'pedigree' remains more important than wealth. Brahman brides generally wear less gold, while affinal payments are more modest and are given discreetly.

13. Attempts to discuss which food which would be acceptable in inter-caste situations never led to articulation of formal distinction between types of food, such as the north Indian *pacca/kacha* categories. In practice, a clear difference exists between fruits and manufactured and purchased items, generally widely acceptable, and items – whether fried or boiled – taken from the house, their acceptance limited.

14. Bride and groom's side arrange separately for photographic and video coverage; often resulting in two sets of video crew and photographer. The resulting videos and albums remain with the respective families.

CHAPTER 4 CONSUMPTION: PROMISES OF ESCAPE

1. *Chettu* is a slang word in common use among young people. Its literal referent is to toddy-tapping, *cettuka*, and to the toddy-tapper's knife (cf Gundert 1872: 381 cols 1 and 2). The slang concept picks up notions of sharpness, knife-like-ness, cutting; so to be *chettu* is to be, in English idiom, a 'sharp' dresser. *Jada* is another slang word, whose literal meaning is shiny: to be *jada* is to be, in English idiom, a flashy person.

2. Baggy, oversized clothing derived from 'ragamuffin', via Jamaican dancehall-style and urban north Atlantic black styles. A famous exponent is Apache Indian, a UK-born Sikh popular in UK, Caribbean and India alike.

3. Bourdieu's 'culture of necessity' and theories of 'dailiness' (e.g. Fernandes 1997) may provide an explanation of the reality behind this stereotype.

4. Price (1996: 100ff) notes the growing importance in nineteenth-century Tamil Nadu of cash as a tool in politics and alliance-making.

5. Houses do not generally actually have basements; the myth clearly refers to the 'underhand' or 'base' methods involved in accumulating cash (cf. Taussig 1980).

6. Called blades because their high interest rates 'cut' like a razor. Sometimes in conversation somebody will refer to their loan as a Seven O'Clock, like the famous brand of razor blades.

7. Although this is being resisted by the artisans themselves, who periodically try to make the case for jewellery being valued as craft, not as mere gold.

8. One 'government model upper primary' with attached pre-primary schools; eight lower primary schools; three upper primary schools. The three private schools are Christian owned and run.

9. Matriculation (SSLC) examinations are taken in six subjects: Malayalam, English, Hindi, Science, Mathematics and History. Each paper is worth 100 marks, and SSLC results are expressed as marks out of 600. A pass is 210/600; 360+ is 1st class; 480+ is a 'ranking'. Rank-holders' names are published in the newspapers,

and they are usually able to attend the college of their parents' choice without paying capitation fees.

10. Primary Healthcare Centre, with five 'junior' sub-centres under its jurisdiction spread throughout the village. The centres are funded by the state government and by central government, under the World Bank Indian Population Project, and have received some help (steam sterilisers, medicines) from UNICEF in the past. The monthly budget in 1993 was around Rs 3000–4000.

11. Death and birth are widely associated: deaths in one arena are births into another, dramatic examples of general processes of union and separation, when what is held together is broken apart and spilled, yielding both regenerative seeds of new life and also some residues (Beck 1969; Kapferer 1991: 298; Ostor 1980: 180–1).

12. For details of Kerala Hindu funerary rituals, see Osella (1993) and Uchiyamada (1995).

13. At Nayar funerals we have seen banana at the south (head) side, coconut in the stomach (central) side, and a tuber at the north (feet) side; at Izhava funerals we have seen coconut and tapioca (*kappa*) planted.

14. An Izhavati (barber-priest to Izhavas, who conducts weddings and funerals) told us that the coconuts grown from 'burial trees' are in demand by sorcerers, and can be sold for ten times the market price.

CHAPTER 5 RELIGION AS A TOOL FOR MOBILITY

1. LMS missionaries are recorded as having supervised destruction of shrines by the newly converted, and building in their place chapels and churches (Kooiman 1989). Ironically, today some of Kerala's largest and most successful shrines to Chattan are owned by Nambutiri Brahmans (Tarabout 1992, 1997).

2. A member of Alummoottil family told us that after Sankaracharya had revived Hinduism and casteism, some people had sided with kings and priests and been rewarded with the status of 'Nayar'. Those – including the Izhavas – who had resisted, retaining Buddhist and anti-caste sympathies, had been ostracised. In contrast to Maharashtra, where Ambedkar's explicit championing of Buddhism for untouchables as anti-caste has flourished, Buddhism is usually seen in Kerala as a 'dead' religion, replaced by reformed twentieth-century Hinduism. While Narayana Guru added Buddhist rationalist arguments to modernist and neo-Hindu rationalisms about caste, founding in 1923 a Dharma Sangha order of *sannyasins;* and while C. Krishnan, founder in 1916 of the Cochin Izhava Samajam and editor of the newspaper *Mithavadi,* urged conversion to Buddhism, leading the poet Kumaran Asan (in 1923) to address the SNDP on the matter, very few actually took this up. Both Buddhist philosophical principles and neo-Buddhist ideas and strategies were freely drawn upon by founders of Izhava movements; sympathies for Buddhism remain. However, in the 1930s when mass conversion was being debated, the pragmatic option of joining the prosperous and respectable Christian fold was more attractive than the prospect of joining ranks with Dalit Ambedkarites, while most Izhavas held fast to the promise of a reformed and revitalised 'New Hinduism', eventually joining with Nayars in struggles for Temple Entry.

3. *Sammaddhi* is not exactly a death anniversary: the achievement of *sammaddhi,* managed by a very few extremely spiritually advanced people, implies

transcendence of the life–death process and entry into a permanent state of meditation.

4. Yellow (not saffron or orange) is the colour particular to Izhavas. *Gurumandirams* and SNDP branch offices are generally painted yellow.

5. Sivagiri, near Varkala, south of Kollam, is where Narayana Guru sits in *sammaddhi*, site of his shrine and an *asram*.

6. One Nayar headmaster argued, in a common idealised Hindu view of Christianity, 'You have to attend every Sunday morning, not just if and when you feel like it ... if you break church law you cannot marry, be buried, or have your children named ... you listen to advice from your priests ... this discipline is what we Hindus lack.'

7. This is a common story. We almost never hear the term *tapas* used. *Sakti* and *siddhi* (magical powers) are commonly received through the agencies of a great *sakti*-ful being, whether given as a blessing, transferred through long and intimate contact, or by teaching the (sometimes secret) techniques of *sakti* increase. Meditation and austerities merely make one's body a fit vehicle (by refinement) to receive these divine boons.

8. While troupe members are expected to be recruited purely on the basis of devotion, many are also professional performing artists (singers, drummers, stage and television actors) who view participation in *kuttiyottam* as simultaneously an extension of their professional life and a form of devotional service.

9. *Kuttiyottam* singing and dancing troupes tour the region giving paid displays during the festival season (December to June), boosting *Puthenkulangara's* growing reputation. Each season new songs are written, new dance steps composed, and audio cassettes recorded for sale: competition between troupes is high, and talented individuals defect to more successful troupes. Many increasingly rely upon *kuttiyottam* as income. One troupe has been filmed by national television; the lead singer of another has used the fame gained through *kuttiyottam* as a springboard for his recording career; a third troupe's leader has appeared on state television in vernacular soap-opera.

10. Sivaratri, according to the myth recounted in Valiyagramam, following a Puranic story, commemorates the time when Siva, in order to save the universe, swallowed poison emitted from the mouth of the serpent which the deities used to churn *amritha* (ambrosia). Other deities kept vigil for the whole night, saving Siva's life. As a result of swallowing poison he developed a blue complexion: in this form he is known as Nilakanthan (Blue-Throated).

11. This point obviously relates to debates on Dalit consciousness which we have chosen not to address since it seems to have run its course (for example Parry 1970; Moffatt 1979; Randeria 1989; Deliege 1992, 1993; Vincentnathan 1993; Mosse 1994; Charsley 1996; Parish 1996).

12. This, like other sacrifices, 'replicates the primal act of Prajapati who produced creation by the sacrificial dismemberment of his own body' (Parry 1982: 77; cf. Heesterman 1959; Malamoud 1975; Herrenschmidt 1978).

13. Village festivals reproduce, albeit less explicitly, big 'royal' festivals, such as Navaratri, Dussera and Ram-Lila (Stein 1980: 385–92; Fuller & Logan 1985; Kapur 1985; Breckenridge 1978; Schechner 1985: Ch. 4; Dirks 1987: 39–43), which celebrate the victory of deities (either of the goddess or Rama) over demons (cf. Fuller 1992: 139–42) and the restoration of *Dharma* over the universe.

14. Part of the relative success of Durga's *navaham* as opposed to the *saptaham* at Sivamuri might lie in the increasing popularity of Durga (Fuller 1996a).

CHAPTER 6 MOBILITY AND POWER

1. Before Martanda Varma, victorious Rajahs established supremacy over defeated rulers by demanding allegiance and tributes, without affecting the internal political and economic status quo. With Martanda Varma this changed: he directly annexed territories of defeated rulers depriving them of political and economic power. He also curtailed the power of local chieftains in annexed territories by diminishing land under their control (cf. Fuller 1976a: 18). According to villagers'stories the Nayar chieftain's family women went to plead with Martanda Varma to have land returned. He returned part of the land on condition that it stayed in the name of the family women.
2. For discussion of the role of the *jajman* see Fuller (1989).
3. The form and wording of these types of moderate protest correspond exactly to Scott's (1990: 96ff) 'not-so-naive monarchism', in which subordinated groups attempt, remaining within frameworks of dominance set by existing social systems, to assert some rights, couching grievances in the form of an appeal to a monarch who is flattered as being assumed to be benevolent and just, but simply unaware of his people's suffering.
4. Old Izhava communists in Valiyagramam remembered rumours that the *Dewan*, delighted by the SNDP leadership's new course, donated some land for building the SNDP headquarters and the first Izhava college.
5. In Kuttanad 75 percent of workers belonged to Izhava and Pulaya communities, while 83 percent of farmers were Nayars and Forward Christians (V.M. Nair 1978: 631).
6. Analyses of Kuttanad's agrarian movement can be found in Oommen (1971, 1985), Tharamangalam (1981) and George (1984).
7. An organisation founded by a group of Dalit intellectuals, activists and social critics in 1972 in Maharashtra, taking inspiration directly from Dr Ambedkar, and modelled around the US Black Panthers.
8. Similar processes of fission have been examined by several authors: see, for example, Cohn (1955, 1959), Srinivas (1966), Rudolph & Rudolph (1967), Hardgrave (1969), Lynch (1969), Parry (1970).
9. While the *kalari* is the province of Nayars, Brahmans are believed to practice *yoga* regularly.
10. Beef-eating is common in Kerala, practised even by Nayars, the dominant (*savarna*) caste. Cow respect is especially associated with north India and with Brahmans.

CHAPTER 7 MICRO-POLITICS, OR THE POLITICAL IN THE PERSONAL

1. Thereby insisting that *jatis* such as Nayar, Izhava, were mis-labels: for Narayana Guru, the scientifically identifiable *jati* was *maushyajati*, the species of human-kind.
2. Once good faith has been proven, external physical contact is enough and cigarettes are no longer shared. Sharing of a cigarette in this way may be an initiatory rite, and appears to forge physical intimacy in the same manner as the sharing of vessels and food practised by bride and groom at weddings (cf. Busby 1997).

3. Initial love-letters from girls to boys frequently begin, 'my dearest respected elder brother'.

4. This may be partly due to the increasingly important public/private distinction and defence of the private against the enforcement in public of anti-discrimination laws. That hypergamy is the usual marriage preference for those who can afford it may have a bearing on senior women's conservatism in matters of caste within the home: having 'gained' in the prestige and power stakes through hypergamous marriage, and having the pleasure of producing children who will come from a 'better' family than the maternal grandparents, they may be unwilling to relinquish their investment in caste (cf. Bourdieu 1990: 155). We might posit a 'caste bargain' analogous to the 'patriarchal bargain' which fixes women, prime socialisers of children, as prime reproducers of inequality (cf. Kandiyoti 1994).

5. A (Christian) city-based CPI(M) activist pointed out to us that this is actively fought against at top levels in the Party, where intellectual and ideological commitment is high. Party activists travel around Kerala and stay in the homes of other activists without enquiring what community they are. He also suggested that caste matters less in the city. On the other hand, an academic colleague, member of the Pulaya (SC) caste, employed at a left-wing city-based teaching and research institution, told us privately that he is still subject to caste discrimination, for example finding it impossible to rent a house on campus or to invite colleagues home to dinner.

6. While many Brahmans are (generally discreet) BJP supporters, they remain apparently aloof from the RSS, whose backbone of activists is Nayar-dominated.

7. *Janniccu*, past participle of the verb *janikkuka*, to be born, derives from *janmam*, birth (Gundert 1989: 402). *Samsa* derives from *samsara*, which in Malayalam holds meanings of life-cycle, 'moving about, world, life in the world, the succession of births and deaths, worldly concerns, wife, family, communication, meditation' (Gundert 1989: 1044 col. 2).

8. Ayurveda, which exerts strong influence on local theories of the body and the person, constantly stresses the importance of environment (cf. for example Obeyesekere 1976, 1984a: 40; Daniel 1984; Kakar 1986: 224; Trawick 1992).

9. As well as one-off conversions, from the 1890s to the 1930s, many Izhava families undertook mass conversion to the Marthoma church in protest at untouchability.

10. The attitude of these *valiya* (lit. big, 'forward') Christians (Syrians) is in contrast to the two local groups of *ceriya* (small, 'backward') Christians: the Latin Catholic Mukkuvar (fishing caste) and the CSI (Church of South India), Jacobite, Pentecostalist or other denomination Pulaya (agricultural labourer) converts. These two groups of untouchable converts continued to be identified with their original caste, had separate churches in their own areas of the village, and neither intermarried nor interacted on equal terms with the forward Christians (cf. Fuller 1976b and Mosse 1994 on stratification among South Indian Christians). Only Izhavas (OBC *avarna jati*) and Nayars (locally dominant *savarna jati*) have assimilated.

11. During the early days of our first fieldwork, when we still took at face value people's assertions that caste prejudice had disappeared from Kerala. The motivations of Madhu for accompanying us must have been highly complex, perhaps connected to wanting to test his abilities at 'passing' and evading identification.

12. We find that the degree to which considerations of untouchability have diminished is often exaggerated: in 1990s Kerala, people are often kept at thresholds – gates, compound walls, verandahs – for considerations which can only be rooted in the supposedly disappeared nineteenth-century 'distance pollution'.

13. From 1984 various Hindu nationalist organisations launched a campaign for the 'liberation' of the alleged birthplace of Lord Rama in Ramkot, the centre of Ayodhya, occupied by a mosque. In the late 1980s the campaign provoked a series of violent riots between Muslims and Hindus; eventually, in December 1992, a Hindu mob marched on Ayodhya and destroyed the mosque. Subsequently, bloody communal riots erupted in many north Indian cities, Bombay in particular. During 1990 and 1991 violent demonstrations took place in many parts of India against proposals to implement the Mandal Commission's positive discrimination recommendations.

14. The organic metaphor's wide historical and geographic spread makes this privileging of mind and sight not, then, a specifically post-Enlightenment phenomenon.

CHAPTER 8 CONCLUSIONS

1. A symptom of this is the increasing presence of compound walls, at times as high as 2 m, enclosing and protecting house and land plots.

2. This is not to deny that such a preoccupation with hierarchy may be historically recent and contingent (Fuller 1996c: 6; Muralidharan 1996).

3. These divisions were made on the basis of access to public temples; 'A' castes were permitted inside the walls, 'B's were just outside, at a little distance, while 'C's were obliged to stand far away.

4. Within the Marxist tradition, debates arise on whether the persistence of 'traditional' relations signifies either a partial transition to capitalism (for example, Byres 1982, 1991) or an articulation of different modes of production, albeit within a hegemony of wider, national and international, capitalist relations of production (for example Alavi 1975). Others have argued that capitalist relations of production might not be in contradiction, but in fact rely on and reproduce pre-capitalist relations (for example Harriss 1982). Alternatively, debates have highlighted the new, modern face of caste, whereby traditional hierarchies based on religious status are displaced by differences in economic achievements, educational levels or 'culture' (Beteille 1996). More recently, authors belonging to the Subaltern Studies circle have suggested that apparently pre-modern relations are not just the left-over or debris of processes of incipient modernisation, but are, on the contrary, an indication of subaltern resistance against the progressive intrusion of either capitalism or the state (colonial and postcolonial) into their lives (for example Guha 1982, 1983). Yet another approach suggests the ideals of modernity – democracy, bureaucratic efficiency, universal justice – have only been partially interiorised by Indian citizens, leading to a tension between new and older identities and allegiances. This position is clearly articulated in recent debates on the apparent crisis of the Indian state, whose democratic credentials are believed to be undermined by corruption and nepotism; by the proliferation of caste-based politics; and by resurgence of

religious nationalism. The theoretical roots of this position are to be found in theories of 'compartmentalisation', as proposed by Milton Singer in his influential 1972 book *When a great tradition modernises*. Compartmentalisation suggested a schizoid (hence ultimately non-modern, non-unified) self which left caste and other aspects of village identity at the door of the workplace and resumed them on going home, in a strategy permitting comfortable movement in different arenas. Workers could develop class consciousness within the factory without losing their caste consciousness, operative outside it.

5. The reflexive nature of these representations is crucial to our understanding of modern gendered identities, whereby, for example, western/British masculinity is constructed in opposition to an 'effeminate' Oriental other (see for example Sinha 1995).

6. For example censuses were first developed in colonial contexts (Cohn 1987; Dirks 1989, 1992; Appadurai 1993; Ludden 1993).

7. Van der Veer has recently argued against the trend towards the 'replacement of an idea of modernity by a notion of a multiplicity of "modernities" ' (1998: 285). While we find ourselves agreeing with his suggestion that 'modernity should in the first place be understood as a project' (1998: 285), it seems to us that, by stressing the importance of the spread of colonial power and insisting upon the singular centrality of the nation state as harbinger of modernity, he ultimately undermines his desire to distance himself from modernisation theorists such as Gellner (1983).

8. Recent work indicates that commodity production and wage labour might pre-date capitalist penetration and thus cannot be the exclusive domain of western modernity (Piot 1999). Debates on the origins of industry in India suggest that in pre-colonial times there was a range of people producing for markets; and production was not only by artisans but also industrial. Meanwhile, we are beginning to realise that 'unfree labour' might not be a left-over indicating the persistence of pre-capitalist relations of production, but a phenomenon generated by capitalism in the West as elsewhere (see for example Brass 1994; Kapadia 1995).

GLOSSARY

aal person
aanu is
aaru who
abkari liquor trade
achan father
adharma cosmic disorder/chaos
adiparasakti universal undifferentiated cosmic power
adjust/adjustment change
adukkulla kitchen
advaita non-duality
advaitin non-dualist
agent person who provides tickets and visas for migration
agni homam fire sacrifice
air-force derogatory term for Izhavas
akkani newly-drawn palm sap
almirah lockable cupboard
aluckal people
amani collection of revenue by government officers directly from
    cultivators/producers of toddy and arrack
amma mother
ammavan/(pl.) ammavanmar mother's brother
ammavi mother's brother's wife
ammumma grandmother
amritha ambrosia
andarajanam Nambutiri Brahman woman
anpoli five-fold offering
anugreham blessing
appam rice-batter pancakes
appuppan grandfather
ara wooden granary
Araby a person from West Asia
arat holy bath
arishtam alcohol-based tonic

274

arppuvili/arpoy - oh! oh! oh! men's auspicious shout
artist person with artistic talent or of artistic sensibilities
asan master, expert
asari carpenter
ashtamangalyam eight auspicious objects
asram place of religious retreat for Hindus
asura demons
atmopadesha-satakam 100 verses of self-instruction
atu that
avagasham/ (pl.) avagashangal exclusive rights by tradition
aval her
aval dish of flaked rice with honey and coconut
avarna not belonging to the *varna* division
avatar incarnation
ayudhava protection

backward rustic, uneducated
bakery items manufactured baked or fried snack items
bakery shop selling bread, cakes, and packaged fried snacks and small
     groceries
ballet burlesque
BAMS Bachelor of Ayurvedic Medicine
bandham affinity, link
bandhukkar affines; people to whom one is linked
baniya derogatory term for shopkeeper, trader
banyan pipal tree
beedi local cigarette
bhagati half
Bhagavatham Bhagavad Gita
bhaiankara extremely (lit. ferociously)
bhajan devotional songs
bhakti religious devotion
bhasmam sandalwood ash
bhavan dosam problems/illnesses caused by problems in the house
bimbam movable image of a temple deity
bindu auspicious red powder on the forehead
biryani white rice and meat dish, associated with Christians and Muslims
BJP Bharatiya Janata Party
black/on the black within the informal economy
blade high-interest informal loan company
block administrative division, sub-division of *panchayat*
Block Member representative of the block
brahmaswam tax-free land belonging to Brahmans

capitation fee paid for admission to employment or education *cash* money

cash-plucker charger of extortionate rates

cassava mundu gold-bordered cloth 'traditional' to high-caste Hindu communities

cent 1 *cent* is a hundredth of an acre

cerippu sandals

chammandi coconut and green chili condiment

chance luck

chapati unleavened bread

charakku commodity, good

charayam distilled arrack

chaturvarnya the four *varnas* system

chembu Ceylon yam

chena Arum yam

chenda drums

chetti Izhavas who work as toddy-tappers; derogatory term for Izhavas; flashy or showy (adj.)

chettu sharpness, knife-like-ness, cutting

chettuka verb indicating the action of toddy-tapping

chilli chicken chicken cooked with extra dried chili powder; speciality of Kerala generally eaten outside the home, and especially in drinking places (toddy-shops, bars)

chitty fund mutual savings and loan find

choodu hot

choru double-boiled rice

chorunnu first feeding ceremonies for babies

chumma irrikkunnu sitting for no reason

churidar young women's loose long tunic and trousers

chuttu top of a coconut branch

citta low, bad

cold store shop with deep-freezes, where frozen meat, ice-cream and so on are sold

colony single-community residential area

community endogamous group

company private-sector employer, especially factory

compounder doctor's assistant

Congress Congress Party

cool bar shop with fridge, where cool drinks are sold

CPI Communist Party of India

CPI(M) Communist Party of India (Marxist)

cultural programme entertainment

culture high culture; good manners or 'breeding'

daivam/devanmar gods

daksina ritual cash payment

Dalit Panthers Dalit organisation and political party
deeparadhana circling a camphor flame in front of a deity
devadasi temple dancer; prostitute (also *thevithisi*)
devaprasanam astrological diagnosis of deity's wishes
devaswams temple properties
Dewan Prime Minister
dharma/dharmic cosmic/ moral order
donation fee paid for admission to employment or education
dosa rice-flour pancake
dosham fault, imbalance, imperfection
drama popular play
Dravidian south Indian indigenous population
duplicate fake copy
dusta evil/bad
dusta sakti power for evil
duskarmam bad sorcery
DYFI Democratic Youth Federation of India

ellavarum everyone
enangar ritual affines/allies
ennikku vayya I can't do it; I can't bear it

fanam old currency
farmer someone who owns paddy land
fashion-show ostentatious display of clothing and jewellery
filmi related to Bollywood cinema
foreign opposed to *nadan*, what comes from this locality (contextual)

ganjavu cannabis
goonda thug
government-joli/government-job employment in the public sector (as opposed
    to a *company*)
gramam village
Gulfan migrant to West Asian Gulf countries
gunam quality
guru teacher/preceptor
Gurudevan the deified Sree Narayana Guru
gurukal indigenous school held in the compound of a house
gurumandiram shrine dedicated to Sri Narayana Guru

half-sari young women's dress of long, full skirt, long blouse, and chiffon
    scarf tied across bosom
halva sweet
Harijan colony area of the village inhabited by '*Harijans*'
Harijan 'son of god'; ex-untouchable; Dalit

head-load portering work
helper assistant
Hindu (used by members of *avarna jatis* and Christians to mean) Nayar
homam vedic sacrifice
hotel cafe/restaurant
hotty alcoholic drink

IAS Indian Administrative Service
idangezhi small measure of paddy
idli steamed rice cakes
illa negative; is not; does not; there is no
illam Brahman house
ISD/STD booth small shop with metred telephone facilities for local, long
    distance and overseas calls
ishtadevata family chosen deity

jajmani patron–client relations
janmam life
janmi landowner holding tax-free land
janniccu related to birth
janiccu gunam qualities by birth
jari/zari gold thread
jati Hindu endogamous community
jawan army private
jayanthi birth anniversary
jivatmavu unique individual soul
jivitham decorated palanquin used to carry images of deities in procession
joli salaried, permanent employment (often, but not necessarily, in public
    sector)
JSS Janadipatiya Samrakshana Samidhi; Committee for the Protection of
    Democracy
jubba muslim-style loose, long-sleeved shirt

kabbadi South Asian game akin to 'tag'
kaffir derogatory term for non-Muslim
kairali relating to Kerala; in a Malayali style
kakka crow
kala decorated wooden oxen; usually in pairs, one red and one white
kalari martial arts gymnasium and training ground, associated with Nayars
kalaripayyattu Kerala's martial art
kallan thief; liar; dishonest person; a lie; cheating
kallu fresh toddy
kalyanamandapam canopy under which bridal couple stand or sit
kamadhenu mythical wish-fulfilling cow
kambavakali dance in which pairs of men cross sticks

kangany plantation labour broker

kanian astrologer caste

kanji rice gruel

kannukittuka putting the evil eye

kanyadanam gift of a virgin

kappa tapioca

kara neighbourhood

karakkar people of the *kara*

karanavan head of a matrilineage/family group

karayogam local assembly

karikku vellam water/juice of green coconut

karshaka farmer

karutta black

kashayam liquid Ayurvedic medicine

kassavu-mundu white, gold-bordered waist-cloth

kathakali Kerala theatrical form claimed as 'classical' and associated with higher castes

kavadi attam ritual possession trance in which devotees pierce their faces and upper bodies with hooks and skewers

kavu an uncleared patch of forest; a shrine to the serpent deities

kazhakamtullal dance/temple art involving men dancing while balancing pots of blooms on their heads

khadi handspun cloth

koolipani casual day-labouring

kottaram palace; see *ksatriya*

kotti derogatory nickname for Izhava

kozhivettu cockerel-sacrifice

Krishi Bhavan government office dispensing agricultural advice, subsidies and small grants

krisipani agricultural work

ksatriya house

KSSP Kerala Sastra Sahitya Parishad, a rationalist organisation for the promotion of science

kuli day's wages for labourers; labour

kulipani manual labour

kundalini sakti root power, energy compacted at the base of the spine

kunnamma mother's younger sister

kuriala ancestors' shrine

kurta long loose tunic worn over loose pajama trousers

kurudi blood sacrifice

kuruva women's auspicious ululating call

kutti child

kuttiyottam ritual for Bhadrakali; symbolic human sacrifice

kuttuvilakku oil lamp which always precedes a deity in processions

kutumbam family group

ladies' items/ladies' sadanangal hair ornaments, beauty products, imitation
     jewellery and so on for girls and women
ladies' shop store specialising in *ladies' items* and fancy goods (given by
     women as wedding presents to female friends)
lakh Rs100,000
lakshamdeepam 100,000 lights; small oil lamps at temple
LIC Life Insurance Corporation of India
licence permission
lingam Siva's aniconic symbol
love-marriage marriage of self-chosen partner as opposed to arranged
     marriage
lunacy mental disturbance
lungi coloured waist-cloth; associated with working men and women, and
     with lower castes

madam respectful address for older woman
madamma European woman
mahotsavam a temple's main annual festival
mahout elephant keeper (also *pappan*)
mala pradesham mountain-land
mala necklace; neck-chain
mala/i mountain; hill
malar parched rice
mamam mother's brother
mami mother's brother's wife
management quota admissions quota at the discretion of an establishment's
     management
management school school funded under public system but run by a private
     management committee
manam prestige, dignity, status
manasilla don't/doesn't have the will;
mandala puja 41-day period in Vrischigam (Scorpio) month especially for
     temple festivals and the Sabarimala pilgrimage
mandapam canopy
mandiram see *gurumandiram*
mangalastri auspicious woman
Manglish Malayam spoken with a large spattering of English words
mantram a Sanskrit formula
mantravadam sorcery
marumukkattayam matrilineal inheritance system; lit. sister's son's share
masala seasoning; mixture
Math religious sect
matram only
medical store pharmacist
member elected representative

mikksu fried snack ('Bombay mix')

mimics' parade impersonations and satire

mixi electric mixer/blender/ grinder

MLA Member of Local Assembly

modern opposed to 'backward'; connotations of being too 'forward'

mol daughter; young girl

mosham very bad

mrtiyanjaya homam victory over death vedic sacrifice

muhurtam auspicious period or time

mukku corner; junction

mundu white waist-cloth

muracherukkan male cross-cousin to a female; lit. the right man

murapennu female cross-cousin to a male; lit. the right woman

naadu this place; homeland

nadan of the *naadu*

nageswaram wind instrument associated with temple arts

nakshatram 'star-day'; lunar asterism

nalla good

nalukettu 'traditional' upper-caste teak wooden house, built in accordance
 with *taccasastram*

naluvittumar 'people of the four houses'; an Izhava group claiming slightly
 higher status

namaste/namaskaram greeting with palms together

nammal we (inclusive)

nammude our (inclusive)

naranga bali sacrifice of limes

naranga vellam lime water

naranga vilakku oil lamp made with half lime

nathoon husband's sister

nava rasas nine essences or emotions

navaham nine days reading of passages from the *Devimahatmyam* (the text
 concerning the goddess)

nellu paddy

nercha vow

nidhi pot full of gold

nighty women's house dress

nira sheaf of paddy

nischayam marriage fixing ceremony (Hindu)

nivarttana abstention movement

nokkakaran watcher, supervisor

NSS Nayar Service Society

OBC Other backward Communities: in Kerala, Izhavas, Muslims and Latin
 Catholics

orangumpool while sleeping
oru cheriya hot; a 'short'
oru one; a

pacca green; raw; untreated (e.g. *pacca vellam*, unboiled water); true, real
    (e.g. *pacca* Malayalam, good Malayalam)
paccari white rice (as opposed to double-boiled rice)
panchabhutas five elements
panchayat administrative division
pandy derogatory term for Tamil people
pani daily-waged agricultural or manual labour; labour
panigraham 'catching the bride's hand'; part of Hindu wedding
papad/papadam crisp lentil-flour cake
pappan elephant keeper/trainer
para full measure of rice (5 litres)
parakku' ezhunellattu procession for collection of paddy from devotees'
    houses
parambu garden land
parippu lentils
party person; political party; tea-party
patient invalid
pattadar rentier
pattu song
pavada young girl's full, gathered skirt
pavam poor person; innocent person
pavan 'sovereign'; unit of measure for precious metals, equal to 8 g
pavan-mala necklace made of a line of gold 'sovereigns'; also known as
    'cash-mala'
payasam sweet pudding
payyan vangikkuka to buy a boy; neologism for dowry
payyan/ (pl) payyanmar young unmarried men (from around 8 to 25)
pazhangal bananas
PDP People's Democratic Party
Peerless Peerless Assurance
penpakam bride-viewing; (lit. ripened female)
peon factotum
pey fierce deity once particular to lower castes; now often termed a 'demon';
    also means 'rabid dog' or 'rabies'
peyvaliyacchan 'pey grandfather'; ancestor who died of rabies?
pidam wooden three-legged stool of the goddess
pisachu evil spirit
pisakkukku stingy; petty-minded
pithrukkal ancestors
planter plantation owner
pothu water-buffalo

pothu-malakkar 'ignorant hillbillies' (like mountain buffaloes)
pottu red dot (*bindu*) on girl or woman's forehead
prasadam left-overs from worship of deity, given to devotees
private doctor doctor in private practice who takes fees
private-bank loan company
progress upward social mobility; escape from 'backward' condition
progressinu vendi for the sake of progress
PSC Public Service Commission
puduvakoda giving of cloth; from unrelated man to woman, marked the
    beginning of a sexual relationship; still carries similar connotations
puja worship of Hindu deities
pujari Hindu priest
Pulaya pokkunnu mukku the corner where the *Pulayas* go
pulisseri sour-curry
punja one-crop paddy land
puranic of the Puranas; later Hindu texts
puttu steamed rice-flour cake

rahu kalam inauspicious period
rakshassu Brahman ghost
rasnadipodi Ayurvedic powder
ration state-government ration system
rebel party defector; floor-crosser; rebel
reception greeting with music, fireworks, coloured lamps and so on
RSS Rashtriya Swayamsevak Sangh
rupam metal figurine

Saar sir; school-teacher; person in authority
saari okay; alright
sahippu European man
sahitya literature, arts
sakti power, energy
samarvartanam part of Brahmanical initiation
sambandham sexual relationship
sambar lentil and vegetable stew
sambhashanam spoken exchange/dialogue
sammadhi death anniversary
sammanam gift
sammatala pradesham mid-land
sammiddhi committee
samrakshana protection
samsa environment; life, being-in-the world
samsa gunam environmental quality
samudayam community
sannyasi renouncer

sappadu vegetarian rice feast

saptaham-vayana reading a sacred text over seven days

sari women's dress

sarpam snake god

sattva/sattvik one of the three qualities

satyagraha hunger-strike

savarna belonging to the higher Hindu castes; within the four *varnas*

SC Scheduled Caste

serious not frivolous; responsible and trustworthy; associated with values of
    permanence

settu-mundu women's white *mundu* with top-cloth

seva service

sharppu toddy-shop; unlicensed house-based still

shawl veil; *dupatta*

shopping complex row of shops

siddhan tantric adepts

simpatia (it.) attraction, empathy, 'fellow-feeling'

sincere sincere; related to serious

sindooram red powder in the parting of married women's hair

sishya pupil

sit-out verandah

Sivaratri Siva's main festival, the night of Siva

SNDP Sri Narayana Dharma Pariplam Yogam; society for the preservation
    of the moral law of Sri Narayana Guru.

sneham love/affection

soappu 'greasing' a relationship; flattery;

social-work public service

social-worker person involved in public life

sound good; trustworthy

srikovil sanctus sanctorum of a Hindu temple

SSLC Secondary School Leaving Certificate

stanam position/reputation

streetil tharikidathom falling in the street

stridhanam women's share of ancestral properties; dowry

style style; fashion

sudram sorcery, bad magic

sudram sakti power of sorcery

sumangali auspicious married Hindu woman

supermarket non-specialist shop selling a full range of items

swabhavam/angal one's own particular nature/qualities

swami Hindu holy man

swaraj home rule; self-determination

swarnam 22 carat gold

taccasastram Hindu building science

tadika knotted black thread

talapoli metal trays of coconut flowers and an oil lamp

tali small gold ornament worn by married women

talikettu tali-tying ritual

talikettukalyanam tali-tying ritual

taluk administrative division above *panchayat*

tamogunam one of the three qualities

tantri high priest adept in *tantra*

Tantric one of Hinduism's streams (with Saivism and Vaisnavism), prominent in Kerala

tapas empowering meditation

tea party pre-wedding snack meal where cash gifts are solicited

thala mother (vulg.)

thalayude mackal children of one mother (i.e. uncertain or different paternity)

thamburan/(pl.) thamburanmar master/lord; twice-born Hindu landowners

thankam 24 carat gold

tharavadu house and land and family temple unit associated with Nayars

thirumeni Brahman; priest

Thiyya community related to Izhavas in north Kerala

tindal jati Hindu community 'below' the untouchability line

tira pradesham shore-land; coastal strip

torrtu coarse white cloth used as towel, headgear, shoulder cloth

tozhilali labourer

travel agency shop where air tickets, visas and jobs in the Gulf are arranged

treat footing the bill for a meal or drinks

trigunam the *samkhya* philosophy's three qualities system

TTC Technical Training College

tukkam tullal hook swinging

tullal possession; also dance

tuni cloth

two-in-one a radio-cassette player

uchi fontanelle

UDF United Democratic Front

ugra extremely powerful and blood-thirsty

upanayanam Brahman initiation

utsavam/mahotsavam annual temple festival

vadam painful joints

vaidyan Ayurvedic practitioner

val sword

valiyammavan mother's mother's brother

vallam pattu snake-boat songs

vandi vehicle

varna Hindu four-fold division of society
vattu distilling
vayya nokkan layabout
vazhakku row, possibly violent
vedanta Hindu texts dealing with non-duality; Upanishads
velichappadu oracle of the goddess
verumpattadar sub-tenant
VHP Vishwa Hindu Parishad
videsi foreigner
vilakku oil-lamp
virippu double-crop paddy land
viswakarmakkar artisan castes
vittukari woman of the house; housewife
vratam fast; abstinence

ward division of a *panchayat*
well-wisher client; friend

yajman sacrificer
yogam association
yogishwaran ancestor deity; deified holy man

zillah district

BIBLIOGRAPHY

Achaya, K.T. 1994 *The food industries of British India*. Oxford University Press: Oxford.

Addleton, J.S. 1992 *Undermining the centre: the Gulf migration and Pakistan*. Oxford University Press: Karachi.

Ahmad, A. 1992 *In theory: classes, nations, literatures*. Verso: London.

Aiya, Nagam (1906) 1989 *The Travancore State manual* (3 vols). Reprint by Indian Educational Services: New Delhi.

Aiyappan, A. 1935 'Fraternal polyandry in Malabar'. *Man in India*, vol. 15: 108–18.

Aiyappan, A. 1941 'The meaning of the tali rite'. *Bulletin of the Rama Varma Research Institute*, vol. 9, part 2: 68–83.

Aiyappan, A. 1944 'Iravas and culture change'. *Bulletin of the Madras Government Museum* (ns), vol. 5, no. 1. Government Press: Madras.

Aiyappan, A. 1965 *Social revolution in a Kerala village*. Asia Publishing House: Bombay.

AKG Centre for Research and Studies 1994 *International Congress on Kerala studies: Abstracts*, vols 1–5. AKG Centre: Thiruvananthapuram

Allahabad, Uttar Pradesh', in I. Ahmad (ed.) *Caste and social stratification among the Muslims*. Manohar Book Service: Delhi.

Alavi, H. 1975 'India and the colonial mode of production'. *Economic and Political Weekly*, Special Issue (August).

Alexander, K.C. 1968 *Social mobility in Kerala*. Deccan College: Poone.

Alexander, K.C. 1980 'Emergence of peasant organisations in South India'. *Economic and Political Weekly* (Annual Review of Agriculture), pp. 72–84.

Amjad, R. (ed.) 1989 *To the Gulf and back: studies on the economic impact of Asian labour migration*, International Labour Organisation: Geneva.

Andersen, W. & S. Damle 1987 *The brotherhood in saffron*. Vistaar Publications: New Delhi.

Appadurai, A. 1981 'Gastro-politics in Hindu South Asia'. *American Ethnologist*, vol. 18, no. 3: 494–509.

Appadurai, A. 1986 'Introduction: commodities and the politics of value', in A. Appadurai (ed.) *The social life of things: commodities in cultural perspective*. Cambridge University Press: Cambridge.

Appadurai, A. 1990 'Disjuncture and difference in the global cultural economy', in M. Featherstone (ed.) *Global culture: nationalism, globalisation and modernity*. Sage: London.

Appadurai, A. 1993 'Number in the colonial imagination', in P. Van der Veer & C. Breckenridge (eds) *Orientalism and the postcolonial predicament*. Oxford University Press: Delhi.

Appiah, K.A. 1992 *In my father's house: Africa in the philosophy of culture*. Oxford University Press: New York.

Arunima, G. 1995 'Matriliny and its discontents', *India International Centre Quarterly*, vol. 22, nos 2–3: 157–67.

Athreya, V. 1987 'Identification of agrarian classes'. *Journal of Peasant Studies*, vol. 14: 147–90.

Athreya V., G. Djurfeldt & S. Lindberg 1990 *Barriers broken: production relations and agrarian change in Tamil Nadu*. Sage: New Delhi.

Ayar, S. 1918 'The Cochin State: Watakanchery (Talapilii Taluk)', in G. Slater (ed.) *Economic studies: some South Indian Villages*, vol. 1, Oxford University Press: London.

Baak, P.E. 1997 *Plantation, production and political power*. Oxford University Press: Delhi.

Babb, L. 1981 'Glancing: visual interaction in Hinduism'. *Journal of Anthropological Research*, vol. 37, no. 4: 387–401.

Babb, L. 1983 'The physiology of redemption'. *History of Religions*, vol. 22: 293–312.

Babb, L. 1987 *Redemptive encounters: three modern styles in the Hindu tradition*. Oxford University Press: Delhi.

Barnard, H. 1990 'Bourdieu and ethnography: reflexivity, politics and praxis', in R. Harker, C. Mahar & C. Wilkes (eds) *An introduction to the work of Pierre Bourdieu: the practice of theory*. London: Macmillan, 58–85.

Barnes, R.H., D. de Coppet & R.J. Parkin (eds) *Contexts and Levels: Anthropological Essays on Hierarchy*. (JASO Occasional papers no. 4) Oxford: JASO.

Barnett, S. 1977 'Identity choice and caste ideology in South India', in K. David (ed.) *The new wind*. Mouton: The Hague.

Basu, T., P. Datta, S. Sarkar, T. Sarkar & S. Sen 1993 *Khaki shorts and saffron flags*. Orient Longman: Delhi.

Bateson, G. 1958 *Naven: a survey of the problems suggested by a composite picture of a culture of a New Guinea tribe drawn from three points of view*. Stanford University Press: Stanford, CA.

Bauman, Z. 1991 *Modernity and ambivalence*. Polity Press: Cambridge.

Baumann, G. 1996 *Contesting Culture: Discourses of identity in multi-ethnic London*. Cambridge University Press: Cambridge.

Bayly, S. 1984 'Hindu kingship and the origin of community: religion, state and society in Kerala, 1750–1850'. *Modern Asian Studies*, vol. 18, no. 2: 177–213.

Bayly, S. 1992 (1989) *Saints, goddesses and kings*. Cambridge University Press: Delhi.

Beck, B. 1969 'Colour and heat in South Indian ritual'. *Man*, vol. 4: 553–72.

Beck, B. 1976 'The symbolic merger of body, space and cosmos in South Indian ritual'. *Contributions to Indian Sociology*, vol. 10, no. 2: 213–43.

Beck, B. 1981 'The goddess and the demon: a local South Indian festival and its wider context'. *Purusartha*, vol. 5: 83–136.

Berreman, G.D. 1972 *Hindus of the Himalayas: ethnography and change*. University of California Press: Berkeley.

Berreman, G.D. 1979 *Caste and other inequities: essays on inequality*. Manohar: Delhi.

Berreman, G.D. (1975) 1993 'Himalayan polyandry and the domestic cycle', in P. Uberoi (ed.) *Family, kinship and marriage in India*. Oxford University Press: Delhi.

Beteille, A. 1965 *Caste, class and power: changing patterns of stratification in a Tanjore village*. University of California Press: Berkeley.

Beteille, A. 1974 *Studies in agrarian social structure*. Oxford University Press: Delhi.

Beteille, A. 1983 *The idea of natural inequality and other essays*. Oxford University Press: Delhi.

Beteille, A. 1991 'The reproduction of inequality: occupation, caste and family'.

Contributions to Indian Sociology, vol. 25, no. 1: 3–28.

Beteille, A. 1992 'Caste and family in representations of Indian society'. *Anthropology Today*, vol. 3, no. 1

Beteille, A. 1996 'Caste in contemporary India', in C.J. Fuller (ed.) *Caste today*. Oxford University Press: Delhi.

Bhatia, G. 1991 *Laurie Baker: life, work, writings*. Viking: New Delhi.

Biardeau, M. 1976 'Le sacrifice dans l'Hindouisme', in M. Biardeau & C. Malamoud (eds) *Le sacrifice dans l'Inde ancienne*. Presses Universitaires de France: Paris.

Biardeau, M. 1984 'The sami tree and the sacrificial buffalo'. *Contributions to Indian Sociology*, vol. 18: 1–23.

Biardeau, M. 1989 *Hinduism: the anthropology of a civilization*. Oxford University Press: Delhi.

Billig, M. 1992 'The marriage squeeze and the rise of groom price in India's Kerala State'. *Journal of Comparative Family Studies*, vol. 22, no. 2: 197–216.

Birks J.S., I.J. Seccombe & C.A. Sinclair 1986 'Migrant workers in the Arab Gulf: the impact of declining oil revenues', *International Migration Review*, vol. 20, no. 4: 799–814.

Bloch, M. (1971) 1994 *Placing the dead*. Waveland Press: Prospect Heights, Illinois.

Bourdieu, P. 1977 *Outline of a theory of practice*. Cambridge University Press: Cambridge.

Bourdieu, P. 1984 *Distinction: a social critique of the judgement of taste*. Cambridge University Press: Cambridge.

Bourdieu, P. 1990 *The logic of practice*. Polity Press: Cambridge.

Bourdieu, P. 1992 'Legitimation and structured interests in Weber's sociology of religion', in S. Whimster and S. Lash (eds) *Max Weber, rationality and modernity*. Allen & Unwin: London.

Bourdieu, P. 1994 *Raisons pratiques: sur la théorie de l'action*. Éditions du Seuil: Paris.

Bourdieu, P. & L.J.D. Wacquant 1992 *An invitation to reflexive sociology*. Polity Press: Cambridge.

Bouveresse, J. 1995 'Régles, dispositions et habitus'. *Critique*, vol. 51, no. 579–80: 573–94.

Bradley, H. 1996. *Fractured identities: changing patterns of inequality*. Polity Press: Cambridge.

Brass, T. 1994. 'Some observations on unfree labour, capitalist restructuring, and deproletarianisation'. *International Review of Social History*, vol. 39, no. 2: 255–75.

Breckenridge, C. 1978 'From protector to litigant: changing relations between Hindu temples and the Rajah of Ramnad', in B. Stein (ed.) *South Indian temples*. Vikas Publishing House: Delhi.

Breman, J. 1974 *Patronage and exploitation: changing agrarian social relations in south Gujarat, India*. University of California Press: Berkeley.

Breman, J. 1985 *Of peasants, migrants and paupers*. Oxford University Press: Delhi.

Breman, J. 1989 *Taming the coolie beast*. Oxford University Press: Delhi.

Breman, J. 1991 'A note on the colonial state', in J. Breman & S. Mundle (eds) *Rural transformation in Asia*. Oxford University Press: Delhi.

Brittan, A. 1989 *Masculinity and power*. Basil Blackwell: Oxford.

Brochmann, G. 1992 'Sri Lankan housemaids in the Middle East: an avenue for social and economic improvement?', in F. Eelens, T. Schampers & J.D. Speckmann (eds) *Labour migration to the Middle East: from Sri Lanka to the Gulf*. Kegan Paul: London.

Brochmann, G. 1993 *Middle East avenue: female migration from Sri Lanka to the Gulf*. Westview Press: Oxford.

Brown, P. & S.C. Levinson 1987 *Politeness: some universals in language usage.* Cambridge University Press: Cambridge.

Busby, C. 1997 'Of marriage and marriageability: gender and Dravidian kinship'. *Journal of the Royal Anthropological Institute,* vol. 3, no. 1: 21–42.

Byres, T.J. 1982 'Agrarian transition and the agrarian question', in J. Harriss (ed.) *Rural development: theories of peasant economy and agrarian change.* Unwin Hyman: London.

Byres, T.J. 1991 'The agrarian question and differing forms of capitalist agrarian transition: an essay with reference to Asia', in J. Breman & S. Mundle (eds) *Rural transformation in Asia.* Oxford University Press: Delhi.

Campbell, C. 1995 'The sociology of consumption', in D. Miller (ed.) *Acknowledging consumption.* Routledge: London.

Caplan, L. 1993 (1984) 'Bridegroom price in urban India: class, caste and "dowry evil" among Christians in Madras', in P. Uberoi (ed.) *Family, kinship and marriage in India.* Oxford University Press: Delhi.

Carrier, J. & J. Heyman, 'Consumption and political economy'. *Journal of the Royal Anthropological Institute,* vol. 3, no. 2: 355–72.

Carsten, J. 1989 'Cooking money', in J. Parry & M. Bloch (eds) *Money and the morality of exchange.* Cambridge University Press: Cambridge.

Carsten, J. & S. Hugh-Jones (eds) 1995 *About the house: Lévi-Strauss and beyond.* Cambridge University Press: Cambridge.

Chakrabarty, D. 1989 *Rethinking working-class history: Bengal 1890–1940.* Princeton University Press: Princeton, NJ.

Chandavarkar, R. 1994 *The origins of industrial capitalism in India: business strategies and the working classes in Bombay, 1900–1940.* Cambridge University Press: Cambridge.

Charsley, S. 1996. 'Untouchable: what is in a name?' *Journal of the Royal Anthropological Institute,* vol. 2, no. 1: 1–23.

Chatterjee, P. 1993 *The nation and its fragments: colonial and postcolonial histories.* Princeton University Press: Princeton, NJ.

Chatterji, P.C. 1996 'Reservation: theory and practice', in T.V. Sathyamurthy (ed.) *Region, religion, caste, gender and culture in contemporary India.* Oxford University Press: Delhi.

Chaudhuri, K.N. 1985 *Trade and civilisation in the Indian Ocean.* Cambridge: Cambridge University Press.

Chaudhuri, K.N. 1990 *Asia before Europe: economy and civilisation of the Indian Ocean from the rise of Islam to 1750.* Cambridge University Press: Cambridge.

Chiriyankandath, J. 1993 'Communities at the polls: electoral politics and the mobilisation of communal groups in Travancore'. *Modern Asian Studies,* vol. 27, no. 3: 643–65.

Classen, C. 1996 'Sugar cane, coca-cola and hypermarkets', in D. Howes (ed.) *Cross-cultural consumption: global markets, local realities.* Routledge: London.

Codd, J. 1990 'Making distinctions: the eye of the beholder', in R. Harker, C. Mahar & C. Wilkes (eds) *An introduction to the work of Pierre Bourdieu: the practice of theory,* Macmillan: London.

Cohn, B. 1955 'The changing status of a depressed caste', in McK. Marriott (ed.) *Village India: studies in the little community.* University of Chicago Press: Chicago.

Cohn, B. 1959 'Changing traditions of a low caste', in M. Singer (ed.) *Traditional India: structure and change.* American Folklore Society: Philadelphia.

Cohn, B. 1987 *An anthropologist among the historians and other essays.* Oxford University Press: Delhi.

Collins, E.F. 1997 *Pierced by Murugan's lance: ritual, power and moral redemption among Malaysian Hindus*. Northern Illinois University Press: DeKalb, Illinois.

Comaroff, J. 1996 'The empire's old clothes: fashioning the colonial subject', in D. Howes (ed.) *Cross-cultural consumption: global markets, local realities*. Routledge: London.

Comaroff, J. & J. Comaroff 1993 'Homemade hegemony', in J. Comaroff and J. Comaroff, *Ethnography and the historical imagination*, Westview Press: Boulder, CO.

Crook, J.H. 1984 *The evolution of human consciousness*. Oxford University Press: Oxford.

Daniel, E.V. 1984 *Fluid signs: being a person the Tamil way*. University of California Press: Berkeley.

Daniel, E.V., H. Bernstein & T. Brass (eds) 1992 *Plantations, peasants and proletarians in colonial Asia*. Cass: London.

Das, V. 1995 *Critical Events: An Anthropological Perspective on Contemporary India*. Oxford University Press: Delhi.

Deliege, R. 1992 'Replication and consensus: untouchability, caste and ideology in India'. *Man* (ns), vol. 27: 155–73.

Deliege, R. 1993 'The myths of origin of the Indian untouchables'. *Man* (ns), vol. 28, no. 3.

DiMaggio, P. 1994 'Social stratification, life-style and social cognition', in D. Grusky (ed.) *Social Stratification, Class, Race and Gender in Sociological Perspective* (Social Inequality Series). Westview Press: Boulder, CO.

Dirks, N. 1987 *The hollow crown: ethnohistory of an Indian kingdom*. Cambridge University Press: Cambridge.

Dirks, N. 1989. 'The invention of caste: civil society in colonial India'. *Social Analysis*, vol. 25: 45–52.

Dirks, N. 1991 'Ritual and resistance: subversion as a social fact', in D. Haynes & G. Prakash (eds) *Contesting power: resistance and everyday social relations in South-Asia*. Oxford University Press: Delhi.

Dirks, N. 1992 'Castes of mind'. *Representations*, vol. 37: 56–78.

Donnan, H. 1993 (1988) 'Marriage preferences among the Dhund of northern Pakistan', in P. Uberoi (ed.) *Family, kinship and marriage in India*. Oxford University Press: Delhi.

Dumont, L. (1970) 1980a *Homo hierarchicus*. University of Chicago Press: Chicago.

Dumont, L. (1961) 1980b 'Caste, racism and "stratification": reflections of a social anthropologist', in *Homo Hierarchicus* (Appendix A). University of Chicago Press: Chicago.

Dumont, L. 1983 *Affinity as a value*. University of Chicago Press: Chicago.

Duncan, I. 1990 'Bourdieu on Bourdieu: learning the lesson of the leçon', in R. Harker, C. Mahar & C. Wilkes, (eds) *An introduction to the work of Pierre Bourdieu: the practice of theory*. Macmillan: London.

Eelens, F. & T. Schampers 1992 'Survival migration: the Sri-Lankan case', in F. Eelens, T. Schampers & J.D. Speckmann (eds) *Labour migration to the Middle East: from Sri Lanka to the Gulf*. Kegan Paul: London.

Eelens F., T. Schampers & J.D. Speckmann 1992 *Labour migration to the Middle East: from Sri Lanka to the Gulf*. Kegan Paul: London.

Erikson, R. & J.H. Goldthorpe 1994 *The constant flux: a study of class mobility in industrial societies*. Clarendon Press: Oxford.

Fanon, F. 1986 *Black skin, white masks*. Pluto: London.

Featherman, D.L. & R.M. Hauser 1994 'A refined model of occupational mobility', in D. Grusky (ed.) *Social Stratification, Class, Race and Gender in Sociological Perspective* (Social Inequality Series). Westview Press: Boulder, CO.

Fernandes, L. 1997 *Producing workers: the politics of gender, class, and culture in the Calcutta jute mills.* University of Pennsylvania Press: Philadelphia.

Franke, R. 1992 'Land reforms versus inequality in Nadur village, Kerala'. *Journal of Anthropological Research,* vol. 48, no. 2: 81–116.

Franke, R. (1992) 1994 *Life is a little better: redistribution as a development strategy in Nadur village, Kerala.* Westview Press: Boulder, CO.

Franke, R.W. & B.H. Chasin (1992) 1994 *Kerala: development through radical reform.* Promilla & Co./Institute for Food and Development Policy: New Delhi.

Freeman, J.M. 1979 *Untouchable: an Indian life history.* Stanford University Press: Stanford, CA.

Friedman, J. 1990 'Being in the world: globalization and localization', in M. Featherstone (ed.) *Global culture.* Sage: London.

Friedman, J. 1994 'The political economy of elegance: life cycles in Cameroon', in J. Friedman (ed.) *Consumption and identity.* Harwood Academic Press: Chur, Switzerland.

Fruzzetti, L. (1982) 1990 *The gift of a virgin: women, marriage and ritual in a Bengali society.* Oxford University Press: Delhi.

Fuller, C.J. 1975 'The internal structure of the Nayar caste'. *Journal of Anthropological Research,* vol. 31, no. 4: 283–312.

Fuller, C.J. 1976a *The Nayars today.* Cambridge University Press: Cambridge.

Fuller, C.J. 1976b 'Kerala Christians and the caste system'. *Man* (ns), vol. 11: 53–70.

Fuller, C.J. 1980 'The divine couple's relationship in a South Indian temple: Minakshi and Sundaresvara at Madurai'. *History of Religions,* vol. 19: 321–48.

Fuller, C.J. 1985 'Royal divinity and human kingship in the festival of a South Indian temple'. *South Asian Social Scientist,* vol. 1: 3–43.

Fuller, C.J. 1989 'Misconceiving the grain heap: a critique of the concept of the Indian jajmani system', in J. Parry & M. Bloch (eds) *Money and the morality of exchange.* Cambridge University Press: Cambridge.

Fuller, C.J. 1992 *The camphor flame.* Princeton University Press: Princeton, NJ.

Fuller, C.J. 1996a 'Brahman temple priests and Hindu revivalism in contemporary Tamilnadu'. *South Indian Studies,* vol. 1, no. 1: 1–34.

Fuller, C.J. 1996b 'Hinduism and the politics of religion in contemporary Tamilnadu'. Unpublished paper.

Fuller, C.J. 1996c 'Introduction: caste today', in C.J. Fuller (ed.) *Caste today.* Oxford University Press: Delhi.

Fuller, C.J. & P. Logan 1985 'The Navaratri festival in Madurai'. *Bulletin of SOAS,* vol. 48: 79–105.

Gaborieau, M. 1975 'Transe rituelle dans l'Himalaya Central: folie, avatar, meditation'. *Purusartha,* vol. 2: 147–72.

Gardner, K. 1993 'Desh-bidesh: Sylethi images of home and away'. *Man* (ns), vol. 28: 1–16.

Gardner, K. 1995 *Global migrants local lives: travel and trasformation in rural Bangladesh.* Clarendon Press: Oxford.

Gath, A. 1998 'Varieties of pilgrimage experience: religious journeying in Central Kerala'. Unpublished PhD thesis, University of Edinburgh.

Gatwood, L.E. 1991 *Devi and the spouse goddess: women, sexuality and marriage in India.* Manohar: Delhi.

Gell, A. 1986 'Newcomers to the world of goods: consumption among the Muria Gonds', in A. Appadurai (ed.) *The social life of things: commodities in cultural perspective.*

Cambridge University Press: Cambridge.

Gell, A. 1988 'Anthropology, material culture and consumption'. *Journal of the Anthropological Society of Oxford*, vol. 19: 43–8.

Gellner, E. 1983 *Nations and nationalism*. Basil Blackwell: Oxford.

George, J. 1984 *Politicisation of agricultural workers in Kerala*. K.P. Bagchi: Calcutta.

George, T.K. & P.K.M. Tharakan 1985 *Development of tea plantations in Kerala: a historical perspective*. Working Paper no. 204, Centre for Development Studies, Thiruvananthapuram.

Gilbert, D. & J.A. Kahl 1982 *The American class structure: a new synthesis*. Dorsey Press: Homewood, IL.

Gilroy, P. 1993 *The black Atlantic: modernity and double consciousness*. Verso: London.

Good, A. 1982 The actor and the act: categories of prestation in South India'. *Man* (ns), vol. 17: 23–41.

Good, A. 1991 *The female bridegroom: a comparative study of life-crisis rituals in South India and Sri Lanka*. Oxford University Press: Delhi.

Gopikuttan, G. 1990 'House construction boom in Kerala'. *Economic and Political Weekly*, 15 Sept.: 2083–8.

Gough, K. 1955 'Female initiation rites on the Malabar Coast'. *Journal of the Royal Anthropological Institute*, vol. 85: 45–80.

Gough, K. 1959 'The Nayars and the definition of marriage'. *Journal of the Royal Anthropological Institute*, vol. 89: 23–34.

Gough, K. 1961 'Nayar: Central Kerala; Nayar: North Kerala; Tiyyar: North Kerala; Mappilla: North Kerala: the modern disintegration of matrilineal descent groups', in D. Schneider & K. Gough (eds) *Matrilineal kinship*. University of California Press: Berkeley.

Gough, K. 1970 'Palakkara: social and religious change in Central Kerala', in K. Ishwaran (ed.) *Continuity and change in India's villages*. Columbia University Press: New York.

Gough, K. 1981 *Rural society in Southeast India*. Cambridge University Press: Cambridge.

Government of Kerala 1993 *Statistics for Planning 1993*. Department of Economics and Statistics: Thiruvananthapuram.

Grewal, I. 1996 *Home and harem: nation, gender, empire and the cultures of travel*. Leicester University Press: London.

Grusky, B. 1994a *Social stratification in sociological perspective*. Westview Press: Boulder, CO.

Grusky, B. (ed.) 1994b *Social stratification: class, race, and gender in sociological perspective*. Westview Press: Boulder, CO.

Guha, R. 1982 'The prose of counter-insurgency'. *Subaltern Studies II*, Oxford University Press: Delhi.

Guha, R. 1983 *Elementary aspects of peasant insurgency in India*. Oxford University Press: Delhi.

Gulati, L. 1983 'Male migration to Middle East and the impact on the family'. *Economic and Political Weekly*, 23 Dec.: 2217–26.

Gulati, L. 1993 *In the absence of their men*. Sage: Delhi.

Gunatilleke, G. (ed.) 1986 *Migration of Asian workers to the Arab world*. United Nations University: Tokyo.

Gundert, H. (1872) 1989 *A Malayalam and English Dictionary*. Asian Educational Services: New Delhi.

Habermas, J. 1987 *The Philosophical Discourse of Modernity: Twelve Lectures*. MIT Press: Cambridge, MA.

Habib, I. 1995 'Studying a colonial economy – without perceiving colonialism', in I. Habib, *Essays in Indian history: towards a Marxist perception*. Tulika: Delhi.

Hannerz, U. 1980 *Exploring the city: enquiries toward an urban anthropology*. Columbia University Press: New York.

Hannerz, U. 1987 'The world in creolisation'. *Africa*, vol. 57, no. 4: 546–59.

Haraway, D. 1992 'The promises of monsters: a regenerative politics for inappropriate/d others', in L. Grossberg, C. Nelson & P. Treichler (eds) *Cultural Studies*. Routledge: London.

Hardgrave, R. 1969 *The Nadars of Tamilnad*. University of California Press: Berkeley.

Hardiman, D. 1987 *The coming of Devi: Adivasi assertion in Western India*. Oxford University Press: Delhi.

Harker, R. 1990 'Bourdieu – education and reproduction', in R. Harker, C. Mahar & C. Wilkes (eds) *An introduction to the work of Pierre Bourdieu: the practice of theory*. Macmillan: London.

Harriss, J. 1982 *Capitalism and peasant farming*. Oxford University Press: Bombay.

Heesterman, J.C. 1959 'Reflections on the significance of daksina', *Indo-Iranian Journal*, vol. 3: 241–58.

Heimsath, C.H. 1978 'The functions of Hindu social reformers – with special reference to Kerala'. *Indian Economic and Social History Review*, vol. 15, no. 1: 25–39.

Herrenschmidt, O. 1978 'Les formes sacrificielles dans l'hindouisme populaire'. *Systèmes de pensée en Afrique Noir*, cahier 2: 115–33.

Herring, J. 1980 'Abolition of landlordism in Kerala: a redistribution of privilege'. *Economic and Political Weekly*, vol. 15, no. 26: 59–89.

Herring, J. 1983 *Land to the tillers: the political economy of agrarian reform in South Asia*. Yale University Press: New Haven, CT.

Herring, J. 1984 'Economic consequences of local power configurations in rural South Asia', in M. Desai, S. Rudolph & A. Rudra (eds) *Agrarian power and agricultural productivity in South Asia*. University of California Press: Berkeley.

Herring, J. 1989 'Dilemmas of agrarian communism: peasant differentiation, sectoral and village politics'. *Third World Quarterly*, vol. 11, no. 1: 89–115.

Herzfeld, M. 1985 *The poetics of manhood: contest and identity in a Cretan mountain village*. Princeton University Press: Princeton, NJ.

Heuzé, G. 1992 'Les Indiens et le travail: une relation oubliée'. *Purusartha*, vol. 14: 9–30.

Hobbs, D. 1996 (1988) *Doing the business: entrepreneurship, detectives and the working class in the East End of London*. Oxford University Press: Oxford.

Hofstadter, D.R. & D.C. Dennett 1981 *The mind's I: fantasies and reflections on self and soul*. Harvester Press: Brighton.

Inden, R. 1978 'Ritual, authority and cyclic time in Hindu kingship', in J. F. Richards (ed.) *Kingship and authority in South Asia*. University of Wisconsin Press: Madison.

Inden, R. 1990 *Imagining India*. Basil Blackwell: Cambridge.

Isaac, T. 1985 'From caste consciousness to class consciousness: Aleppey coir workers during inter-war period'. *Economic and Political Weekly*, vol. 20, no.4 (Special Issue: Review of Political Economy): 5–18

Isaac, T. 1990 *Evolution of organisation of production in coir yarn spinning industry*. Working Paper no. 236, Centre for Development Studies, Thiruvananthapuram.

Isaac, T. 1995 'Kerala - the emerging perspectives: overview of the International Congress on Kerala Sudies'. *Social Scientist*, vol. 23, nos. 3–4: 3–36.

Isaac, T. & P.K. Tharakan 1986a *Sree Narayana movement in Travancore 1880–1939: a study of social basis and ideological reproduction.* Working Paper no. 214, Centre for Development Studies, Thiruvananthapuram.

Isaac, T. & P.K. Tharakan 1986b *An enquiry into the historical roots of industrial backwardness of Kerala: a study of Travancore Region.* Working Paper no. 215, Centre for Development Studies, Thiruvananthapuram.

Isaac, T. & P.K. Tharakan 1995 'Kerala – the emerging perspectives: overview of the International Congress of Kerala Studies'. *Social Scientist*, vol. 23, nos 1–3: 3–35.

Isaac, T., P.A. Van Stuijenberg & K.N. Nair 1992 *Modernisation and employment: the coir industry in Kerala.* Sage: New Delhi.

Jayawardena, K. 1995 *The white woman's other burden: Western women and South Asia during British rule.* Routledge: New York.

Jeffrey, R. 1974 'The social origins of a caste association, 1875–1905: the founding of the SNDP Yogam'. *Journal of South Asian Studies*, no. 4: 39–59.

Jeffrey, R. (1976) 1994 *The decline of Nayar dominance.* Manohar: Delhi.

Jeffrey, R. 1978 'Matriliny, marxism and the birth of the Communist Party in Kerala, 1930–1940'. *Journal of Asian Studies*, vol. 38, no. 1: 77–98.

Jeffrey, R. 1993 *Politics, women and well being: how Kerala became a 'a model'.* Oxford University Press: Delhi.

Kaelber, W.O. 1976 'Tapas, birth and spiritual rebirth in the Veda'. *History of Religions*, vol. 15: 343–86.

Kaelber, W.O. 1978 'The "dramatic" element in Brahmanic initiation: symbols of death, danger and difficult passage'. *History of Religions*, vol. 18: 54–76.

Kahn, J. 1997 'Malaysian modern or anti-anti Asian values'. *Thesis Eleven*, no. 50: 15–34.

Kaimal, P.K.V. 1994 *Revolt of the oppressed: Punappra-Vayalar 1946.* Konark Publishers: Delhi.

Kakar, S. (1982) 1986 *Shamans, mystics and doctors: a psychological enquiry into India and its healing traditions.* Oxford University Press: Delhi.

Kale, M. 1995 'Projecting identities: empire and indentured labour migration from India to Trinidad and British Guiana 1836–1885', in P. Van der Veer (ed.) *Nation and migration: the politics of space in the South Asian diaspora.* University of Pennsylvania Press: Philadephia.

Kandiyoti, D. 1994 'Bargaining with patriarchy'. *Gender and Society*, vol. 2, no. 3: 274–90.

Kannan, K.P. 1988 *Of rural proletarian struggle: mobilization and organization of rural workers in south-west India.* Oxford University Press: Delhi.

Kapadia, K. 1993a 'Mutuality and competition: female landless labour and wage rates in Tamil Nadu'. *Journal of Peasant Studies*, vol. 20, no. 2: 296–316.

Kapadia, K. 1993b 'Marrying money: changing preference and practice in Tamil marriage'. *Contributions to Indian Sociology*, vol. 27, no. 1: 25–51.

Kapadia, K. 1995 'The profitability of bonded labor: the gem-cutting industry in rural South-India'. *Journal of Peasant Studies*, vol. 22, no. 3: 446–83.

Kapur, A. 1985 'Actors, pilgrims and gods: Ramlila at Ramnagar'. *Contributions to Indian Sociology*, vol. 19: 57–74.

Kelly, J.D. 1991 *A politics of virtue: Hinduism, sexuality and countercolonial discourse in Fiji.* University of Chicago Press: Chicago.

Kelly, R.C. 1993. *Constructing inequality: the fabrication of a hierarchy of virtue among the Etoro.* University of Michigan: Michigan.

Kennedy, J. 1974 'Status and control of temples in Tamil Nadu'. *Indian Economic and*

Social History Review, vol. 11: 260–90.

Kent, S. 1993 'Sharing in an egalitarian Kalahari community'. *Man* (ns), vol. 28, no. 3: 479–514.

Klass, M. 1978 *From field to factory: community structure and industrialisation in West Bengal*. ISHI: Philadelphia.

Knipe, D.M. 1975 *In the image of fire: Vedic experiences of heat*. Motilal & Banarsidas: Delhi.

Kolenda, P. 1990 'Untouchable Chuhras through their humor: "equalizing" marital kin through teasing, pretence, and farce', in O.M. Lynch (ed.) *Divine passions: the social construction of emotion in India*, Oxford University Press: Delhi.

Kondo, D. 1990a *Crafting selves: power, gender, and discourses in a Japanese workplace*. University of Chicago Press: Chicago.

Kondo, D. 1990b 'Mme Butterfly: orientalism, gender and a critique of essentialist identity'. *Cultural Critique*, Fall: 5–28.

Kondos, P. 1986 'Images of the fierce goddess and portrayals of Hindu women'. *Contributions to Indian Scoiology*, vol. 20, no. 2: 173–96.

Kooiman, D. 1989 *Conversion and social equality in India*. Manohar: New Delhi.

Kopytoff, I. 1986 'The cultural biography of things: commoditization as process', in A. Appadurai (ed.) *The social life of things: commodities in cultural perspective*. Cambridge University Press: Cambridge.

Krishnaji, N. 1979 'Agrarian relations and the left movement in Kerala'. *Economic and Political Weekly*, vol. 15, no. 9.

Kumar, S. 1994 *Political evolution in Kerala: Travancore 1859–1938*. Phoenix Publishing House: New Delhi.

Kurien, C.T. 1994 'Kerala's development experience: random comments about the past and some considerations for the future', *International Congress on Kerala Studies*, vol. 1: 21–34.

Kurien, J. 1995 'The Kerala Model: its central tendency and the outlier'. *Social Scientist*, vol. 23, nos 1–3: 70–90.

Kurien, P.A. 1994 'Non-economic bases of economic behaviour: the consumption, investment and exchange patterns of three emigrant communities in Kerala, India'. *Development and Change*, vol. 25: 757–83.

Kurtz, S.N. 1992 *All the mothers are one: Hindu India and the cultural reshaping of psychoanalysis*. Columbia University Press: New York

Kurup, A.M. 1977 'The sociology of Onam', *Indian Anthropologist*, vol. 3, no.2: 95–120.

Kurup, K.K.N. 1988 *Modern Kerala: studies in social and agrarian relations*. Mittal Publications: Delhi.

Latour, B. 1993 *We have never been modern*. Harvester Wheatsheaf: Hemel Hempstead.

Leela Devi, R. 1978 *Influence of English on Malayalam novels*. College Book House: Trivandrum.

Lemercinier, G. (1974) 1994 *Religion and ideology in Kerala*. Centre Tricontinental: Louvain-la-Neuve & Institute for the Study of Developing Areas: Trivandrum.

Lipset, S.M., R. Bendix & M.L. Zetterberg 1994 'Social mobility in industrial society', in D. Grusky (ed.) *Social Stratification, Class, Race and Gender in Sociological Perspective* (Social Inequality Series). Westview Press: Boulder, CO.

Ludden, D. 1993 'Orientalist empiricism', in P. Van der Veer & C. Breckenridge (eds) *Orientalism and the postcolonial predicament*, Oxford University Press: Delhi.

Luhrmann, T.M. 1996 *The good Parsi: the fate of a colonial elite in a postcolonial society*. Harvard University Press: Cambridge, MA.

Lynch, O. 1969 *The politics of untouchability*. Columbia University Press: New York.

Madan, T.N. (1975) 1993 'Structural implications of marriage in north India: wife-givers and wife-takers among the Pandits of Kashmir', in P. Uberoi (ed.) *Family, kinship and marriage in India*. Oxford University Press: Delhi.

Madan, T.N. 1987 *Non-renunciation: themes and interpretations of Hindu culture*. Oxford University Press: Delhi.

Mahadevan, K. & M. Sumangala 1987 *Social development, cultural change and fertility decline: a study of fertility change in Kerala*. Sage: New Delhi.

Mahar, C., R. Harker & C. Wilkes 1990 'The basic theoretical position', in R. Harker, C. Mahar & C. Wilkes, (eds) *An introduction to the work of Pierre Bourdieu: the practice of theory*. Macmillan: London.

Maher, V. 1987 'Sewing the seams of society: dressmakers and seamstresses in Turin between the wars', in J. Collier & S. Yanagisako (eds) *Gender and kinship: essays towards a unified analysis*. Stanford University Press: Stanford.

Malamoud, C. 1975 'Cuire le monde'. *Purusartha*, vol. 1: 91–135.

Marglin, F.A. 1985 'Types of oppositions in Hindu culture', in J.B. Carman & F.A. Marglin (eds) *Purity and auspiciousness in Indian society*. Brill: Leiden.

Mari Bhat, P.N. & S. Irudaya Rajan 1990 'Demographic transition in Kerala revisited'. *Economic and Political Weekly*, 1–8 Sept.: 1957–80.

Marriott, McK. 1968a 'Caste ranking and food transactions: a matrix analysis', in M. Singer & B. Cohn (eds) *Structure and change in Indian society*. Aldine: Chicago.

Marriott, McK. 1968b 'The feast of love', in M. Singer (ed.) *Krishna: myths, rites, attitudes*, University of Chicago Press: Chicago.

Marriott, McK. 1976 'Hindu transactions: diversity without dualism', in B. Kapferer (ed.) *Transactions and meaning*. Institute for the Study of Human Issues: Philadelphia.

Marriott, McK. 1990 'Constructing an Indian ethnosociology', in McK. Marriott (ed.) *India through Hindu categories*. Sage: New Delhi.

Mascarenhas-Keyes, S. 1986 'Death notices and dispersal: international migration among Catholic Goans', in J. Eades (ed.) *Migrant workers and the social order*. Tavistock Publications: London.

Mateer, S. (1870) 1991a *Land of charity: a descriptive account of Travancore and its people*. Reprint by Asian Educational Services: New Delhi.

Mateer, S. (1883) 1991b *Native life in Travancore*. Reprint by Asian Educational Services: New Delhi.

Mathew, E.T. & P.R.G. Nair 1978 'Socio-economic characteristics of emigrants and emigrants' households: a case study of two villages in Kerala'. *Economic and Political Weekly*, 15 July: 1141–53.

Mathew, G. 1989 *Communal road to a secular Kerala*. Concept Publishing House: New Delhi.

Mathew, G. 1995 'The paradox of women's development in Kerala'. *IIC Quarterly*, vol. 22, nos 2–3: 203–14.

Mathur, P.R.G. 1977 'Caste councils of the Ilavas of Kerala'. *Journal of Kerala Sudies*, vol. 4, parts 1–2: 261–87.

Mayer, A. 1966 *Caste and kinship in Central India: a village and its region*. University of California Press: Berkeley.

Mayer, A. 1996 *Caste in an Indian village: change and continuity, 1954–1992*, in C.J. Fuller (ed.) *Caste today*. Oxford University Press: Delhi.

Mencher, J. 1966a. 'Kerala and Madras: a comparative study of ecology and social structure'. *Ethnology*, vol. 5: 135–71.

Mencher, J. 1966b 'Namboodiri Brahmans: an analysis of a traditional elite in Kerala'. *Journal of Asian and African Studies*, vol. 1: 183–96.

Mencher, J. 1974 'The caste system upside down, or the not-so-mysterious East'. *Current Anthropology*, vol. 15, no. 4: 469–93.

Mencher, J. 1980 'The lessons and non-lessons of Kerala: agricultural labourers and poverty'. *Economic and Political Weekly*, vol. 15: 1781–1802.

Mencher, J. 1994 'The Kerala Model of development: the excluded ones'. *International Congress on Kerala Studies: Abstracts*, vol. 2, no. 1. AKG Centre for Research and Studies: Thiruvananthapuram.

Mencher, J. & H. Goldberg 1967 'Kinship and marriage regulations amongst the Namboodiri Brahmans of Kerala'. *Man* (ns), vol. 2: 87–106.

Menon, D.M. 1992 'Conjectural community: Communism in Malabar, 1934–1948'. *Economic and Political Weekly*, 19–26 Dec.: 2705–15.

Menon, D.M. 1994 *Caste, nationalism and Communism in South India: Malabar 1900–1948*. Cambridge University Press: Cambridge.

Menon, K.P. Padmanabha (1937) 1993 *History of Kerala* (4 vols). Reprint by Asian Educational Services: New Delhi.

Menon, P.A. & C.K. Rajan 1989 *Climate of Kerala*, Classic Publishing House: Cochin.

Menon, Sreedhara 1965 *Kerala Districts Gazetteers: Ernakulam*. Government Press: Trivandrum.

Miller, D. 1987 *Material culture and mass consumption*. Basil Blackwell: Oxford.

Miller, D. 1991 ' Absolute freedom in Trinidad'. *Man* (ns), vol. 26: 323–41.

Miller, D. 1994a *Modernity: an ethnographic approach: dualism and mass consumption in Trinidad*. Berg: Oxford.

Miller, D. 1994b 'Style and ontology', in J. Friedman (ed.) *Consumption and identity*. Harwood Academic Press: Chur, Switzerland.

Miller, D. 1995a 'Consumption as the vanguard of history', in D. Miller (ed.) *Acknowledging consumption*. Routledge: London.

Miller, D. 1995b 'Introduction: anthropology, modernity and consumption', in D. Miller (ed.) *Worlds apart: modernity through the prism of the local*. Routledge: London.

Miller, E.J. 1954 'Caste and territory in Malabar'. *American Anthropologist* 56: 410–20.

Mines, M. 1994. *Public faces, private voices: community and individuality in South India*. Oxford University Press: Delhi.

Mines, M. & Vijayalakshmi Gourishankar 1990 'Leadership and individuality in South Asia: the case of the South Indian big-man'. *Journal of Asian Studies*, vol. 49, no. 4: 761–86.

Mintz, S. 1985 *Sweetness and power: the place of sugar in modern history*. Viking: New York.

Moffatt, M. 1975 'Untouchables and the caste system: a Tamil case study'. *Contributions to Indian Sociology*, vol. 9: 111–22.

Moffatt, M. 1979 *An untouchable community in South India: structure and consensus*. Princeton University Press: Princeton, NJ.

Mohandas, M. 1994 'Poverty in Kerala', in B.A. Prakash (ed.) *Kerala's economy: performance, problems, prospects*. Sage: New Delhi.

Mook, T. 1992 'Middle East migration at the micro-level: a village case study', in F. Eelens, T. Schampers & J.D. Speckmann (eds) *Labour migration to the Middle East: from Sri Lanka to the Gulf*. Kegan Paul: London.

Moore, H.L. 1994 *A passion for difference*. Polity Press: London.

Moore, M. 1985 'A new look at the Nayar taravad'. *Man* (ns), vol. 20: 523–41.

Moore, M. 1988 'Symbol and meaning in Nayar marriage ritual'. *American Ethnologist*, vol. 15: 254–73.

Moore, M. 1990 'The Kerala house and the Hindu cosmos', in McK. Marriott (ed.) *India through Hindu categories*. Sage: New Delhi.

Mosse, D. 1994 'Idioms of subordination and styles of protest among Christian and Hindu Harijan in Tamil Nadu'. *Contributions to Indian Sociology*, vol. 28, no. 1: 67–106.

Mudimbe, V.Y. 1988 *The invention of Africa: gnosis, philosophy and the order of knowledge*. Indiana University Press: Bloomington.

Muralidharan, M. 1996. 'Hindu community formation in Kerala: processes and structures under colonial modernity'. *South Indian Studies*, no. 2: 234–59.

Nagaraj, D.R. 1993 *The flaming feet: a study of the Dalit movement*. South Forum Press: Bangalore.

Nair, A.B. 1994 *The government and politics of Kerala*. Indira Publications: Thiruvananthapuram.

Nair, K.S. 1984 *Congress and Kerala politics*. College Book House: Trivandrum.

Nair, P.R.G. 1986 'India', in G. Gunatilleke (ed.) *Migration of Asian workers to the Arab world*. United Nations University: Tokyo.

Nair, P.R.G. 1989 'Incidence, impact and implications of migration to the Middle East from Kerala (India)', in Amjad R. (ed.) *To the Gulf and back*, International Labour Organisation: New Delhi.

Nair, P.R.G. & D. Ajit 1984 'Parallel colleges in Kerala', *Economic and Political Weekly* vol. 19, nos 42–3: 1840–7.

Nair P.R.G. & P.M. Pillai 1994 *Impact of external transfers on the regional economy of Kerala*. Centre for Development Studies: Thiruvananthapuram.

Nair, V.B. 1994 *Social development and demographic changes in South India*. M.D. Publications: New Delhi.

Nair, V.K.S. 1966 'Communal interest groups in Kerala', in D.E. Smith (ed.) *South Asian politics and religion*. Princeton University Press: Princeton, NJ.

Nair, V.M. 1978 'Communal interest groups and socio-economic changes in Kerala 1967–77'. *Journal of Kerala Studies*, vol. 5, parts 3–4: 627–42.

Nandy, A. 1983 'The psychology of colonialism: sex, age and ideology in British India', in A. Nandy, *The intimate enemy: loss and recovery of self under colonialism*, Oxford University Press: Delhi.

Narayana, D. & K.N. Nair 1989 *Heterogenity, mobility and dynamics of contractual arrangements in the agricultural labour market in an irrigated district*. Working Paper no. 230, Centre for Development Studies: Thiruvananthapuram.

Nataraja Guru 1968 *The word of the Guru: an outline of the life and teachings of the Guru Narayana*. Paico: Cochin.

Nataraja Guru 1989 *Autobiography of an absolutist*. Gurukula Publishing House: Varkala.

Nataraja Guru 1990 *Life and teachings of Narayana Guru*. East–West University Publication: Fernhill & Bainbridge.

Nayyar, D. 1989 'International labour migration from India: a macro-economic analysis', in R. Amjad (ed.) *To the Gulf and back*. International Labour Organisation: New Delhi.

Nayyar, D. 1994 *Migration, remittances and capital flows: the Indian experience*. Oxford University Press: Delhi.

Nieuwenhuys, O. 1991 'Emancipation for survival: access to land and labour of

Thandans in Kerala'. *Modern Asian Studies*, vol. 25, no. 3: 599–619.

Nieuwenhuys, O. 1994 *Children's lifeworlds: gender, welfare and labour in the developing world*. Routledge: London.

Nishimura, Y. 1994 'Marriage payments among the Nagarattars in South India'. *Contributions to Indian Sociology*, vol. 28, no. 2: 243–72.

Nossiter, T. 1982 *Communism in Kerala: a study in political adaptation*. C. Hurst & Company: London.

O'Hanlon, R. 1985 *Caste, conflict and ideology*. Orient Longman (for Cambridge University Press): Hyderabad

O'Hanlon, R. 1988 'Recovering the subject: subaltern studies and histories of resistance in colonial South Asia'. *Modern Asian Studies*, vol. 22, no. 1: 189–224.

Obeyesekere, G. 1976 'The impact of Ayurvedic ideas on the culture and the individual in Sri Lanka', in J.W. Leslie (ed.) *Asian medical systems: a comparative study*. University of California Press: Berkeley.

Obeyesekere, G. 1984a *The cult of the goddess Pattini*. University of Chicago Press, Chicago.

Obeyesekere, G. (1981) 1984b *Medusa's hair: an essay on personal symbolism and religious experience*. University of Chicago Press: Chicago.

Oddie, G.A. 1978 *Social protest in India*. Manohar: Delhi.

Oddie, G.A. 1995 *Popular religion, elites and reforms: hook-swinging and its prohibition in colonial India, 1800–1894*. Manohar: Delhi.

Ong, A. 1999 'Clash of civilizations or Asian liberalism: an anthropology of the state and citizenship', in H. Moore (ed.) *Anthropological theory today*. Polity Press: Cambridge.

Oommen, M.A. 1994 'Land reforms and economic change: experience and lessons from Kerala', in B.A. Prakash (ed.) *Kerala's economy: performance, problems and prospects*. Sage: New Delhi.

Oommen, T.K. 1971 'Agrarian tension in a Kerala district: an analysis'. *Indian Journal of Industrial Relations*, vol. 7, no. 2: 229–68.

Oommen, T.K. 1985 *From mobilisation to institutionalisation: the dynamics of agrarian movement in twentieth-century Kerala*. Popular Prakashan: Bombay.

Oommen, T.K. 1990 *Protest and change: studies in social movements*. Sage: Delhi.

Osella, C. 1993 'Making hierarchy natural: the cultural construction of gender and maturity in Kerala, India'. Unpublished PhD thesis, London School of Economics and Political Sciences.

Osella, C. & F. Osella 1998 'On flirting and friendship: micro-politics in a hierarchical society'. *Journal of the Royal Anthropological Institute*, vol. 4, no. 2: 189–206.

Osella, C. & F. Osella 2000 'Seepage of divinised power through social, spiritual and bodily boundaries'. *Purusartha*, vol. 21: 183–210.

Osella, F. 1993 'Caste, class, power and social mobility in Kerala, India'. Unpublished PhD thesis, London School of Economics and Political Sciences.

Osella, F. & C. Osella 1996 'Articulation of physical and social bodies in Kerala'. *Contributions to Indian Sociology*, vol. 30, no. 1: 37–68.

Osella, F. & C. Osella 1999 'From transience to immanence: consumption, life-cycle and social mobility in Kerala, South India'. *Modern Asian Studies*, vol. 33, no. 4: 989–1020.

Osella, F. & C. Osella 2000 'Migration, money and masculinity in Kerala'. *Journal of the Royal Anthropological Institute*, vol. 6, no. 1: 115–31.

Osella, F. & C. Osella (forthcoming) 'The return of king Mahabali: the politics of morality in South India', in C.J. Fuller & V. Benei (eds) *The Everyday State and Society in India*. Social Science Press: Delhi.

Osella, C. & F. Osella (forthcoming) 'Points de vue malayalis sur l'inné et l'acquis', in V. Bouiller & G. Tarabout (eds) *Le Corps en Inde*.

Osmani, S.R. 1986 'Bangladesh', in G. Gunatilleke (ed.) *Migration of Asian workers to the Arab world*. United Nations University: Tokyo.

Ostor, A. 1980 *The play of the gods: locality, ideology, structure and time in the festivals of a Bengali town*. University of Chicago Press: Chicago.

Ouwerkerk, L. 1994 *No elephants for the Maharaja: social and political change in Travancore 1921–1947*. Manohar: Delhi.

Pandian, M.S.S. 1992 *The image trap: M.G. Ramachandran in film and politics*. Sage: Delhi.

Pandian, M.S.S. 1995 'Beyond colonial crumbs: Cambridge School, identity, politics and Dravidian movement(s)'. *Economic and Political Weekly*, vol. 30, nos 7–8: 385–91.

Panikar, P.G.K. 1992 'High cost of medical care in Kerala'. *Economic and Political Weekly*, June: 1179–81.

Panikkar, K.M. 1918 'Some aspects of Nayar life'. *Journal of the Royal Anthropological Institute*, vol. 48: 254–93.

Panikkar, K.N. 1995 *Culture, ideology, hegemony: intellectuals and social consciousness in colonial India*. Tulika: New Delhi.

Parish, S.M. 1996 *Hierarchy and its discontents: culture and the politics of consciousness in caste society*. University of Pennsylvania Press: Philadephia.

Parkin, F. 1979 *Marxism and class theory: a bourgeois critique*. Tavistock Publications: London.

Parmeswaran, P. 1979 *Narayana Guru, the prophet of renaissance*. Suruchi Sahitya: New Delhi.

Parry, J. 1970 'The Koli dilemma'. *Contributions to Indian Sociology*, vol. 4: 88–104.

Parry, J. 1974 'Egalitarian values in a hierarchical society'. *South Asian Review*, vol. 7, no. 2: 95–121.

Parry, J. 1979 *Caste and kinship in Kangra*. Routledge & Kegan Paul: London.

Parry, J. 1982 'Sacrificial death and the necrophagous ascetic', in M. Bloch & J. Parry (eds) *Death and regeneration of life*. Cambridge University Press: Cambridge.

Parry, J. 1985 'Death and digestion: the symbolism of food and eating in north Indian mortuary rites'. *Man* (ns), vol. 20, no. 4: 612–31.

Parry, J. 1986 'The gift, the Indian gift and the "Indian gift" '. *Man* (ns), vol. 21, no. 3: 453–73.

Parry, J. 1989 'On the moral perils of exchange', in J. Parry & M. Bloch (eds) *Money and the morality of exchange*. Cambridge University Press: Cambridge.

Parry, J. 1994 *Death in Banaras*. Cambridge University Press: Cambridge.

Parry, J. & M. Bloch 1989 'Introduction: money and the morality of exchange', in J. Parry & M. Bloch (eds) *Money and the morality of exchange*. Cambridge University Press: Cambridge.

Pereira, J.J. 1989 *Narayana Guru: a social educator*. R.R.Publishers: Varkala.

Piot, C. 1999 *Remotely global: village modernity in West Africa*. University of Chicago Press: Chicago.

Pocock, D. (1954) 1993 'The hypergamy of the Pattidars', in P. Uberoi (ed.) *Family, kinship and marriage in India*. Oxford University Press: Delhi.

Pocock, D. 1973 *Mind, body and wealth: a study of belief and practice in an Indian village*. Basil Blackwell: Oxford.

Pottekkat, S.K. 1980 *Vishakanyaka*. Kerala Sahitya Akademi: Trichur.

Prakash, B.A. 1978 'Impact of foreign remittances'. *Economic and Political Weekly*, 8 July: 1107–11.

Prakash, G. 1996 'Science between the lines', in *Subaltern Studies IX*, Oxford University Press: Delhi.

Prakash, G. 1999 *Another reason: science and the imagination of modern India*. Princeton University Press: Princeton, NJ.

Price, P.G. 1996 *Kingship and political practice in colonial India*. Cambridge University Press: Cambridge.

Quigley, D. 1993 *The interpretation of caste*. Clarendon Press: Oxford.

Radhakrishnan, P. 1980 'Peasant struggles and land reforms in Malabar'. *Economic and Political Weekly*, vol. 15, no. 52: 2095–102.

Radhakrishnan, P. 1983 'Land reforms and social change'. *Economic and Political Weekly* (Special Issue: Annual Review of Agriculture) pp. 143–50.

Radhakrishnan, P. 1989 *Peasant struggles, land reforms and social change: Malabar 1836–1982*. Sage Publications: Delhi.

Radhakrishnan, P. 1991 'Ambedkar's legacy'. *The Hindu*, 19–20 Jan.

Radhakrishnan, P. 1993 'Caste, politics and the reservation issue'. Unpublished paper presented at the Centre for South Asian Studies, SOAS, UK, 'Workshop on Caste', 12–13 July.

Radhakrishnan, P. 1995 'Putting society together again', *The Hindu* newspaper weekly magazine, part 1, 27 Aug.

Raghavan, V.P. 1994 'Kerala's development experience: an overview in historical perspective'. *International Congress on Kerala Studies: Abstracts*, vol. 2: 14–15, AKG Centre for Research and Studies: Thiruvananthapuram.

Raheja, G. 1988 *The poison in the gift*. University of Chicago Press: Chicago.

Rajendran, G. 1974 *The Ezhava community and Kerala politics*. Kerala Academy of Political Sciences: Trivandrum.

Randeria, S. 1989 'Carrion and corpses'. *Archives Européennes de Sociologie*, vol. 30: 171–91.

Rao V.N., D. Shulman & S. Subrahmanyam 1992 *Symbols of substance: court and state in Nayaka period Tamil Nadu*. Oxford University Press: Delhi.

Rao, M.S.A. (1979) 1987 *Social movements and social transformation: a study of two backward classes movements in India*. Manohar: Delhi.

Rao, M.S.A. 1986 'Gastro-dynamics', in R.S. Khare & M.S.A. Rao (eds) *Food, society and culture*. California Academic Press: Durham, NC.

Ravi Raman, K. 1991 'Labour under imperial hegemony: the case of tea plantations in South India', in S. Bhattacharya et al. (eds) *The South Indian economy: agrarian change, industrial structure, and state policy c. 1914–1947*. Oxford University Press: Delhi.

Reynolds, H.B. 1991 'The auspicious married woman', in S. Wadley (ed.) *The powers of Tamil women*. Manohar: Delhi.

Roediger, D. 1994 *Towards the abolition of whiteness: essays on race, politics, and working-class history*. Verso: London

Rofel, L. 1999 *Other modernities: gendered yearnings in China after socialism*. University of California Press: Berkeley.

Roland, A. 1988 *In search of self in India and Japan: toward a cross-cultural psychology*. Princeton University Press: Princeton, NJ.

Rosaldo, R. 1993 *Culture and truth: the remaking of social analysis*. Routledge: London.

Rowe, W. 1968 'The new Cauhans: a caste mobility movement in North India', in

J. Silverberg (ed.) *Social mobility in the caste system in India*. Mouton: The Hague and Paris.

Rowland, M. 'The material culture of success: ideals and life cycles in Cameroon', in J. Friedman (ed.) *Consumption and identity*. Harwood Academic Press: Chur, Switzerland.

Rudner, D.W. 1994 *Caste and capitalism in colonial India: the Nattukottai Chettiars*. University of California Press: Berkeley.

Rudolph, L. & S. Rudolph 1967 *The modernity of tradition*. University of Chicago Press: Chicago.

Said, E.W. 1978 *Orientalism*. Routledge & Kegan Paul: London.

Schechner, R. 1985 *Between theatre and anthropology*. University of Pennsylvania Press: Philadelphia.

Scott, J.C. 1990 *Dominance and the arts of resistance: hidden transcripts*. Yale University Press: New Haven, CT.

Searle-Chatterjee, M. & U. Sharma 1994 'Introduction', in M. Searle-Chatterjee & U. Sharma (eds) *Contextualising caste: post-Dumontian approaches*. Basil Blackwell: Oxford.

Sekar, R. 1992 *The Sabarimalai pilgrimage and Ayyappan cults*. Motilal & Banarsidas: Delhi.

Seth, P. 1995 'Initiation of a temple velichapadu'. *India International Centre Quarterly*, vol. 22, nos 2–3: 115–31.

Shahnaz Kazi 1989 'Domestic impact of overseas migration: Pakistan', in R. Amjad (ed.) *To the Gulf and back: studies on the economic impact of Asian labour migration*. International Labour Organisation: Delhi.

Sharma, U. 1984 'Dowry in North India: its consequences for women', in R. Hirschon (ed.) *Women and property-women as property*. Croom Helm: London.

Shulman, D. 1980 *Tamil temple myths*. Princeton University Press: Princeton, NJ.

Singer, M. 1972 *When a great tradition modernizes*. Vikas: Delhi.

Sinha, M. 1995. *Colonial masculinity: the 'manly Englishman' and the 'effeminate Bengali' in the late nineteenth century*. Manchester University Press: Manchester.

Sivan, M.N. 1977 'The Mahabali myth: a study in the sociology of religion', in K. Thulaseedharan (ed.) *Conflict and culture*. College Book House: Trivandrum.

Sivanandan, P. 1979 'Caste, class and economic opportunity in Kerala'. *Economic and Political Weekly*, Special Annual Issue, pp 475–80.

Sivaramakrishnan, K. 1995 'Situating the subalterns: history and anthropology in the Subaltern Studies project'. *Journal of Historical Sociology*, vol. 8, no. 4: 395–429.

Smith, B.K. 1986 'Ritual, knowledge and being: initiation to Veda study in ancient India'. *Numen*, vol. 33, no. 1: 65–89.

Smith, B.K. 1988 *Reflections on resemblance, ritual and religion*. Oxford University Press: New York.

Sobhanan, B. 1977 'Macaulay and Christianity in Kerala'. *Journal of Kerala Studies*, vol. IV, part IV: 603–8.

Sorensen, A. 1994 'The basic concepts of stratification research: class, status and power', in D. Grusky (ed.) *Social Stratification, Class, Race and Gender in Sociological Perspective* (Social Inequality Series). Westview Press: Boulder, CO.

Sorokin, D.A. 1994 'Social and cultural mobility', in D. Grusky (ed.) *Social Stratification, Class, Race and Gender in Sociological Perspective* (Social Inequality Series). Westview Press: Boulder, CO.

Sreenivasan, K. 1981 *Kumaran Asan: profile of a poet's vision*. Jayasree Publications: Trivandrum.

Srinivas, M.N. (1966) 1988 *Social change in modern India*. Orient Longman: Hyderabad.

Stein, B. 1980 *Peasant state and society in medieval South India*. Oxford University Press: Delhi.

Stirrat, R.L. 1989 'Money, men and women', in J. Parry & M. Bloch (eds) *Money and the morality of exchange*. Cambridge University Press: Cambridge.

Stivens, M. 1996 *Matriliny and modernity: sexual politics and social change in rural Malaysia*. Allen & Unwin: St Leonards, NSW.

Stoler, A.L. 1995 *Race and the education of desire: Foucault's 'History of Sexuality' and the colonial order of things*. Duke University Press: Durham, NC.

Strathern, M. (1988) 1990 *The gender of the gift: problems with women and problems with society in Melanesia*. University of California Press: Berkeley.

Subbarayappa, B.V. 1966 'The Indian doctrine of the five elements'. *Indian Journal of the History of Science*, vol. 1, no. 1: 61–7.

Tambiah, S.J. 1973 'From varna to caste through mixed unions', in J. Goody (ed.) *The character of kinship*. Cambridge University Press: Cambridge.

Tambiah, S.J. 1985 *Culture, thought and social action: an anthropological perspective*. Harvard University Press: Cambridge, MA.

Tanaka, M. 1991 *Patrons, devotees, and Goddesses: ritual and power among the Tamil fishermen in Sri Lanka*. Institute for Research in Humanities, Kyoto University: Kyoto.

Tapper, B.E. 1979 'Widows and goddesses: female roles in deity symbolism in a South Indian village'. *Contributions to Indian Sociology*, vol. 15: 1–31.

Tarabout, G. 1986 *Sacrifier et donner à voir en pays Malabar: les fêtes de temple au Kérala (Inde du Sud): étude anthropologique*. Publication de l'EFEO, vol. 147: Paris.

Tarabout, G. 1990 'Traces de foundation'. *Bibliothèque de l'École des Hautes Études: Section des Sciences Religieuses*, vol. 113: 211–32.

Tarabout, G. 1992 'Quand les dieux s'emmêlent: point de vue sur les classifications divines au Kérala'. *Purusartha*, vol. 15: 43–74.

Tarabout, G. 1993 'Ritual rivalry in Kerala', in H. Brückuer, L. Lutze & A. Malik (eds) *Flags of fame: studies in South Asian folk culture*. New Delhi: Manohar.

Tarabout, G. 1997 'Maîtres et serviteurs: commander à des dieux au Kerala', in A. de Surgy, A. Padoux & P. Lory (eds) *Religion et pratiques de puissance*. L'Harmattan: Paris.

Tarabout, G. 1999 ' "Psycho-religious therapy" in Kerala as a form of interaction between local traditions and (perceived) scientific discourse', in M. Carrin (ed.) *Managing distress – possession and therapeutic cults in South Asia*. Manohar: Delhi.

Taussig, M. 1980 *The devil and commodity fetishism in South America*. University of North Carolina Press: Chapel Hill, NC.

Taussig, M. 1993 *Mimesis and alterity*. University of Chicago Press: Chicago.

Taylor C. 1995 'Suivre un règle'. *Critique*, nos 579–80: 554–72.

Templeman, D. 1996 *The northern Nadars of Tamil Nadu: an Indian caste in the process of change*. Oxford University Press: Delhi.

Tharakan, M. 1978 'Dimensions and characteristics of the migration of farmers from Travancore to Malabar, 1930–1950'. *Journal of Kerala Studies*, vol. 5, part 2: 288–305.

Tharakan, M. 1984 'Socio-economic factors in educational development: the case of nineteenth-century Travancore'. *Economic and Political Weekly*, vol. 19, no. 45: 1913–28 (part 1) & vol. 19, no. 46: 1959–67 (part 2).

Tharamangalam, J. 1981 *Agrarian class conflicts: the political mobilisation of agricultural labourers in Kuttanad, South India*. University of British Columbia Press: Vancouver.

Thurston, E. & K. Rangachari 1909 *Castes and tribes of southern India* (7 vols).

Government Press: Madras.

Thurston, E. (1906) 1989 *Ethnographic notes in southern India.* Asian Educational Services: New Delhi.

Toren, C. 1990 *Making sense of hierarchy: cognition as a social process in Fiji.* Athlone Press: London.

Toren, C. 1993 'Making history: the significance of childhood cognition for a comparative anthropology of mind'. *Man* (ns), vol. 28: 461–78.

Toren, C. 1994 'All things go in pairs, or the sharks will bite: the antithetical nature of Fijian chiefship'. *Oceania*, vol. 64, no. 3: 197–216.

Toren, C. 1996 'Transforming love', in P. Gow and P. Harvey (eds) *Sex and love.* Routledge: London.

Trautman, T. 1981 *Dravidian kinship.* Cambridge University Press: Cambridge.

Trawick, M. 1990 *Notes on love in a Tamil family.* University of California Press: Oxford.

Trawick, M. 1992 'Ayurveda, cosmopolitan medicine and other traditions in South Asia', in C. Leslie & A. Young (eds) *Paths to Asian medical knowledge.* University of California Press: Berkeley.

Uchiyamada, Y. 1995 'Sacred grove (*kaavu*): ancestral land of "landless agricultural labourers" in Kerala, India'. Unpublished PhD thesis, London School of Economics and Political Sciences.

Van der Veer, P. 1994. *Religious nationalism: Hindus and Muslims in India.* University of California Press: Berkeley.

Van der Veer, P. 1998 'The global history of "modernity" '. *Journal of the Social and Economic History of the Orient*, vol. 41, no. 3: 285–94.

Varghese, T. 1970 *Agrarian change and economic consequences.* Allied Publishers: Bombay.

Vera-Sanso, P. 1995 'Community, seclusion and female labour force participation in Madras, India'. *Third World Planning Review*, vol. 17, no. 2: 155–67.

Vijayamohan, T.K. 1979 'Col. Macaulay, the Political Resident of Travancore (1800–1810)'. *Journal of Kerala Studies*, vol. 5: 287–91.

Vincentnathan, L. 1993 'Untouchable concepts of person and society'. *Contributions to Indian Sociology*, vol. 27, no. 1: 53–82.

Visvanathan, S. 1989 'Marriage, birth and death: property rights and domestic relationships of the Orthodox Jacobite Syrian Christians of Kerala'. *Economic and Political Weekly*, vol. 24, no. 24: 1341–6.

Wacquant, L.J.D. 1992 'The structure and logic of Bourdieu's sociology', in P. Bourdieu & L.J.D. Wacquant, *An invitation to reflexive sociology.* Polity Press: Oxford.

Wagner, P. 1994 *A sociology of modernity: liberty and discipline.* Routledge: London.

Wagner, P. 1999 'The resistance that modernity constantly provokes: Europe, America and social theory'. *Thesis Eleven*, no. 58: 35–58.

Wallerstein, I. 1979 *The capitalist world economy.* Cambridge University Press: Cambridge.

Warner, L., M. Meeker & K. Eells 1994 'Social class in America', in D. Grusky (ed.) *Social Stratification, Class, Race and Gender in Sociological Perspective* (Social Inequality Series). Westview Press: Boulder, CO.

Washbrook, D.A. 1988 'Progress and problems: South Asian economic and social history c. 1720–1860'. *Modern Asian Studies*, vol. 22, no. 1: 57–96.

Wilk, R. 1989 'Houses as consumer goods: the Kelkchi of Belize', in B. Orlove & H. Rutz (eds) *The social economy of consumption.* University Press of America: Lanham, MD.

Wilk, R. 1994 'Consumer goods as dialogue about development: colonial time and television time in Belize', in J. Friedman (ed.) *Consumption and identity.* Harwood Academic Press: Chur, Switzerland.

Wilkes, C. 1990 'Bourdieu's class', in R. Harker, C. Mahar & C. Wilkes (eds) *An* introduction to the work of Pierre Bourdieu: the practice of theory, Macmillan: London.

Willis, P. 1977 *Learning to labour*. Saxon House: Farnborough.

Wolf, E. 1982 *Europe and the people without history*. University of California Press: Berkeley.

Yalman, N. 1967 *Under the Bo tree: studies in caste, kinship and marriage in the interior of Ceylon*. University of California Press: Berkeley.

Yati, N.N. 1991 'An intelligent man's guide to the Hindu religion'. Narayana Gurukula Foundation: Nilgiris.

Yelvington, K.A. 1996 'Flirting in the factory'. *Journal of the Royal Anthropological Society*, vol. 2, no. 2: 313–33.

Yesudas, R.N. 1977 'Colonel John Munro in Travancore'. *Journal of Kerala Studies*, vol. 4, parts 1–2: 363–411.

Zarrilli, P. 1979 'Kalarippayattu, martial art of Kerala'. *Tulane Drama Review*, vol. 23, no. 3: 113–24.

Zarrilli, P. 1989 'Three bodies of practice in a traditional South Indian martial art'. *Social Science & Medicine*, vol. 28: 1289–309.

Zarrilli, P. 1999 *When the body becomes all eyes: paradigms, discourses and practices of power in Kalarippayattu, a South Indian martial art*. Oxford University Press: Delhi.

Zimmermann, F. 1987 *The jungle and the aroma of meats: an ecological theme in Hindu medicine*. University of California Press: Berkeley.

INDEX

Compiled by Sue Carlton